# Aftersight
## *and*
# Foresight

# Aftersight
## *and*
# Foresight

## *Selected Essays*

## Gerhart Niemeyer

FOREWORD BY
## William F. Buckley, Jr.

INTRODUCTION BY
## Michael Henry

University Press of America
The Intercollegiate Studies Institute, Inc.

Copyright © 1988 by

The Intercollegiate Studies Institute, Inc.

University Press of America,© Inc.

4720 Boston Way
Lanham, MD 20706

3 Henrietta Street
London WC2E 8LU England

Printed in the United States of America

British Cataloging in Publication Information Available

Co-published by arrangement with
the Intercollegiate Studies Institute, Inc.

Library of Congress Cataloging-in-Publication Data

Niemeyer, Gerhart.
Aftersight and foresight : selected essays / Gerhart Niemeyer :
foreword by William F. Buckley, Jr. : introduction by Michael Henry.
p. cm.
1. Political science—Moral and ethical aspects. 2. Ideology. 3. Communism.
4. Conservatism. 5. International relations. I. Title.
JA79.N46     1988     320.5—dc19     87–33418 CIP

ISBN: 0–8191–6841–6 (pbk. : alk. paper)
ISBN: 0–8191–6840–8 (alk. paper)

All University Press of America books are produced on acid-free
paper which exceeds the minimum standards set by the National
Historical Publications and Records Commission.

# Contents

v

**The Struggle Toward the Good**

. . . and urge the mind to aftersight and foresight.

T.S. Eliot, *Little Gidding*

# Foreword

IN HIS LEARNED introduction to this book of essays, Michael Henry seeks to decoct from the work of Gerhart Niemeyer just what it is that most adamantly asserts itself. It is the imperative need for a continuing search for order and wholeness, in the absence of which, Niemeyer believes and Henry and others cited affirm, we become desiccated beings, living on heady transfusions of solipsism; self-concerned, bored and boring, incapable of the kind of joy we feel on experiencing the irradiations of a cosmic order, intelligently contrived.

Mr. Henry's introduction is provocative, and causes me to think back to a haunting theme I have for years thought to write about. Probably I never will (sheer funk). But here I adumbrate it in connection with Gerhart Niemeyer.

I am talking about moral character. And here I note that I dispose of only one advantage, in having been selected to write this brief foreword. It is, to be sure, a singular advantage: that of having known Mr. Niemeyer for a very long time. There have been professional associations: he did us the honor, at *National Review*, to serve for a time as our philosopher-at-large, succeeding the late Frank Meyer whose regular column, "Principles & Heresies," was an integral part of our editorial enterprise (Niemeyer changed its logo to "Days & Works"). I was in touch with him when he worked for the State Department and, later, for the USIA as chairman of its Board of Foreign Scholarships. We have labored together on ad hoc projects at the National War College, at Notre Dame, and at *National Review*. I am familiar with his work, even if lacking the technical equipment fully to exploit it; indeed some of what appears in this volume appeared first in *National Review*.

The question I have often been perplexed by is this: how is it that

ix

we all believe (and indeed preach) that education is ennobling, enhancing of character and of moral imagination–and yet we all guard a dirty little secret, which is that among the intellectuals we all know, creatures of considerable learning, we are no likelier to find ourselves among morally civilized men and women than when in the company of ignorant folk.

How can this be? I began to ask myself when I was very young, observing some of my professors at work and at play. Nor does it require personal familiarity with the ways of the intellectuals to come by this knowledge. One can read what they write in the serious journals, and note what they do and say about each other. And then of course there are the novels. Randall Jarrell writing about them in his novel, *Pictures From an Institution*; or Mary McCarthy on Vassar; or almost anybody on the New York intellectuals. There are of course moral stars out there, but also a great deal of surrounding blackness, which after all accounts for the singularity of stellar light. Why is it that the graduate of a university, Phi Beta Kappa, often proves to be less satisfactory, defined as a human being engaged by virtuous ambition, than–well, the milkman?

Gerhart Niemeyer, Mr. Henry instructs us, has something to say about all this. Well, he has an approach, if by no means an answer. Niemeyer believes it unlikely that the thoughtful man who does not understand the wholeness of the human experience can draw joy from life, or indeed enjoy a true understanding of it. And yet I know (and so do you; and so does he) merry and lovable pagans whose company I prefer, in whom I would confide the virtue of my wife, the safety of my children, and the intactness of my worldly goods, sooner than I would many who proclaim themselves as Christians and in doing so dramatize a great problem Christianity needs to cope with, which is of course Christians undirected by right reason. Some pagans appear to come by it naturally. What accounts for the dismaying lack of charity in Professor Jones? Or for the tormenting envy of this Nobel Prize winner? Or for the petty lying and cheating of Nancy, Ph.D.? They know so much–and yet so little of the tender of personal virtue comes from them. Granted that without this Nobel Prize winner's meteorological contributions we would need to struggle without the key to the formation of tropical hurricanes: still, all that scientific knowledge and he cannot be civil (or faithful) to his wife, honest with his colleagues, or kind to his servants. And it isn't merely that the Nobel Prize winner knows not God. I am not a bit sure that life with St. Jerome would have been all that pleasant.

I had dramatic occasion to ponder the paradox when, seven years ago, I attended the ordination of Gerhart Niemeyer as an Anglican priest. There must have been working on me that late afternoon singular vibrations: elderly men have been ordained before, and I have attended other memorable liturgical services. But there was something riveting in the figure of this medium-build, venerable scholar, prostrate on the floor before the altar, making his solemn affirmations. Now he combined, as one of his colleagues remarked, the ultimate blend: *studium, imperium, sacerdotum.*

I thought back to the sunny afternoon in Washington, D.C. when I met Gerhart Niemeyer. It was in 1951. I was pretending to be in Washington for the purpose of using the Congressional Library to do research on academic freedom. Actually, I spent my days in safe houses being instructed in the arts of covert intelligence for the CIA. My friend and tutor Willmoore Kendall took me to meet his old friend Gerhart Niemeyer, and we spoke in the garden about academic freedom and he instructed me in the distinctions common in German and indeed European culture.

He was emphatic in his pedagogical style. Gerhart is humble and inquisitive, but never a mincer. *That* is the way it is done in Germany, take it or leave it. He would enrage our disputatious friend Willmoore from time to time by simply declining to argue, when he believed Willmoore was arguing for the sake of doing so. But he would take infinite pains to communicate a point the apprehension of which rested on elusive subtleties.

Although Germans are not thought to be the most humorous race in town, Gerhart's love of laughter has always been a distinctive characteristic. While acutely sensing the tragedy of this most awful century, he could always laugh, even as Whittaker Chambers laughed right through the Weltschmerz he memorialized. I do not know Solzhenitsyn, but I like to think that the man who has the stomach to paint the definitive portrait of Gulag has been given the grace of laughter. And there are different kinds of laughter, Gerhart's being of the generous kind, the laughter of gratitude: to the person who makes him laugh, and to the protocols of the cosmos that permit laughter, a divine revel. Fulton Sheen would preach that grown men must know to laugh, even as they must know to cry. One weeps most profoundly for others; and one laughs most salvifically to express thanks.

*"As a priest it will be your task to proclaim by word and deed the Gospel of Jesus Christ, and to fashion your life in accordance with its precepts. You are to love and serve the people among whom you work, caring alike for young and old, strong and weak, rich and poor. My brother, do you believe that you are truly called by God and his Church to this priesthood?"*

*"I do,"* Gerhart Niemeyer said. The supreme act of that dominating love, experienced by all who have known him, as friends, as students, as family.

But he continues to exercise his special philanthropy, helping his students – his readers – to cope with the great mysteries about us. He does this by exhibiting his successful resistance to T.S. Eliot's "dissociation of sensibilities," the cleavage between the life of the mind and the life of the heart. He shows us how to draw strength from confusion, and pleasure from the working of the mind. The odd reader, waiting the special vibrations Niemeyer can generate, will perhaps find in these essays a key to the good life, the life he has led on earth. The special vindication of learning, turned by him into an instrument of virtue.

"We thank you," the bishop at South Bend addressed the altar, "that by his death he has overcome death [and] has poured his gifts abundantly upon your people, making some apostles, some prophets, some evangelists, some pastors and teachers." How specially fortunate we are who have known Gerhart Niemeyer, but fortunate also those who know him through his works.

*William F. Buckley, Jr.*
*National Review*

# Introduction

Being human is a risky business, beset on all sides with insecurities and pitfalls.

> — Gerhart Niemeyer

Mounds of human heads recede into the distance,
I am diminished there—they won't notice me;
But in tender books and the games of small children
I shall rise again to say the sun is shining.

> — Osip Mandelstam

Joy is praise of the whole.

> — Thornton Wilder

IN THE MIDDLE of the discussion of immortality in the *Phaedo* Socrates remarks to his friends that he is in danger of losing "a philosophical attitude," that he might be more concerned with persuading them of his own belief in immortality than with seeking the truth, be what it may. So he asks them to think not of him or their desire to believe in immortality but of the truth and to pose whatever arguments and objections occur to them. For Socrates the fulfillment of the soul's nature that is happiness is in abandonment of illusion for the single-minded pursuit of truth as it can be discovered by sound rational argument.

As the paradigmatic philosopher for the Western tradition Socrates represents the life of the spirit, a psyche animated by wonder, by a loving trust in the goodness and order of the whole, and engaged in a tireless search for truth by carefully examining his own and others' beliefs, experiences, and ideas. Well aware of the insecurities and pitfalls of the human condition, Socrates' concern is to avoid them by seeking only, through constant questioning, to gain the self-knowledge necessary to participate in the order of the whole, on the assumption that an unfailing openness to truth is the best antidote to error. To Socrates the love of wisdom, the mind's passionate belief in and search for truth, begets such joy in existence that loss of the philosophical attitude means a kind of inner death, a loss of "education," a lapse from the loving search for participation in truth to the fearful isolation of the desire only to persuade. Until his death Socrates maintains his philosophical attitude because, in the profoundest sense of the expression, he believes in the gods.

Unfortunately, since the onset of modernity the philosophical ability to live in the tension of uncertainty while searching for the truth has become largely a lost art. Philosophy has become a rather grim, joyless, often nihilistic enterprise, knowing neither gaiety of spirit nor love of what is, because, bereft of faith in the order of the whole, it has plunged headlong into the pitfalls of an egocentric need for certainty and craving for power. Although the pursuit of certainty proclaims itself the way to Truth and happiness, it succeeds only in transmogrifying the joyous participation in the whole into a nihilistic isolation in which man, deprived of self-knowledge, is diminished to a kind of deified beast. The persistence of modernity's lust for certainty and its concomitant rejection of the faith in the whole at the heart of the tradition has meant that those in whom the tradition survives must engage in what T.S. Eliot called "the fight to recover what has been lost/ And found and lost again and again."

Among those contemporaries of Socratic spirit who prefer celebrating truth and reality to apotheosizing fantasies, who believe in the order and goodness of the whole of which we are a part, and who seek by questioning and searching to attain an ampler existence through a fuller participation in the whole is Gerhart Niemeyer. Although the essays collected in this volume cover a wide range of topics, problems, and philosophers, they are unified by Niemeyer's love for truth and his concern for the recovery of a wholeness in human existence that has been lost or fragmented, particularly but not exclusively by totalitarian ideologies. The various questions, subjects, and experiences he discusses converge on the single purpose of restoring or reawakening a sense of order and tradition in this ideologically ravaged age, bringing into focus, with clinical precision, the morbidity of ideology.

The central, unifying assumption of Niemeyer's thought in general and his critique of ideologies in particular is participation, or what Gabriel Marcel called "the ontological need," that is, an innate need for wonder and mystery, for the sense that we are participants in a larger order beyond our comprehension. The suppression or denial of the ontological need characteristic of ideologies produces a spiritual disorder that manifests itself as emptiness, melancholy, and despair, for, as Socrates well knew, the questioning born of wonder is the breath of the spirit. Therefore, to remedy the ills of modernity and reawaken a sense of participation Niemeyer has focused on a recovery of the tradition and a therapeutic *Nosce te ipsum*. Enjoyment of the fullness of our humanity requires an examination of reality as it is given to us in the whole of our experience, and this in turn depends upon a critical concern for the tradition, where past experience is preserved.

Through his efforts to restore an appreciation of the tradition Niemeyer has long been prominent among American conservatives, a group which he characterizes, almost ironically, as "a forward-driving force, an innovating force, one might even be tempted to say, an up-turning force." Contemporary conservatives have perforce become virtual revolutionaries through their opposition to the liberal intellectual Establishment status quo, "an amalgam of socialism, positivism, progressivism, and anti-Christian humanism." These Western "isms," as well as Communism, share in an attack on tradition, experience, common sense, religion, and the sense of identity we have, or should have, inherited from the past. To reject the tradition, the accumulated wisdom of countless human beings who reflected on their human experience and on the tradition they received is to turn ourselves into amnesiacs, "hollow men," incapable of significant communication, self-knowledge, understanding of the past, or realistic expectations of the future. And, as history has all too abundantly demonstrated, the more diminished our self-knowledge, the more fragmentary our grasp of the human, the more limited our perception of others as participants in the same human condition with ourselves, the more evil we do.

The twentieth century, "the wolfhound age [that] hurls itself at my shoulders" in Osip Mandelstam's graphic image, has thoroughly documented the catastrophic results of a lack of self-knowledge and rejection of the tradition. In a century of ideological death marches towards the fata morgana of an earthly paradise, Niemeyer, like many others of his generation, felt these totalitarian mass movements as "an all-overshadowing experience," because there was no theory adequate to explain such monumental abdications of rationality. Since, as Niemeyer and others have been well aware, the struggle to ascend to wisdom and self-knowledge requires a descent into the psychological underworld of ideologies, particularly Communism, now by far the most dominating and dangerous ideology, much of Niemeyer's work has been devoted to elucidating both the nature of Communism and the true intellectual and spiritual order of which Communism is a perversion.

This spiritual order of the whole is a given, an assumption, a fundamental faith, if you will, but a faith essential for significant communication about a common world. Niemeyer begins from the assumption that since such thinking, questioning, and reflecting take place, since we have had experience of significant communication, there must be an order of meaning or goodness or truth which both permits and requires rational reflection and discourse. Without such an order we are reduced to monologues.

> There is an order of goodness in the universe, and human knowledge can attain to it. The proposition is made here as an assertion and an affirmation. In the context of the question raised by this paper ["What Price 'Natural Law'?"] it comes as a premise which, if we did not have it, would leave us without anything to talk about.

For Niemeyer not only can human knowledge attain to the order of goodness in the universe, but we ourselves and our search for knowledge are part of this order. Without this faith in the existence, order, and meaning of the whole the scope of reason is limited to private sensations because the universe is merely, in Hobbes's words, "the aggregate of all bodies," discrete entities scattered in space that do not and can not participate organically in a whole. Conversely, reason provides faith with the architectonics necessary for us to understand it and to contemplate the whole.

Philosophy provides a structure in which faith finds confirmation of its reasonableness, in turn providing that structure with depth and height in which consciousness attains wholeness.

Faith's essential vision of the order of the whole is perceived only through the eyes of wonder, praise, and thanksgiving, and faith expresses itself through the questions of reason, as we assume that reason has the power to illuminate faith.

The critical point distinguishing the freedom of the philosophical love of wisdom from the imprisonment of the ideological love of power is that the questions reason asks about the order of the whole and the ultimate significance of our existence cannot and should not be answered, at least not fully, as Niemeyer points out in "The Glory and Misery of Education."

Assuming that we are part of a whole is an integral part of our thinking. . . . The whole . . . has no context: there is no place beyond on which we could stand, even in imagination, to look on the whole as if it were an object. Our wonderment about the whole therefore can have no end. The whole has inescapably the character of a mystery, and our place in it likewise must remain mysterious. Questions concerning it cannot be answered by way of experiment, nor can they be silenced by a compelling proof. If there were such proof our questioning would be stopped once and for all; we should be enclosed by a confining wall of "fact" imprisoning us beyond endurance.

For Niemeyer, as for Socrates and Marcel, without wonder and the sense of participation in mystery human existence becomes sterile, boring, unendurable. The search for wisdom and knowledge that gives life depth and meaning requires faith in a reality which we cannot grasp, for, in Marcel's words, "knowledge is contingent on a participation in being for which no epistemology can account because it continually presupposes it." It is the ground on which we stand. Or, to put it differently, the life and freedom of the spirit are possible only in the experiential tensions between time and eternity, nature and transcendence, the world and heaven, the sacred and the profane, which, as Niemeyer says, "cannot and should not be resolved."

The rejection of the sense of participation that grows out of wonder and searching, the attempt to conceive meaning and certainty parthenogenetically in one's own isolated psyche leads only to sterility and death. The sterility is obvious in the mind-numbing boredom of ideological propaganda, which is so stupefyingly dull that even the rulers in the Soviet Union have complained about its soporiferousness. Truly interesting ideological propaganda is, however, a contradiction in terms, not only because the propagandists are unimaginative, but because the ideology is itself inherently boring, for the reason that it is a spiritual prison. The ideologist announces the end of all questions and abandons the demanding task of careful, painstaking rational analysis of reality for the ego-gratifying triumph of the will over a flattened or diminished reality. The result is, in Steven Mosher's apt phrase describing Communist China, "a flatland of the mind." The logic of this willful refusal to participate in a reality that is in any way subject to the will of another requires that propaganda be nothing but a relentless campaign to force human consciousness into the desired mold, that is, to convince people that what their experience tells them is not true, to impose a "second reality" on the true reality.

Therefore, the anti-ideological recovery of the tradition is vital because the participation in the order of the whole that is essential to the spiritual health of rational beings requires the imperfect knowledge gained through wonder and questioning, and, as Niemeyer puts it, echoing Plato, Augustine, and Eric Voegelin, knowledge is memory, the anamnestic recovery of experience, or "the return of the past." He elaborates on this theme in his book *Between Nothingness and Paradise* in a section entitled "The Public Past," in which he begins with personal experience and extrapolates to public experience.

Underlying the public past is the cognition of each individual self through the awareness of the past. Consciousness of self emerges in and through the consciousness of objects and experiences. Only after having perceived does one become aware of the self as perceiving; only after an experience has

occurred does attention focus on the subject of the experience.

As T.S. Eliot put it, "We had the experience but missed the meaning." The past, as Niemeyer understands it, is anything but dead or
obsolete. Its meaning and structure actively reveal themselves
over time, as we gain distance and perspective: "Something that at
the time was rejected now stands revealed as a landmark;
something which the will classified at its time in one way now
shows itself in a completely different light." The past, asserting its
significance, vitality, and power in memory, "moves us to present
being, to experiences of remorse, contrition, elation, or joy." And
here, precisely in the discovery of the past, is the discovery of
ourselves. "Confronted with the unwilled and unplanned return of
the past, we experience the I to whom all this happened and who,
enduring in the stream of time, proves his being." In reflecting on
the past that by returning "uncovers itself" to us we reflect on "the
order that makes itself felt" in the power of memory beyond the
control of our will.

However, this process of self-discovery does not occur in isolation because the past of the individual is inextricably interwoven
with the pasts of family and friends. And ultimately, as a member
of a society, a man requires a public past to give his existence order
and meaning as a member of that particular group. In the "public
memory" of tradition we find the matrix for the questions about the
whole essential to our humanity. Niemeyer's position is the refutation of ideology, which assumes that we (or at least the ideologist)
can stand outside the whole and observe it as an object, that our
place in it can be fully explained so that no further questions will be
necessary or even possible. Ideology is a prison. (There is a certain
logic in the frequent use of "truth-seeking" to diagnose
"schizophrenia" in Soviet dissidents. Since all truth is supposedly
already known to man, only an insane person would insist on seeking it as though it were not known.) In short, without searching into the past of personal memory and cultural, intellectual, and
spiritual tradition we cannot grasp who we are, either as individuals or as a people. In Eliot's line, "A people without history/
Is not redeemed from time. . . ."

Eliot himself puts this thesis into the context of art in his famous essay "Tradition and the Individual Talent." To Eliot it was obvious that it is impossible to produce a work of original art by attempting to reject the tradition. The originality and worth of the artist's work depend upon a participation in or dialogue with the *entire* tradition, reaching back through Shakespeare to Homer and even the "Magdalenian draughtsmen." Although the specific material of art changes, art itself does not improve, just as philosophy and the essentials of human experience do not improve or "progress." There is deepening insight, but the questions remain perennially the same. Consequently, with a *Zeitgeist* that is hostile to tradition and favorable to anything labelled progressive the intellectual tradition seems "irrelevant" to the present because, as John Stuart Mill complained about moral philosophy, it makes "little progress."

A kind of confirmation of Eliot's thesis that originality roots in a caring for the tradition is the work of the late Eric Voegelin, whom Niemeyer, one of his principal interpreters and critics, described in 1979 as "the most original, furthest advanced political theorist living today," and shortly after his death in 1985 as "one of the greatest minds of our times." Voegelin was so original and so advanced precisely because of his constant endeavor to understand the intellectual tradition (of both West and East) as deeply and comprehensively as possible, not only for the sake of understanding the tradition but as an "undertaking of self-discovery." He entered into this work because of the experience of the seemingly incomprehensible horror of totalitarianism, and by the time of his death he had mapped out a theory of the history of order and a theory of consciousness which ground an analysis of the classical tradition and of the spiritual disorders of modernity.

As one of the prime modern disorders Communist ideology represents itself as the epitome of all that is good because it is, supposedly, the most progressive, the movement most intent on leaving behind a superannuated past, with all its recognition of human limits. But as Niemeyer points out, the rejection of the past accompanied by the refusal to recognize the inexorable limitations of reality is motivated by hatred, not love, of what is and entails the loss of humanity and the death of the spirit. To contain this spiritual malignancy we need to understand clearly what it is and how its exponents think. Beyond the core of ideological irrationality are the specific considerations that govern Communists' decision-making in the practical sphere. We cannot win the struggle with Communism and preserve our heritage and our freedom unless we understand how the assumptions, world-view, and thought processes of Communists differ from our own. To this end Niemeyer has written *An Inquiry into Soviet Mentality* and *Deceitful Peace* and a large number of articles, four of which are included in this book.

In these works he elaborates on the workings of the Communist mind with its distortions and irrationality, its rejections of the past, of human experience, and of human nature in the name of a dogmatic insistence on an unreal state of human perfection. Regardless of the precise extent to which the dictators in the Soviet Union sincerely believe in all of the ideology, there is no doubt that their entire mind-set and world-view have been shaped by Marxist-Leninist assumptions, categories, and doctrines. Once it is understood that Communism is doctrinally driven to dominate the world, the West might be less inclined to hope that the rulers of the Soviet Union might be seized with ordinary reasonableness. As Leninists the Soviets can and do compromise on specifics as a tactical maneuver, but the ideological goal of the USSR remains that of ultimate world domination, as, for instance, the former Soviet general Petro Grigorenko states at the end of his *Memoirs*. As the Soviets see it, the Communist nations and the capitalist nations are locked in a desperate struggle to the death, with Communism assured as the ultimate victor. (Although at the rate the Soviet government keeps postponing the realization of Communism in just the Soviet Union it is clear they do not anticipate total victory in the very near future.) The West, however, particularly the liberal Establishment, more complacent in its enjoyment of freedom and material prosperity, and lacking the conviction of an ideological mandate to dominate the world, resists facing the true predatory nature of Communism, as half a century ago the democracies resisted seeing Hitler for the radical, irrational nihilist that he was.

In "Reason and Faith: The Fallacious Antithesis," Niemeyer quotes Alfred North Whitehead's description of evil as "the brute motive force of fragmentary purpose," with the fragmentary purpose a consequence of fragmentary reality and fragmentary human nature. In ideologies which reject reason, imagination, and memory, along with questioning based on an appreciation of tradition and a sense of participating in an order of goodness ("total critiques") humanity is crushed beneath a new and absolute "Truth." However, after a sweeping rejection of the past there is really nothing left to say except the negation of the tradition and accumulated human experience. An ideology restricts itself to willing a fantasy that is essentially *not* what is or has been, and the attempt to bludgeon reality into being its opposite leads only to death and destruction.

For instance, Communist ideology, for all its seductive predictions that "the free development of each is the condition for the free development of all," entails no such thing. The dimensions of humanity and human experience will actually be bounded by the short and narrow procrustean bed of productive labor so that man can become master of nature and his own god. But according to the absolutist logic of ideological thinking the deification of man requires the abolition of man, or his reduction to the bestial level. "Communist man" is not some wondrous new divine being, but simply a negation of the human – not a being that thinks abstractly, not a being that questions or seeks wisdom, not a being that believes in a higher reality or immorality, not a being with a unique spiritual identity, not a being that makes moral decisions, not a being that suffers the tensions of limitations and uncertainties, and so on. In positive terms "Communist man" is little more than a labor-loving primate that always knows where the next meal is coming from. Underneath all the orotund rhetoric "Communist man" represents the refusal to be human.

The reciprocal of the determination with which the second, ideological reality is imposed in the Soviet Union and other "Socialist" countries is the significance of "dissidents," a term often ridiculously inadequate to describe the reality, for it reduces the essence of what these people have to say to "disagreement" with the state's version of truth. This is sometimes the case, but often it is as much a diminishing of the reality as would be labelling Socrates a "dissident." The most notable such case is, of course, Solzhenitsyn, whom Niemeyer celebrates in "The Eternal Meaning of Solzhenitsyn" as well as in several other essays included here. Unlike such great and therefore persecuted twentieth-century Russian writers as Mandelstam and Pasternak, Solzhenitsyn never knew Russia before Communism but grew up imbibing the ideology. This makes his work all the more remarkable and significant because it testifies to the tenacity of spiritual life which manages to rise from beneath the rubble of a culture to rejoice in the sunlight, as Solzhenitsyn describes Oleg Kostoglotov's feelings at being released from the hospital in *Cancer Ward*, a passage Niemeyer quotes as descriptive of the spiritual effects of human experience in that Oleg insists on being what he is—a human being—rather than forcing himself into the mold of the "new man" tirelessly and mindlessly and joylessly struggling against capitalism in the service of the juggernaut of history.

> [Oleg] looked about. This was a young world, turning green. He raised his head. The sky spread out, rosy from the sun rising somewhere behind the horizon. A string of feathery clouds—centuries of the finest workmanship had gone into their making—stretched out across the whole sky. . . . This was the morning of Creation! The world was being created anew solely for Oleg's return! Go! Live!

Given the context in which it was written, Niemeyer reads this and other passages in Solzhenitsyn as descriptive of a regenerative experience that reawakens a man to real human existence, freedom, and spiritual life after escaping from the prison or cancer ward of ideology. As Niemeyer explains, Solzhenitsyn's achievement in restoring the concept of man to the fullness of humanity is a recovery from not only the pseudo-reality of Communist ideology but also from the fragmentation, truncation, and reduction of man for the past three centuries. Since Thomas Hobbes, "humanity" has been rather arbitrarily restricted to only part of the full range of human experience and motivation. The wholeness of our nature and existence has been fragmented, and we have yet to see the end of the horrors this deformed humanity is capable of wreaking.

In accordance with Whitehead's definition of evil, good could be understood as something like "the healing force of a wholeness of purpose, or the wholeness of reality." (As one character observes in Thornton Wilder's *The Eighth Day*, "There is no happiness save in understanding the whole.") The emphasis here is on wholeness, a fullness of experience that to Niemeyer certainly and necessarily includes transcendence and the order of good created by a transcendent God. It is Niemeyer's fundamental conviction that our understanding of our humanity is inseparable from our understanding of transcendent reality, and it is his further, unfashionable but quite sensible belief that liberal education should concern itself with the study of Christianity because "Christianity has been the source and center of our culture, the ultimate truth that has shaped our past and is still shaping our present, regardless what attitude to it particular persons may have." Our culture and tradition simply cannot be fully or even adequately understood without a grasp of Christianity that requires knowledge of its doctrines, liturgy, history, and institutions, and of its sense of "life in tension" between time and eternity.

Gerhart Niemeyer's work, in his writing and his teaching, has been the recovery of order and wholeness, the conservation of the tradition, and the awakening of reason and the life of the mind. Like Richard Hooker he has labored "for no other cause but for this; that posterity may know we have not loosely through silence permitted things to pass away as in a dream." What he wrote of his teacher Hermann Heller in 1941, that he was "a man to whom the rational mastery of political reality meant a profound human responsibility and thus a personal task," is true of himself and his own work. It is the constant concern with preserving the philosophical attitude of openness to truth, order, meaning, and transcendence that Niemeyer considers "an imperative of the highest rank" that "imposes on us a duty to serve humanity, in the truest sense of that word, humanity which is not defined by bread, power, or superstition, but only by the awe-filled love of truth and goodness." Through his love of truth which enables him to penetrate experience with the clarity of the spirit Niemeyer serves his readers by communicating the essential regenerative experience of the wonder and joy of being human.

*Michael Henry*
*St. John's University*
*Jamaica, N.Y.*

# Part I
# The Loss of Order

# The "Autonomous" Man

IF ONE WERE to select for our time a single watchword, in the manner of the popularizing paperbacks covering a couple of centuries as "The Age of Faith," "The Age of Reason," or something similar, one might come closest to the target with "The Age of Autonomous Man." The dominant passion of the now generation seems to raise the banner of human autonomy ("man having come of age"), the news being preached by intellectuals and emotionalists, symbolized in countless signs and gestures, manifested through an appropriate "life-style." There are those who insist that this is nothing new; some trace the growth of "autonomy" back to the Renaissance, others to Francis Bacon and Galileo, still others to Rousseau, or the American Revolution. It is true that these and related milestones of human consciousness do seem to add up to a steady retreat of—how can one put it?—"authority" before "autonomy." But then autonomy as a self-conscious slogan was not used before the nineteenth century where we find it, in a variety of versions, dominating the works of Feuerbach, Max Stirner, Kierkegaard, Karl Marx, Friedrich Nietzsche. In his deep-probing study of this period, Henri de Lubac has given it a strikingly suitable name, when he titled his book *The Drama of Atheistic Humanism*, making clear that the intoxicating experience of "autonomy" centered on man's severing himself from God, the ground of being.

If the nineteenth century produced most of the idea systems through which various thinkers sought to secure man's self-reliant glory, the political and cultural manifestations of human autonomy belong only to the twentieth century, breaking out along a broad front in the rebellion—not of the young—but of students, young intellectuals. We have heard it said that student rebellions are nothing new. The late medieval centuries reverberate with riots

3

and even pitched battles generated by student unrest, and a Notre Dame professor recently uncovered evidence of a revolt in Plato's Academy, Plato himself, in his old age, being unequal to the situation and having to rely on his more energetic assistant to restore order. What is noted here, however, amounts to nothing more than external similarities. For everyone who sees in the present situation "nothing new," there are others who find it wholly unprecedented. The concluding paragraphs of the Epilogue in Hans Jonas' *The Gnostic Religion* may be mentioned as a representative example. The political phenomena stemming from the message of human autonomy today are centered in "the total critique of society," the wholesale condemnation and rejection of all norms, institutions, authorities, and allegiances of the present. Historically speaking, this total critique has two prongs, of which the first is a sweeping attack on religious faith in God, first initiated by Machiavelli and Hobbes, continued by Pierre Bayle, Voltaire, Helvetius, Holbach, the current then picking up volume and speed as later intellectuals derive boldness and radicality from their predecessors. In the nineteenth century there are a number of ideologies based on man as an autocrat, creating and governing himself without a divine origin, judge, and ruler. The movement was prepared not merely by scoffers and rebels. In the seventeenth century Pascal already spoke of those "vast spaces which know me not." Aristotle's geocentric cosmos, related to human meaning and human action, had given way to the centerless expanses of Galileo and Kepler which seemed to some seminal thinkers to elude human comprehension and evade any significance. The man's thought contracted to an exclusive concern with first human society, as already taught by Locke in his *Essay on Human Understanding*, and later with the contracted human self, so characteristic of the Romantics.

This is when the second prong of the total critique developed, in total condemnatory attacks on the social order, from Meslier, Morelly, Mably, to Babeuf, Fourier, Saint-Simon, Owen, Louis Blanc, Proudhon, Bakunin, Marx – the list of the founding fathers of socialist thought through two centuries. The attack on religion had come to its climax when first Hegel and then Nietzsche pronounced God dead, and Feuerbach and Marx capitalized on this news. Even then, however, the social structure preserved in its traditions, institutions, and allegiances many hints about the order and meaning of being. One recalls the "grizzled old stager of a captain" in Dostoevsky's *The Possessed* who, on hearing his drinking companions make "short work of God," got up and left, saying: "If there's no God, how can I be a captain then?"

The appeal to society's order was first prominently made by Edmund Burke, reacting to the "atheistic Humanism" of the French Enlightenment not with a creative philosophical effort resembling that of Socrates and Plato in the age of Greece's Enlightenment, but rather with a metaphysical endorsement of England's traditional order. The continuity, the slow growth, the affirmation by succeeding generations were seen by Burke as evidence of ontic truth and cosmic rightness. Not by accident did this thinking come out of England, for it was England which had weathered the first profound crisis of modernity, the onslaught of Puritanism, by working out that marvelously flexible and informal relationship between Church and State initiated by the Elizabethan Settlement and so eloquently defended by Richard Hooker, in his *Ecclesiastical Polity*. The Establishment, with the laws of England, seemed to him to combine Revelation and Reason in what amounted to the totality of a Christian Commonwealth. Hooker's and Burke's England, then, could speak to men of universal truth through concrete historical institutions. Even in the midst of nineteenth-century ideologies, this message of England continued, somewhat diluted, through the Victorian ideal of the "Christian gentleman," and, still more diluted, the near-ridiculous formula "cleanliness is Godliness." From Victorian England the modern world learned to look on its civilization as something embodying transcendent meaning, as witnessed by the semi-religious overtones attending that period's colonial ventures. It is during the same period that various other nations began to refer to themselves in terms of slogans claiming metaphysical significance for their national culture: *La Grande Nation*, *"Es soll am deutschen Wesen die ganze Welt genesen,"* *Italianità*, *Hispanidad*, *Manifest Destiny*.

As the total critique of society gathered momentum, all aspects of society being condemned as totally false and inhuman, all human authority as a sham, all norms as suspect of hidden self-interest, all power as masked violence, man was denuded of the last vestiges of order. Nothing was left to mediate between each person's subjectivity and universal reality. Universal order and meaning could no longer be found through any concrete manifestations, it had no more standing in this world and thus vanished into unreality. Man found himself isolated in a meaningless and irrelevant setting, far more isolated than Pascal in the vast cosmic spaces. Kafka's work testified to this experience of utter solitude. A word used by both Hegel and Marx seemed to fit the new situation and gained wide popularity: alienation. First in the semi-philosophical works, then in literature, man was described as "alienated" from his species, society, other men, and from any meaningful activity. He began to think of himself as existing in the midst of "the Absurd." All that is left to him is his solitary subjectivity, at best expanded to just one other intimate companion. The world reduced to "me and my girl," to lonesomeness à deux, preferably on a palm-studded speck of sand in the Pacific, came to be the last word of writers, film-makers, painters. Anarchism provided the fitting political foil for this mood, and the anarchic denigration of society, the public norm, the common good, and authority instituted extended into other fields, notably education. Already since the early nineteenth-century Wilhelm von Humboldt and J.S. Mill had pointed to the creative individual as all that needed cultivation, with society counting but for little. In Existentialism, we reach the full expression of man's endeavor to fashion life's order entirely out of individual sub-jectivity, invalidating whatever may have been called "objective," or "real," and thus elevating every person to the rank of creator of his own world.

A kind of composite portrait of the autonomous man might be drawn by adding up his attributes, or attitudes. Above all, the autonomous man will not be dependent on a Creator. One recalls the representative words of Marx, in his *Economic and Philosophical Manuscripts of 1844*: "A man who lives by the grace of another regards himself as a dependent being. But I live com-pletely by the grace of another if I owe him not only the sustenance of my life, but if he has, moreover, *created* my *life*." Marx con-tinues: "Since for the socialist man the entire history of the world is nothing but the begetting of man through human labor . . . the question about an *alien* being, about a being above nature and man . . . has become practically impossible." One recalls also Nietzsche's proud exclamation: "If there were a god, how could I bear not being God?" With divinity, the autonomous man also has thrown out any higher norm. The death of God means that "anything is permitted," as Ivan Karamasov concedes. Speaking more precisely, norm is absorbed into will. This pattern is found already in Rousseau, where the general will is proclaimed good by definition. It thus becomes the source or embodiment for every norm of society. All the same, in Rousseau one notes persistent traces of Socrates' "God is the measure," or Aristotle's "right by nature." By the turn of the century, however, utterly different notes are sounded in the writings of those two "autonomous" characters, the Marquis de Sade, and Lord Byron. (cf. Mario Praz, *The Romantic Agony*) Here the will, deliberately embracing the demonic and anti-natural, emancipates itself from normative barriers. Later, Nietzsche elevates the will of the superman to sovereignty over all norms, the sole remaining discipline being the "eternal return," a repetition freely willed. Incidentally, Nietzsche's pattern has its corollary in contemporary twelve-tone music in which the norms of harmony are discarded, the composer setting down at the beginning a sequence of notes which then, in serial recurrence, becomes the order of the piece. With the will in sole ascendancy, gone (or suppressed) is the conscience that used to be taken as evidence of a moral structure of being, gone is the Kantian universality. Each will now constitutes the scope of whatever order prevails, with power alone mediating between self-enclosed subjectivities. This is what among the young generation is meant by "emancipation," the systematic flouting of any normative structure by the unbounded will. Hans Jonas has deftly characterized the pertinent "life-style," "the idea that in sinning something like a program has to be completed, a due rendered as the price of ultimate freedom, [which] is the strongest doctrinal reinforcement of the libertinistic tendency inherent in gnostic religion and turns it into a positive prescription of immoralism." (*The Gnostic Religion*)

Next, philosophically speaking, we have the denigration of ontology and the substitution of psychology in its place. Ontology, man's rational orientation towards being, nature, cosmos, divine transcendence – all these have abided at the core of philosophy from the very first. Through two millennia, man has carefully put together and evaluated all the bits of evidence and insight from which he could conclude in what kind of larger reality he found himself set. Equipped with a free, restless, and ever-doubtful mind, man could not exist or act except by mapping out some landmarks telling of the constitution of that reality which he knew not to have created himself. Ontology, metaphysics, were the discursive formulations of this orienting knowledge regarding that which *is* in a more eminent sense than man feels himself to be. The present age has disdained ontology. Into the void psychology has moved, the speculative panorama of man's drives, emotional needs, and something called "the unconscious." That which *is* no longer is contemplated; that which one supposedly feels or desires now counts as the Alpha and Omega. Feuerbach psychologized religion, attributing the "creation of god" to man's subjective emotional needs; since then theology and religion have rarely been protected from the psychologizing approach. Politics, laws, ethics, and other normative disciplines have likewise been made subject to psychological premises. Need one wonder that Madison Avenue has developed into one of the foremost public institutions?

At this point one might remark that there seem to be two radically opposed premises which are relevant to the views here discussed. On the one hand we find the inquiry into the *arche*, the beginning. In the beginning, something *is*: "In the beginning – God." "In the beginning was the Word." Back before all appearances, said Plato, there are the Ideas, the eternal forms. Aristotle holds that prior to everything there is its nature. All this, in a variety of versions, points to something like a ground of everything that exists, so that life's endeavor would seek to discover the norm of that ground, to re-establish the link to the origin, and to avoid and remove any habit or attitude alienating us from the ground of our being. The opposite view sees no ground of beginning. It assumes something like an original accident, or accidents; it fastens its whole attention rather on the process of coming-to-be that goes on toward ever-increasing complexity and refinement, promising to culminate in some sort of perfection. The stream of becoming, and its eventual goal, orient man's activities and aspirations toward the future, the point being to remove and destroy all traces of the past, to free life for the onrushing movement, to be a part of the "upward" thrust. These two orientations constitute the most significant watershed of our time, a line from which run down mighty currents in opposite directions.

It is the second of these views which goes with the next character feature of autonomous man: valuing imagination above knowledge. Let there be no misunderstanding: imagination is an integral aspect of all knowledge; there could be no science without imagination. For the autonomous man, however, imagination replaces knowledge which to him appears confining, unbending, demanding. Imagination, by contrast, has all the freedom of creating. Much is made in our time of "dreaming," which many regard almost as an activity bringing forth something new. "Dreams" is sometimes used as a synonym for "ideal," "ideal" formerly deriving its meaning from Plato's ideas, forms of ultimate reality. Those who confuse "dream" and "ideal" relate these words rather to subjective urges and wishful desires. This is part of a shift, in much of contemporary thinking, from "real possibilities" to "possible realities." A characteristic of this shift is to substitute "the impossible" for what used to be "the difficult," so that The Impossible Dream can attain great popularity as a hit song. Another manifestation of the same kind is the campus cult of William Blake, the poet, painter, and myth-maker of the early-nineteenth century. Blake was supremely representative of that romantic intoxication with the imagined; he created an entire mythical world for himself, but also sought to impose new mythical meaning on various aspects of the existing reality. There are many who discover in Blake's autonomy a strong kinship with their own souls.

"Imagination" over "knowledge" is closely related to the elevation of "making" over "acting." The distinction is Aristotle's: "making" brings something into existence that did not exist before and either could or could not exist. An artisan thus "makes" things after his own plan and purpose. "Acting," by contrast, occurs in the midst of things which are what they are by nature; it means choosing conduct, or actions, bearing in mind what befits the natures of men and things. The distinction is obvious and would seem commonplace if it were not for the fact that today the autonomous man looks on politics not as a field of "acting" but rather as an opportunity for "making." Aristotle's insistence that politics belongs to the field of "acting" means that one chooses among the "real possibilities" of conduct which any given situation, and the nature of things and men, contain. The autonomous man, by contrast, looks on political power as the "maker" of things and men, on politics as the business of "creating" societies and culture, and on history as the process of "making dreams come true." The power of organization and technology, then, serves to set aside the limitations of nature, including human nature, which autonomous man finds insufferably confining.

Man's vaunted autonomy, then, centers on will, imagination, feeling, the subjective, in the name of all of which norms, hierarchies, and structures of reality are negated. Such assumptions lead to two distinct attitudes. The first may be called the *mega-self*. Here, characteristically, we find the intellectual, or the man of will, who marshalls all available methods, intellectual, organizational, and technical, for the support of his conclusion that "nothing is impossible." The pattern is manifested weekly by the TV show "Mission Impossible." Electronics, chemistry, medicine, ordonnance, and, above all, organizational efficiency combine to give to a small group of men supreme mastery over apparently inconquerable obstacles. No limit is acknowledged, no failure contemplated. This kind of attitude is often attributed to the notion of science as power. Science, however, has always been governed by a true deference to reality and subservience to truth. Scientists are typically humble. The mega-self does not flourish in the soul of the dedicated scholar. Its sources are found in the self-deification of autonomous man, and its bid for irresistible power stems from a blind confidence in both technology and organization, honed and perfected to the point of unfailing efficiency. In this context it is interesting to note that the word "philosophy," which literally means "love of truth," is being used as denoting something like "basic operating principles" of an organized enterprise or manipulation.

Alternatively, autonomous man develops an attitude that may be called the *micro-self*. It characterizes the person who, feeling too weak or unenergetic to accomplish a "Mission Impossible," drops out from the common world of society into his own private world. On a mini-scale, this world consists either of himself alone, or at best of "me and my girl." The scale is so small as to give him a sense of mastery over all, as witnessed by the term used to describe this situation: "life-style." Life-style means, of course, an unbounded freedom to give to human existence any shape, direction, or form, including formlessness, which imagination may dream up. One used to hear: "My right to my opinion is as good as yours." Later, this mutated to: "My truth is as good as yours." The present slogan runs, "My life-style is as good as yours." All governing criteria, all norms, and ultimately all distinctions are swamped in the invertebrate subjectivity. The raw feeling of subjectivity was exemplified by Janis Joplin, emotion without any other meaning, shape, or structure, a voice of someone howling in emptiness. In art, too, unlimited subjectivity has entailed the end of communication. The public is left to supply subjective interpretation to what has remained totally encapsuled in the artist's own subjectivity. Each work is contracted to a minuscule cell of a micro-self, devoid of any communicable content. The cutting of any objective or public bond between artist and onlooker is deliberately sought as a mode that does not encroach on subjective freedom. Going beyond art, we find anti-social dress, hair-style, and general appearance manifest the micro-self, as do drugs, the ultimate means of withdrawal from any structured reality into personal shapelessness.

BOTH THE MEGA – SELF and the micro-self essentially seek freedom as power. The mega-self dreams of limitless possibilities to manipulate nature, men, and circumstances according to any imaginable dream, using technology, psychological manipulation, and organization. The micro-self attains full power by reducing his world to the tiny dimensions in which everything can be wholly his, and nothing and nobody can encroach. In both cases, then, the will must be satisfied in that nothing obstructs its mastery. From the soul any limiting norms and any fear of judgment have been cast out; no sense of sin or guilt is allowed any more; any trace or hint of dependence is radically rejected. The craving for power will be satisfied on whatever level, the very large or the very small, appears feasible.

In the course of his many negations, the autonomous man has cast aside not only traditional limitations but also ideological strictures, above all, the discipline of the Communist Party, and the narrow severity of positivism. Such resistances one must credit as gains. One might think of gain also the new interest in the religious that manifests itself in so many different forms at the present time.

It seems for the most part, though, that this is interest in religious expression rather than in God, or Christ; one might even call it flirtation with religious flavors, the more exotic the better. One cannot generalize, but it would seem that there is little if any genuine commitment to any faith, cult, or discipline behind these flirtations. The people who chant Hare Rama, Hare Krishna, or copiously quote the *I Ching*, or join the followers of a Hindu guru may be fascinated, excited, titillated, but are hardly in any real sense devoted. Moreover, the varieties of religious interest today stem often from totally psychologized persons, which means that what drives them on is not a quest for the ground of being, but the question of what religion could do to one's emotional condition. Such people do not care what it is they chant, worship, or admire, and they hardly distinguish between religion, the occult, or satanism, all of which they readily equate with "mysticism," and any variety or mixture of varieties of which they welcome. Truth or reality do not matter where vague emotional surges are sought above all. One sees the symbols of various mutually exclusive religions displayed together, incompatible cultic actions are mingled, and signs adopted without any sense of meaning. Observers of these syncretistic phenomena frequently point to the hellenistic centuries at the beginning of our era as a precedent. The parallel, however, does not hold. Hellenism had engendered a wide-spread and genuine yearning for salvation, to which the Oriental mystery cults could appear as a direct response. The modern autonomous man, however, feels no need of salvation whatsoever, he being his own savior in any case. His own will is his norm, he acknowledges no sense of guilt, and he personally has moved beyond good and evil. Many of the imported cults of our day, then, seem to amount to nothing more than what Pascal called "divertissements," devices to stir up the lassitude of vastly bored souls.

THESE OBSERVATIONS should not be understood to say that everybody in our age can be described in terms of the autonomous man. Many people at present live essentially peacefully in a world that has meaning, structure, and direction. Autonomous men, however, are found in bureaucracies, businesses, laboratories, universities, governments, in sufficient numbers to warrant giving this period their name. Their appearance forces the rest of us to think through the intellectual and spiritual premises of their attitudes; a very great effort of mind and soul is required first to find out in what kind of mental world such people live and how to prevent their attitude from spreading to others. That, however, is the subject of another article. At this time we conclude that the autonomous man is 1) man without a father, having divested himself not merely of his heavenly Father, but also of his earthly parents, his forebears, and the past in general; 2) man without a Creator, who finds creatureliness something impossible to accept and live with, who, with Marx and Nietzsche, refuses to acknowledge any dependence of his on anyone or anything, particularly for his life; 3) man without any judge, either in heaven, or on earth, who deems himself unaccountable either to his fellowmen, or to a divine judge, or for the meaning of his life, in the moment of death, who has eliminated all potential measures or yardsticks, such as *physis* (nature, in Aristotle's sense), or *nomos* (civil law), or *ethos* (custom). We have not to look too far to encounter a specimen of this super-race, and when we find one and are curious from where he might be coming, all we have to do is to retrace his steps to the classroom, where unbounded human freedom is taught, as if it were the truth, in many varieties of lectures. In that sense the colleges and universities of our society are the infectious boils on which, surely, the greatest efforts of therapy should be concentrated.

# Loss of Reality:
# Gnosticism and Modern Nihilism *

"LOSS OF REALITY" is a concept introduced by Eric Voegelin's philosophy of consciousness, where it is applied on a historically and topically broad scale. In this essay the concept will be used only in the context of modernity, and there only as focused on the *histoire en philosophe*, the enterprise initiated by Turgot and Voltaire in which history was turned into a hypostasis at the same time at which it was confined to entirely world-immanent factors and forces, to the exclusion of any kind of divine transcendence. It has been pointed out frequently that the anti-Christian thrust of this enterprise was not anti-religious. Rather, the rejection of the traditional view of history which goes back to St. Augustine, St. Paul, and Israel went hand in hand with initiatives to find an anti-Christian religion, openly in the case of Saint-Simon and Comte, concealed in the case of Hegel and Marx.

The theological element in modern "philosophy of history" has been called "gnostic." The concept is, of course, analogous. Hans Jonas has given us a detailed account of how the knowledge of ancient gnosticism enabled him, by analogy, to grasp the nature of Heidegger's existentialism.[1] Once introduced the term tended to become a slogan and occasionally even an epithet. There is an inclination to feel that one has said everything when one has called a modern movement "gnostic." In fact, however, one has not said everything. An analogy has limitations. Modern ideological movements are not organized bodies of worship, nor do they worship a radically transcendent god who is alien to this world. Heuristically the term "gnostic" has been most productive, but it must not cut short the detailed analysis of modern thought structures and cultural phenomena. This essay is meant as a kind of

15

outline of a study of modern alienation and modern nihilism insofar as they differ from ancient gnosticism, by tracing the course from modern "philosophy of history" to the eventual loss of the intelligibility of being, man, and history itself. This result could be plausibly expected where history is construed wholly in terms of material or subhuman forces, but this essay will focus on constructions of history centering on the mind, adducing the three cases of Turgot, Hegel, and Comte.

## Three Systems of History

TURGOT saw genius as the instrument of progress. In order to do its work, however, circumstances had to provide a favorable environment, mainly a rich, i.e. mixed, language. This was brought about chiefly by wars, conquests, revolutions, turmoils involving much misery. "Interest, ambition, vainglory change every moment the scene of the world and flood the earth with blood; and in their midst, customs (morality) become softer, the human mind clearer, the isolated nations approach one another; commerce and politics finally unite parts of the globe, and the total mass of mankind marches, through alternative phases of quiet and disturbance, of good and bad, slowly but steadily toward ever greater perfection.[2] In this passage, history is defined as a "steady march" and its goal as "ever greater perfection," but the process of perfection is merely asserted. Insofar as its causes are mentioned, they are not primarily in the realm of consciousness but in turbulent events brought about by passion. At the other end we find the subject of progress mentioned as "the total mass of mankind" which evades any concreteness,[3] and thus must be called an imaginary subject. There is sufficient empirical content in Turgot to mask his escape from reality, as in this passage:

> The first beginnings of men, the formation and merging of nations, the origin and the revolutions of governments, the progress of languages, of physics, of morals, of sciences and arts, the revolutions which made empires succeed empires, nations succeed nations, religions succeed religions, – mankind, always the same through its upheavals, like the water of the sea through storms, and always advancing toward its perfection.[4]

Again, the "mankind" mentioned at the end appears as a subject both having and not having history, combining attributes of god and man, and resembling a thing of nature, something beyond reality.

Hegel began by radically abstracting from everything that exists, i.e. with thought in the void. Engendering concepts, he obtained an analyzable object by introducing into the concepts movement which necessarily had to be self-movement. History's subject (meaning man) is declared identical with substance (meaning Spinoza's God). The movement, transferred from logic to history, is described as the self-mediated "transitions from one state or position to the other."[5] By "state or positions" Hegel means states of consciousness which thus seem to be equipped with an existence of their own. The "self-mediated transitions" occur through the energy inhering in the opposite of what exists, which leads to "negation," so that the first phase of the movement goes from something to nothing. Out of that *nihil* there then arises something new by way of the "negation of the negation" which thus takes the place of divine creation. Like Turgot, Hegel attributes creative force to destructive processes, except that Hegel uses the term *aufheben* which has the triple meaning of liquidating, raising up, and preserving.

In Marx, incidentally, the "positions" are no longer states of consciousness but rather social conditions, and the transition is characterized not as *aufheben* but rather as "destruction." The system is closed in terms of these concepts over which, Kierkegaard said, Hegel had "forgotten, in a sort of world-historical absentmindedness, what it means to be a human being. Not, indeed, what it means to be a human being in general; for this is the sort of thing that one might even induce a speculative philosopher to agree to; but what it means that you and I and he are human beings, each for himself."[6] In other words, the system has nothing to say to a man living in the world who must die. Thus the reality of man is lost and likewise the reality of existing things, as well as the historical existence of living men among things in the world. Kierkegaard admits that "in a speculative-fantastic sense we have a positive finality in the system. . . . But this sort of finality is valid only for fantastic beings."

Comte started out with an initial experience in 1822, and his system centers on a supposed evolution of the human mind. On closer examination one finds, however, that the "experience" consisted in his hitting on a two-part dogmatic formula. The first part elevated the method of the physical sciences to ontological status, something like a substitute for the concept of being. There followed a hierarchical classification of the sciences, the pride of place moving historically from mathematics to sociology, as the latter would become "positivist." Sociology then would provide a new social order free from any doubt, loopholes, or open questions. Comte's second dogma resembles Hegel's transferrence of movement from concepts to history: the "three stages" formula, the "necessity" of the mind's development from theology through metaphysics to positivism. This movement would culminate in the perfect future society, governed in indubitable certainty by both a spiritual and a temporal authority. That society required the affective bond of a religion, designed to replace Christianity, centering on the worship of the *Grand Être* of humanity and "altruism" as an ethics replacing charity.[7] That Comte, unlike Hegel, conceived the need for an ethics, is to his credit. All the more one is struck by the lack of reality in "the whole of the positive concepts" which, as he says, "is condensed in the single notion of an immense and eternal being, Humanity, whose sociological destiny develops throughout under the necessary preponderance of biological and cosmological fatality."[8] This humanity is defined as "the ensemble of human beings past, future, and present, . . . but only those who are really assimilable."[9] In spite of this note of manipulated inclusion and exclusion, Comte insists that "this true *Grand Être*" is "the immediate mover of each individual or collective existence, (around which) our affections gather as spontaneously as our thoughts and actions."[10]

## Imaginary Concepts and Imaginary Reality

THE THREE constructions of history resemble each other in that they contain considerable empirical material which not only provides a certain amount of *prima facie* plausibility but also apparent grounds for a claim to the character of science, or, respectively, philosophy. Nor can one say that empirical material has been stretched on a bed of Procrustes. Rather the problem is in the structural concepts that provide the framework of unity for the empirical material. In the Augustinian construction we find a series of symbols of eternity which stem from spiritual experience and also enabled Augustine to attain the intelligibility of history. They are such symbols as *Deus creator omnium,* the Eighth Day, the Judgment, Heaven and Hell, the Kingdom of God, Providence. It is significant that he rejected the millennium as a symbol, because of its intramundane realization. The structural concepts used by Turgot, Hegel, and Comte do not have the character of symbolic expressions of either spiritual or other experiences. Nor do they belong to the category of *a posteriori* abstractions. They seem to float in mid-air and would be the same if they were wholly detached from the empirical materials. Turgot's "total mass of mankind" and Comte's *Grand-Être* represent nothing that has existence, yet both are pivotal concepts. The descriptions of historical process are vague and question-begging. The structural concepts do hang together, to use Kierkegaard's words, in a kind of "positive finality" but that finality has no more than a very tenuous relation to reality. The modern *philosophes* of history can arrive at either the unity or the intelligibility of history only by means of "imaginary concepts," if one may coin a term analogous to the imaginary numbers in mathematics.

In mathematics imaginary numbers constitute an artificial system that permits the asking of an infinite number of questions even though the links to reality are removed. One wonders whether that procedure is permissible in a science having to do with concrete human beings and their experiences and actions. All three thinkers mentioned emphasize that the closed logic of their system has for the first time explained the "laws of history" not only for the past but also for the future. The "positive finality" of the system itself thus takes the place of any concreteness and reality. The imaginary character of that reality is evidenced in many ways, in the absence of an ethics in Hegel, in the utter irrelevance of Marx's system to the human problem of death, in Hegel's merging of subject and substance, in the evasiveness of the key concepts of all three.

If one construes history of imaginary concepts with a resulting imaginary reality, the system must necessarily clash with the reality experienced in ordinary life. That clash takes the form of a total critique of "all that exists" (Marx), since the system appears with the claim of novel discovery and logical consistency. As a yardstick of judgment it must necessarily throw the societies of historical growth out of court. The gnostics rejected the world by the yardstick of a radically transcendent divinity. Their total critique expressed itself in asceticism or else a subjective antinomianism. Modern philosophy of history, however, criticizes history with history, or rather, living history with imaginary history. The imaginary concepts speak of causations, creative forces, final destinies, elements of a definitive order, all locked into this world to the exclusion of a divine transcendence. The total critique therefore splits people against people, generates causes in which people enlist, and produces political hostilities.

### Three Types of Alienation

MODERN philosophy of history incites a combative "critique" that may take the form of intellectual destruction or physical destruction by revolutionary armed forces. The imaginary reality thus cannot remain a mere academic structure of concepts but must proclaim itself as a "new world," the "real history," even a "new man." Accepting a closed system of this kind therefore amounts to alienating oneself from one's society and fellow-citizens, from one's past and present.

The speculations of ancient gnosticism concerned things that happened in a divine sphere not only "beyond" the cosmos of things and men, but actually before that cosmos and man ever existed. Gnostic alienation thus rooted in the hypostatization of the "beyond." The gnostic saw two different realities: a divine and good reality wholly alien to this cosmos and this world, and a cosmic and human reality alien to the absent divinity. The gnostic felt alienated insofar as his esoteric knowledge taught him the speculatively established total incompatibility of God and created existence. While gnostic speculation was complex to the point of monstrosity, there is no denying that gnostics lived in some kind of faith. Whatever alienated them had not been brought upon them by themselves or any other men but had occurred in the beyond, before all creation.

Modern ideological alienation is of another type. The modern futurist becomes alienated by his own act of accepting an idea structure that implies a declaration of war by some men on the historical existence of all men. The idea structure is one that he can take or leave. It is known to him as the work of some contemporary or at any rate modern author which carries none of the halo of ancient truth attending the myth, even the contrived myths of ancient gnostics. The ideological system bears the stamp of an imperious pretension in rebellion against that which exists. The symbol of Prometheus, perverted into a modern hero of rebellion, is present in all modern thinking. Thus modern alienation is based not on faith but on choice. It consists in the hypostatization of an historical "against," and thus entails an irreconcilable polarization of social forces, particular human beings, and even ideas and emotions. The alienation is intentionally entered and its maintenance deliberately cultivated. Its character is willfull rather than experiential.

There is a third type of alienation which seems to be the oldest variety, one that has consistently occurred in typical human experience and is widely documented. It stems from sorrow at being separated from God, the source of truth, order, and peace. It is probably best represented by the *Lamentations of Jeremiah*. Here one finds no hypostatization; rather a suffering awareness of a distance between God and man for which man feels he himself is to blame. While gnostic alienation comes from going excessively *beyond* the world, and ideological alienation from going excessively *against* the world, the third type of alienation has nothing excessive about it. One may call this type of alienation "real," in that it roots in the experienced reality of God who is alien neither to the creation nor to man, and of man who has both the capacity for the infinite and a tendency toward the finite. This alienation is not experienced as essential and thus can be, and is often, resolved in reconciliation.

## Three Movements in Modern Art

WITH THE GLANCE at alienation we have left the realm of a critique of concepts and entered that of ensuing existential attitudes and disturbances of social order. In that respect, most critics of modern ideologies have confined themselves to pointing out the manifest disorder of the Fascist, Nationalsocialist, and Communist movements and their terror regimes. I shall here essay a brief appraisal of schools or movements of modern art where attitudes and practices similar to those of the political ideologists can be found. The analysis of modern art movements is useful for two reasons. First, these movements formed independently from the political movements, to some extent even preceding the latter, so that the evidence indicates the prevalence of alienation and rebellion in the entire culture. Secondly, the art movements appeared, developed and declined much faster than the political movements and thus supply quantitatively more material.

The question of when to begin is not easily answerable. I shall here arbitrarily decide on Fauvism (1905) as a starting point. That movement was quickly followed by Cubism, with Picasso's *Les Demoiselles d'Avignon* as the opening trumpet blast, in 1907. Then came the largely Italian movement of Futurism, beginning in 1909, with new waves in 1910, and a Russian branch in 1914. The wartime phenomenon of De Stijl (Mondrian, 1917) led to the postwar Constructionism (1920). In Germany, 1919 was the beginning of the Bauhaus movement, while in France Dada had originated already in 1918. Surrealism developed in 1924 but it has a precursor in Max Ernst (1919). After the Second World War there formed a Dutch group called CoBrA (1949). In 1951 there occurred a revival of Dada, and in 1960 we have both the New Realism and Pop Art. The list is by no means exhaustive but suffices for our purposes. In practically all cases the first step is the publication of a manifesto, containing a declaration of war against both past and present and a sketch of the imaginary reality to which the group of artists consider themselves committed. Frequently, further manifestos accompany waves of artistic production of the school. The manifestos authoritatively prescribe what is and what is not to be experienced.

Tristan Tarza wrote the *Dada Manifesto of 1918*.[11] It begins:

To put out a manifesto you must want:
ABC
to fulminate against 1,2,3
to fly into a rage and sharpen your wings to conquer and

disseminate little abcs and big abcs, to sign, shout, swear, to organize prose into a form of absolute and irrefutable evidence, to prove your non plus ultra and maintain that novelty resembles life just as the latest appearance of some whore proves the essence of God. His existence was previously proved by the accordion, the landscape, the wheedling word. To impose your ABC is a natural thing—hence deplorable. Everybody does it in the form of crystalbluff-madonna, monetary system, pharmaceutical product, or a bare leg advertising the ardent sterile spring. The love of novelty is the cross of sympathy, demonstrates a naive *je m'enfoutisme*, it is a transitory, positive sign without a cause.

Futurism produced a number of manifestos. The original manifesto, by F.T. Marinetti (1909) contained these passages:

Let's break out of the horrible shell of wisdom and throw ourselves like pride-ripened fruit into the wide, contorted mouth of the wind! Let's give ourselves utterly to the Unknown, not in desperation but only to replenish the deep wells of the Absurd! . . . Courage, audacity, and revolt will be essential elements of our poetry. . . . Except in struggle, there is no more beauty. No work without an aggressive character can be a masterpiece. Poetry must be conceived as a violent attack on unknown forces, to reduce and prostrate them before man. . . . We will glorify war—the world's only hygiene—militarism, patriotism, the destructive gesture of freedom-bringers, beautiful ideas worth dying for, and scorn for woman. We will destroy the museum, libraries, academies of every kind, we will fight moralism, feminism, every opportunistic or utilitarian cowardice. . . . Take up your pickaxes, your axes and hammers and wreck, wreck the venerable cities, pitilessly![12]

A third example is the first manifesto of Surrealism, written in 1924 by André Breton:

So strong is the belief in life, in what is most fragile in life—*real* life, I mean—that in the end this belief is lost. Man, that inveterate dreamer, daily more discontent with his destiny, has trouble assessing the objects he has been led to use . . . he will hardly succeed. This is because he henceforth belongs body and soul to an imperative practical necessity which demands his constant attention. None of his gestures will be expansive, none of his ideas generous or far-reaching. In his mind's eye, events real or imagined will be seen only as they relate to a welter of similar events, events in which he has not participated, *abortive* events. What I am saying: he will judge them in relationship to one of these events whose consequences are more reassuring than the others. On no account will he view them as his salvation.[13].

Even where there is no manifesto, there has nevertheless been a deliberate intellectual destruction of past and present. Logically, this is followed by actions with destructive intent. The British writer and critic Edward Lucie-Smith[14] comments on Picasso's *Demoiselles d'Avignon*: "Everything leads us to suppose that it was a large part of Picasso's intention to produce a picture which any middle-class spectator would find unacceptably hideous." (p.14) He quotes Barnett Newman: "In 1940, some of us woke up to find ourselves without hope, to find that painting did not really exist. Or to coin a modern phrase, painting . . . (like God) . . . was dead. The awakening had the exaltation of a revolution. It was that awakening that inspired the aspiration . . . to start from scratch, to paint as if painting had never existed before." (p. 76) The movements in each case consisted of only a small group of men, each of whom would mingle his personal development with the publicly proclaimed school dogma. Hence all of these movements were relatively short-lived, the reason being that the "awakening" and "exaltation" and intoxication with novelty were followed by the discovery of an abyss of nothingness. Lucie-Smith quotes Adolf Gottlieb: "The situation was so bad that I know I felt free to try anything. . . . What was there to lose? Neither Cubism nor Surrealism could absorb someone like myself – we felt like derelicts." (p. 76) Likewise L. Fontana: "Beyond the perforations of a newly gained freedom of interpretation awaits us also, and inevitably, the end of art."

## The Pattern of Nihilism

ONE CAN discover a repeated pattern, beginning with destruction, moving to the illusion of new creation, and ending in nihilism. The initial rejection of everything that exists by the mind entails a determination actively to destroy. Upon destruction follows the illusion of a new, untrammeled freedom, particularly the freedom to create a new "world," be it of art or of existence. In art, production implies a kind of proof. The expected new worlds do not materialize. Soon the impulse dies in disillusionment which may refer to that particular movement or even to art as a whole, which for an artist would be equivalent to life as a whole. The process throws light on a number of temporary phenomena. First, there seem to be two varieties of nihilism. The announcement of nothingness at the outset ("to find that painting did not really exist") amounts not so much to a description but rather to a statement of intention to annihilate.

It is, then, an annihilating nihilism. After the new untrammeled freedom has run its brief course and ended in illusion, however, there is the shattering experience that one finds oneself plunged into nothingness, either as regards the hopes for a new world, or else as regards the whole of human endeavor, in this case, art. This is, then, an annihilated nihilism. At the outset there is nihilism by intent, and the result is nihilism by discovery. In either case, however, the nihilism remains no mere subjective feeling but a publicly spreading position and attitude. Secondly, one notes that the act of destroying what exists and the illusion of untrammeled freedom do generate and enhance creative capabilities, even if they express themselves in a frenzied way and have but a meteoric career. Modern art undoubtedly is characterized by a destructive and nihilistic mood. All the same, a considerable public finds its work at least fascinating and exciting, and can derive enjoyment from them. We discover that the demonic as well as the divine can appear with a kind of beauty of its own, and that nothingness has a perverse kind of aesthetic appeal, – that discovery of beauty's ambiguity which left its mark on Dostoevsky's anthropology. In this sense modern art bears out Plato's contention that the degeneration and perversion of a true human order result not in the dissolution or cessation of existence but precisely in a perverted variety of order, something that in its perversion centers on a governing principle which observers as well as protagonists can accept as "thinkable" and novel. Perversity and degeneration do not so clearly manifest themselves that we can consider ourselves excused from the task of sorting out truth from untruth.

## The Recovery of Reality

THERE REMAINS the question of how to return from the wasteland.
For the ancient gnostics the step seems not to have been particularly difficult. There is the case of the two day public disputation which St. Augustine had with the Manichaean Elect Felix, in
404. Felix, at the end, conceded defeat and signed a protocol curs-
ing Mani, after which Augustine admitted him to the Church.[15]
Twelve years before that date Augustine had carried a similar victory over the local Manichaean leader Fortunatus who in utter
humiliation left the town. Nothing as simple as that is conceivable
in the modern world. The gulf is not breachable by discussion. For
the particular intellectual, Eric Voegelin has suggested that
"whoever has had enough of rebellion against the ground and
wishes again to think rationally needs only to turn around and
toward that reality against which the symbols of rebellion aggress.
It seems that the rebellion itself can become the guideline for the
seeker, inasmuch as that against which he rebels is precisely that
which he is seeking."[16] That road is indeed the one which Voegelin
himself has walked. Others, however, have not found it easy to
enter it. They frequently grope for the symbols of what they have
lost, but the symbols no longer speak to them, so that they fail to
perceive incompatibilities and tend to a kind of desperate eclec-
ticism. In the same context Voegelin seems to indicate another way
when he asks: "From where did Albert Camus get the strength that
sustained him for decades in the tension of his meditation and
enabled him to look through the perversion of rebellion and to overcome it?" His answer is: "For Camus it came from the [Greek]
myth."[17] Again this road has not proved viable for all people. It did
not help Robert Graves. In the case of Tolkien, who wrote nar-
ratives with a high level of reality in the mode of the myth, it seems
that he personally had never suffered from loss of reality. T.H.
White, on the other hand, while using the myth skillfully, wrote ancient legends into which he carried the entire baggage of his
modern alienation.

There is one contemporary example, one is tempted to say
paradigm, of a return from modern nihilism achieved not primarily
by an intellectual effort or by way of the myth, but rather as the
result of personal primary experience. It is the case of hundreds,

maybe thousands of Soviet labor camp prisoners who were driven to the brink of personal annihilation and regained the reality of man in the reality of transcendence through a spiritual wager of their life. Solzhenitsyn has written about his personal case. As a wider phenomenon it is described by Mihajlo Mihajlov in his article "Mystical Experiences in the Labor Camps."[18] Basing his findings on the written testimony of Solzhenitsyn, Panin, Shiffrin, and Tertz (only one of them a Christian), Mihajlov comments on the astonishing number of prisoners who experienced a strong and sustaining spiritual force: "descriptions of an intense, concentrated life . . . a life which, despite all torment, was oddly precious." The very experience itself forced a rethinking "not only of the psychology and psychoanalysis of the twentieth century, but also of Marxism in contemporary Western sociology," a process which "explodes the very foundation on which modern science and philosophy are built." Here, indeed, is the intellectual retracing of steps which Voegelin suggests. In these cases the road proved viable because at the outset there was not a mere intellectual decision but a totally renewing experience of militantly accepted suffering in soul, body, and mind. One is driven to the conclusion that as deep a loss of reality as modern man experiences cannot be retrieved at any lower cost.

*This article is based on a paper given at the Conference on Gnosticism and Reality, held at Vanderbilt University in April of 1978 under the direction of Dr. Richard J. Bishirjian and Dr. William Havard. Sponsors were the Earhart Foundation, the Vanderbilt Research Council, and the Intercollegiate Studies Institute, Inc. This article shall subsequently appear as a chapter in a book to be published by the Louisiana State University Press.

[1] *The Gnostic Religion*, 2nd ed., Epilogue (Boston: Beacon Books, 1963).
[2] *Oeuvres de Turgot*, Schelle, ed., 5 vls., 1913-23, vol. I, p. 215.
[3] On Turgot's "progress" and "total mass of humanity" cf. Eric Voegelin, *From Enlightenment to Revolution* (Durham: Duke University Press, 1975), pp. 90ff, 92ff, 98.
[4] *Oeuvres*, vol. I, p. 276.
[5] *Phenomenology of Mind*, Baillie, tr., p. 80.
[6] *Concluding Unscientific Postscript*, thesis attributable to Lessing, B.

[7]On Comte's *Grand-Être* cf. Eric Voegelin, *From Enlightenment to Revolution*, ch. VII.

[8]*Catéchisme Positiviste* (Paris, 1891), p. 54.

[9]*Ibid.*, p. 65.

[10]*Ibid.*, p. 55.

[11]*Dadas on Art*, Lucy R. Lippard, ed. (Englewood Cliffs, 1971).

[12]*Futurist Manifestos*, Umbro Apollonio, ed., Engl. tr. (New York, 1973).

[13]*Surrealists on Art*, Lucy R. Lippard, ed. (Englewood Cliffs, 1970).

[14]*Art Now* (New York: Morrow, 1977). See also H.B. Chipp, *Theories of Modern Art* (Los Angeles: University of California Press, 1968).

[15]F. Van der Meer, *Augustinus der Seelsorger*, German tr. (Cologne: Bachem, 1951), p. 152.

[16]*Anamnesis* (Notre Dame: Notre Dame University Press, 1978), p. 188.

[17]*Ibid.*, p. 189.

[18]*Kontinent 2*, American edition, 1977.

# The Loss and
# Recovery of History

PHILOSOPHY OF HISTORY is a concept coined by Voltaire, who can be said to have originated this form of consciousness in the middle of the eighteenth century. From the beginning, philosophy of history had an anti-theistic character. The tableau of world-immanent developments and evolutions which Voltaire constructed was meant as a substitute for the concept of Providence that still had dominated Bossuet's *Histoire Universelle*. We have Voltaire's word for it: "Let us respectfully leave the divine to those who are its keepers, and attach ourselves solely to history."[1]

After Voltaire created the first model of what he called history *en philosophe*, his successors, with Hegel and Marx at their head, went even further in deliberately making of philosophical history an alternative to religious faith. They relied on history to provide man with a destiny and a goal, and the goal, both of time and in time, served as a replacement for all moral values. The philosophy of history, therefore, cannot be understood properly except in terms of its negative relation to Christianity. That is not the same as a negative relation to religion. Philosophy of history is not in itself hostile to religion.

First, among the great systems of philosophy of history constructed between 1750 and 1850 there are a few in which a deist god figures as the absentee landlord of Nature. Second, at least two of these systems of history, those of Saint-Simon and Auguste Comte, supplemented the scheme of successive ages of history with a newly invented civil religion expressly designed to displace Christianity. Third, in Hegel's system, history figures as a kind of biography of the Absolute Mind, which is Hegel's formula for god, no longer "the maker of heaven and earth" but rather a god coming to be himself through the development of human consciousness. Philosophy of history, then, far from being anti-religious, pretends to the status of an "ersatz religion," a new religion proposed to take the place of faith in God, the Father of Jesus Christ.

Philosophy of history is a form of the loss of reality. "Loss of reality," a concept coined by Eric Voegelin, has a profound meaning in the context of Voegelin's philosophy of consciousness, a meaning which it would take too long to explain fully at this point. As I am going to steer this paper in the direction of empirical evidence, I hope that the phenomena will speak for themselves and illustrate the concept.

At this point I should like to remark only that the sentence "philosophy of history is a form of the loss of reality" can be taken in two meanings. First, it can mean that philosophy of history is a symbolic form giving expression to the experience of having lost consciousness of reality. In other words, human beings, feeling themselves threatened by a sense of sliding into nothingness, grab hold of history in a desperate effort to construct some meaning of human existence and to save themselves from dying by boredom, or melancholy. Second, the sentence could mean that the construction of a philosophy of history in itself entails a deliberate contraction or reduction of reality, so that the reality that goes into the image is less than the full reality. Let us, for the time being, dwell on this second meaning.

Let me describe a few varieties of the "loss of reality" as a function of the partial destruction of reality by the philosopher of history. The construction of history *en philosophe*, as Voltaire named it, relies on a more or less arbitrary selection of facts. Voltaire expressly stated that he obtained something like a unified picture of history only as he chose from the record "what is worthy to be known" and "what is useful,"[2] and that only by so choosing could he make "out of this chaos a general and well-articulated tableau."[3]

Likewise Friedrich Schiller, who in 1789 gave a lecture on universal history at the University of Jena, remarked that the record of past events showed wide and obvious gaps, but rejoiced in this as an advantage to his enterprise, since it allowed him to fill the space between the fragments using materials of his own imagination. Only in this way, he said, would he be able to arrive at a totality of universal history that had the quality of "concealing the narrow boundaries of birth and death," in other words, "expanding his brief and oppressive existence into an infinite space, and to merge the individual into the species,"[4] i.e. into a man-made ersatz immortality. Voltaire and Schiller thus knew that their constructions contained no more than fragments of reality, combined with products of their own fabulation. The result, part fact and part fiction, nevertheless claimed to be the whole of reality, so that the reduction of reality was undertaken deliberately by the authors.

A reduction of a different kind stems from the selection of one causal factor as a key to the entire course of history. After Voltaire, philosophical constructions of history confined themselves to efficient causation as the propellant of change and progress, rejecting the other three of Aristotle's causes, above all, final causes. This, in itself, is a reductive idea, claiming exclusive reality only for what can be explained as the effect of efficient causation. Besides, the selection of one causal factor as containing the key to the knowledge of history reduces other causal factors or aspects of existence to an inferior grade of reality or to unreality.

We refer, by way of example, to Marx's *German Ideology*. The single and permanent cause of history, Marx says there, is the change from one mode of economic production to another. "Morality, metaphysics, all the rest of ideology and their corresponding forms of consciousness, thus no longer retain their semblance of independence. They have no history, no development. . . ."[5] This, of course, is Marx's vaunted correction of Hegel, who had attributed history exclusively to the developments of human consciousness. Marx, then, reduces consciousness to a derivative of economic factors which alone have the character of historical reality. Hegel's selection of consciousness as the sole factor of history, however, is no less a reduction than Marx's selection of economic structures, for Hegel reduced God to his incarnation in human affairs and to the evolution of human consciousness.

Incidentally, the fallacy of Marx's reduction shows up only a few pages after he had proclaimed it, when Marx, having said that there was only the history of modes of economic production, introduces the history of the class struggle, which obviously pre-

supposes some degree of an autonomous consciousness, the proletariat's consciousness "of its historic mission," as mentioned later
in *The Communist Manifesto*.

The problems stemming from Marx's approach to history are immediately evident: the reduction of history to the succession of
modes of economic production resulted not only in the neglect of
political order by the socialists, but in their demonstrated inability
to construct anything like a political theory, as becomes clear when
one looks at the frantic but unsuccessful efforts of Engels, Lenin,
Stalin, and Khrushchev to arrive at principles of political order, on
the basis of Marxian premises. It just could not be done.

A third variety of reduction stems from the concept of a goal, in
the form of a future society in space and time, a society that would
constitute a full, harmonious, and perfect human existence. Incidentally, this idea of a goal is what distinguishes philosophy of
history from a philosophy of process. The latter, a doctrine about
change as such, requires no goal concept. To refer again to Marx,
his teaching on revolution as "the locomotive of history" does not
require the idea of a culmination, a final goal. Revolutionary
change could be expected to go on indefinitely. That would be a
philosophy of process.

Marx, however, postulated an end to this process, by introducing
into his series of revolutions one revolution that differs from all the
others. The proletariat, unlike all other revolutionary classes, has
no property of its own, so that its victory will mean the end of all
class societies and the end of the class struggle. This means, of
course, that Marx attributes to that socialist society a quality of being which he denied to all previous societies. To use the language of
Parmenides, only in the socialist future can Marx find being (or
"issing"), so that by comparison all previous ages must be seen as
nothing but "coming-to-be," provisional and instrumental existence.

This differentiation of societies corresponds to a similar image of
man, in the Marxian mind. Marx believes that the reality of man is
wholly dependent on the social conditions. In any one of the
societies prior to the final socialist society, then, man is not man.
Marx sees man as separated from his own essence, separated from
his fellow beings, and from himself, a mere fragment of a man, a
being wholly determined in its existence, like an animal. That

means, among other things, that all of man's attempts to know himself cannot be anything else but speculations on the utopian future, that neither the present nor the past can give us any clues about our own humanity.

An interesting confirmation of the loss of reality can be found in the concept of a spark of reality having persisted through all the past dark ages. Auguste Comte, who divided history into the theological, the metaphysical, and the positivist age, the latter being his concept for the society of the imminent future, attributes to the past a weak trace of inchoate positivism mixed both with the theology of the first and the metaphysics of the second age, and accounting for the forward momentum.

A similar concept is that of the so-called forerunners of communism, such men as Spartakus, John Ball, Thomas Muentzer, Jean Meslier, and Morelly. If we look at these concepts we find that the past is not depicted as either society, or man, in an embryonic or inchoate stage of early development. Rather, it is only a tiny little spark, a segment of the whole, that is considered real because it prefigures the future, meaning that all the rest of the past does not have the character of even inchoate reality.

It will have become clear that philosophy of history, far from philosophical in character, is an enterprise of modern myth-making. The totality of history, made imaginatively out of fragments of facts and assertion of causes has the character of a myth. Certainly the alleged goal of history, to occur in space and time, as the fulfillment of human destiny, is a myth. The human agency or enterprise through which this denouement is to be brought about, has likewise mythical character. The philosophy of history transgresses the bounds of genuine classical philosophy both in front and in back, expressing its meaning through images of speculation which pretend to historical reality. This brings up the problem of the difference between ideological myths serving as the "cause" of movements and the myths that have ordered civilizations.

Sacred myths of all cultures acknowledge the givenness and mystery of the reality in which humans participate. By the naming of the gods and the telling of mythical stories they seek to grasp the relatedness or unity as well as the fittingness of the parts in the whole. Whatever is experienced is thus accounted for. There are the life processes of generation, decay, and renewal, the returning cycles of growth, seasons, days, and nights. There is man with his powers of speech, arts, and action, the mysterious terminals of his birth and death, the struggle of good and evil in his life. There are human societies with their hierarchical order, the ups and downs of their existence, their endurance through changing generations of individual members. The cosmos is full of wonders, and thus full of gods, as Thales put it.

The myth-making mind neither denies nor destroys the experienced reality and man's participation. His myths subtract nothing that is experienced, and they contribute the communicability of meaning, through stories, and rites. They fully acknowledge the facts of reality, its tangibilities, visibilities, usabilities, terribilities, together with the partly hidden wherefores and uncertain wheretos, the uncanny powers and unstable frailties of reality.

This kind of mythical fabulation does not have the character of willful fantasy, and thus can provide for a rational being a basis of operation in a cosmos which man acknowledges not to have made himself. It furnishes the human mind with a hypothetical order of the cosmos and existence which makes sense and thus supports thought, and also serves man's practical needs as effectively as did the explanation of the pump through the notion of *horror vacui*. Sacred myth, then, is fabulation in the attitude of deference to, and full awareness of, the reality that is not man-made and in which man experiences himself as participating.

We have already seen that the myths created by the philosophy of history imply a loss of reality, to a large extent through a willful intellectual destruction of reality, a contraction of its scope and character. At the beginning of this lecture, I allowed for the possibility of an original experience of lost reality to which these myths might seek to give expression. Such experiences were indeed recorded in the seventeenth and eighteenth centuries. One thinks of Pascal's horror of "the infinite immensity of spaces . . . which know me not."[6]

Undoubtedly, there must have been countless cases of a loss of faith, of the resulting disorientation and confusion, during the Enlightenment. One might look on philosophy of history as possibly the expression either of such lamentable and lamented experiences

of a reality lost, or maybe of the jubilant experience of a new reality
having been found. There is some evidence of the latter, as when
Feuerbach's assertion that gods were the projections of man's own
noble attributes to some phantasmal set of beings, touched off a
wave of enthusiasm among young Hegelians. One also recalls the
atmosphere of religious awe gripping the audience at Hegel's lectures, or the lectures of Hegel's successor, Professor Gans.

Precisely this evidence, however, tells us that what we have here
are secondary experiences, i.e. experiences touched off by the con-
trivance of ideas rather than primary experiences of reality. In
other words, if we look for evidence of a newly discovered
reality – symbolization of both experiences in and through
ideologies, we find that actually the series is reversed.

Pascal, who did have an experience of cosmic loneliness, reacted
by regaining his Christian faith. Voltaire, who rejected Christianity, never seems to have had an experience similar to Pascal's. In
Voltaire's case his formula "the human mind, left to itself,"[7] is an
axiom of his philosophy of history and, as such, a deliberate and aggressive choice rather than a primary experience. It suggests that
philosophy of history does not have the character of a remedial
system to comfort man as he feels left to himself. Rather, it begins
by creating the position of "the human mind, left to itself," and then
begins the enterprise of drawing philosophical and
historiographical results from its own creation.

The replacement of Providence by efficient causation, of a self-
enclosed human mind for a participating soul, of human self-
salvation for divine salvation, all bear the stamp of grim and combative eristic rather than of jubilant discovery. In other words, a
new reality was not discovered in the soul's experience but rather
defiantly made up of deficient parts and, with full knowledge of the
deficiency, passed on as if it were the whole. The experience followed from the astonishing success of the trick, rather than from
meditation preceding it. Or, to put it in other words, the experience
was a response to the artifice of a system, rather than to a
manifestation of reality.

Philosophy of history, as a system, is a whole consisting of three
parts: the fixed element in it is a permanent causal factor alleged to
bring forth the succession of history's phases; the variable element
is the utter plasticity of man seen as a function of progressively

higher social arrangements; the third element is neither variable nor fixed but rather an anticipated product of human making: the future utopia.

Once this kind of thinking is around and accepted as if it were reality, it touches off its own experiences. The experiences are roughly two: the jubilant lust of apparently limitless power, and the complaint of abysmal alienation. The lust of power manifests itself in the intellectual postulate of "certain knowledge" replacing the former uncertainty of faith and the fuzziness of moral philosophy. Hegel triumphantly proclaimed "certainty of knowledge" as the attribute of his speculation, replacing Plato's "love of truth." Feuerbach's bid to "take back" from a non-existing deity the noble attributes which in truth are man's own implies the same character of certain possession. "Certainty:" Marion Montgomery muses, "the death of love, and so of poetry, since it is the death of the possible or probable. Certainty destroys wonder, desire, joy, sorrow – those inclinations swayed from love to love."[8]

The resulting lust of power, or lust of certain possession, eventually found its supreme expression in the phrase "God is dead." One should note that in Nietzsche's *Froeliche Wissenschaft* this formula is embedded in philosophy of history, as manifested by the following sentences: "We have killed him – you and I! We are all his murderers!"[9] The murder is an historical event, dividing a before from an after. Thus philosophy of history shifted the order of human action from the truth of goodness to the goal of history, or, as Camus put it, "from vertical to horizontal transcendence."[10]

The "horizontal transcendence," history's utopia, appearing as the highest product of human salvific enterprise, entailed the corresponding depreciation of the past and the present. Man's sense of uncertainty made a roundabout turn. It used to be that from the past there came a sense of solidity and direction. The common-sense man is "a boatman," who "moves intelligently forward as he looks backward,"[11] to use the words of John A. Mackay.

The lust of power and certainty, however, now flamed up over the prospect of a salvific future, to be built by human forces and efforts. Consequently, the future was invested with certainty, while past and present were subordinated to that future not only as prolegomena, but also as antitheses. It is instructive to find Marx praising his "forerunner," Fourier, not for any of Fourier's constructive ideas, but rather for Fourier's scathing and, indeed, total criticism of the present, which implies a similar disdain for the past.

The curious result of this reversal of certainty is the loss of that history which philosophy of history sought to construct. The future, which has not yet occurred, governs the ideas of the present and the past. So the past, no longer providing a solidity of background, becomes infinitely malleable, subject to re-writings, deletions, additions, whatever is needed to justify the movement toward the utopian future. Similarly, the present is described as nothing but darkness inhabited by monstrous human types.

However, the future, which alone is supposed to shed light, actually recedes further and further as the years go by in unmitigated bleakness.

Something similar happens to the concept of man. The concept of human nature does play, or is meant to play, a central role in the philosophy of history, depicted as the movement toward the ultimate realization of human nature. First of all, however, man's coming-to-be in the course of historical ages requires the concept of man's infinite malleability, through changing social arrangements. Second, since the present, as Ernst Bloch put it, is darkness wholly unintelligible, and the past is utterly lost, no experience is available to tell us about human nature. To put it in other words, a concept of human nature could only be drawn from the future utopia. That utopia, however, has not yet occurred, and, what is more, such ranking Marxists as Lenin and Ernst Bloch consider the real possibility that it may be missed. Thus the entire three-partite system fails to fit reality, to explain reality, to draw meaning from reality. On the contrary, it finds itself in open conflict with reality on three of four fronts.

Its myths neither support nor are supported by man's existence, man's experience of the limits of birth and death, man's experienced transcending of his natural existence, man's depth of memory, man's sense of being. Instead, the myths of philosophy of history go together only with the human will to power in its Promethean defiance of the divine.

It is because of their perennial conflict with human experience and reality that these myths have been surrounded with intellectual and physical means of enforcement. They have been converted into dogmas, in open contradiction to their own claim to constitute a "science." Dogmas do have their place in human affairs, but are wholly out of place when the matter supposedly is science, empirically founded and based on strict logic. The rigid dogmatism of an ideology presenting itself in the language of science thus insults the critical sense of even the man in the street, whose day-by-day experiences give the lie to those dogmatized myths. The myths, however, the less tenable they are, are all the more tenaciously enforced, imposed, and inflicted as the monopoly of truth. For by their own destruction of past and present, and of the concept of man, they have opened up behind and around them the abyss of nothingness and the corresponding anxiety of alienation.

These myths are deliberately accepted only by a minority. To the others who still continue to be guided, more or less, by common sense, the dogma of history that is no history constitutes a web of lies. Russia has become a country deprived of its history. On this condition, Solzhenitsyn remarks as follows:

> One cannot help fearing that the abnormality of the conditions which underlie the study of Russian history, similar to a general displacement of geological strata, creates . . . a common *systematic* error, as mathematicians would say. The error displaces and distorts all the results of research. The abnormality I speak of lies, first of all in a paradox: the fact that the country studied is your contemporary – it leads a real and stormy existence – and yet, at the same time, it behaves like the archeologist's prehistory: the spine of its history has been fractured, its memory has failed, it has lost the power of speech. It has been denied the possibility of writing the truth about itself, to tell honestly how things are, to discover itself.[12]

Solzhenitsyn points here to a condition affecting scholarship, which he has tried to counteract by his own scholarly novels on Russia's history, as well as by his *Gulag Archipelago*.

In the life of the ordinary citizen, however, this same "displacement" manifests itself as the necessity of lying in order to live:

> The permanent lie becomes the only safe form of existence, in the same way as betrayal. Every wag of the tongue can be heard by someone, every facial expression observed by some-

one. Therefore every word if it does not have to be a direct
lie, is nonetheless obliged not to contradict the general, common lie. . . . But that was not all: Your children were growing
up! . . . And if the children were little, then you had to decide
what was the best way to bring them up; whether to start
them off on lies instead of the truth (so that it would be *easier*
for them to live) and then to lie forevermore in front of them
too; or to tell them the truth, with the risk that they might
make a slip, that they might let it out, which meant that you
had to instill in them from the start that the truth was
murderous, that beyond the threshold of the house you had to
lie, only lie, just like papa and mama.[13]

Summing it all up, Solzhenitsyn adds: "And the lie has, in fact, led
us so far away from a normal society that you cannot even orient
yourself any longer; in its dense, gray fog not even one pillar can be
seen."[14]

"Russia is a country that has officially been deprived of its
history." This sentence is not a metaphorical statement but a fact
of life in Russia. One piece of evidence is the list of official text-
books that have been issued for use in schools at the university
level. The first is a book on political economy: that, according to
Marx, is the essential though truncated reality of man. A second
textbook is called *Marxism-Leninism*; it contains the communist
ideology and the ideological version of society. Its companion is a
textbook on Marxist philosophy, presenting dialectical
materialism, the only philosophy taught in Soviet Russia. Then
there is the history of the CPSU, in other words, a history of the
Party in lieu of a history of Russia: Russia had history only until
1917, then its place was taken by the history of the Communist Party numbering less than five percent of the Russian people. The last
textbook is called *Scientific Communism*; it surveys on the one
hand, the forerunners of the Communist Party in the past of
Western civilization, and, on the other hand, the problems of the
transition from capitalism to communism, especially the transition
of the present phase of socialism to the final phase of communism,
in the Soviet Union. This last book, then, puts the CPSU, the Communist Party of Russia, in the framework of a wider past and a
universal future, attributing all dimensions of history exclusively to
the communist enterprise.

Russia as an agglomeration of people without history. What does that mean in day-by-day reality? Solzhenitsyn tells us:

> In half a century we have not succeeded in calling anything by its right name or thinking anything through. . . . For decades, while we were silent, our thoughts straggled in all possible and impossible directions, lost touch with each other, never learned to know each other, ceased to check and correct each other.[15]

It is in Russia, however, that a movement has begun to which we must attribute the quintessential character of a recovery of history in our time. It is a movement composed of intellectuals to whom the Western world refers by the belittling name of "dissidents."

The movement owes its cohesion to the catalytic effect of Solzhenitsyn's publications. Solzhenitsyn has also coined the appropriate descriptive title of the movement, the name of his lead article in *From Under the Rubble*: "As Breathing and Consciousness Returns." In what way is consciousness returning to this increasingly articulate group of Russian writers and thinkers? Solzhenitsyn again is the one who provides the answer, through the whole of his work and life. Neither his life nor his work are governed by a note of dissidence, which has a chiefly negative connotation. Solzhenitsyn's achievement is, above all, to have re-gained, in experience, thought, and word, the reality of man, God, and history.

The experience came as he began to accept the hardly imaginable degradation of his existence in prison camp and, simultaneously, to re-discover his own humanity in the surrounding humanity of all others, his own torturers included. Under conditions of near-annihilation he learned to be grateful for the tiniest manifestation of life, so that, years later, he could sincerely write: *"Bless you, prison*, for having been in my life."[16] The experience revealed to him, all at once, both man and God, the re-discovery of God occurring in the same motion of his soul as the re-discovery of human reality.

What followed upon that experience was hard intellectual work: "As breathing returns after our swoon, as a glimmer of consciousness breaks through the unrelieved darkness, it is difficult for us at first to regain clarity of vision, to pick our way among the clutter of hurdles, among the idols planted in our path."[17] "The rubble" is ideology, the willed falsehood of consciousness, which to remove is tantamount to the recovery of history. "Our present system," writes Solzhenitsyn of Russia, "is unique in world history, because over and above its physical and economic constraints, it demands total surrender of our souls, continuous and active participation in the general, conscious *lie*."[18] Hence, he concludes, "the absolutely essential task is not political liberation, but the liberation of our souls from participation in the lie forced upon us."[19] This lead article in *From Under the Rubble* is a profound criticism of Sakharov, who, far more than Solzhenitsyn, deserves to be called a "dissident," a man who differs with the Soviet rulers on policy but is not deeply concerned with what his soul participates in. Solzhenitsyn's critique is hard and inexorable: "No one who voluntarily runs with the hounds of falsehood, or props it up, will ever be able to justify himself to the living, or to posterity, or to his friends, or to his children."[20]

The problem, as Solzhenitsyn sees and describes it, emerges with life-and-death urgency in Russia, but is a concern of the entire modern world. In the West, it is no less the burden of foreign policy than it is in Russia the burden of false participation. The political dimension of the problem turns out to be secondary to the religious aspect, and the latter turns out to be a revelation to those who have lived in the man-made hell of *Gulag Archipelago*. Thus the Russians have the advantage over us of having suffered more deeply, and having reaped from their suffering the experienced ripening of their souls.

The movement began, in Russia, in the personal experience of sundry prisoners. It took on the shape of a group movement with the publication of Solzhenitsyn's *One Day in the Life of Ivan Denisovitch*, which appeared as a bright light in the darkness of Soviet life. Solzhenitsyn has neither in Russia nor abroad tried to form anything like a political conspiracy. His endeavor is to induce others to join in "the return of consciousness." Hence the publication of the volume *From Under the Rubble*, a book that relates itself to the 1909 publication called *Vekhi* (*Landmarks*), and, like *Landmarks* is a joint publication of a group of authors. Solzhenitsyn is also a contributor to *Kontinent*, a periodical publication edited by Vladimir Maximov. All these, and other works, address primarily

Russians but at the same time also the non-Communist world. Among these writers, Solzhenitsyn is the one person fully aware of that and how his breathing and consciousness have returned, and that that return to reality is the recovery of history. Without any trace of vanity, but in deep seriousness, he can state: "History is us – and there is no alternative but to shoulder the burden of what we so passionately desire and bear it out of the depths."[21]

[1]François Voltaire, "Essai sur les moeurs et l'esprit," *Oeuvres complètes*, vol. 2, ed. E. de la Bédolière and Georges Avenal (Paris: Bureau du Siècle, 1867), p. 65.

[2]*Ibid.*, p. 4.

[3]*Ibid.*, p. 48.

[4]Friedrich Schiller, "Was heisst und zu welchem Ende studiert man Universalgeschichte?", *Saemtliche Werke*, vol. 4 (Munich: Carl Hanser Verlag, 1962), p. 765.

[5]Karl Marx, *The German Ideology* (New York: International Publishers, 1947), p. 14.

[6]Blaise Pascal, *Pensées* (New York: E.P. Dutton, 1958), no. 205, p. 81.

[7]Voltaire, "Essai," p. 9.

[8]Marion Montgomery, *Fugitive* (New York: Harper and Row, 1974), p.5.

[9]Friedrich Nietzsche, *Die Froeliche Wissenschaft*, 1881/2, Aphorism, no. 125.

[10]Albert Camus, *The Rebel* (New York: Vintage Books, 1965), pp. 142, 233.

[11]John A. Mackay, *Heritage and Destiny* (New York: Macmillan, 1943), p.12.

[12]Aleksandr Solzhenitsyn, *Solzhenitsyn Speaks at the Hoover Institution on War, Revolution, and Peace*, May-June 1976, Stanford, California.

[13]Aleksandr Solzhenitsyn, *The Gulag Archipelago 1918-1956*, III-IV (New York: Harper and Row, 1975), p. 646f.

[14]*Ibid.*, p. 649.

[15]Aleksandr Solzhenitsyn, *From Under the Rubble* (Boston: Little, Brown & Co., 1975), pp. 3, 4.

[16]Solzhenitsyn, *Gulag*, III-IV, p. 617.

[17]Solzhenitsyn, *From Under the Rubble*, p. 12.

[18]*Ibid.*, p. 24.

[19]*Ibid.*, p. 25.

[20]*Ibid.*, p. 25.

[21]*Ibid.*, p. x.

# The Homesickness
# of the New Left

BY THE END of the Fifties it seemed—did it not?—that the leftist ideologies of the nineteenth century had run their course. Germany's Social Democrats had foresworn Marxism, the anarchist movement had met a violent death during the Spanish Civil War, even Leninism appeared to have reached a kind of plateau and run out of new ideas and methods. One of America's noted social scientists published a book proclaiming *The End of Ideology*.

But then a new upsurge of ideology made itself felt in a number of Western countries. Its first spectacular outbreak occurred at Berkeley in 1964, the Free Speech Movement with Mario Savio and Bettina Aptheker. Since she was a Communist, it seemed at first that this might be a new Communist tactic. But subsequent developments made it clear that the situation was not that simple. In Germany the former student organization of the Social Democratic Party had broken away from the mother party and set itself up as the more radical autonomous SDS. In the United States, another SDS, the Students for a Democratic Society, had been founded at Port Huron in 1962. A left-wing student group within the civil rights movement, the Student Nonviolent Coordinating Committee (SNCC), turned into an exclusively black radical organization. A still more radical group, the Black Panthers, emerged on the West Coast. Among white students, the Youth International Party (Yippies) was formed while the SDS has

recently split into a number of different groups, one of them
Maoist. German students rioted repeatedly in 1966-67, French
students in 1966 and the spring of 1968. In '68 they succeeded in
pushing the French workers to a revolutionary general strike and
occupation of some factories. Italian students, with a long
background of radicalism, particularly at Bologna, occupied Rome
University, and Spanish students followed suit in Madrid.

The first salient feature of the New Left, then, is its character as
a movement of radicalized students and professors, except in the
United States where there is also a black New Left. Secondly, the
movement cannot be said to operate under the effective command
and discipline of the Communist Party and has not produced
anything like the tightly knit centralized organization of Communism or even democratic socialism. Third, it puts revolutionary
action as such above carefully planned revolutionary strategy and
will engage in riots, demonstrations, occupations, and confrontations even when the Marxist parties want to avoid such spec-
taculars. Fourth, the ideology of the New Left is complex, eclectic
and, by derivation, one step removed from that of the Old Left.
Fifth, beside and behind the New Left, there is also a broader
rebellious culture, something which the Old Left could never boast.

On the other hand, Old Left and New Left both are aware that
they are moving toward the same ultimate goal. The New Left has
focused most frequently on university issues, but it has also
mobilized its cadres on the more general issues of Indochina and
military armaments; occasionally it picks special events like the
visit of the Shah of Iran to the United States or a merger enlarging
the West German press empire of Axel Springer, for their symbolic
value. All of these issues however, as numerous New Left leaders
have openly admitted, are secondary and merely serve to advance
toward the real goal which is the destruction of the entire social
order and the reversal of all values in Western countries. In this
sense the New Left knows it is pulling in the same direction as the
Communists, Trotskyists, Maoists, Castroites, with all of whom it
would like to work.

The Old Left was usually discussed in terms of alleged underlying
material causes. This kind of approach won't get us very far in
understanding a movement composed of the sons and daughters of
affluence. Their radicalism must be understood as rooted in

ideologized ideas – irrational thinking about history, society, and the human condition. We must have a critical grasp of the ideology of the New Left. Its ideological manifestations are of two kinds: unsystematic, spontaneous outbursts of ideological language, imagery, prejudices from the rank-and-file, and the coherent and systematic ideological writings of the intellectual leaders. In the Old Left, the ideology was first created in writing and then it began to shape the consciousness of rank-and-file members.

The New Left, then, is a second growth, as it were, on ideologically contaminated soil. A phenomenon like ideological spontaneity would not be possible had not the teachings of Marx, Lenin, Bakunin, and others spread through our culture so that they were absorbed by the young from parents, teachers, newspapers, and communications media. One must also go beyond the apostles of the revolutionary Left: the revolutionary student movement of our time has derived many of its concepts, slogans, imagery, expectations and prejudices from Nietzsche, Freud and Jüng, Heidegger and Sartre, Blake and Breton, and ideas for its tactics from Sorel and McLuhan. One might say that it constitutes a potpourri of all the major ideological currents of the past century and a half, not all of which one can place on the Left. It might be better, then, if we could think of another name for the new movement – possibly, it might be "the New Emancipation."

## Revolution: Relative or Absolute?

EMANCIPATION is the main accent in most of the ideological writings, a contrast to the nineteenth century which produced apparently scientific analyses of society's structure and dynamics. That kind of semi-rationality is now gone. "The Revolution" is taken for granted; no elaborate argument is needed to establish it; rather, it appears as a "self-evident" truth around which one cannot build other conclusions, but also from which one can deduce other premises.

Herbert Marcuse, who has contributed more books to the new movement than anyone else, begins with Marx's assertion of total revolution as an axiom from which he himself has removed Marx's supporting evidence. For Marx, the Revolution followed from the instability inherent in the proletariat's ever-deepening misery; indignation and growing class consciousness would arouse it to the final triumphant battle against its capitalist masters. Marcuse admits that the proletariat has not sunk and will not sink into misery, that its consciousness is not revolutionary, that capitalism has bestowed considerable wealth on all classes, and that its economic crises are not likely to result in a wholesale collapse. He admits that the capitalist economy satisfies human needs on an unprecedented scale. Such abandonment of Marx's analysis, however, does not lead him to abandon Marx's conclusion, but rather to think of a substitute set of supporting reasons for the central concept of total revolution. The Revolution turns out to be the absolute, its explanations merely relative.

Marx assumed that the evolution of economic forces followed from the pressure of human needs, in which he saw a kind of rock-bottom driving energy. Marcuse, by contrast, looks on human needs as artificial contrivances of the capitalist system, invisible threads by which the system enslaves men and falsifies human existence. Marx accepted the value of industrialization and confined his critique to the system of appropriation. Marcuse rejects the industrial system to which he attributes what he regards as an entirely false system of values and men's "false" contentment in the present society. Everything in our society must be turned into its opposite. The tolerance in our country is actually a powerful means of oppression, our freedoms are nothing but chains of enslavement, our ideas mere mental perversions.

## One-Upmanship

THE REVOLUTION and its radical negation, on the other hand, are man's creative expression, intolerance is a moral duty, physical uncleanliness an "unsoiled" condition of the body, obscenity the mark of the emancipated human being. What matters is total newness, which will spring from total rejection and destruction of all that exists. There is a dialectic relation between total newness and the alleged total evil that is supposed to prevail today. The road to newness then goes through an intellectual destruction of the present order in one's mind to an eventual practical destruction in the political and social sense. In dialectic opposition, since the present is depicted as totally evil, the new world is postulated as wholly good.

Marcuse's radical indictment of present-day society is a kind of one-upmanship on Marx. Marx boasted of having discovered grounds for a critique of society far deeper and more basic than political oppression and social injustice. Marcuse piles Freud on Marx and depicts alienation in psychic terms, thus discovering cause for profound discontent even in the midst of affluence and security. He has no need of Marx's proletarian misery; in the heart of contentment he finds slavery, oppression, and indignity. Unlike Marx, Marcuse is not forced to play down any positive features of present-day society. They all serve to prove man's dehumanization.

Marcuse uses Marx minus his historical materialism; similarly, Norman Brown, having discovered Freud in the mid-Fifties, derives from him a message of emancipation that does away with Freud's own pessimistic analysis of civilization. To this end, Norman Brown adds to Freud the nineteenth-century visionary Blake, as well as Nietzsche. "Freud is the great emancipator from the reality principle." Norman Brown wants to join Freud, Marx, and Pope John XXIII for the "unification of mankind"; unity is of bodies, thus social organization is ultimately sexual. "The endless task; to achieve the impossible, to find a male female (vaginal father) or a female male (phallic mother). It is to square the circle; the desire and pursuit of the whole in the form of dual unity or the combined object; the Satanic hermaphroditism of Antichrist." In these terms Norman Brown proclaims emancipation from "this world of generation and death," which we "must cast off" in its entirety. Again, such condemnation of present reality far exceeds Marx's rather instrumentalist critique. All morality and religion, even being itself, is called before the bar and rejected out of hand. An emancipation is postulated that will liberate bodies and passions from frustration, separateness and any sense of guilt or imperfection.

On a far lower intellectual level Abbie Hoffman bears witness to the new emancipation by writing books in the language of absurdity and by using obscenity as the mark of the new freedom. Hoffman, like Brown and others, celebrates his escape both from the normative and from rationality, which are to him a cultural prison. Demonstrative madness is the form this celebration takes, the

display of mind unchained from logic, reason and structure—language gleefully splashing in nonsense. Similarly, among
the French students, Sartre is worshipped as the bringer of absolute freedom, for he has shown that being is nothingness and
thereby taken from man the most fundamental limitation his mind
has to acknowledge, that of reality itself.

We have already moved from the politically revolutionary movement to what Theodore Roszak calls the "counter-culture": patterns of living chosen in pointed opposition to the customary,
moral, aesthetic, religious traditions of our civilization. The Old
Left never knew anything like this. Neither socialists nor Communists could draw support from any culture other than that of the
society which they sought to combat, and even to this day the
Soviet Union has not produced a specifically Soviet culture, for
even the vaunted Soviet realism merely imitates art forms
developed long before the Communist revolution. Behind and
beside the student revolutionary organizations, however, young
people on both sides of the Atlantic are clustering together under
the slogan "turn on, tune in, drop out." "Turn on" refers to the anti-
rational state of mind produced by hallucinogenic drugs, "tune in"
to rock music and the life-style that goes with it, "drop out" to the
extant order of society and culture.

Rock, sex, drugs and unbounded subjectivism characterize the
varieties of "life-styles" and their manifestation in the absence of
norms for dress, hair, and cleanliness acceptable to these youths.
Certain cultural productions complete the picture: besides rock
music, absurdist poetry and absurdist art. Finally, there is a pervading preoccupation with exotic religiosity, borrowing freely from
a diversity of Oriental religions as well as from shamanism, magic,
and astrology.

## The Counter-Culture

WHAT IS the significance of this "counter-cultural" phenomenon?
First, it provides the political activists with a broad substratum of
support and sympathy, as well as a supply of recruits. More importantly, however, it maintains a public impression that something
new is actually growing, something that serves as conclusive proof
of a coming society after the destruction of the present one. The

counter-culture seems to substantiate the claim that we are in the presence of cultural creation and that the new freedom can already be discerned at least in dim outline. If it were not for this impression generated by the counter-culture, the New Left would seem like the emperor without his new clothes, a rebellion bare in its nihilistic refusal. The counter-culture provides an apparent justification for the political revolutionaries, it nourishes their self-righteous confidence and optimistic resort to total destruction. In its confrontation with democracy, the New Left feels entitled to claim rights in the name of human creativity, demanding freedom to express its ideas and "do its thing," justified by a cultural promise vaguely identified by the god-words, "peace" and "love."

Alas, the claim is false. What we are witnessing is not the creation of a new culture but merely the reversal or withdrawal symptoms of nihilism. The counter-culture consists of nothing but the principle of negation, of which it has made a cult. It deeply distrusts any form, any norm, any kind of structured present. It seeks perpetual restlessness, dynamism without pause, destination or fulfillment. Rebellious youth "drops out" not merely from a political, economic, or cultural system, but from goodness, reason, and being as such. LSD has been embraced as an instrument of anti-being, a vehicle for phantasmic flight from reality and all its structures. The acknowledgment of reality implies all kinds of limitations, but "dropping out" means escape into the boundless freedom of undefined non-reality. Similarly, the metaphysical enchantment of subjectivity amounts to a thrust into a dreamlike nothingness. All alone, the subject feels capable of creating worlds, moralities, societies, because he finds himself freed from otherness, the otherness of God, nature, or fellow men, having risen from the *esse cum* to a freedom that has no qualities, where he feels like God.

The one aspect of the counter-culture that might seem to contain some germs of a new growth is youth's pervading interest in religion, its discovery of depths of life that were ignored by its liberal and positivist parents. Alas again, the appearance is deceptive. In the indiscriminate invocations of Hindu or Buddhist deities, the mixing of Christian, pagan, shamanist and magic rites, there is little evidence that the human condition of creatureliness in a divinely created world is taken seriously, or that there is anything like serious worship. Such practices indicate, rather, a disposition to flirt with any kind of myth or ritual in playful combinations of religions, high and primitive, thereby incidentally annihilating the past with its leaps from compact to more differentiated orders.

The apparent culture of the new religiosity thrives largely on the excitement of fascination with whatever is strange as well as on its shock value, even though behind it there may well lurk a genuine yearning. The genuineness, however, turns to counterfeit when religious symbols are perverted mainly for rebellious purposes. No norm of human conduct, no ordering orientation, no moral obligation, no structure of society flows from the counter-culture. Roszak's designation seems to be a misnomer; one should rather speak of an anti-culture. The only believable claim of the anti-culture is youth's desire to do, feel, think in any way that negates Greco-Judaeo-Christian morality, aesthetics and understanding of reality. There is in it no power to bring forth a higher or even alternative order of existence. One possibility remains: The widespread fascination with the culture of primitives, including shamanism, archetypal myths, also the absence of dress and shoes, the possession of amulets, and the practice of ritually painting the body suggests something like Vico's *ricorso*: After the "barbarism of reflection," which in our time would be the same as the wasteland of positivism, men might return to a barbarism pure and simple, a life below civilization which, however, might imply the chance of a genuine turning to God.

Short of such speculations, however, our immediate interest bids us focus on the relation between the anti-culture and student revolutionary movements. One cannot assume that one is necessarily a function of the other; witness England where the anti-culture has flourished long and vigorously while political student movements have remained relatively unexplosive. The reverse can be observed in France, where the student movement brought the nation to the brink of civil war, but the anti-culture is not as noticeable as in the United States. In France as well as Germany, revolutionary students seem to draw slogans and motives more from Marxist-Leninist Communism and Bakunist and Kropotkinist anarchism, while new ideological writings have been produced mostly in the United States.

### The New Left Credo

AT THIS POINT, one may venture some generalizations about the
New Emancipation in both its revolutionary and cultural aspects:

1) The ideological crux of all student revolutionary movements is
the total condemnation of their own community, be it the university, the society, or the civilization as a whole. Even though such an
indictment usually comes replete with particular illustrations, the
underlying intention is not to change for the better this or that
practice, institution or norm. Rather, the condemnation is its own
end. Whatever concrete demands the students present do not adequately express their limitless discontent; they are instruments to
attain further power positions. The French students coined the
slogan: "Be realistic, demand the impossible!" German student
leaders wanted something they called "protest in permanence." All
student movements reject the strict discipline of strategy and tactics observed, in different ways, by both trade unions and the Communist Party; instead they all desire revolutionary action as such,
for its own sake.

One group of students talked about a mystical "revolutionary
synthesis of food and dispute" and wanted to destroy all comfortable homes, which bar "total man" from "space opening on him." In
May 1968, the Paris students wrote on the walls: "It is forbidden to
forbid!" The limitless character of the total critique is evidenced
also by the multitude of sweeping descriptions of society's evil
which seem to be interchangeable. Our society is simultaneously
defined as a "world of death," a "world of violence," of materialism,
racism, constraint, a system of exploitative capitalism, oppressive
imperialism, a culture of repressive tolerance, oppressive consciousness, mindless power. No detailed analysis of society's evils is
required any more. The equation of society with evil is an *a priori*
one, not to be proved, but simply evident in any example one
chooses to pick. Society amounts to instituted evil.

2) Defining the Establishment as the totality of evil establishes
the innocence of all revolutionary action. As all conceivable evil has
been attributed to the Establishment, such a sweeping *j'accuse* implies ultimate self-justification. He who pronounces such global

judgments, denouncing an entire society rather than particular actions, can speak only from Beyond Good and Evil, which position provides a metaphysical warranty of his innocence. It is the *a priori* innocence of total condemnation and total destruction that dispenses the revolutionary student from any requirement to define their goal even in terms of a utopia. While they admit that they cannot see what will come after the destruction of the present society, they are supremely confident that the destruction will be good.

There results a kind of ontological and moral division between two kinds of people: *they* – the supporters and beneficiaries of the Establishment who are all guilty – and *we* – the radical revolutionaries who have dropped out from the instituted evil. "IBM, Mobil and AT&T are enemies of all life," said those who planted bombs in the New York offices of the three firms, implying that the planting of bombs in such places was a cleansing and righteous work of the avenger of life itself. When men make such fundamental distinctions between themselves and others, it amounts to a refusal to share a common civic life, even more, a refusal to share the human condition as such ("The Great Refusal"). The revolutionary students, by charging the totality of evil to extant society, to "them," have moved out, as it were, from "being in the same boat" with their fellow men, and consequently cannot be reconciled to any human order. As a consequence, they feel that they should affirm their solidarity with the enemies of order, the heroes of total revolution and destructive activism: Che Guevara, Mao Tse-tung, Fidel Castro, Ho Chi Minh.

3) From the sense of their own innocence flows a notion of limitless power, limitless both in the normative and factual sense. The students cannot conceive that revolutionary power should be subject to any limiting norm, principle or objective, or that it could be conceived as a mere means to an end. On the other hand, they are convinced that revolutionary power and the power of the Establishment are just not in the same class, since the power of revolutionary action is innocent while that of the Establishment is guilty. Even in a purely factual sense, the two powers are incommensurable. The revolutionary students have no sense of defeat, even when the other side is stronger. An acknowledgment of defeat is always a mental process implying an acknowledgment

that the other side is a human being like oneself who can be powerful in the same way as oneself, which is tantamount to perceiving
power limitations.

When one begins by denying that the other side shares the same
condition of existence as oneself, however, one cannot see one's
own power limited by that of the others, and cannot accept a settlement in terms of power relativity. The only time the relativity of
power seems to become real to revolutionary students is when the
jail doors close behind them. Otherwise their inability soberly to
assess power relations has manifested itself both in a reckless lack
of inhibition and in a quixotic overestimation of gestures, slogans
and resolutions. It is precisely on this point that the revolutionary
students have most sharply diverged from the Communist Party,
which, obedient to Lenin's teaching, has always clearly understood
power realities. Still, the ultimate goal of Communism also consists
in obtaining limitless power for the dictatorial Party, a goal which
comes close to the student revolutionary spirit.


## The Revolutionary Cadre

A CRITICAL analysis of the revolutionary student movement by one
of its former members (Jens Litten, *Eine verpasste Revolution*,
1969) predicts that the movement will die from internal emotional
exhaustion. That may well be; what is sure, however, is that it cannot be satisfied by appeasement, concessions, or reforms. A late
and hybrid ideology has been spawned in the soil of Western
civilization and it will be a source of disorder for a considerable
time. Many are confused because the revolution appears as one of
youth as such; the anti-culture appears to have become *the* way of
life for the people under thirty. This, of course, is very far from the
truth. The impression is created by the fact that the anti-culture is
widely scattered and seems to have taken hold in practically every
town and most schools, and that between the anti-culture and
revolutionary movements there are many affinities. It is important
to remind ourselves again and again that the cause of disorder is
not youth as such, but a radical ideology, a body of irrational ideas,
notions, slogans, and the ensuing attitudes. All this forms a cult,
the adepts of which range from seventeen to seventy; the cult is

more characteristic of uprooted Western intelligentsia, Julian Benda's *clercs*, than of youth.

The activist part of the movement is bent on destruction rather than reform of our society; one should remember that both Lenin and Hitler began with less than a dozen. Unlike Lenin and Hitler, the radical students are not well organized, they are poorly armed, and they have had scant success in breaking out of the gilded ghetto of social privilege. In any kind of frontal assault, they would be no match for the forces that preserve the order of society. If they could attract the urban masses, as seemed possible for a moment in the Paris of May 1968, their power might loom more formidable, but the possibility still seems remote.

### Enter Fortinbras

TWO OTHER courses are left to them: urban guerrilla warfare and provocative confrontations. The first would result in much material damage and some loss of life, but it would tend to consolidate the moral and political force of society, and to isolate the revolutionists. Provocative confrontation has been the chosen technique of revolutionary students on both sides of the Atlantic until now, and it presents democracy with its greatest challenge. The technique relies on the myth of an abstractly perfect democracy, a myth frequently invoked by the slogan "participatory democracy," which myth is used as an ideal yardstick to measure the historical legal guarantees of the citizen: freedom of speech and assembly, freedom of the press, due process and equal protection before the law. The technique consists in demonstrating *ad oculos*, i.e., on TV, that the present society not only falls far short of a perfect democracy but actually is a regime of oppressive power that ought to be destroyed. The means the students have chosen to bring this about is to misuse various civil liberties: freedom of speech is misused for obscenity, irrationality and subversive appeals; defendants in court misuse their rights, to disrupt and discredit the judiciary process; freedom of assembly is misused by the physical obstruction of others.

Such practices hit democracy at its weakest point. In the last hundred years democracy has defined itself more and more in terms of mere procedure, progressively neglecting or even banning problems of moral and intellectual substance. By 1970 Paul Eidelberg could make the assertion that "intellectual and moral anarchy" prevails in American society, because of the unwillingness or inability of the nation's leaders to make significant distinctions. "No society can endure unless its members are capable of feeling disgust or indignation, hence of being intolerant of certain kinds of behavior and sometimes of the ideas which encourage such behavior. The situation is characteristic not merely of the United States but prevails as far as the influence of Western positivism reaches. Much earlier, the Weimar Republic stood committed to the idea that democracy existed in the quantitatively widest possible extension of the sameness of procedure; it therefore gave the same security to the destroyers of the republic as to its defenders."

Some political scientists, it is true, insisted that freedom of speech made sense and was effective only within a community of values and rationality. Others pointed out that civil rights were meaningful only within a continuum of political obligation. There were some warnings that free elections as such could not guarantee a free government. The courts, however, on both sides of the Atlantic have taken the strictly positivistic line. For a long while they have refused to make substantive distinctions between bona fide and perverted uses of civil rights. By now a significant number of leaders in our society are actually incapable of making such distinctions. Eidelberg pointedly quotes Justice Douglas in the Ginzburg case, where he put the words "good," "bad" and "truth" in quotation marks, thereby indicating that he no longer could make any rational statements regarding pornography. A similar inability seems to have befallen academic administrators who fail to distinguish between academic freedom and student license, freedom of expression and the use of words for destruction, rational dialogue and the clash of irrationalities, speakers who communicate ideas and others who incite to rebellious action. Where such deep uncertainty and confusion manifests itself, weakness spreads from society's leaders to all citizens, and strength accrues to the forces bent on ending it all.

The real challenge to democracy in our time lies, therefore, not in the streets or on some battlefield, but in the hearts and minds of those on whom it is incumbent to make decisions in the name of the whole. For too long they have allowed the substance of order to atrophy within their souls. Now they are confronted with tests which threaten to expose the hollow shell of what was once a rational public understanding of right and wrong, high and low, real and unreal, decent and indecent. The truth is that during the last thirty years we have allowed the basis of public rationality to erode. Unless we succeed in stopping and reversing that course, and in recovering some knowledge of "the things that belong to our peace," our intellectual and moral anarchy may well end in a scene strewn with corpses, waiting for a Fortinbras in full armor to enter and take over.

# Two Socialisms

"THE ISSUE TODAY is between socialism and freedom." Those who state their conviction in this way fear that the gradual expansion of government here at home will ultimately turn out to have been the road to communism. Is their fear well-founded? What precisely is socialism? Strictly speaking, the term connotes public ownership of the means of production. Today in the United States, socialism is a derisive name for any tendency of Washington to plan what must not be planned, to organize what should regulate itself, to regiment what ought to move in freedom. The fear of government invasion in certain areas of life bespeaks the premise that government has proper limits, that wide areas of human life should remain beyond its reach. We speak of a public and a private sphere. "Private" is not only the life of each individual person, and his relations with family and friends, but "private" designates also an entire system of social order in which not the government but the decisions of numberless individuals and their action upon each other keep house. The fear of "socialism" implies that this pattern of individual decisions constitutes a genuine order, an order that is valuable not only because it has intrinsic merit but also because its unhampered functioning guarantees the freedom of personal autonomy to all competent individuals who can exercise responsible self-control.

Public discussion of these problems is emotional and somewhat fuzzy. Clarity can be achieved only when one penetrates beyond the slogans to the underlying problems. The problems are institutional, but the institutional concepts are formed by theoretical premises. Thus when we speak of the limited state, which has been one of the perennial political problems of Western civilization, we must go further and examine the assumptions on which the notion of the limited state is founded. This takes us to the basic ideas about man,

57

his ultimate destiny and his aspirations in life. The concept of man, in turn, inspires that of an order of life that lies beyond government action. In modern times, this idea has taken the form of a "natural order." No more can be done here than roughly to indicate the direction of this kind of inquiry. Thus we shall explore the connection between the modern notion of the limited state and socialism, the difference between the welfare socialism of the Western variety and Marxist socialism, and the role which both socialisms play in the crisis of Western civilization. I shall try to show that socialism in the West, being a variety of liberalism, differs both in fundamental philosophies and policies from communism, but that both socialisms constitute relations between rulers and ruled that are alien to the spirit of freedom and friendship.

## I

ARISTOTLE SAID the political community is the highest and most comprehensive of all communities. He argued that every community among men exists for a particular good, but the political community aims at the good of the whole life. Hence government, the art of politics, is the master art of them all, for it determines the respective importance and scope of all the other arts. There is nothing limited about this concept of the state. The limited state is a creation of Christian thinking, particularly of Augustine. It arose from the fundamental experience of the Incarnation, the appearance of God in human form at a definite place and time of human history. Christian thinking about politics was based on a new discovery about the destiny of man: man lived in order to attain fellowship with God. Augustine distinguished in this world two great communities among men: those who were drawn to each other by the common love of God, and those who understood each other in the similarity of the love for themselves. The first he called the City of God. In its orientation toward eternal life, this community ranks highest among all human associations. Augustine, in other words, could not share Aristotle's idea that the purely temporal institution of government represents the royal order, the master order. The City of God ranks higher. The state cannot be its master and director. Thus Augustine, for the first time in human history, assigned to the state a merely practical task of procuring a rudimentary sort of peace and a modicum of justice.

As a result, an entire sphere of human life, the spiritual sphere, was not only distinguished from the temporal order but deliberately put beyond the reach of the government. The spiritual and moral life of man, with its purpose of salvation, was left to the autonomous authority of the Church. The significant feature of this arrangement was that the center of gravity shifted from the state to the non-political aspects of life. Man's chief purpose in life was pursued in an order which the government had not created and did not direct. The government, in turn, provided what amounted to a mere auxiliary framework of temporal peace and justice. Its function was limited not only in scope but also in dignity. The state's proper activity is legislation, and legislation cannot save men's souls. In the autonomy of the spiritual sphere from government Western man achieved both the social order characteristic of our civilization and the Western form of freedom. For the limitation of government to peace, public order, and justice also permitted and facilitated the freedom of human reason, represented by the Western institution of the university.

A decisive change in this pattern occurred when the rationale of the limited state was secularized by John Locke. Locke taught that "the great and chief end of men uniting into commonwealths" is property, the acquisition of wealth. This teaching, which was almost universally accepted in the West, shifted the center of gravity of human life from man's relation with God to man's relation with nature, from the concern for his soul to the concern for his estate. Man's economic activity was seen as that for the sake of which governments performed their auxiliary functions. Thus Locke continued to think of the state as an order limited in scope and in dignity. Instead of being limited in favor of the autonomous order of salvation, however, he conceived it to be oriented to the service of men's economic purposes which antedated the state. The state was seen as an order of peace, public safety, and judicial certainty, which enabled men to acquire wealth more effectively than would have been possible otherwise. Beyond the state lies the great private sphere of economics, a sphere which the state with its laws has not created and cannot create because the state has been created by it. This secular sphere of men's chief end differed from the spiritual order in more than one respect. Above all, unlike the spiritual order, it could not be conceived or experienced as a community beside the state. Rather, it was a sphere of self-seeking activities of a multitude of men, each pursuing his own advantage, an aggregate of private personal interests. The relation of the social order to these interests was one of means to end, so that the purpose of society would be attained as the private interests of multitudes of individuals were more or less satisfied, according to each person's abilities. The contribution of the state to this end was the procurement of suitable conditions that would facilitate each individual's success as much as is possible.

To this new version of the limited state Adam Smith contributed the idea that the total aggregate of self-centered individual economic activities constitutes a natural pattern of order. Smith's symbol was the "Invisible Hand," the force that in the circulation of goods produces a general harmony. As each individual "intends only his own gain," he is "led by an invisible hand to promote an end which was no part of his intention," and "by pursuing his own interest he frequently promotes that of the society more effectually than when he really intends to promote it." Individual self-interest thus was seen as a social function, the motor which propels not merely individual wealth but the wealth of nations. As self-seeking individual activities produced an ordered pattern for the whole, unhindered economic initiative must eventually result in the widest possible individual satisfaction. This is the concept of a natural economic order, an order on which the intentional pursuit of society's interest by the government could not possibly improve. Locke had said that man's economic purposes constitute the *raison d'être* of the state. Smith added that these purposes were unconscious parts of a self-executing harmony which could function perfectly only when left autonomous, and which would procure the end of society, namely the best possible satisfaction of individual material welfare. Thus the economic natural order and its laws now turned into the ultimate cause for the sake of which the state should be limited to minimal activity.

The Locke-Smithean limitation of the state involves also a concept of man that differs radically from that of the Christian tradition. Augustine's limitation of the state had derived from a psychology that sees men's loves as the decisive factor in any community, and the love of God as the most significant fact of human life. The community formed by the love of God is then recognized as that which embodies man's highest destiny. By contrast, Locke's psychology sees man as significantly self-centered and self-seeking. This follows from the assumption that man's essential relationship is not that with God but rather that with nature. Foreshadowing Marx, Locke centers man's social interests in property, and derives property from human labor creating value out of nature's matter. We have here the difference between what Mircea Eliade has called "religious man," the man who conceives his entire existence in the light of the Creation and his relation to the Creator, and modern man, who vaunts his mastery over material nature. To these two concepts of man correspond two concepts of the limited state. For Augustine, the community of men in the love of God is a fact of life. As the highest conceivable community, its order lies untouchable beyond the reach of merely temporal authority. For the modern *homo oeconomicus*, the natural order of the Invisible Hand is his proper realm, an order of intrinsic value which involves the actuality of human freedom as well as the promise of human welfare. One cannot possibly overemphasize the importance of this change from the traditional to the modern notion of the limited state. The state is limited now for the sake of unhindered economic production rather than for the sake of the love of God; the autonomous realm limiting it is no longer the spiritual order of salvation but the natural order of economic harmony.

The difference is not merely philosophical. Unlike the order of salvation, the Invisible Hand implies a pragmatic postulate. It is supposed to function here and now, and there are tangible criteria of its functioning. What is more, the idea that the economic system's harmonious functioning entails benefits for all arouses certain definite expectations. These soon begin to take the form of demands which people make on their society. We have noted that the task assigned to government was to procure the conditions under which individual interests could attain maximum fulfillment. Society thus became an arrangement for the ultimate purpose of a well-functioning economic order. A corresponding change occurred in the concept of the common good. Traditionally identified with justice, it now takes the form of a macro-economic perspective of society, in which individual material welfare is a function of the over-all balance of productive forces. The new orientation, however, has taken a most ironic turn. For the same concepts which first instructed government to stay within limits drawn more narrowly than ever before in history later prompted an ever-expanding role of government in the management of the economic system. It is the concern with the health of the economic system as a whole, for the sake of its expected benefits for the individual members of society, that has brought about the gradual incursion of the government into the economic realm and created Western welfare socialism.

## II

THE LIMITATION of the state, as postulated by Locke's concept of man and Smith's concept of the natural order of society, has a tendency to give way to ever expanding government interference in the economic system. This is the thesis I am here submitting, a thesis that can of course not be adequately substantiated in so brief a space. Only the main arguments can be briefly sketched.

The role of government is to ban from human existence certain evils. When the limits of government are circumscribed by man's ultimate spiritual destiny and the autonomous life of moral and spiritual order, the business of government will be seen in the "punishment of wickedness and vice, the maintenance of true religion, and virtue." When man's purpose, however, is seen as the acquisition of wealth, and the aggregate of individual pursuits of wealth postulated as an order of natural harmony, the evil on which government should concentrate must be found wholly in external conditions which somehow are disturbing the natural harmony of things. Government thus becomes increasingly a device to procure favorable circumstances. The concept of evil is externalized, the source of evil no longer sought in the human heart but in certain undesired conditions that can be removed in order to achieve a more perfect functioning of the social order. Once this is the accepted notion of government's role, there is room for widely divergent opinions on what precisely are the disturbing circumstances, and what should be done to eliminate them. The limitation of government will be prescribed by these opinions.

Locke, for instance, felt that the only thing man lacked for his existence was the assurance of a smooth-functioning judicial system. It was not so much justice that he demanded but rather the predictability in human relations that comes from publicly promulgated laws, impartial judges, and assured enforcement. In other words, men could live well, if only government would see to it that society observed certain "rules of the game." Now this is one idea of the conditions which man needs in order to live the good life, but not the only one. Other conditions can be postulated, particularly when attention has been drawn to the macro-economic context of the good life. When one begins to wonder under what conditions the economic system as a whole would probably operate as postulated, one may hit upon all kinds of things. The government may be called upon to provide tariffs or other means of protection, to regulate credit, even to lend a supporting hand to the pricing system, – all in the name of macro-economic health. Such measures will of course be disputed by those who say that here the government is no longer engaged in the business of securing favorable basic conditions but is rather trying to run the economy, thereby disturbing the laws of the natural order. The point, however, is not whether such government interferences are or are not well-conceived and compatible with premises of the Invisible Hand. Once the entire problem of order and disorder has been shifted from the human heart to external conditions, and men begin to blame circumstances rather than themselves for the evils of their social existence, and expect their government to change these circumstances, there is really no cogent reason why any external condition should be kept from government's correcting hand. Thus the dispute between classical liberals and modern liberal socialists is one conducted on common premises. The premises are that the over-all economic order of society is the basis of the good life, that it has inherent value, and that its functioning depends on certain basic conditions to be secured by the government. Given this assumption, the decision of what conditions are an impediment to the system's smooth operation and what means are required to remove them is one on which opinions may vary widely.

A tendency toward socialist policies thus is built into the assumptions underlying our modern world, since with Locke we see man as the *homo oeconomicus* whose habitat is the acquisitive society. A socialist government is one that concerns itself authoritatively with the functioning of the economic system. The economic order of which Adam Smith spoke is supposed to engender its own equilibrium, but it is also, on the Lockean premise, supposed to provide individual welfare. The concept of welfare in terms of material well-being is a thoroughly modern one, differing from Aristotle's happiness as identical with virtue, and Augustine's goal of fellowship with God. Welfare is what modern man expects of society. The promise of welfare as the result of a well-functioning economic order can almost be called the charter of modern society. Once this promise was grasped by the masses in an age of universal suffrage, the voters would build up enormous pressures on the government to make up for any failures of the Invisible Hand to fulfill it. The welfare state is thus the psychologically and politically unavoidable consequence of the welfare concept of society that stems from John Locke.

One should distinguish between the problem of human welfare and welfare as the utilitarian rationale and purpose of the political order. The latter results from the turn which political philosophy took in the seventeenth and eighteenth centuries. The modern welfare problem, by contrast, is a product of the industrialized and urbanized society as it emerged in the nineteenth century. Masses of individuals found, and are still finding, themselves exposed to indigence of health and estate which they are unable to handle with the resources of rented apartment dwellings and wage income. Facilities larger than those at the command of the urban family are required to cope with many personal emergencies that typically arise in modern existence. We are still groping for the most humane forms of organization capable of dealing with these problems. There is, then, a modern welfare problem. One must, however, resist the temptation of jumping from the awareness of a welfare problem to the conclusion of the welfare state. The welfare state is more than an answer to an urgent need: it embodies a concept of man's purpose in life and the function of political association that far antedates as well as transcends the welfare task in an industrial society. Western welfare socialism has arisen from the relatively recent merger of urban welfare problems and utilitarian political philosophy, compounding the fallacies of the latter with a fallacious intellectual shortcut that makes government instrumental to the solution of almost any human task.

Socialism in the West thus is merely one of the possible variants of Western liberalism, the concept of society centered in the individual and his material aspirations. It is an ultimate concern for private utility and individual welfare that converts itself here into an expanding public management of economic processes and resources. To be sure, the "Individual" is not the concrete living person, whom nobody really consults, but rather a type that is authoritatively defined, together with his presumed needs and aspirations, by the political thinker or government planner. Still, the motivation of Western welfare socialism stems from the same sources as that of Western classical liberalism. It is an individualist rather than a collectivist approach to man and society. It conceives of government as the servant of the ultimate value, acquisitive individual self-interest, and merely occupies one of the extremes of a wide range of conditions that can be conceived as meeting the postulate of welfare.

## III

THE SOCIALISM of Marx and Lenin roots in entirely different ideas. To begin with, its underlying concept of human nature is collectivist rather than individualist. Marx saw man as being wholly defined by the process of labor. To Aristotle's formulation "More than anything else, reason is man" Marx might have retorted: "More than anything else, labor is man." Man is a being whose distinctive feature is that he creates his own life through the objects that he makes out of nature, and who becomes himself in the relations with the objects of his creation. Any kind of separation between him and the fruit of his labor, or between him and his labor process, deprives him of his humanity. This view of man leads Marx into the concept of a collectivist order of labor as man's proper way of life. For in any other economic system, man would be alienated from his fellow beings and himself, by being alienated from his labor and its products. Private property of the means of production, for instance, enables one man to make another work for him.

It also entails a division of labor by which a person is constrained to do the same kind of work all his life, so that he becomes functionally dependent on others. Only if labor were organized under the management of the entire community, and the means of production became the property of all, could man become the master of his own labor process as well as of nature and nature's laws. It is clear that the Marxist view of man differs as much from that of Locke as from that of Augustine or of Aristotle. The individual as a separate entity is rejected. Freedom and a human life is seen possible only in a collective arrangement of the labor process. All individualism, above all however acquisitive individualism, is condemned as injustice, oppression, and dehumanization. Marx, together with Locke, looks for man's "chief end" in his relation with nature, but unlike Smith does not assume that there is a human self-executing order of economic production, as long as private property and individual self-interest is the basis of the economic system.

Marxist socialism, however, is more than the postulate of a collectivist order of labor. More than anything else, it centers in a view of history that asserts a necessary movement of history from one type of society to another by means of revolution. Marxism-Leninism assumes that the conceivable types of society are limited, in fact that there are only five such types, and that the last of these, which is still to come, is the collectivist society in which human nature finally comes into its own. This last society of history will grow out of the revolution of the proletariat, the class of propertyless workers that arises in the last but one society in the series, the capitalist society. The struggle of the proletariat against the class of the bourgeoisie, i.e. the owners of the capitalist means of production, is thus the decisive struggle of history. Through it, the proletariat will overthrow its masters and then use political power dictatorially to "expropriate the expropriators." The proletariat is described as the only "really revolutionary class" because it fights not for the establishment of any interests of its own but for the radical destruction of the bourgeois society and all its vestiges. Thus Marxist socialism is more than merely a vision of collectivist production. It is also a doctrine of protracted and irreconcilable struggle, a declaration of total war against every now existing social order. It proclaims the action of revolutionary forces, of revolutionaries who pride themselves in having nothing in common with all other fellow-beings and are committed to a radical attitude of hostility until every trace of the now existing society has been eliminated.

For the same reason, Marxist socialism is not a doctrine of state supremacy, particularly not of state management of the economic system. Marx, Engels, and Lenin agree in characterizing the state as merely an instrument of class rule which will disappear when class society gives way to classless socialism. The ultimate vision of these communists includes a society with no political order, a society held together only by the discipline of collective labor. This is not the place to pass judgment on that vision. The point is to note that Marxist socialism, unlike Western welfare socialism, sees no role for the state in the ultimate order of economic harmony which it expects. The state is, however, extremely important in the period of transition from capitalism to communism. This is the period in which the Communist Party is still relatively weak, the forces hostile to it still powerful, the dangers of a relapse into the past lurking everywhere, and the new socialist society still in gestation. Man is still beset by the habits acquired under capitalism, and therefore he is still selfish, individualistic, acquisitive, obstreperous. In this period the state must be powerful to hold down the enemies of the Revolution, to enforce labor discipline, to destroy what Lenin called the "terrible force of habit," and to press men into a new mold. Thus in Marxist communism the state is above all an instrument of combative power, the major weapon in that protracted struggle that is to fill the entire period of transition from capitalism to communism. It must be totalitarian because the Communist Party is engaged in a total struggle against everything that has existed, because its power is supposed to be adequate to the task of re-making human beings into something they never have been, and, as far as we know, do not want to be. The communist state is totalitarian because the Communists want to play God. They intend to master the human soul, to converge all its powers of loyalty on the Party, to create the world according to their idea of what it should have been. In this enterprise, the state's monopolistic management of the economy plays an important role, but it is the role of engendering more and more power for the Party. In the period of transition, unlimited and unlimitable power is the Party's main concern. State management of labor and production represents not yet the way of life, the social order for which communism ultimately hopes. Rather, it is another manipulative operation designed above all to suppress and eradicate everything in the hearts and minds of men that is not wholly amenable to the Party's leadership.

## IV

THERE IS, then, a Western socialism distinct from the Marxist variety. Between the two there are fundamental differences in assumptions and motivations. The socialism that is a noticeable tendency in this country stems from the liberal tradition of Locke-Adam Smith-John Stuart Mill. Its basis is the concept of the acquisitive individual who expects from society the satisfaction of his material interests. Its orientation is toward a nebulous value called welfare. Marxist communism comes from the tradition of speculations about history that runs from Fourier and Saint-Simon to Hegel and Comte. Its basis is the expectation of a wholly new and transfigured world that is to emerge from the revolution of the proletariat. Its orientation is toward the requirements of the struggle that precedes the coming of that world. The difference of assumptions and motivations results in different policies and legal forms. Western socialism emphasizes the supremacy of government in the economic process, but one may say that with all that it is not wholly committed to the abolition of private property or the free labor contract, so that it is likely to retain these institutions while putting an ever heavier hand of government regulation on the freedom of their use. Marxist communism can never reconcile itself with any part of the existing order, but it will readily make use of existing institutions to further its power strategy. One could trace these differences in many details, and one is likely to come out with the clear-cut result that, no matter how objectionable Western socialism may be, it is in no way a road to the regime of Communists. That is an enterprise of quite a different nature.

The differences, however, should not induce us to overlook the similarities among all kinds of socialisms. After all, one could possibly discover still more varieties of socialism around, for instance, the unity-oriented socialism of the Fascists, and the modernity-oriented socialism of Nehru and Nasser. What characterizes all socialism in an institutional respect is the combination of political power with the power of controlling the means of material existence. Political power, we all would agree, consists in the authority to make laws that bind people's wills in conscience and obligation. Thus, the individual citizen can properly be said to be *subject* to political authorities. Now if the same set of people or the same agency that makes laws also holds the key to every person's livelihood and material betterment, the individual is not merely subject to, but *dependent* on, the government. There is quite a difference between subjection to authority and dependence on controlling power. Not only does a government combining both political and economic power become impossible to control, but it also acquires the means of manipulating people into unresisting subservience. It does not even require the open and harsh methods of compulsion, such as penalties, jails, police force. It needs only to withhold employment, deny advancement, raise the bread basket or lower it, as its interests may require. Instead of addressing the citizens, through the command of laws, as moral beings capable of rational obedience, it controls them as natural creatures who cannot escape their animal needs for food, shelter, cover. In a socialist system, the entire relation between rulers and ruled is changed. A normal political relationship is cast in terms of rational moral assumptions and persuasion within that framework. Under the socialist type of authority, the relation between ruler and ruled is based on the people's dire necessity, a necessity to which the government alone holds the key. Even should a socialistic government conceive of itself as the servant of people's needs rather than the exploiter of people's dependence, it would still be that government which determines which needs should be recognized, and in what way people should be served. The entire public order is distorted when it centers in the material aspects of life where men are by necessity unfree, rather than in the rational-moral order where man, by virtue of the spirit, is free.

In conclusion, we may ask the question why socialism, seeing that it perverts the public order, attracts so much support. The answer can be submitted only in the form of a hypothesis which cannot be proven. It has nothing but plausibility to recommend it. It claims that socialism is a reaction meant to counteract the void left by a state limited on a purely secular basis, a void that left Western man without any order or guidance for his soul and his spirit.

The limited state has been created by Christian political thought. In the Christian order of things, it was man's community in God that imposed limits on government. Because God himself had created this community, the government was reduced to the practical function of procuring peace, public order, and a modicum of justice. But throughout the Christian era, the government discharged this function side by side with the Church. Thus the realm beyond the temporal order was also a kind of public order, one concerning the spiritual and moral aspects of human life. The temporal and the spiritual order together covered the fullness of human life. The two realms were separate but co-ordinate, and this arrangement allowed for greater human freedom than had ever been achieved before. The limited state could operate within its bounds because beyond its limits the Church provided guidance and community.

The modern era began when the Church first was split, and then rejected by the European intelligentsia. A number of perceptive thinkers then noticed that, with the dropping out of the Church from the public order, a dangerous gap had opened. There was now no publicly recognized spiritual and moral community. Hobbes and Rousseau, among others, attempted to fill that gap by the creation of a "civil theology," a minimal public philosophy that would be substituted for the spiritual community of the Church. These attempts, as we know, came to nothing. Instead, the place of the former autonomous order of the Church was taken by the autonomous economy. It is for the sake of the system of production that limits were now imposed on government action. This provided for a rationale of the limited state, but not for community. For in his economic activities, man is centered on himself, competing rather than communing with others. And the economic system as a whole is a pattern of regularities rather than one of common values. The new limitation thus placed the state side by side with a realm of public order that spiritually is a void. Man, insofar as he was left to himself by the state, found himself individually alone, or at most embedded in a business company. Society outside of the state became a statistical universe rather than an experienced community. The modern world presents itself to individuals as a medium through which one must claw one's way to individual goals. As the last remnants of the former community fell victim to the freedom of modern *homo oeconomicus*, complaints about the emptiness of human existence began to multiply. Man's loneliness, that is, his lack of community with others, has become the dominant theme of our time, from Riesman's sociological analysis to the elevation of loneliness to a philosophical axiom by the Existentialists and its endlessly varied representation in modern art.

In this situation, socialism has offered itself as a kind of patent medicine to cure man's illness. It postulates an extension of the state's order to embrace the whole man, through the medium of the care for individual material welfare. There is a feeling that somehow, if only the economic system can be managed by the government as the common authority, the economy can become the vehicle of true community. Needless to say, this hope is illusory. Under socialism, man's loneliness has not decreased. Rather, it has been compounded by boredom resulting from the absence of risk, adventure, and personal achievement which are characteristic of an individualistic economy. We are gradually beginning again to recognize that community among men is a matter of the spirit. It resides only in the acknowledgment of common truths, common meaning, common values, which in turn are rooted in a publicly shared theology or philosophy, a recognized view of what is man, society, nature, and the meaning of life.

The characteristic feature of Western political order is the "civil government," that is a government barred from publicly entertaining theological or philosophical orthodoxies. The state that is thus limited can administer a true social order only in combination with an autonomous unity representing spiritual truth, be it spontaneous or directed. Our limited state in itself is unable to provide a full social order, and it cannot represent a communal order if supplemented by nothing but the economic system. People can be united only by a shared view of the meaning of life. In other words, the limited state makes sense only in combination with religious community. This does not mean a community of abstract contemplation or mere cult: in the West, spiritual community must always entail active brotherhood and mutual help. The sharing of transcendent truth creates common responsibilities of practical

love. It is in the framework of a spiritual community that the task
of providing for the welfare of the needy must be solved if that task
is not to degenerate into an occasion for the soulless bureaucratic
power of an apparatus over dependent beings.

This view could be criticized as a mere personal preference if it
were not for the massive evidence of the totalitarian movements
that have threatened us in our time. In both cases, we have a kind
of substitute church, the totalitarian party, designed to take its
place beside the state to provide meaning and coherence to the
whole. Needless to say these parties are profound perversions of
what a church is and should be. The question is not how we should
judge them. The question is why so many millions have acclaimed
these perverted churches as filling a deeply sensed need. We cannot have any doubt as to the answer, for the evidence is over-
whelming: the people recoiled from the social structure of the West
in which they failed to find satisfaction for their spirit's hunger. We
have traditionally kept the authority of faith and that of reason
apart from political authority. This order, the glory of the West,
worked as long as "separate" meant also "coordinate" and
"together." The crisis of the West cannot be solved merely by falling back from totalitarianism to the system of free enterprise.
There must be a re-creation of an order of the spirit, in conjunction
with which limited government alone is capable of ordering human
life.

# The Communist Mind

THE WEST is still groping to comprehend the nature of the Communist threat. By and large, the effort at understanding our enemy
is still lacking in system and purpose. Most writings on Communism presuppose, rather than aspire at, knowledge of what it is
that endangers us. Uncritically held assumptions about Communism separate schools of thought from each other. Thus, one
school of thought posits that the Communist threat is that of an
ambitious great power pursuing an expansive policy in the style of
nineteenth-century imperialism. Another presupposes that the
threat stems from the existence of the "Communist system," meaning the collectivized economy as such. These are the assumptions
underlying our various approaches to the Communist problem.
This essay is an attempt to challenge both of the already-mentioned
presuppositions, even though both point to important elements in
the situation. It is submitted that neither the power of Russia nor a
foreign collectivist economy endangers our national security and
way of life, but that the threat stems from the mentality of the people who are organized in the Communist Party and, through choice,
association, and discipline, acquire attitudes of profound and irremediable irrationality. Such people, when in possession of
political power, constitute a perennial disturbance to the peace of
nations and of the world.

What is it that shapes and orients the Communist mind? Communists feel linked to each other and to the Party by the tenets of
belief which go under the name of the Communist ideology. This is
a complex structure with many component elements of which the
socialist, or collectivist, element has attracted Western attention
more than any other. And yet, if one asks whether there is one
thing in the ideology that constitutes the key to the Communist

mind, it would be the theory of history rather than the doctrine of collectivist economy. Characteristically, the theory of history of Communism is the part that has encountered little objection and less intellectual resistance in the West, even though, for the Communist, it is the doctrine of historical necessity which replaces religion, ethics, and philosophy.

One can reduce the Marxist-Leninist speculation about history to a simple formula: History is a chain of cause-and-effect successions of certain types of society, each following the preceding one with inexorable necessity. The entire course of history thus is said to obey objective "laws" which can be "scientifically" known. Knowledge of these "laws" enables man not only to understand the past, but to gauge the future, and thus to find the "correct" line of action for the present. Surveying the whole of history from beginning to end, Communism avers that history moves not merely forward but also upward, toward a climax which will constitute the fulfillment of everything that has gone before. Communists believe that history culminates in the fight of the proletariat against capitalism, of which the Communist Party considers itself the cadre organization.

COMMUNISTS thus look at history in a way which radically differs from that of other people: from the vantage point of the ultimate end, retrospecting the present from the future. The certainty of things to come furnishes the Communist point of view for all problems of the present. Communists claim to know, with "scientific" accuracy, where mankind must eventually arrive. The present and all its aspects assume in this perspective the character of a mere period of transition. To Communists, the future is more real than the present, because it is the ultimate destiny toward which everything present is moving. This way of reversing the normal human perspective of present and future marks a turn from rational to irrational thinking about politics. Something that exists, like man, cannot look upon its own existence from the point of view of a future completion of time, as the Danish philosopher Kierkegaard has reminded us. Existence means to have an open future with a variety of possibilities. To regard the whole of history as if it were already realized, retrospectively, is something not given to man. It is the prerogative of God. Communists, in claiming a foreknowledge that can only be that of a Being above and beyond time, cast themselves in a role not befitting the human situation. This is the deepest source of Communist irrationality. Let us observe that irrationality in some of its applications.

The future is knowable – but only to those trained in its "science": Marxism-Leninism. Marxist analysis has "proved" that a fully human life can be expected not in the present but only in the future that will emerge from the victory of the proletariat over its enemies. The Party has styled itself the "Vanguard" of the proletariat, the organization that is doing unremitting battle against the resisting forces of the present. The Party and its forces are "good," its use of force is justified, its wars are holy, its cause triumphant. Instead of judging in terms of criteria of intrinsic goodness, the Communists judge themselves and others by the yardstick of the "forward movement of history." If anything or anyone is identified with the anticipated future, the verdict is "progressive," meaning "good" because justified by history. Identification with the present or even the past results in a judgment of "reactionary," meaning bad because condemned by history. Motion in time has taken the place of ethics.

THE FUTURE is already known – that means that, for the Communist in the present, the future is not a matter of open possibilities. Only one kind of road leads from here to the anticipated there. To know this road is the task of political thinking. All Communist thinking therefore turns on the problem of the "correct" choice, the choice of that one road to the future. Compared with all others, the Communist Party claims to know most about this "correct" choice. Being the "Vanguard," the element that is furthest advanced in consciousness of the future course of history, the Party is ahead of others in the motion toward the destined goal. It can see what is yet hidden from others. From its insights into things to come, it knows the "true" interests of peoples, classes, and nations, and has the right to overrule the illusory interests which people mistakenly assume to be theirs. The truth unfolds as history moves on. All those who dissent from the Party today will not be able to realize their mistake until the morrow has vindicated its Communist servants.

The "Party Line" is thus more than expediency. It appears to

Communists like the blazing of a trail by a competent guide who alone is familiar with the terrain and aware of the detours that must be taken to arrive at the yet unseen goal. Communists would not necessarily claim that the Party is above mistakes. But they do regard it as in fact infallible, for in comparison with the Party there is nobody who could claim to be more "advanced," nobody with even equally valid insights into the road to be traveled, nobody who could conceivably improve on the Party's judgment. Because the truth that is history becomes accessible through struggle against the forces of reaction, the body which leads in this struggle must, by virtue of its forward position, have superior knowledge. The Party, in Communist eyes, is therefore more than a mere power organization. It is the fountainhead of truth, a truth which, in Lenin's words, is "always concrete." It is a spiritual home. It is the only available framework for meaningful individual action, if the meaning of human action is tied to the promotion of mankind's future destiny. It is the sole structure of order in an otherwise chaotic world. Outside of the Party, there is nothing but darkness, reaction, corruption, and hopelessness. Thus even a Communist who has come to doubt the Party's ideology finds it a matter of heartbreaking difficulty to sever himself from the Party and from there to go out into a world where no similar organization links his daily action with universal meaning and a hopeful future.

"THE PARTY AND THE MASSES" is a chapter by itself. Only the Party can have knowledge of the anticipated future and the road leading there. The masses, caught up in the present and its concerns, cannot sufficiently detach themselves from reactionary influences. The Party, therefore, must "lead and not follow." It must never adjust to people and their interests but rather adjust people to itself and its interests. The proper role for the masses is one of "support" for Party policies. Being unable to appeal to the masses in terms of what the Party alone can know by virtue of Marxism-Leninism, the Party can gain mass support only by playing on the masses' present grievances, discontentments and needs. One could call this a kind of adjustment of the Party to people and their feelings. But the adjustment is not made in good faith. The Communists are fully and articulately aware that they arouse hopes and make promises which they intend to deny once their strategic objective has been attained thanks to the masses' support. The Party's faithlessness, however, does not trouble the Communist conscience. If the Party deceives and manipulates the masses, it will eventually turn out to have been for the good, as all increases in the Party's power will move history nearer to the anticipated future. The masses, who are incapable of being moved by the "truth" must be led by the Party as children are led by parents.

A similar relationship exists between Party leadership and Party rank-and-file. The Communist term for this relationship is "democratic centralism." It means in practice that all Party members take part in endless debates and discussions about foregone conclusions. The Communists cannot approach the process of discussion as one of open possibilities, which approach would alone guarantee respect for the minds that converge in give-and-take. Since for the Communists history admits of only one "correct" road, the discussion can also have only one "correct" outcome, and the discussion process is one of attunement to this single choice. Any failure to take "the" correct path is for him necessarily a "deviation," and a deviation is a betrayal of "progress," and thus "reaction." A discussion is for Communists not a process of finding the materials for a forthcoming decision, but rather one of making the members understand the necessity and rationalization of a decision already taken. This is logical only when one pretends to have scientific knowledge of history's "Laws."

The same orientation underlies the typical Communist "toughness." Present shortcomings or setbacks cannot daunt a mind that has made its habitat entirely in the future. The present, from this perspective, must appear nothing but imperfect, hostile, and transitory. From here to the future the road is one of struggle, and the struggle is a "protracted" one, replete with victories and defeats, periods of contention and of lull, battles and campaigns, advances and retreats. The Communist manages to see in present imperfections the expected perfection of the future, as did the Russian lecturer who told Professor Gollwitzer a report on Russia saying that Russians live in beautiful new homes was true, even though at present many Russians do not yet live that way. "To see the future in the present means to think dialectically." (Gollwitzer, *Und Fuehren Wohin Du Nicht Willst*) For a Communist it is one of the basic facts of life that the Party, as long as it exists, must expect to struggle against enemies of superior strength. No campaign, no battle can be considered final except the one that puts its last enemy at its feet. Since the Party has been appointed by History as the instrument to move mankind forward toward the fulfillment of its destiny, the Party's eventual victory is assured. Khrushchev's "We shall bury you!" was meant not as a declaration of intention but as a confident reference to fact, a statement of "knowledge" concerning what will be the end of it all.

The Party's leadership consists of those people who, by virtue of their ideological "correctness," know most about the road that history must take. These people, and the small minority that belongs to the Party, are assumed to be surrounded by hostile influences of vastly superior strength. Organization and strict Party discipline are considered the recipe to the Party's eventual success over even the strongest enemy. Communists trust nobody and believe in nothing, except the Party and its mission. Thus the highest Communist duty is discipline. It is this discipline, permeating the entire personality, which renders Communists so formidable as enemies. The Communists' discipline has its roots in ideological convictions, for the ultimate enforcement consists in the threat of expulsion from the Party. Only those who assume that the Party alone is the enterprise of Progress, and that outside of the Party there is nothing but selfishness and Reaction, will fear expulsion as the Christian fears excommunication. The secret of Communist discipline is the Communists' belief in a world divided between bourgeois reaction and socialist revolution in which the Party leads the forces of progress.

THE COMMUNIST attitude toward people is based on the assumption that, as there are two ages, the present of capitalism and the future of socialism, there are two ideologies and two kinds of people, the "progressives" and the "reactionaries." The "progressives" are those who help the revolution which is the path toward the future age. All others are reactionary. The Communists' condemnation of all people classified as "reactionaries" follows from their total rejection of present-day society. They compare the present bourgeois and the future socialist society. Of these two, only the future one is considered real human life. It is seen as an age in which all tensions, disharmonies and shortcomings of human existence will disappear. Man will be fully himself, his thoughts will be one with his actions, his individuality will harmonize with society, his days will no longer be darkened by poverty, oppression, and war. The future alone is the full realization of truth, freedom, and humanity. By contrast, the present age is for Communists totally "false." It is an existence characterized by exploitation, wars, the rule of money, political and economic oppression. Philosophy, religion, and government do not represent truth but merely the interests of the ruling class strife. Each individual's life is distorted by false institutions and hostile powers. His labor belongs to someone else. His mind is enslaved by false notions. Thus all those who have their interests in the present age rather than in the socialist future are seen as the enemies of truth and humanity. The dividing line between revolutionaries and reactionaries is razor-sharp. For, as Lenin did not tire to point out, there are only two ideologies in the world, bourgeois and socialist, since "mankind has not created a third ideology." Anyone who fails to be socialist, even unwittingly, actually stands on the side of the bourgeoisie. Whether one is "progressive" or not is thus not a matter of intention but "objective" identification – either with the interests of the Party, or else with those of the class enemy.

In Communist eyes, the world is thus bipolarized. This is the characteristic feature of the period of "transition" or "protracted struggle" between Communists and their enemies, a period that constitutes for Communists the framework of their lives and actions. The "period of transition" is filled with the struggle between "two camps." This notion splits everything in two: classes – the bourgeoisie and the proletariat; ideologies – the bourgeois and the socialist ideology; people – the progressives and the reactionaries; nations – the "peace-loving" and the "imperialist" nations; wars – imperialist wars and wars of liberation; and similarly, laws, philosophies, even methods of science. The criterion of distinction is objective support. He who by his thoughts and actions supports the bourgeoisie does not deserve respect or even existence. He who objectively supports the Party is approved. Since the Party Line, by design, zigs and zags, mere revolutionary conviction alone will not do. One must be able to step fast when the Party changes tactics and to guess right while the change is taking place. What is more, the Communists recognize and accept the support of non-Communist elements. These are officially called "vacillating" elements, who, purely for tactical purposes, constitute a kind of third force between the battle lines. According to the Communists, a third force cannot endure long, for sooner or later it will split, one part coming down on the bourgeois and the other on the Communist side. Until then, these "vacillating" elements can be effectively "neutralized" or even used as allies, albeit with the full knowledge that eventually they must be fought and liquidated as ideological enemies.

There are only two ideologies, the bourgeois and the socialist ideology, but of these the bourgeois is still considered by far stronger. Lenin established the dogma that bourgeois ideological influences would powerfully linger long after the abolition of private property and that they constituted a besetting temptation even to Communist Party members. Hence the proper attitude of Communists toward all people is a basic universal suspicion. The bourgeois ideology is seen lurking under every bed, in every human foible, behind every appearance of slackness or self-interest. Communists characteristically struggle not merely on external battle lines but also against the "enemy within." All people deserve to be distrusted: Trust must be earned by unwavering Party loyalty and can never be securely enjoyed. On the same showing, one can call the Communist attitude toward people one of basic and primary hostility. The Party imagines itself surrounded by enemies on all sides. There may be occasional allies, which are even considered essential to the Party's strategic achievements, but every ally, according to Lenin's admonition, must be "watched as if he were an enemy." In the entire world, only those who have succeeded in fully detaching themselves from the present and its lure can be considered reliable. All others are enemies, if not open, then disguised. The latter, in order to be fought, must first be "unmasked."

COMMUNISTS have put between themselves and all other people a deliberate and profound alienation, or estrangement. They postulate that all who have not cast their will and thought into the mold of the socialist future cannot live in the same world with Communists. Communists cannot and will not accept the world in which, on their showing, all non-Communists actually live. Thus their design with respect to these other people is to re-make them into the Communist image. Communists adopt a totalitarian attitude toward people under their rule because they deny the right of these people to be what they are and want to be, and aim at the forceful creation of an entirely "new man." This is a long educational process, for the duration of which the human material under Communist hands is still considered shaped by bourgeois influences and thus hostile to the Party. The totalitarian plan of recreating man must therefore be supplemented by the Party's dictatorial power, that is, power "organized for war." (Lenin) The Communist quest for power is thus no ordinary desire to enjoy the distinctions and perquisites of command. It is an enterprise to create the world according to the Communists' idea of what it should have been, and to make men into something which they are not now, never have been, and do not want to be. Communist totalitarianism springs from the arrogation of the role of God.

A Communist, even though he might not be able to quote Marxist scripture and verse for his statements, might sum up his own view of the world as follows: A future socialist society is a certainty. The present bourgeois society must be rejected as totally unworthy and inhuman. Among all men, only a small group, the Communists, possess clear and scientific knowledge of the future while all others are still captive to the prejudices of the present. Between Communists and non-Communists there is thus no community of values. Under these conditions, life, and all politics, must be a continuous struggle. To assume that there could be harmony and unity in the present world would be but a reactionary illusion. Revolutionary realism emphasizes rather than mitigates the conflict. This does not bar stratagems of "coexistence" with the enemy, with the purpose of capturing, through the enemy's own institutions, the loyalties of people still under his influence. No inner reconciliation with the present society and its defending forces, however, can be considered anything else but treason of the Revolution. The good life can come only in the future. The future that is good will emerge from the victorious struggle of the Party against its reactionary enemies. The Party's power, its militant enterprise, its strategies and tactics, its use of force and ruse, its ongoing conquest of loyalties and institutions are sacred, as the entire revolutionary course of history is sacred. Any resistance to the Party is utterly unjustifiable. One does not measure the Party and its opponents with the same yardstick. The Party alone represents progress and hope; its enemies represent the total evil of the present. Thus, there can be no right to resist the Revolution. Khrushchev, in this sense, told Walter Lippmann that Western opposition to the ongoing Communist world Revolution is impermissible "interference."

A Communist is a man who has the outlook just described. He has steeped himself in it by inclination, choice, and ceaseless indoctrination. The outlook is also bolstered by official Party enforcement. The combination of attraction, semi-rational persuasion, and enforcement is extremely strong. To see people and situations, the Party, and oneself in the perspectives laid down by dogmatized ideology becomes second nature to a Communist. The grip of the ideology is all the firmer since Communists are not likely to be confronted with any articulate alternative. At one point alone a different set of ideas might make an opposing claim on him: The traditional standards of morality, demanding good will, charity, veracity and faithfulness, pose a conflict with the Communist norm of the class struggle. The struggle-hardened Communist is likely to win this argument with his conscience by persuading himself that since the course of history is known as certain, helping the course of history is the only moral conduct, compared with which traditional morality is nothing but bourgeois sentimentality. Once he commits himself to the belief that history treads an objectively knowable path, all the other arguments of the Party ideology follow with grim but inescapable logic. With regard to this fundamental dogma, the Communist not only finds no alternative view available in the contemporary world, but actually finds himself aided and abetted by Western thought. Positivism, Progressivism, Historicism have left deep marks on most Western intellectuals. These intellectual patterns are first cousin to the Communist ideology in that they, too, posit a knowable and predictable course of historical causality, the progressive movement of history to higher forms of life, the key role of revolutions, the struggle against the heritage of the past in the name of the future. Opposite views have not yet been sufficiently articulated in the West.

ONE CAN SAY, therefore, that in the West, too, ideologies hold sway and that between the prevailing ideologies in the West and Communism there are certain affinities and similarities. From all other ideologies the Communists differ by a trait of character which under different circumstances would be considered admirable: They take their beliefs seriously and expect at all times to act upon them. The Communists are above all ideological activists. This is why they constitute a more deadly threat than others whose thinking may also be irrationally distorted. Any ideology, since it proceeds from irrational premises, is apt to cause profound disturbances in the social order. In the Communist case, the character of the disturbance is a militant hostility towards men and existing institutions, a design to subvert, uproot, and destroy everything that exists. This flows from the fact that Communists live in a dreamworld, of the coming realization of which they are yet "scientifically" convinced. When dreams are carried over into the sober light of the day and become confused with reality, human action loses the quality of sobriety and adopts quixotic features. The substitution of a fictitious future age for the world of actual experience must entail irrationality of action. The irrationality of Communists manifests itself in their self-willed alienation from the world in which, after all, they also live.

One must distinguish between substantive and pragmatic rationality, the first concerning basic views of man, society, nature, and life, the second concerning the suitability of means to given ends. The Communists are irrational in a substantive sense. It is their construction of ends, and the realities on which ends are based, which is arbitrarily distorted and contrived. The pragmatic conclusions drawn from these ideological assumptions, however, are quite rational, given the basic postulates. The Communists, in daily life, are concerned almost exclusively with the full range of these pragmatic principles. Their problems are those of the protracted struggle, the Party and its leadership, the strength and weaknesses of the enemy, the assessment of various social forces from the point of view of the strategy, and the expediency of this or that policy to be adopted by the Soviet Union. Assuming the need to destroy the present-day world, the Communists have developed the art of destroying social structures to a previously unknown high level. This one must call pragmatic rationality of a sort, just as the "perfect crime" is a variety of pragmatic rationality. What is more, a certain amount of constructive rationality has room within the substantive irrationality of the Communist world view. Even a ruler committed to a dreamworld can succeed in commanding resources and skills which produce missiles, spaceships, and steel presses. Political madness is capable of creating an illusion of genuine and rational purpose and may even spur the output of great energy applied to ways, means, and instruments.

No amount of technical rationality, though, can remedy a deficiency of substantive rationality. The Communists are and remain in a basic and irremediable conflict with reality. It is, of course, impossible to escape from reality, and the Communists run their heads against its walls all the time. On those occasions, they have a choice of trying to suppress resistant reality by sheer power or making concessions in the interest of continuing their struggle. By and large, they have preferred the second course, a course that was initiated by Lenin when he accepted the Peace of Brest Litovsk and, three years later, instituted the NEP. But Lenin also taught them that such concessions must never be made in the spirit of a change of mind. Rather, they are mere temporary retreats. This determination to continue believing in a world of their fancy rather than accepting the lessons taught them by reality bars the Communists forever from the achievement of peace. Not even where they have established total power over men and society have they created anything that could be honored by the name of order. Wherever Communists are organized for power there is hostility, suspicion, insecurity, and disintegration. Nor have they accomplished even within their own Party anything like relations of trust and friendship.

The present age of humanity is deeply disturbed, nations are threatened, institutions and traditions subverted, humanity suppressed, because a movement given to a cult of unreality has organized itself as a political army. There is a widespread misconception that Communists are engendered by conditions of social misery. This is quite contrary to the facts. The truth is that Communists are made by Communists. Tempted by visions of fancy, bribed by a pseudo-scientism, they come to believe the reality of dreams, submerge themselves in a world of their own intellectual making, and pretend to be masters of creation. As long as such people are effectively organized for political action, the world can have no peace. Socialism might be conceived as an order of society. The might of Russia may disturb the sleep of other nations' rulers. Neither, however, can be called a fundamental threat to human order and people's existence. That threat comes solely from the irrational, alienated, destructive mind that has taken political shape in the Communist Party.

# Communism and the Notion of the Good

THE QUESTION, "Communism: is it or isn't it a threat?" continues to disturb us. It has been phrased in this manner: "Do they behave like human beings? Certainly. Do they behave like Russians? Indeed. Do they behave like Communists?" If the last question is answered affirmatively, it brings up further questions: "Often?" "always?" "occasionally?" "typically?" and, above all: "What does 'behaving like a Communist' mean?" This last question should be narrowed down, for our present purposes, to: "In what way is Communist politics moved by goodness?" This formula already structures the answer, since it removes the problem from the ground of psychology. To the extent to which the practices of Communists differ significantly from that of other human beings we must look for an explanation not in conditions but in ideas, the ideas shaped into an ideological system by Marx and Lenin. Both insisted that ideas and practice should be united, that the point of ideas is not to explain the world but to change it, and that the appropriate type of practice must be revolutionary.

There is no denying that a strong moral element is present in the Communist call for action. The call draws its power from both moral indignation and a moral vision. The initial appeal of communism to outsiders is always moral. On the other hand, the fear of communism is also primarily moral. It is not primarily a concern of rich men for their wealth. Quite the contrary: rich men have tended to either observe an attitude of indifference toward communism or else have sympathized with it, from a distance or, on occasion, even actively. Nor is it an aversion to rapid change as such. Among those who fear communism have been many socialists who themselves have initiated systemic changes of society. What is feared is, first, Communist terror, Communist unscrupulousness, Communist untrustworthiness. Deeper down we find the fear of Communist godlessness and of the "public falsehood." If, then, the initial Communist impulse has been moral, the Communists have encountered a resistance no less moral. This induces us to take a closer look at the moral element in Communist theory and practice.

A modern movement appeals from the later Marx to "the early Marx," supposedly the "humanist Marx." As we pick up Marx's early writings what strikes us is the negative form of his morality. His emphatic concern is with "critique," a watchword of all left-Hegelians. "Critique" was exalted as the process of negation which, as the "negation of the negation," would open the way to higher realities. Among the left-Hegelians Marx alone pushed on, from "Critical Critique" to "radical critique" and "practical critique," i.e., revolution. In other words, he moved from an epistemic negation to practical-subversive negation. The present system, he wrote, "dehumanizes" men, the "feeling of man's dignity [has] vanished from the world," and thus the world is in "a dream" from which it must be "awakened." "Social truth" cannot be found in men's consciousness but can be "developed everywhere out of this conflict of the political state with itself."[1]

Marx's critique of "the political state" became, almost immediately, a total critique of society, as he rejected a *merely* political revolution" on the grounds that it "would leave the pillars of the house standing."[2] Moreover, he praised the French "critical and utopian socialists and Communists," whose ideas he in general rejected, for "the critical element" in their writings: "They attack every principle of existing society. Hence they are full of the most valuable materials for the enlightenment of the working class."[3] This emphasis leads Marx to his concept of a "negative representative of society" as the carrier of the revolution. It must be "a class with radical chains, a class in civil society that is not of civil society, a class that is the dissolution of all classes, a sphere of society having a universal character because of its universal suffering and claiming no *particular* right because *no particular wrong* but *wrong in general* is perpetrated on it."[4] The burden of the accusation could not be graver. It amounts to deriving evil as such from the institutional structure of society. The tone of the indictment reminds one of the prophets of Israel, and thus a moral standpoint is strongly implied.

It is implied but never explicitly set forth. In the case of Israel's prophets, their starting point is the covenant between Yahweh and his people. Yahweh is the God whose concern is righteousness, and his commandments are no mere implication but a clearly defined way of life. Marx, who had embraced Feuerbach's "critique of religion," would not draw his indignation from a divine source. But when speaking of "dehumanization" he certainly invokes something akin to "human nature" in Aristotle's sense. He quotes Aristotle in the context. His total critique of society, however, has the side-effect that it negates not merely the present but all of the past, and thereby eliminates any experience of human nature. If no humanity has ever been actual, Marx might dream of a human nature but could not claim any knowledge of it. He did say explicitly that he hoped to discover "the social truth" in the course of revolutionary practice. In terms of the historical record, however, Communists must profess agnosticism with regard to human nature.

The "implied moral standpoint," then, has no basis other than that of radical negation, the total critique of society. The good is chiefly seen as the opposite of that which now exists. Present society is bourgeois and capitalistic, so the good must be proletarian and socialistic. Hence, as Bakunin put it, destruction is to be held a "creative force." Goodness is not now, nor has it been, but will be, after radical revolution, in the future. On the other hand, not much is known about the future, but, since it will be utterly different from the inhuman present, it must by definition be good. The resulting moral justification chiefly supports the historical struggle as "absolute" (Lenin's term). The struggle as such carries hope,

since by virtue of the total critique of present society it is necessarily a struggle against what is seen as wholly inhuman, unjust, and
alienated: an apocalyptic war against wickedness as such, to the
end of its final elimination.

Fourteen hundred years before Marx, Augustine had criticized
the "present society" of Rome in terms as radical as those of Marx,
but without losing the foundation of his positive morality. A total
critique of society, then, does not always have the undesirable side-
effects that showed up in Marx's case. One is led to inquire into
Hegel's system as the likely cause of this devouring negativity.
Hegel made history into the ultimate reality of everything. In all
the great cultures of the world, however, morality seems to have
been experienced as an aspect of some ultimate "givenness." One
thinks of the Hindu concept of *rta* and *dharma*, of the Chinese *tao*,
of Plato's *Ideas* and Aristotle's *Nature*, of the Stoics' *Cosmos* and
the Hebrews' *Creation*. Buddhism, it is true, does look for a *Nir-
vana* that can be seen as the annihilation of everything given, but
still the Boddhisattva's *compassion* is positive goodness.

Nor is this "givenness" denied by the obvious fact that good
character requires a process of formation. For learning, not only of
good moral habits but of other kinds of habits as well, seems to be
attended by an intuition of rightness. A child is taught words, and
all of a sudden begins to speak entire sentences never heard before.
An athlete is shown the various motions of hurling a ball but then,
all at once, intuits how the parts combine into a single motion. A
musician faces many notes, but the wholeness of the music comes
to him beyond these particulars. A detective sees the unity of a
multitude of facts, in a flash which has no explanation. Such experiences are at the back of the manifold symbols of givenness,
e.g., the idea that knowledge is above all memory. Morality, then,
is conceived as attached to such constants as gods, essences,
nature, being. More important, though, "the good" itself, i.e., its
content, is experienced as something given rather than something
consciously invented or subjectively preferred, so that Plato refused to define it. In the common law tradition we still say that the
judge is supposed to find the right measure rather than to make it
up. Nor is this experience of givenness incompatible with the
philosophy of process. If Aristotle had no trouble in conceiving a

nature as the development of an entelechy, the perception of a chain of events is likewise not incompatible with structure.

All givenness vanishes, however, when such concepts as being, nature, creation are replaced by history. History differs from "process" in kind, process being eminently analyzable in relations and successions, while history is characterized by the play of countless singularities whose ensemble defies any kind of universal concept. In no ways can history serve as a substitute for such a concept as, e.g., nature. In its Hegelian meaning, which underlies most of contemporary thinking, it stands not for "process" but rather for "coming to be," a coming to be not of existing things, but rather a coming to be culminating in some perfected future kind of being. Thus it both requires and entails a claim to "knowledge" of the future. This is not the kind of knowledge that enables one to predict the outcome of an ongoing project, but rather knowledge of a future condition that contains all of history's meaning.

All the same this humanly foreknown future sheds no light. It does appear bright, but its brightness casts deep shadows over past and present human existence. As for the past, it tends to disappear in the abyss of "not at all"; as for the present, it lingers in the twilight of "not yet." (cf. Ernest Bloch, *The Principle of Hope*) Thus Camus wrote: "Nothing is pure: that is the cry which convulses our period. Impurity, the equivalent of history, is going to become the rule, and the abandoned earth will be delivered to naked force, which will decide whether or not man is divine."[5] At this point, defenders of Hegel and Marx like to point to the Christian faith which believes in a Kingdom of God yet to come. The comparison, however, is misplaced. The Kingdom of God is also "at hand," and the faithful endeavor to live now in a manner worthy of it. The Kingdom of God was "opened to all believers" by Christ's death on the cross, so that it is also indissolubly linked to the past. The Kingdom of God is both given and coming. It bears no likeness to a reality which is supposed to have no being at all until some future generation will be able to say that it has "become."

In that perspective nothing can be said to be real except becoming, the coming to be of being which is not yet. That becoming was given by Hegel the character of negation, and by Marx that of revolutionary struggle. Now a struggle that carries the becoming of reality is of such transcending importance that it must divide all humanity into two opposing groups. On one side is the very small group of those who, possessing the key knowledge of the ideology, have anchored their consciousness in mankind's future, who are therefore conscious of their own "historical mission" and, by virtue of this consciousness, detached from all "spontaneity." Aware of that which is to come they form "the vanguard," not merely of the proletariat or even of mankind, but of history itself. On them lies the burden of bringing about mankind's destiny. The others, bulking in numbers, are all counted as the vanguard's opponents, not necessarily by intention, rather by situational definition. Social origin makes them into opponents, spontaneity makes them into opponents, so does attachment to the present, or even a merely passive trust in history's self-movement; for the vanguard, having apprehended what is yet to come, must actively lead. The struggle being defined in such terms, nothing remains that these two groups could have in common. A Manichaean gulf divides them, as the forces of light from the forces of darkness. Again, this terminology bears no comparison with "children of light" and "children of darkness," which says something about subjective orientations that may yield to conversion, while the Communist concept of embattled class forces postulates a situation that can change only in the moment of the vanguard's total victory.

Now one of the basic assumptions of morality is an acknowledgement of sameness, or equality, between humans. Martin Buber has insisted that the well-known Biblical commandment should be translated: "and (love) thy neighbor as *one like* thyself." A realization that we share an ontic or transcendent equality – whether we call it "the human condition," "human nature," a "divine image," or a common "fatherhood of God" – lies at the root of what Bergson has called "absolute morality." This is the attitude of the "open soul," which experiences obligation beyond what is relatively owed to a particular society.

> Suppose we say that it embraces all humanity: we should not be going too far, we should hardly be going far enough, since its love may extend to animals, to plants, to all nature. And yet no one of these things which would thus fill it would suffice to define the attitude taken by the soul, for it could, strictly speaking, do without all of them . . . it has not aimed at this

object; it has shot beyond and reached humanity only by passing through humanity.[6]

Nothing of this attitude has a place in the Communist mind
which, rather than opening the soul, closes it in on a small part of
humanity and its "historical mission." All the same, their "narrow-
ing of the soul" has, paradoxically, a moral character for it is
motivated by the vision of "human emancipation." Some call it a
peculiar "love of mankind." It would seem more correct to speak of
a "love for Communism's 'sublime vision' of the future." As far as
mankind short of that future is concerned, Communists see in it
nothing but a basic and unremediable inequality between the two
opposed groups. There can be no rights for the enemies of history,
but the Communist party has the historical right to make sure that
all others support it unconditionally, for the future's sake.

Thus we are thoroughly mistaken if we attribute to communism
an advocacy of equality and justice. Marx rejected both principles
in his scathing criticism of Proudhon, *The Poverty of Philosophy*
(1847), and, later, in *The Critique of the Gotha Programme* (1875).
There is no need to appeal to authority, though, for the concept of
Communist inequality follows logically from a morality centering
on history's coming to be and on revolution as the mode of that
becoming. In Communist eyes their commitment to two standards
has the same moral character as the initial impulse of the revolution. Still, Communists are quite aware that they do not share a
common conscience with the rest of humanity, so they feel the need
to keep the principle of Communist inequality hidden, and to play
publicly on the conscience of "the others." Thus history does make
liars of us all.

On the same grounds the struggle itself, seen in terms of light
against darkness, enjoys exemption from all moral restrictions.
The "sublimity" of the goal justifies any method required to reach
it. Lenin explicitly enjoined on the comrades both violence and
trickery, dissimulation and brutal force, concessions and deception.
He also succeeded in giving to foreign affairs the color of the class
struggle, in which the class enemy has no right to exist. One may
say that Communist operations are characterized by moral immorality, immoral practice that is moral in its ultimate justification. The immorality is real, though, while the moral justification is

merely implied. After all, the future is not yet. Communist "moral immorality," then, is composed of a moral element amounting to a begged question and an immoral aspect that is consummated practice. If one should wonder why the moral *petitio principii* is still socially effective and appealing to outsiders, one should remember that our age tends to deify humanity and to exalt politics to the rank of a redemptive enterprise. The Communist vision therefore touches the deepest hopes of many who, though not sharing the Communist ideology, look for cultural perfection in this world.

It may not be superfluous at this point to look briefly at the merits of the Communist vision of the good, as if it were conceived as a utopian blueprint – which, in fact, it is not. The only feature of the future order that Communists profess to know is its socialism, i.e., social ownership of the means of production. The concept looks for the overcoming of human egotism through collective economic production, secured by appropriate institutional arrangements. A book by the Yugoslav philosopher Svetozar Stojanovic, *Between Ideals and Reality*,[7] criticizes the Communist ideology by pointing to the way in which things have gone wrong in practice. The condition now prevailing in the Soviet Union he calls "statism" rather than socialism, arguing that socialism would have required self-management and self-determination by the workers. The main thrust of his critique is that a wrong kind of institutional arrangement was chosen for the new society. One asks, why? To which question a possible answer is that institutional arrangements were not, and can never be, entirely under the control of social planners, since all institutions have a momentum of their own that is never fully predictable. Likewise, the relation between institutions and their effect on personal morality are not known and possibly not knowable. This answer is underscored by the fact that Stojanovic's criticism comes late, long after the fact. That implies that at the time of the choice no prediction of the moral effect of new institutions was possible, so that the experiment amounted to nothing more than a wager.

Another way in which things have gone wrong bears the Communist name of "opportunism," the persistence of petty self-seeking and self-advancement even in the framework of socialist collectivism. Complaints about opportunism in the ranks of the party itself continue to be voiced, implying the acknowledgement that, in spite of the "correct" institutional change, no transformation of personal morality has occurred. This entails basic doubts whether any moral regeneration can be expected from a reshuffling of institutions. Moreover, Marxist-Leninist analysis of extant immorality rests on the premise that avarice is the root of all human evil. The ineradicability of selfishness, even in a socialist economy, strongly suggests that there are other roots of evil in the human soul.

Finally, one doubts the entire notion of the merging of human individuals with the social whole. That notion, we remember, was in modern times set forth by Rousseau, who asserted that a "collective moral being" would result if every person "alienated" his individuality to the community. Now we are all aware that self-centeredness is something to be overcome and that, to be saved, we must give ourselves to the service of a higher and better reality. The question whether a collectivity is better than the individual, however, is begged. A social whole is still a whole of human beings. Even on the level of collectivity, humanity is still imperfect. Rousseau and Marx were wrong. Collectivism is no salvation.

After this brief excursion into the realm of socialism as a utopia, we return to the ideological edifice that Marx and Lenin erected. Both in their analysis of the present society and in their prefiguring of the future, their thought concentrates wholly on the economic order. It is political order, however, which is measured by the concept of the good. Communist ideology has failed to produce, and probably will not be able to produce norms, principles, and concepts regarding the good political order of existence. One reason for this failure is Marx's insistence that power consists in ownership of the means of production, an apolitical concept that he himself found not applicable to the "Asiatic Society" which drew his attention in the middle 1850s. The other reason is the ideology's emphasis on history's coming to be. Marx and Lenin, with Engels and Stalin thrown in for good measure, produced principles of political action only in the form of principles of revolutionary strategy and the "dictatorship of the proletariat," the latter being political order in "the period of transition." Lenin added to this a strategy of "the socialist camp" in the setting of politics among nations. Strategy, by definition, aims at the preconceived goal of victory, which means that it also aims at the peace of victory. The

Communist concept of peace, however, is futuristic, vague, and speculative. Most definitely it is not peace in the present setting, i.e., peace between socialists and the forces and units of the present-day society.

Strategy is the Communist manipulation of these forces to the end of ultimate and total victory, but peace will come by eventual social evolution, and that evolution is speculatively asserted. Peace is something for which Communists typically are waiting, even while continuing the prime duty of the struggle. That same waiting also applies to Communist domestic policies. "Building" there is, but always in the expectation of effects which no man can fully predict, e.g., the coming of "the new Soviet man." Since the building is done in the period of transition, one does not build primarily in order to live in the present. All Communist building is strategic. Therefore, no state concept is presently possible, and, as for the future, the state is said to wither away. At any rate, all good, for Communists, still lies in the future, except "the good" of the struggle itself. Some point to the welfare aspects of the Soviet system as a modicum of common good, but then one also remembers that state-administered welfare was in fact introduced by Bismarck as early as the 1880s, when there was not even a parliamentary government in Germany.

Soviet rule, then, labors under the absence of a concept of political order. It does have a concept of the party's rule, the supremacy and highest authority of the party over the state, the people, and the entire Russian tradition. But one bears in mind that the party regards itself as a "movement," implying the very opposite of the word "state." Human law, as Boethius rightly perceived, imitates eternity, as laws are designed not strategically but normatively. Since the Soviets have no political theory, in spite of repeated efforts in that direction by Marx, Engels, Lenin, Stalin, and Khrushchev, they have found it impossible to conceive of abiding principles setting limits to state action. Whatever limitations are occasionally conceded must appear, in the words of Zhores Medvedev, as "humane forms of arbitrariness." As long as Communist ideology continues to motivate Russia's rulers, the idea of government as a servant of present human good, common good, will remain a dream. For the same reason, an effective and realistic notion of peace will elude the Soviet leaders. One may say that they are doomed to continue, until the day of the great conversion, in the peaceless and restless prison of their dogma of history's movement.

# Communist Ideology:
# The Sixth Age

THE TITLE derives from Augustine's *City of God*, where he mentions mankind's six ages. The Communist ideology likewise can be said to have gone through five ages and entered the sixth and last one, the *saeculum senescens*. Born in the storm of the Second Party Congress in 1903, tempestuously shaking itself free from its parent in 1912, seizing power in Russia 1917, battling its fellow-revolutionaries and then dividing in internal strife between the Left and the Right, 1920-7, after collectivization entering into a period of violent purges, 1934-8. With Stalin's death began the sixth age. The great times of dramatic changes are over, the convulsions have yielded to tensions underneath a crust of relative stability, the system no longer generates large "movement." The ever hopeful West asks whether now a mentality of management, routine, ripening form has replaced the breathlessness of ideological conniptions. If so, does an ideological spark abide in the casing? If revolutionary passion is a thing of the past, whom or what do Soviet rulers represent, in their own understanding?

Empirical methods cannot avail in trying to answer such questions: Soviet leaders do not answer questionnaires, and, if they did, would look on their answers as means to produce a dynamic political effect. The documents of ideological thought are still the materials from which to extract an answer, although the answers must not conflict with observed conduct and practice. It will not do merely to generalize, saying: "They denied people freedom but promised economic plenty; that promise has proved false, ergo the ideology is dead." Communist leaders come back with their "superior" knowledge that rising societies always live frugally, while declining societies waste their substance in luxury. We do know that Communist persuasion is not found among the masses of population outside the Party, but that tells us nothing about Communist persuasion within, above all, in the innermost circle.

Research in this field has found increasing value in a distinction between the mythical core and the semi-scientific mantle of this idea structure. Leonard P. Wessell, Jr., in his book *Prometheus Bound: The Mythic Structure of Karl Marx's Scientific Thinking* (Louisiana State University Press, 1984), has shown the powerful emotions issuing from "ontomythical" convictions. The qualifier "onto" signals the role of the myth as a replacement of philosophical ontology, the "myth" figuring as a substitute for religion. Thus mankind is seen in fetters through all "hitherto existing history" which is described as but a series of obstructing and distorting conditions that effectively prevent human nature from realizing itself. At present, the great Promethean deed of delivering mankind from its chains is at hand, in the form of the proletariat's self-emancipation. This movement will have universal effects: for the first time true humanity will be possible, freedom and unity will kiss each other in a new society. The convergence of historical circumstances and revolutionary consciousness has put this millennium within the reach of the living generation. Strong stuff, this. No merely progressivist message from the Enlightenment can hold a candle to it. It took German Romanticism to produce this most poisonously seductive *fleur du mal*.

The reverse of the coin carries the practical and temporal aspect of the message. It makes sure that its halo is not that of a far away ideal. Indeed, the process of accomplishment is already now arranged by history, forces presently at work are destined to prepare the necessary conditions for social explosion and the human masses moved to decisive action. It would be more fitting to say that this is the cutting edge of Marx's message, for he never said much about the goal – except that it would be socialistic – but spoke all the more about the process of its coming-to-be. Into the concept of the "cunning of reason," so named by Hegel but prefigured in Kant, Marx threaded the notion that revolutionary intent would come to the right subjects at the right time. Thus his vision did not have the vacant stare of perfection but the blazing eye asserting man's own responsibility for the future of the race, in collusion with history's mighty movements. Marx's great power was, indeed, the conviction that at this moment mankind would at long last take the making of its destiny in its own hands, fashioning liberating conditions out of extant materials. In this work, both prediction and human will have their role, as men discover their duty towards history's motion in the direction of the "most sublime" reality to come. Presented in this way, we perceive the power of a myth. Marx, however, surrounded it with the penumbra of "scientific" concepts: base and superstructure, commodity and its production, use value and exchange value, surplus value and exploitation, accumulation and immiseration, centralization, falling rate of profits, industrial reserve army. Through an analysis based on these concepts, the "present day society" is both hailed as the mighty accelerator of history's march toward the great emancipation, and cursed as the greatest destroyer of human values. The "scientific" mantle silenced doubt and apparently removed the need for faith. The greatest moral undertaking combined the driving forces of human indignation and of material necessity. How can it fail?

If research has found it useful to isolate this mythical core for special attention, one of the reasons is that in the many changes of the ideology, this core has remained untouched. Differently put: When Soviet leadership allowed such "bourgeois" concepts as value, commodity production, the division of labor, the differentiation of town and country, into the socialist system, they all the same ceased not to be moved by the onto-mythical conviction. *A fortiori* less structural concepts, e.g. the long-range revolutionary strategy, the character and duration of the "period of transition," the link between national class struggles and the global struggle, concepts that from the outset were held adjustable to circumstances, could be twisted, added to and deleted from, without affecting the core conviction.

We come to a different kind of problem, however, when focusing on the role of judgment in this process. Human judgment, in its nature, is free. Just how free can it be in the presence of an elaborate ideology? Would Communists judge things in the light of what we call "the nature of things"? Would they assess circumstances by something like common sense? This general question runs into further complication through Lenin's introduction of the principle of utmost flexibility in Communist tactics: use any and all means and methods, if you want to be a serious revolutionary. This is the point at which Western observers of Soviet Russia tend to beg the question by assuming that circumstances are circumstances which elicit essentially the same kind of judgment from every intelligent person, and that therefore Soviet leaders must be presumed to act by assumptions largely similar to the rulers of other nations. If the Soviets were indeed ideologically motivated, they argue, that motivation would show up as rigid dogmatism. These observers assume that Communist ideology leaves no freedom to human judgment, so that it cannot be present where Soviet actions do not appear to be dogmatic. "If we do observe these leaders using free judgment, they cannot have ideological convictions." One wonders whether this kind of syllogism is not characteristic of people who themselves often have no fundamental beliefs of any kind, so that a mind formed by belief appears strange and even quaint to them, and that they cannot imagine someone with unvarying beliefs to act other than as a manifest bigot. By contrast Lenin was emphatic: "Our doctrine is no dogma but a guide to action." He himself created the model of a Communist leader using free judgment in pursuit of fixed goals.

There remains the further question to what extent the judgment of Communists, even though relatively free from dogma, might be clouded in its perception of realities. Judgment does not form in a vacuum. It belongs to a mind that entertains an overall understanding of the matter to be judged and is also informed by philosophical intelligence about the reality in which all humans participate. It is in this perspective that Aristotle raises the question, "What is the good of man?" Communists ask questions in a totally different perspective. They believe that man is not yet, that man will be in the future, that they themselves are the leaders of mankind's universal movement from present non-being to future being. Hence a question like "what is the good of man?" can make no sense to them. If asked about the good, they would point to that huge historical movement which is their Promethean enterprise. The sole end which they can conceive in regard to man is the temporal completion of that movement. Their judgment plays on givens within a general assumption of the revolutionary transformation of the world, the sole reality bearing on any concept of goodness. If Communists have often impressed others by their realism, it is because they have become past masters in judging, with a long view, the power of their opponents compared with their own. Here they judge uninhibited by any dogmatic notion, yet with utter fidelity to the mythical goal and the ideological road toward that goal.

If the Communists were to judge things in a way we call "sound," they would have to assume that fully human men live now, that there have always been fully human men in history, and that that judgment concerning the good of man would be of the same character now as judgment in the past about men then living. The difficulty, for Communists, of learning to rely on such philosophical assumptions baffles the imagination. For as soon as their inner eye would begin to encompass men, the past, the world, nature, in this fashion, their own enterprise together with its hopes and fears would turn into utter nonsense. All they could then do would be to fold their tents and steal away.

## Communist Ideology and Real Circumstances

THE IDEOLOGY, whether one takes it from Marx or Lenin or both, contains no accurate prediction of real circumstances to come. Marx's idea that the Revolution would occur only at a certain stage of economic development is obviously more myth than prediction: the myth of the historical formation of revolutionary forces. Marx has from the outset been charged with error in his predictions. If one takes them for what they pretend to be, elements of scientific thought, he was in error. If they, by contrast, are read as part of the myth, the charge of error fails, for a myth conveys truth only in poetical rather than in analytical fashion. If the predictions are mythical, however, the Communists must find themselves poorly equipped when encountering new historical situations. The first socialist revolution occurred in a country that had neither much of a proletariat nor a developed capitalism, and succeeded only through the revolutionary mobilization of the peasantry. Worse, Marx had not conceived either an economic theory or a political theory for the post-revolutionary society. His definition of power as residing essentially in the ownership of the means of production and his prediction that revolutionary expropriation would end both exploitation and contradictions in the economic system did little to help Lenin to face practical problems. By 1920 Lenin wrote that, while the overthrow of the capitalist masters was easy, the Communists now faced the far more "terrible force of habit" in the peasantry, which could not be vanquished by a frontal assault. Nor would the economy switch to socialism without fatal damage. In other words, the ideology, which "to belittle *in any way*, to *deviate from in the slightest degree* means strengthening bourgeois ideology," had run up against recalcitrant reality. Lenin concluded that a detour was the only passable road towards the ideological goal.

Lenin's judgment aimed not at "the good of man," but at an estimate regarding the future course of history. Such discussions as between Plekhanov and Lenin in 1904, Kautsky and Lenin in 1918, Trotsky and Stalin in 1924-6 all turned on guesses about the influence of Communist decisions on the supporting forces of future history. That is the sole criterion of ideological "correctness," a matter which otherwise appears irrelevant to the Communist mind. Communist judgment, therefore, is essentially one of strategy. Moreover, the Party is the locus of ideological correctness, because it represents the cutting edge of history, in Communist eyes. No solitary Communist thinker opposing the Party can be ideologically correct, seeing that the Party, by definition, is mankind's "Vanguard." No metaphysical truth is available to one who wants to be more correct than the Party. Concretely speaking, history's future course must be guessed, and nobody's guess can replace that of the Party.

## Ideology and Detours: Part I

THE COMMUNIST ideology centers on a specific view of history. History, however, looks decisively different to the Party of 1985 than it looked to Marx in 1848 or to Lenin in 1903. Up to the Revolution, the Party had only one idea of history: All of the past looked provisional, so provisional that it had no record of any genuine humanity. The Party of 1985, however, sees also half a century of the first Communist regime, beginning with the dramatic explosion that "turned all human affairs into a new direction." All the same, in practice the following 68 years have turned out to bring no kind of fulfillment, but nothing more than an extended "period of transition." Though a transition must by definition be considered provisional, it yet bears no comparison with the "pre-history" of all the previous past. For in 1917 real history is said to have begun, even though it is still racing along the runway. For Communists, since 1917, there is no more history of Russia as a country, but only a history of the Communist Party of the Soviet Union, the concretely inchoate element of true human being. While all previously existing history is dismissed with a global verdict of "not yet," their own history is examined in detail, with concrete judgments not excluding moral verdicts. A chief example of the latter is the 20th Party Congress, with Khrushchev's indictment of Stalin. The Party found then that a) its history included excessively hard measures of terror, and b) the institutionalization of the Party in the Soviet system had not changed at all. The implied moral verdict was not sidestepped, as witness the period of "thaw" with mitigation of Gulag practices and rehabilitation of many *zeks*. That condemnation, however, had narrow limits, even as regards Stalin's person. One cannot report of Russia a phenomenon like that of Dubcek in Czechoslovakia, whose concept of moral duty demanded a complete turning around of the system.

One must speculate on why there was no Russian Dubcek, and psychological methods can not get us to the root of the matter. For there is a decisive difference between Russia and other Communist-controlled countries in that the Russian revolution of 1917 appears to all Communists as *the* historical turning point. We have seen that Communists, like all people, have moral sensitivity; they are willing to admit that the CPSU had made mistakes and in such cases deserves blame. But much, very much – mass killings, the Party's claim to total power, the absence of any tolerance, the diminution of human dignity – can be justified in terms of the grand "necessity" of history. A Communist conscience moves in the framework of the great cause of human emancipation. Their inner voice speaks somewhat in this way: "With so absolutely obligating a goal – no less than *making true man possible* for the first time – one might feel justified to put at stake the whole which is anyway not worth the candle without it." (Hans Jonas, *The Imperative of Responsibility* [Chicago: University of Chicago Press, 1984], p. 185)

Add to that their total rejection of any version of the Christian message, the forgiveness of sins, and one sees that Communists, even when they admit their mistakes, *must* endorse, as a whole, the Revolution of 1917 as well as the Party history since then. The burden of guilt that would come into sight were the Party's regime and its history morally rejected would seem to be beyond any human capacity to bear. A Christian could even then rely on the "wideness of God's mercy," since in his eyes the forgiveness of sins won by Jesus Christ is absolute. Communists, ruling out God's existence and Christ's redemption, have no means of protecting themselves from monstrous guilt except to cling with all their might to the world view that exonerates those who help history's forward march from any moral culpability. In this case justification is not personal; it is collective and historical. It also depends on the retention of the core of the ideology.

At this point, one may state some intermediate conclusions. The Communists, it seems, have effectively separated Marx's scientific penumbra from the mythical core. That has happened not only since 1917: the early struggle within the Social Democratic Party of Russia was between the Mensheviks who accepted Marx, myth, scientific penumbra and all. The Bolsheviks even at that time took Marx's myth and ran vigorously ahead, fortified by Lenin's various principles of revolutionary activism. They made a revolution in a country which according to Marx's materialistic interpretation was not ready for one, and with mass support that was overwhelmingly peasantry, which Marx had declared a non-class. Subsequently they acted with sovereign disregard for Marx's classifying and scientific concepts. They did, however, retain the notion of the myth's predictable certainty, a mark left on it by its scientific wrapping. Thus, when reality turned out to be obstreperous, the Party of Lenin had no difficulty in taking a detour. One of Lenin's concepts of activism was precisely a readiness for compromise with obstructing realities, as long as the core of revolutionary conviction was not abandoned. That core, precisely, is Marx's Promethean myth. Fundamental beliefs, in this as in many precedent cases, turn out to be the strongest motivating powers in human history. One may assume that those who in the last half century were either in responsible positions in the Party, or close to those in responsible positions, will more strongly cling to the fundamental beliefs than

Party members on the periphery. This explains the possibility of a Dubcek in Czechoslovakia and the absence of one in Russia. It follows, then, that the judgment of Party leaders must be ideologically clouded. Of the four basic experiences, "God and man, world and society [which] form the primordial community of being" (Voegelin), the Communist mind knows none. Its judgment of things, persons, and situations, its direction of practice, are contracted on one point, the "making" of man by the Communist Party collaborating with the "progressive" forces of history. This yields a small field of vision, and consequently a large area of possible conflicts with reality. All the same, the power that holds Communists riveted to this vision stems from the exclusionary effect of their moral sensitivity which could in no case assent to a plea of "guilty" regarding the Party's history. A "change of heart" might occur in the Kremlin on this or that aspect of their thinking and practice, but not on their concept of history as authored by the Party.

## Ideology and Detours: Part II

SO FAR we have focused on ideological concepts by themselves. A different problem arises when from the ideology or its lack of it institutions arise which possibly have their own kind of influence on men and society. After all, the entire Marxian argument consists in the assertion that human nature in the past has been utterly distorted by economic and social institutions, and that in the future "good" institutions will generate "good" human beings. When recalcitrant reality forces the Communist Party to take a detour passage, there must be some fear that the resulting institutional changes might thwart the entire Communist enterprise. Still, the Party has authorized considerable changes in its economy: The NEP, varieties of incentives, commodity production, the acceptance of the concept of "value," the so-called Libermann reforms, Khrushchev's decentralizing decrees. Yugoslavia has introduced a modicum of workers' democracy, Poland has returned part of its agriculture to private enterprise, Hungary permits a considerable amount of free market transactions, the Soviets themselves are now considering "profit sharing" as well as fewer planning indicators. Much more radical institutional changes are being tried in Communist China. What possibility of a "return to capitalism" by way of such institutional experiments can we, who look at the matter with non-ideological eyes, discern? And, if there are such possibilities in sight, would a regained capitalism necessitate a return to freedom of the human person, in the Western sense?

To remove a possibly distorting bias of Western observers, if capitalism in the West has helped freedom, that relation is not a necessary one. If freedom has been realized through the political forms of democracy, again this is not a necessary relation. Marx, after all, foresaw state-capitalism as a first and non-emancipating result of a socialist revolution, and warned against it. State capitalism characterized the Nazi *Third Reich* and Mussolini's corporate state. The history of freedom has coincided to some extent with that of capitalism but cannot be reduced to it. More than market prices, freedom of enterprise, and competition, it was the inviolability of private property which gave to the acquisition of wealth that protection which shielded freedom. Property, in turn, would not have been inviolable had it not been for the century-old respect, forced on kings, for the "vested rights" that composed the power-structure of feudal lords in their relation to the king. Neither vested rights, nor security of private property, nor personal liberty can be economically explained. After all, private property did exist in the East (India, China) but remained subject to periodical and systematic raids from on high.

Mention has been made before of the fact that Marx said little about the future society except that it would be socialistic. That is still an integral part of the onto-mythical core. Thus it may be ideological core-conviction which has kept the Communists so far from any re-introduction of private property as the mode of production, and from any fundamental guarantee of personal freedom. Some people have, indeed, derived benefits from the economic changes we have mentioned. Whoever did, peasants, workers, managers, traders, still continue in personal insecurity of position and possession. In the absence of any inviolable property they cannot form a "class" in Marx's sense. Marx never conceived of the bureaucracy as a class, although Hegel had made him fully aware of its operation and mentality. In the Soviet Union, the Party's monopoly on central power disposes of countless means of stopping, isolating, damaging, or destroying any political enemy, thereby preventing the formation of a hostile sector in society. One may, then, conclude a) that changes of economic institutions in Communist systems will not necessarily conduce to the emergence of insuperable forces of resistance; and b) that in the absence of guaranteed private property no such changes will amount to instituted personal freedom and human rights.

Among the authors of "detour" changes, Dubcek alone proposed political changes denying to the Communist Party the totality of power. His idea was to have the Party share power with other groups, parties, and forces. If any such political change materialized, it might indeed lend to changed economic institutions an important role in developing freedom. A downright disestablishment of the Communist Party, however, would no longer seem to fit the category of "detour." It can occur only to a mind which has already dismissed the "necessity of history" and the Party's duty to create the "good" man by means of "good" institutions. Short of such an abandonment of the ideology, economic changes can amount to no more than a little running distance granted by the cat to the mouse.

### Ideology and Detours: Part III

THE COMMUNIST ideology posits two phases after the socialist Revolution: socialism and communism. Since 1917 the higher phase of "communism" was announced twice, by Stalin in 1936, and by Khrushchev in 1961. Later on, however, this brave talk gave way to the idea of more phases, most importantly, an "incipient" communism and a "mature" communism. Gorbachev, on coming to power, proclaimed with great emphasis that the system was now solidly in the midst of "socialism," the first phase. Difficulties in moving from one to another were reflected by the creation, in 1962, of a new academic discipline of "Scientific Communism." As this science is supposed to deal with the problems of the transition from capitalism to socialism and communism, what is remarkable is that it was established only 45 years after the Revolution. It is a silent acknowledgement that the expected forward movement of the new society has not yet materialized. To arrive at "communism," at least three conditions would have to be present: economic production would have to accelerate to the point of yielding plenty rather than scarcity; the "new Soviet man" who holds labor to be the "prime want of life" would have to emerge, and the state would begin to wither away. Only then does the injustice of distribution vanish, only then can "the free development of each" be "the condition for the free development of all." Since the collectivization of agriculture, there has been no major social movement in the direction of the higher phase. The fact that one now emphasizes the achievement of the lower phase without mention of the higher one must be read as an admission of this fact. Still, Communism is an ideology of the movement of history and the movement of the Party towards the fulfillment of man's destiny.

If the Soviet system has not moved noticeably, there still has been movement of a revolutionary kind, in the Third World. One recalls Khrushchev's emphasis on "popular uprisings" (e.g., Cuba) and "national liberation wars" (e.g., Vietnam). Both of these indicate grand social movement primarily in colonial and semi-colonial countries. Here is where Soviet power has made its presence felt: Cuba, Guyana, Surinam, Grenada, Nicaragua, Ethiopia, Mozambique, Angola, Vietnam, Laos, Cambodia, and Afghanistan. In such places a transition to socialism would occur in a most dramatic fashion, from a sleepy pre-capitalist pattern to Communist total organization. Could this be considered a detour by Soviet leaders? If it were so considered, this would imply a recognition that not merely this or that social or organizational element had obstructed the advance of history, but that the entire Soviet system had failed and thus become an obstacle. Furthermore, if the shifting of the theater of revolution from the Soviet Union to other countries had been chosen as a detour, that would differ from other detours, e.g. the NEP, where a later return to the straight road of progress remained under Party control. The places in the Third World above mentioned, however, are mostly exposed to power influences other than Soviet power. In each theater, the Communist Party is subject to severe reversals, as e.g. in Chile. From theaters of the Revolution they may even turn into obstacles to further Communist progress. If Vietnam, in the United States, was frequently called "the wrong war, at the wrong time, in the wrong place," could some of these choices not be similarly mistaken for the Soviet Union? And why should the resulting strategic world map turn out to be necessarily favorable to an ultimate Communist success?

## Soviet Rule and the Problem of Representation

WE OWE the conceptual structure of the problem of representation to Eric Voegelin's *The New Science of Politics* (1952). He distinguished "elemental," "existential" representation, and "representation of truth." Representation is a matter of a society's self-understanding. Voegelin used precisely the Soviet Union as a case of "existential" representation, in that "the legislative and administrative acts of the Soviet government are domestically effective . . . the governmental commands find obedience with the people . . . [and] can effectively operate an enormous military machine fed by the human and material resources of the Soviet society." (p. 36) The body effectively governing the Soviet Union, however, is the Communist Party, and it understands itself to represent the truth of history as revealed by Marx, in relation to which the "human and material resources of the Soviet society" function as mere instruments. The Party's truth is admittedly not shared by the Party and the people. Objectively, the people "support" the party; subjectively the Party's truth is believed by hardly more than five percent of the population.

What is the truth that is represented by the Party? A generation ago, in *The First Circle*, Solzhenitsyn portrayed Rubin, a Communist unjustly imprisoned, as embodying that Communist "we"-consciousness which, in spite of rejecting the ends-justifies-the-means principle in private life, holds that "it's different in a social sense. Our ends are the first in human history which are so lofty that we can say they justify the means by which they've been attained." The Party, then, knows itself to represent history's goal. Since that time, official Communist talk about the goal has been lacking in power and conviction. Particularly after Gorbachev's heralding "the midst of fully developed socialism," the first phase, as a great achievement, one may conclude that the Party's self-understanding has shifted from representing the goal to representing the way. "The way," of course makes no sense apart from the goal. It may well be that the goal figures in the concept of the way like an "as if." One might compare the situation to the waning of the Christian concept of God to the remote and semi-irrelevant idea of God in Deism. If Deism, for most people, proved to be just one

step short of agnosticism, might something similar apply to the
CPSU? Again, the figure of Rubin, in *The First Circle*, can instruct
us. From the profundity of his unjustified suffering, this *zek* says:
"Intelligence is objective. Just because our lives have been
wrecked, because our destinies have not worked out, why should
we change our convictions?" There is also the case of Wolfgang
Leonhard, a man with serious misgivings about the Soviet system
under Stalin, working in Berlin where he regularly reads the
Western press. "Their arguments," he writes, "persuaded us of
nothing, for in most cases where the younger and politically
educated generation was in sharp opposition to the Stalinist
system, this by no means implied approval of the Western system
. . . the frequent attempts to refute Marxism in tones of ill-
concealed superiority made no impression at all on Party officials
like ourselves." (*Child of the Revolution*, 1958, p. 382f) Communist
convictions are based, collectively as well as personally, on the
deliberate rejection of previous convictions held in common with
the West. Even in a mood of deep disillusionment, the path of
return is effectively barred to Communist minds. Given this fact,
the fading of the goal may be considered merely an unfortunate cir-
cumstance, while the importance of "the way" remains unaffected.
This is precisely why Western observers so often have surmised
that Communist beliefs are dead, their place having been taken by
lust for power. The same view came also from a Russian pen,
Michael Voslensky's. (*Nomenklatura: The Soviet Ruling Class—An
Insider's Report*, 1984) "The way," of course, as conceptualized by
Lenin, has consisted exactly in the winning of one power position
after another, by decomposing, paralyzing, and force-defeating the
class enemy. Lenin's interest in power, nevertheless, was wholly
other than, let us say, Napoleon's. The Communist striving for
power can never have the primary meaning of satisfying a nar-
cissistic ego. Meaning, in Communist eyes, still attaches to the Party alone, the head-column of history.

## The Demise of the Ideology

THE RESULT of these speculations is that enough of the motivating
power of the ontomythical Communist belief remains to spur Communists on to maintain Party unity even in the midst of Party

strife, to maintain energy of action even in the midst of relative disillusionment, to conceive expansion even in spite of relative failure at home. Soviet leadership will therefore continue measures of repressive total power, internal terror, public deceit, perversion of justice, militarization, compulsion of human thinking, human creativity and human emotions, all with quietness of conscience. There could be change in all these practices only were the ideology to be abandoned. This would imply not merely a long period of gnawing and persisting doubt, not only reversal after reversal in Party attempts to control all things of life, but also the emergence of a bold mind and courageous character like Dubcek. A Soviet Dubcek would have a chance only in a public atmosphere in which the nonsense of the ideology has become manifest in loud whisperings and secret jeers. Nor would a Russian Dubcek be able to draw on a national experience in democracy, as a Slovak was able to do.

The doubts would have to be radical enough to realize that Communists are running not merely into this or that obstruction of reality, but that history as a whole has failed them. If history itself appears to be the obstacle, the Party's assumption of justification cannot be saved. Alternatively, one could envision a collapse of the system if, for one reason or other, the Party itself were to fail to keep collective unity. If two factions emerged, both disposing of armed might and a part of the administrative apparatus, the military might intervene, as they did in China. But, in Russia as well as in China, military rule might break down into a number of semi-independent warlord regimes. In any event, a military rule of Soviet Russia might be more dangerous in the short run. In the long run it would lack both in political imagination and finesse. The threat of Russia's sheer power would remain and so would the danger of imperial expansion. The rulers' conception of reality, however, would be different, making for greater predictability of Russian moves. Above all, a merely military regime in Soviet Russia could not count on any moral appeal abroad, and would dispose of no ideological support among its foreign victims.

After the French Revolution a person who was asked what he had done in it replied: "I survived." In the present world, with its profound distortions of international relations and extremes of methods and weapons, the same might be the future historian's reply regarding Western civilization and the nations defending it.

These are the conceptual elements from which Augustine shapes his doctrine of the justification of war, i.e., of military action aimed at killing enemies for the sake of public defense. His justification of war is remarkable in that he denies justification of killing to which a private person may resort in individual self-defense. Confronted with an armed robber who threatens my life, I may still not seek to kill him, says Augustine, for this would put an inordinate value on my own life, something that should not be loved more than it is worth, i.e., more than God. Augustine remarks that the law permits killing in individual self-defense but points out that the virtuous man is not enjoined by the law to kill under such circumstances. The soldier, however, is in a different situation. The law bids him kill the enemy and punishes him if he does not do so. Moreover, when engaged in military action, the soldier acts not in his own interest but as an "agent of the law." He takes life not for his own good but for the common good, the peace and order that is endangered by the enemy. And his is an action prompted by the common love through which he is a part of his people. Thus it is in the spirit of service to good and sacrifice for others that killing is justified. The background of all this, of course, is the assumption that wars will occur, for, as Augustine says, "It is the wrongdoing of the opposing side that compels the wise man to wage just war." This is no cause for moral celebration, for the war is caused by wrongdoing but not justified by one's own high justice, and both war and wrongdoing are occasion for deep grief for all of us.

# National Self-Defense and Political Existence

OUR EXISTENCE as a nation is threatened today, not only from without but from within, by moral erosion and civic disintegration. Two decomposing forces are at work: the Marxist condemnation of our entire social structure, and the pacifist rejection of our right to national self-defense. Both attacks compel us to rethink problems to which we have given little attention for many, many years. The problem of modern war is confusing enough in its technological aspects. It is also maintained that the technology of modern war has totally changed the relation between war and political order, so that now political order could no longer be maintained if the price of its maintenance is war. On the other hand, our time has revived the doctrine of just war, both on the Communist side and on our own, although the two doctrines are quite different. At any rate, clarity about the problem of war in its moral aspects belongs to the intellectual equipment the modern citizen needs.

A footnote first: One does not consider the problem of morality and war in timeless abstraction but rather in the setting of a singular historical situation. Our situation is singular in that we are living in a political order created by Western civilization under assault by the hostile force of Communism. Both sides are armed with nuclear weapons. There are those who would also mention the United Nations among the features making up the singularity of our historical situation. I personally would not do this, on the grounds that the UN, while designed to alter the nature of international politics, has in fact not done anything of the kind and has played by and large a minor role in contemporary affairs. That leaves Western civilization, Communism, and nuclear weapons as the salient features, as far as the problem of war is concerned. One more prefatory remark concerning the approach to morality: We take it for granted that nobody today thinks of morality in the terms of that caricature drawn up in the eighteenth century, a body of cut-and-dried abstract principles valid unchangeably for all times and places. Rather, we approach moral problems as Aristotle suggested: as the mature man's rational response to reality, both the fundamental reality of being and his own nature, and the changing reality of time and place. (Cf. Eric Voegelin, "Das Rechte von Natur," *Oesterr. Zeitschrift Für Öffentliches Recht*, XIII, pp. 38-51)

As children of Western civilization, who cannot cut ourselves off from our own shadows, we cannot overlook what the great minds of the West have found out about war and morality. Among the remarkable products of this civilization of ours is a doctrine of just war, or, as Paul Ramsey suggests, "justifiable war." (Paul Ramsey, *War and the Christian Conscience*, 1961) There is no need to study the history of this doctrine in detail, but it may be useful to recall that there are at least three different versions of it and that the distinction between them may help us considerably. Augustine, the originator of the doctrine, did *not* say that war was justified if and when one side defended a just cause. He had too low an opinion of the justice of human causes to take that position. We remember his argument against Cicero who had claimed that a people was constituted by "common interests and a common acknowledgment of right," i.e., "true justice." Augustine demolished this view, pointing out that "true justice" is the property of God rather than of fallen man and that a people was held together by "a common agreement as to the objects of their love," as were, e.g., the Romans by their common love for liberty and the praise of men. Augustine's definition of a people is a far more existential one. Whatever it is that a people may love, they are a people insofar as they agree on a common object of love. Furthermore, a people and the government that it produces are the existential foundation of peace and order and justice, "such as this mortal life can afford." This peace, imperfect as it may be, all the same participates in the perfection of God's peace. Any created nature requires peace and seeks peace even through strife. Augustine clinches this point by observing that even bandits maintain peace in their gang, but then hastens to add that the peace of the wicked "does not deserve to be called peace."

THE TYPE of doctrine of just war of which all of us tend to think automatically was not developed until the sixteenth and seventeenth centuries. It is linked with the names Victoria and Grotius who developed the concept that a nation can be justified in going to war only if it acts to punish a wrong or vindicate a right. All nations together were assumed to constitute one legal community in which the enforcement of justice lay within the particular nations. (Cf. Walter Schiffer, *The Legal Community of Mankind*, 1954) In a sense this is a return to Cicero's idea. But it also amounts to the idea that wars arise over cases which can be catalogued and handled in terms of particular rights and particular wrongs and that wars are necessary because there is no supranational agency to adjudicate these cases and enforce the judgments. This idea came to the fore again after World War I when it served as the foundation for the League of Nations and, later, the United Nations. The new concept was that of "disputes" which, if not settled, presumably forced nations to go to war. Accordingly, the League of Nations established machinery for the "peaceful settlement of disputes" and sought to make use of this machinery obligatory for all nations. The doctrine of just war in the sense of Grotius was now converted into another one in which war in defiance of this international machinery was termed "aggression," and resistance to aggression was called "sanctions." As we know, the peaceful settlement machinery of the League, or that of the UN, was never fully accepted and thus the sole concrete substance of the concept of "aggression" was removed. All the same, the concept has played a major role in modern times as a general term of condemnation in connection with military action.

Between Grotius' doctrine and the modern idea of "aggression" and "sanction" another view of war was developed. It stemmed from Vattel's observation, in the eighteenth century, that since there was no objective way of determining the justice of either side in a war, and since both sides claimed that they fought for a just cause, in effect both sides were equal in that respect. Accordingly, the nineteenth century no longer was interested in justifying war on the basis of just causes but rather talked of power conflicts and the requirements of the balance of power. We have here not so much a justification as a characterization of war. Wars will occur when several units of order and political existence rub shoulders

with each other and occasionally find themselves in a conflict that
to each side appears as a clash of existences. This is a late formulation of an insight that can be found in much earlier writings, even
though in not fully elaborated form: while actions are subject to
moral judgments and are appropriate matters for judicial contention and verdict, existences as such are not. There is no way to adjudicate the claim of one people to exist as compared with that of
another, and a conflict, once it has arisen, is not resolved by the
observation that both have an equal claim. What is more, a clash of
political units involves existence which for many people constitutes
the setting of peace, order, justice, that is, the representation of
the good and true in their lives. If we look closer, it is this same insight that prompted Augustine to justify action in defense of a people which he characterized as no more than a group in agreement
on a common object of love, i.e., an existential community.

There is one other, ultra-modern version of the doctrine of just
war (let the reader note that I use the word "modern" without the
usual overtones of praise); many people doubt the right of our country to go to war, to "impose our will on others" unless and until our
society has become perfect. This notion is ideologically complex,
for it stems from the background of the total critique of society as
taught by Communism, Anarchism, and other radically revolutionary movements of our time. Society, so it is implied, has no
right to do anything, including engaging in war, maintaining public
order through judges and police, and levying taxes, as long as it has
the marks of imperfection upon it. While faulty, everything that a
society does lacks the title of authority. This implies that once
perfect, a society could do no wrong. We must remember that the
Communist and Anarchist ideologies postulate that whatever
society will emerge from the destruction of the present-day society
will by definition be perfect.

Enough of the doctrines by which war has been justified. None of
these doctrines can be ignored when we make up our mind on
morality and war. That does not mean that all of them are equally
valid. I may have already indicated that I regard Augustine's view
as free from self-righteous pretenses as well as clearly aware of
political realities and thus to be preferred, even though the part of
truth that is contained in the others must not suffer neglect. The
doctrine of just war represents our participation in Western

civilization. We must now turn to the second great reality of our time, the Communist attack on our society.

THE CRUCIAL question about Communism is whether we are or are not to regard it as simply one government among others, a government, let us say, with a peculiar economic system. The organization of Communism calls itself a party. A party normally is a group of persons standing ready to run a government. A government, as we have seen, procures peace, establishes order, and administers justice within its realm. In that sense, the Communist Party is misnamed, for rather than running a government it substitutes for government a conflict operation which knows no peace and respects no justice. For Communists postulate the continuation of a bitter struggle against a more powerful class enemy even after · they have assumed power in a country. They expect this struggle to continue for an indefinite time to come. They regard themselves as a minority surrounded by people whose instincts, habits, and traditions are alien and injurious to Communists and whose resistance they cannot possibly conquer by force. They assume that they and their subjects are *not* bound by a common love. Thus the co-existence of Communists with these elements is not peace, even though the struggle may be conducted with the instruments of government rather than those of armies. Lenin coined the concept of "protracted struggle," a struggle that would continue during the entire "period of transition" between the overthrow of capitalism and the emergence of the new society. Stalin characterized this period as "an entire historical era, replete with civil wars and external conflicts, with persistent organizational work and economic construction, with advances and retreats, victories and defeats." During this period, there could be no government. What the Communists put in place of government carries the name of "dictatorship of the proletariat." Lenin emphasizes the difference quite consciously. "The dictatorship of the proletariat," he says, "is not the organization of order but the organization of war." Stalin, too, speaks of this regime in terms of military conflict: "general staff," "strategy," "tactics," "reserves," and so on. The purpose of this regime is not to maintain peace but to wage the "protracted struggle," to combat an enemy with whom one has to co-exist and whom one cannot "vanquish" by force, to maintain the spirit of irrecon-

cilable struggle within the ranks of the Revolution. As the regime
does not serve peace, neither does it look to justice. On Lenin's
showing, the regime is "based on force and not limited by law."
Justice, he insisted, must be subordinated to the requirements of
the class struggle.

The Communist power organization closely adheres to these
ideological concepts. War-like operations have characterized the
Communist regime from the outset. The police is organized and
operates as an army. It has all kinds of weapons, is housed in bar-
racks, and trained to fight in military formation. The regime maintains a host of spies against its subjects. It engages in activities
designed to break the spirit of its subjects. It takes life among its
subjects not on the grounds of wrong-doing but on the grounds of
hostility. If the Communist regime resembles a government, it is a
military government conducted by an occupation force, in the
midst of a hostile country. Military government is part of a general
combat operation, and so is the regime of the Communist enterprise. As no Communist regime yet has brought peace to the people
it controls, so Communist foreign relations have aimed at conflict
rather than peace. The avowed chosen instrument of Communist
foreign policy is a type of conflict defined as "wars of liberation and
popular uprisings." In spite of the definition, these movements of
subversion and unrest are not confined to the cause of liberation
from colonial rule. They continue even in countries that have
already won their independence, until they submit to a Communist
regime. Once under a Communist regime, they do not enjoy peace
but continue subject to the official warfare waged on them by those
in authority.

The reason for the "peacelessness" of Communism lies in the
ideology which has focussed the Communist's attention exclusively
on the destruction of the "inhuman" present-day society. Unlike so-
called "utopian socialism," Marxism-Leninism does not comprise a
blueprint of an ideal society. It does, however, contain a strategy
for the revolutionary destruction of what now exists. Its faith in
the ultimately beneficient "laws of history" claims that nothing but
good can follow from the radical tearing down of the house we now
inhabit. In that it believes that total destruction to be salutory,
Communism, along with Anarchism, should be called an ideology of
destruction. Neither Communism nor Anarchism has developed

theories of a future order. There is no Communist political theory or a Communist economic theory. There is no theory of a Communist culture or of a Communist world order. Some pathetic attempts to lay the foundations of such theories were made by Stalin but did not go beyond the stage of hints. Communists literally "do not know the things that belong to their peace" and could not know them if they wanted to, since their ideology has defined only the struggle, the enemy, and the forces of the Revolution. The precepts of the protracted struggle, of combat organization, and of revolutionary strategy are clear, emphatic, and consistent – but nothing in his ideology tells the Communist when and how to come to rest.

This inability of Communism to arrive at peace is what gives the Communist assault on existing societies its peculiar character. That assault fits into no available pigeonhole. Should it be characterized as "aggression" in the sense of the League of Nations concept? Communists, at least those following Lenin, do not consider war a decisive and preferred instrument of their struggle, although they also reject pacifism as bourgeois reaction. Should one look upon it as great-power aggrandizement in the sense of nineteenth-century politics? Communists are not primarily interested in territory but rather in the control of people and will trade territory for other means of manipulation if necessary. The crux of the matter is that a regime of Communists is a perpetual combat operation and thus an instituted condition of "peacelessness." Societies, which now have governments in the normal sense, pass into the Communist peacelessness if they succumb to Communist forces in any way whatsoever, with or without "aggression" in the form of military invasion. The struggle of "free," i.e., not Communist-controlled, societies against Communism is thus essentially in defense of such peace as these societies have achieved. One can hardly grasp this situation with the help of concepts of international relations such as "aggression," "great power conflicts," or "international disputes." Augustine's peace as the supreme common good of peoples and his justification of fighting for the sake of this good is more to the point, even though Augustine could not have foreseen the present situation. Communism, not only through military action but through its embattled regime, assails that peace on which decent men everywhere depend for their human potentialities.

Now the question arises to what extent the entire justification of war and fighting has been eliminated by nuclear weapons and the indiscriminate destruction to which they are supposed to commit future belligerents. The crux of the discussion in this regard has been the death of "innocents," i.e., non-combatants. Innocents have always fallen victims to warfare. All the same, their death has not affected the justification of war, on the theory of the "double effect." This concept, originated by Thomas Aquinas, distinguishes between the intended effect of an action and secondary or unintentional effect. It is only the intended effect which should be taken into consideration in judging the morality of an action. Thus if military action aims at combatants, seeking to conquer and possibly even kill them, this action is covered by the general justification of the war, if any. On the other hand, the intentional killing of non-combatants is not covered, although if non-combatants are unintentionally killed in the course of justified military action, the whole action does not thereby become unjust. In the case of nuclear weapons, and even in that of obliteration bombing, the argument now goes, this distinction can no longer be made. The death of innocents *must* be intended. The military action thereby turns, at least partly, into murder. War is no longer justifiable.

Another argument is based on the concept of proportionality, also stemming from Thomas Aquinas. He argues for "moderate defense" so that the evil of the remedy should not exceed that of the original wrong. Such proportionality, we now hear, is no longer possible in the age of nuclear armaments. Their use means the mutual destruction of the combatant countries, plus the destruction of other countries, and in the extreme even the depopulation of the earth.

What conclusions are drawn from these assumptions? Some recommend that we rid ourselves of atomic weapons so as to make just wars possible again. Others would commit us to never using the nuclear arms we possess. Still others want unilateral disarmament. And a few do not tire of repeating "Rather red than dead." The conclusions seem to fall into two categories: either a wish that conditions were not what they are or else a refusal to defend the political order under which we live. Neither can be called a moral solution. One is merely wishing for what cannot be. The other is the destruction of the extant common good for fear of some alleged common evils. An apparently moral critique of war turns into an immoral subversion and disruption of society.

The rationale of subversion says that a society that permits war is not worth having, however, it is not the worth or unworth of societies that renders wars possible but the fact that human beings live in many societies that differ from each other in language, culture, and the common love around which they are constituted. Reaching deep into historical roots, each of these societies is a given setting of human life that makes activities, love, purpose, and growth possible. Each of them is particular in the sense of not constituting a class with others, except insofar as it belongs to the class of social orders. "That among particularities accidents will occur is not accidental but necessary," said Rousseau, and Hegel restated the idea in Paragraph 324 of his *Philosophy of Right*. (Cf. K.N. Waltz, *Man, the State, and War*, 1959) Among the particularities of historically grown societies, war is a possibility on which one must count, just as one must count on accidents in traffic in which many cars are driven by particular drivers. Self-defense is thus necessarily an integral part of political existence in a world of many nations, a necessity that could be obviated only by a world state which in turn would make civil wars and uprisings an almost daily occurrence.

When the will to self-defense dies, the "common love" that holds a people together dies along with it. Citizens become fear-struck demi-animals, each scrambling for whatever small tangible possession has the strongest hold on him at the moment. The impression of the disintegration of France in the spring of 1940 must have been General de Gaulle's overriding experience. He perceived then that without the readiness to self-defense there can be no people and no political order and that without a vigorous participation in a common political existence men fall into total disarray. Whatever mistakes de Gaulle may have made subsequently, this insight rather than any cheap nostalgia for past glories of totalitarian design has been his basic motive.

THE IDEOLOGICAL rejection of self-defense by those whose minds are totally obsessed with the fear of nuclear war amounts to a version of nihilism. To say, "In the atomic age, no society is worth defending" is tantamount to saying that sheer physical existence is preferable to the love of the good that constitutes a people. "We lose our values which are worth defending and then lose our arms and language, and with loss of civilizational identity become incapable of governing ourselves" said Vico, in the eighteenth century, and in the twentieth Raymond Aron adds this comment: "The costs of servitude for a people and a culture may be higher than the costs of a war, even an atomic war." The renunciation of a society's self-defense becomes one prong in a multi-pronged nihilistic subversion, others being the tearing down of sexual inhibitions, the undoing of a common religious orientation, the moral condemnation of the entire economic system, the rejection of anything that speaks of authority, of up and down, more important and less important, sacred and profane.

The attempts to establish the immorality of nuclear war have turned out to stem from either wishful or immoral roots. That, of course, does not alter the fact that the deliberate mass killing of innocent people, either through atomic or conventional weapons, cannot be morally condoned. The answer, however, is not the nihilistic decomposition of political order but rather the elaboration of weaponry and strategy which, to speak in Paul Ramsey's terms, makes "just war possible." Efforts in that direction have been made and have proceeded quite far. We have moved along three paths: one toward more diversified and sophisticated weapons enabling us to control nuclear force more and more and to subject it to a clearcut military purpose; the second toward a strategy of nuclear war that has turned its back even on the practices of World War II and is more strictly geared to a "counterforce" concept; third, toward a doctrine of conflict management which has sought to increase and enlarge the situations offering us choices and to avoid situations in which the sole choice is a nuclear strike against an entire country.

No man in his right mind can do anything but grieve at the thought of any war. A "just war" is not something to be sought and celebrated. But the defense of one's peace for the sake of the "common love" which unites men in peoples is so much an integral aspect of our humanity that to deny it to men, insofar as it is defensively justified, means to put nothingness above the good.

# Detente and Ideological Struggle

THOSE WHOSE BUSINESS it is to conduct foreign policy must have in their minds some picture of the reality in which they are acting, as well as some kind of broad principle that guides their action. When Britain and France tried to deal with Italy's war on Ethiopia in 1936, when Roosevelt delivered his "Quarantine Speech" in 1937, when Truman initiated a "police action" in Korea, the prevailing picture was evidently that of a world which by common agreement had renounced war, so that "aggression" could be looked upon as a kind of atavistic abnormality that must be contained lest it spread like a contagious disease. That brave hope did not survive the Korean War, after which there was a return to the imagery and principle characteristic of the nineteenth century, which went under the name of "balance of power." The choice was made somewhat uncritically. Nobody seemed to have considered that the international realities of the mid-twentieth century might possibly be as far from nineteenth-century power rivalry as the nineteenth century had been from the foreign affairs of the Middle Ages. The "balance of power" concept seemed to be the sole available alternative to international idealism.

Could the "balance of power" principle fit the politics of ideological conflict? Balance of power was essentially conceived as an equation with two variables. The first consisted in the comparative and somewhat quantifiable ratio of power instrumentalities (weaponry, manpower, resources, and terrain) which, secondly, was assessed in view of the intuited relation of what Bismarck called "The imponderables," i.e. elements of judgment, intention, and emotion influencing leading statesmen. This much is elemental. There is, however, still one more aspect of the "balance of power" which one may call "the externality" of foreign policy.

125

Nineteenth-century statesmen were able to take the solidarity of their nations pretty much for granted, so that their decisions could confine themselves to the instrumentalities of external power and the imponderabilities of external relations. One's nation's unity for purposes of external action was taken for granted, which meant that foreign affairs was one thing and domestic politics another. *This externality of foreign policies was mutually sustained.* Thus the makers of foreign policy could be specialists in "external affairs," i.e. in relations in which nations figured as given integers, as if they were persons, and the problems of which were characteristically *inter*national.

In an age of ideologies the solidarity of states and peoples can no longer be considered a given. We have been late in acknowledging this fact, even though we had considerable early warning. New ways of looking at politics were proclaimed as early as 1848 when Marx declared that the relevant concept of political unity was not a people but class, that workers have no country, that revolution ignores all boundaries. Lenin's *Imperialism*, published in the year before he came to power, projected Marx's concept of class struggle into world politics. Lenin described capitalism as a single worldwide system, to which he opposed, three years later, a single system of Communist parties bound to the Soviet center in the loyalty of common defense. Lenin distinguished between wars made by imperialist countries for "The distribution and redistribution of the world" and wars between capitalist and colonial countries, the latter conflict assuming the functions of Marx's revolution. Lenin attributed different "class" characteristics to wars, and called for the conversion of an "imperialist war" into a civil war. Lenin thus construed the known facts of world politics as aspects of a revolutionary process in which power between nations was seen not as a problem of equilibrium but rather as a means for turning societies, cultures, and human beings upside down.

Another fact of contemporary life is that the Russian Revolution brought to power not a group pursuing the interests of its own state and people, but rather one engaged in a global enterprise and claiming authority beyond its national boundaries, like a church though not being a church, then again, like a government though not being a normal government. This enterprise has followers in other countries who in turn prepare themselves to seize power over their state. This means that an expansion of Soviet power is both something like an international sphere of influence yet also the subversion of another people's way of life, and the conversion of another state into a venture to "build a communist society resembling the Soviet model." Soviet foreign policy, then, remains "external" only in the sense that Soviet rulers, relying on their monopoly of power, can afford to take the unity of their subjects for granted. On the other hand, any successful expansion of Soviet influence amounts to moral, cultural, and human disasters for the people unfortunate enough to fall under Communist control, so that these results are not merely in the realm of external power, but mainly in the internal order of a state and even of human personalities. The foreign policies of the ideological group controlling the Soviet Union are therefore *subjectively external but objectively internal.*

Communist-controlled countries are not all the ideological reality there is in the world today. Ideological notions clustering around both the Marxist and the Anarchist model are widely spread among the peoples of the world. They give rise to loyalties other than to country and state, yardsticks other than the humanistic respect for life, liberty, property, and dignity. They have aroused extraordinarily intensive passions for disruptive organization and action. Ideologically motivated people no longer care for the order of a common life but give their loyalty to a cause of irreconcilable struggle against the world. A total critique of society, a sweeping condemnation of everything that exists, is characteristically attached to any and every grievance caused by concrete failings or shortcomings. In the eyes of ideologically infected groups, all actions by society's representatives are tainted by what one may call "systematic suspicion." The on-going existence of a people in a system of order and peace is constantly and unfavorably compared with some "possible reality" that has no existence, past or present, except in the heated fantasy of the ideological mind. This attitude gives rise to both an activist-militant and a passive-lethargic variant. The activists see it their duty to join their own country's enemies, display the enemy's symbols, visit the enemy's leaders, support the enemy's cause rhetorically and politically. Thus an internal alienation produces external effects, a domestic dissension becomes a power factor in international conflicts. The politics of ideologies in non-Communist countries are *subjectively internal but objectively external.*

This situation has further domestic consequences affecting the nation's power to act, in that representative leaders, unable to distinguish between ideological subversion and legitimate political argument, become unsure of themselves and tend to suffer from what has been called a "loss of nerve," guilty conscience destroying the ability for action. With the combination of alienation among the citizens, attraction of ideological causes based on foreign countries, and the weakening of leadership, a nation may well decompose to the point of no longer being capable of any external action, and that not for want of power instrumentalities. The manpower may remain the same, the arsenals may be full, the resources available; but in the absence of national one-mindedness the instrumentalities cannot be put to use. Under such circumstances it no longer makes any sense to conceive foreign policy as "the right use of power." Policy then ceases to be amenable to an understanding as an equation with two variables. One may still continue to see a "balance" of external power as desirable, but that can no longer be considered an end of the matter. The various aspects of external power are interlocked, in the Free World, with the complexities of generating and protecting the very conditions of that national unity which underlies national power.

LET US NOW attempt a brief sketch of how the Soviet Union and the West handle themselves in this situation. Soviet strategy combines four aspects: 1) "Peaceful co-existence" (or detente), a complex of limitation and reduction of armaments, trade and cultural exchange pacts, regional declarations of peace, gestures of mutual consultation and apparent good-will; 2) expansion of Soviet influence through the use of "national liberation" movements and wars, and "popular uprisings," and including unsettling deliveries of Soviet arms, active support of native military or paramilitary forces aiming at the creation of leftist regimes, inciting of conflicts between such forces and the United States; 3) stepping up the increase of armed strength of the Soviet Union and its satellites, including conventional forces, nuclear armaments, and acquisition of new bases in various parts of the world; 4) the continuation and intensification of "ideological struggle." Others have written and spoken sufficiently on the first three aspects of this strategy, even though there is a tendency to deal with them separately rather than as a whole. The fourth aspect, however, is usually passed over in silence. Brezhnev said: "Detente does not in the slightest way abolish, and cannot abolish or change, the laws of class struggle." Other Soviet leaders have emphasized that the "Spirit of Helsinki" does not apply to ideological struggle. For twenty years the Soviets have insisted that "peaceful co-existence" is a form of class struggle, and that the ideological struggle must be intensified in the presence of peaceful external co-existence.

What does "ideological struggle" mean? Why has this aspect of Soviet policy been passed over in silence by the West? Could it be because one believes that one can dismiss the phrase as windowdressing? That assumption can be made only by neglecting what social science knows about the continuing identity of cultural structures. Henri Frankfort[1] has introduced the term "form" to designate the enduring principle of unchanged identity that maintains civilizations for very long periods and through changing internal and external circumstances. Frankfort's research, it is true, deals with civilizations. Norman Cohn's work[2] on medieval millenarian movements, however, has shown that such movements also have a "form" and maintain their principle of identity over long periods, and that this identity comes to an end not as a change of the "form" but rather through extermination or attrition of the membership. The "form" of the Communist movement is its universal and uncompromising hostility to the entire existing world, in the name of an alleged new world that must replace the existing one, the replacement to be effected by a protracted but irreconcilable struggle. As historical movements go, the Communist Party is not yet old. All the same, it has gone through considerable internal and external changes while its "form" has continued the same. From it flows the *raison d'être* of the Party. The Soviet insistence on the combination of "peaceful co-existence" with "ideological struggle" is nothing but a manifestation of the enduring "form" of the Communist movement. The Party manifests its concern with dangers threatening its "form" in a period of "peaceful co-existence" which to some might suggest the cessation of class struggle. This concern cannot be dismissed as mere rhetoric. "Ideology" in Communist eyes means not so much attention to a formula but rather a way of existence, existence in hostility to the class enemy and in protracted struggle led by the Party. That existence is predicated on the attribution of the world's evil to the class enemy, and on the presumption that Communists constitute that part of mankind which possesses the alternative to those evils. It is an existence positioning "high terms of separation between such and the rest of the world" (Richard Hooker's words analyzing the sixteenth-century Puritans) so that between the two parts of mankind no common obligation is conceived. It is dangerous to dismiss such attitudes as "mere mythology." Class is, indeed, the Communists' myth, but so was "race" the Nazis' myth, and Dachau still bears gruesome witness to the evil deeds spawned by a "mere myth."

"Ideological struggle," then, means that the axiom of ultimate and universal hostility to the class enemy, meaning us, continues as the background to even the Soviets' peaceful moves, by virtue of the "form" of the movement's continuing identity. Circumstantial evidence corroborates this thesis. We notice, for instance, that the policy of detente has been adopted not only by the Soviet Union, where one could attribute it to reasons of state security, but also by the Communist parties of Italy, France, the U.S.A., and Japan. These parties are not defending a position but rather aspiring to get into power and to control the government. The new strategy calls for a public image of Communists implying reasonableness, respectability, and demonstrative dedication to the people's daily well-being. That image would go far to dispel the strong emotional resistance that so far has blocked Communist ruling power in those countries. On the other hand, one finds that the new strategy is obviously more than a mere expedient to help this or that Communist party to the seats of power, with a view to help solving its own country's problems. Such conferences as those of chairman Miyamoto of Japan's Communist Party with Secretary General Carillo of the Spanish Communist Party (March 30, 1976) and Secretary Marchais of the French Communist Party (April 8, 1976) indicate an international orchestration of the various Communist parties' domestic policies.

"Ideological struggle," we must conclude, means that Communists in the Soviet Union and Communists in Western countries agree in their ultimate expectation of Communist regimes to be established in the leading countries of the world. In that perspective all more immediate policies take their place as partial moves toward a grand objective. It also means that the Communists are giving top priority to the political aspects of power, on the premise that the measure of their power is but a function of our resistance. Their strategy envisages a combination of such pressures and illusions acting on the West as will melt the residue of anti-Communist resistance. It was anti-Communist attitudes which in the past generated NATO, Western re-armament, the deployment of U.S. troops in defense of allies in various parts of the world, and sufficient programs of internal security. Solzhenitsyn has remarked that he, Sakharov, and other dissidents enjoyed a modicum of safety in the Soviet Union because of the pressure of aroused public opinion in the West. If we should ask ourselves in astonishment, what would the Soviets have to fear from the West if they killed Solzhenitsyn, Sakharov, and others who think like them, the answer is that the Soviets have reason to fear a re-kindling of that Western indignation that flamed up when Czechoslovakia was first raped in 1948, when Greece seemed on the point of succumbing to invading Communist guerrillas, when South Korea was invaded, when the West's access to Berlin was blocked. That indignation was the sap of our strength. It provided a will to maintain armaments in such quantity that the Soviets could not afford to disregard them, to set limits to Soviet expansion, to confront them even at the risk of war. Later that Western indignation was officially pronounced obsolete by the same American President who had drawn strength from it in order to force Khrushchev to remove his missiles from Cuba. During the Vietnam War, President Johnson and his advisors, failing to understand the ideological dimension, took deliberate steps not to arouse it again, and thus conducted the war from the outset in a twilight of ambiguity that prevented the people from grasping its meaning. In the climate of well-orchestrated propaganda against America's "imperialism" the Vietnam War was lost primarily on the political home front. "Ideological struggle," in sum, turns around the Soviets' determination to keep their own hostile will at high pitch while weakening ours to the point of ineffectiveness. That requires both steps creating the illusion of "peace in our generation" and avoidance of steps that would renew anti-Communist indignation. The dispelling of anti-Communism as a political force in the West is a matter of highest priority, so stated in the 1961 Program of the CPSU. To that end, the Soviets have officially renounced or postponed both a military showdown between their forces and those of the West, and the overthrow of Western governments by violent revolution. They are willing to seek intermediate changes from which they could hope for better conditions favoring their political operations. "Ideological struggle" in the short run aims at removing institutional, organizational, legal, and emotional obstacles to Communist propaganda and organization. They are convinced that with much patient political preparation, they will need neither an international war nor civil war to pluck the fruit of power in the world's leading industrial countries.

One interpretation of "ideological struggle" seems to be absolutely excluded: it does *not* mean that the Communists, having renounced international war and violent revolution, have placed their reliance wholly on persuasion. They remain aware that the Communist Party is not a ruler one might eventually accept as legitimate, respect, cherish, and willingly obey. They know that a deep gulf separates them not merely from capitalists, but also from socialists in the West, or rather, the Free World. They see that their cause cannot recommend itself to the world by virtue of the justice it might be seeking. They have declared themselves at war with everything that has traditionally made for order in human life. Thus they cannot escape operating on fear and force, falsehood, terror, guile, blackmail, dictatorship, and penal servitude. Persuasion presupposes belief in a humanity participating in common reason by virtue of its participation in a common order of being. That idea is one which no Communist can understand, let alone accept.

NOW LET US likewise examine the conduct of the West. Our policy goes under its own name: detente. If asking ourselves what that is, we are facing greater difficulties than in the case of Soviet policy. Kissinger himself has provided a brief formula: "To create the maximum incentives for a moderate Soviet course." This is admirable, but not very clear. The Truman Doctrine, after all, was a maximum incentive for a Soviet moderate course, so was the Berlin airlift, Dulles' "massive retaliation," and Kennedy's partial mobilization to counter Khrushchev's Cuban missiles. What is more, these and similar measures had the desired results. They manifested our capabilities and signalled our determination to use them, so that while we held this firm course, no major power position was lost, none was added to the Soviet Union, and Azerbeidjan and Austria were even recovered. Detente, having begun before the Nixon era, hit its full stride with the opening to Peking, truly a landmark event. That was followed by the liquidation of the Vietnam War and the subsequent indifference of the United States to Hanoi's violation of the agreements which made the eventual Communist conquest of all of Indochina inevitable. Next came the opening of trade relations with the Soviet Union, leading to the sales of vital wheat and, more important, advanced technology. This went hand-in-hand with Brandt's *Ostpolitik*, implying the West's acceptance of the status quo in Central Europe. The chief attraction to the West was the prospect of an eventual agreement with the Soviet Union limiting and reducing armaments both strategic and deployed, a hope kept alive by a series of conferences the main purpose of which seemed to be precisely to keep alive a hope. The same may be said of the Helsinki Pact, an agreement the nature and meaning of which has remained most unclear, Soviet interpretations differing sharply from those in the West. The entire policy was underscored by the willingness of the United States to lower its requirements of national security, abandoning the criterion of "superiority" and falling back on the standard of "sufficiency," again a term without precision.

The key to the logic holding these main pieces together may be locked forever in the secretive mind of Henry Kissinger. Taken by themselves, the pieces do not fit into a self-evident pattern. We know that containment consisted in the judicious combination of various types and locations of tangible pressures to prevent further Soviet expansion. Detente has claimed to be the opposite of containment. Still, the opening of relations with Communist China may also be seen as the creation of new pressure on the Soviet Union, almost like the opening of a Second Front in World War II. Only in that the new pressure was created wholly by diplomatic means was it novel, a bold and imaginative step. That step, however, did not call for subsequent detente with the Soviet Union. Detente, in that it relieved the Soviet Union of pressures, even nullified the benefits the West had received from Nixon's trip to Peking. Similarly, the policy of negotiations which Nixon proclaimed had no need to include either direct or indirect approval of

Soviet practices, power, and aims. Other countries had previously negotiated and maintained fairly close relations with the Soviet Union while continuing an unwavering opposition to Communism as a potential regime. Again, a moderation of the arms race is an undeniably worthwhile objective, but it does not necessarily entail a lowering of national security requirements for the United States. If, then, the pieces of detente do not fit easily together, there must be an additional and intangible element, probably a psychological element, which has not been expressed but contains the unifying principle. Kissinger's and Sonnenfeldt's presentation to the meeting of American ambassadors in London has been read as a revelation of this so far hidden rationale of detente. The unraveling of detente, however, is not our problem here. We are engaged in an examination of its ideological dimensions.

If detente is the opposite of containment, and if containment relied on tangible pressures, then detente would consist in removing pressures, or at least irritations. One might even surmise that it would seek to create attractions for the other side, which brings to mind the title of one of Pirandello's plays: *As You Desire Me.* Again, if containment operated on conditions under one's own control, trying to shape those conditions into a complex that would give one the most potent leverage in response to the other side's potential actions, detente would amount to a self-adjustment to the other side's moods in an attempt to change the other side's attitudes and priorities. It would operate, then, on the basis of psychological speculations. That would give us a clue to the West's ultimate expectations underlying the policy of detente: it must be an expectation to see an emerging Communist Party of the Soviet Union that is worthy of the West's trust and friendship. Let us keep in mind that the Soviet's ultimate expectation is to see Communist regimes in the leading nations of the world. Detente, then, roots in the psychological speculations that it may be possible to have Communists give up the notion of class struggle, of the class enemy, and of the redeeming mission of Communism, or, alternatively, on the speculation that the Soviet leaders may already have abandoned those notions (a speculation as wishful as conflicting with the record of Soviet conduct).

Detente is a relationship, and thus it must affect both sides. Each side, however, seems to be sure that itself will be immune against any ill effect and that only the other side will be subject to far-reaching changes. There is this difference, however: The Soviets did take positive measures to counteract potentially weakening effects of detente on themselves, precisely their new emphasis on "ideological struggle," while no need for similar precautions seems to have been perceived by Western leaders. Yet it is the West which is ideologically more vulnerable, since it publicly tolerates any degree of ideological dissent including open subversion, while the Communist Party has built into it a principle of ideological discipline. It would seem that the most undesirable effects on the West would occur by way of mutation in its public assessment of Communism.

A parenthetical remark is in order here. In the course of normal foreign relations no moral judgment of other nations is required, because of that mutually sustained "externality" of foreign policy that was earlier mentioned. If such a judgment does take shape among citizens or leaders (as it did, for instance, in Britain regarding Turkey, at the beginning of this century), that is a kind of private self-indulgence of little or no consequence. In the presence of such phenomena as Communism or Nazism, however, the formation of a judgment about them must be called a political necessity. For these movements appear in the world with a claim to universal authority which implicitly sets them up as a potential alternative to every political order in the world. That means that the evil they practice as their official policy of ruling must also be seen as the potential lot of any nation, nay, as a potential personal fate of every man, woman, and child in the world. Thus approval or disapproval of this potentiality is inescapable. By comparison, no moral judgment is a political necessity in relations with, let us say, the Stroessner dictatorship in Paraguay, or the Park regime in South Korea, both of which may be viewed as mere givens in the realm of external affairs, without any actual or potential reach beyond their own boundaries.

Detente, a policy of accommodation to Soviet moods and aspirations, expecting eventually to attain full trust and friendship with Soviet leaders, is bound to affect the public's judgment of Communism. Detente inclines to ignore or even deny the fact that the Communists to this day have not yet learned to live in peace with their own subjects. The decrease of media reporting about the treatment of intellectual dissidents in the Soviet Union, and President Ford's snubbing of Solzhenitsyn are cases in point. In 1963, the term "Communist threat" was declared taboo in the United States; now detente has added any notice of Soviet terror to the taboo. The pattern of public actions under detente implies an image of the Soviets as a normal, respectable, reasonable, peace-loving, right-thinking government. That image is bound to remove the emotional and moral rejection of Communism which has prevailed in the West and has mobilized Western nations to both internal and external resistance. In the course of time, it will become more and more difficult to utter any objection to the admission of Communists into the government, which means that Communists will come into demand as political partners of legitimate parties, and will be able to attain positions of power as members of a coalition. Czechoslovakia in 1948 shows how such ventures end.

Among other effects there would be a growing unwillingness to vote appropriations for armaments and armed forces, to maintain troops at foreign bases, and to shoulder the responsibilities of sharing defense with one's allies. The most serious effects, however, would come through situations in which the requirements of detente would move our leaders to sacrifice the freedom and lives of other peoples to Communist expansion. A case in point is the so-called Sonnenfeldt doctrine which says that in the interest of peace with the Soviet Union the United States favors the conversion of a presently crude presence of Soviet force in Eastern Europe into an "organic relationship." Eventually, dramatic situations would produce themselves, for instance, if we should similarly favor the abandonment of sixteen million peaceful, orderly, and prosperous Taiwan Chinese to "an organic relationship" with mainland Communist rule. Two or three precedents of this kind, each reeking with official cynicism, will cause a real erosion of Western citizens' trust in the protective nature of their society. If today trusting allies can be sacrificed to the expediency of power relations, why would not I be the next? There might emerge a kind of Watergate psychosis in reverse, as everybody feels that he is potentially in line to die on the altar of the god Moloch, which in the government is officially called "peace." A peace agreement with evil demands human sacrifices. Since that evil is not confined to its state boundaries but potentially reaches right into our living room, it is clear that the accommodations of detente may well bring about a protracted crisis of civil confidence in government–any Western government. In the presence of universal, potentially world-conquering ideologies foreign policy has thus an inescapable moral dimension, so that a foreign policy of principled compromise can directly affect the moral foundation of our country.

Into this situation President Carter's emphasis on human rights introduced a moral note which seemed equally suited to protect us against the erosive effects of detente as are the Soviet efforts to maintain "ideological struggle." That new emphasis would once again fan the flames of public indignation about any Communist regime which, never achieving something like peace with its own subjects, and never enjoying the intangible benefits of legitimacy, had to rely on the limitless efforts to attain total power enforced by a lawless police terror. Detente and public emphasis on human rights in U.S. foreign policy therefore are in tension with each other. If the American President insisted on noting the endemic disregard for human rights by the Soviet regime, he would contribute to forces apt to increase Western armaments, strengthen the West's will to resist Communism, and determination to fight if necessary. The test of this policy was identified with the concept of "linkage," i.e. a quid-pro-quo relation between Soviet conduct and either disarmament negotiations or U.S. policies in the Mideast or Africa. Officially, "linkage" has been denied; unofficially it has been effective. Its effect has been ambiguous, so that one must assume that both President Carter's insistence on human rights and his efforts to obtain a SALT agreement will be negatively affected and U.S. policy will be denied success across the board. The Soviets, reacting sharply to criticism of their domestic policies, have been able to force the voice of criticism to become muted and, indeed, intermittent, with the result that the full weight of American moral censure has fallen not on the Soviets but on America's allies who have no leverage by which to tone us down. In one respect this has produced a warping of our foreign policy perspective, in that Rhodesia, South Africa, and post-Allende Chile now appear to be dangers outranking the Communist threat. On the other hand, however, relations with the Soviet Union have not been restored to the openness of the Kissinger period. The impression of confusion in U.S. foreign policy is thus not an assessment of President Carter's personality but rather the observation of several wills conflicting with each other in the design and execution of our foreign conduct. In spite of a declared moral intention, U.S. foreign policy has given the impression of less moral substance than the preceding detente, which had in its favor the doubtful but yet single-minded logic of a "peace-in-our-time" morality.

It was the moral substance of Rome which enabled the Senate, in one hopeless situation after another during the Punic wars, to rise to that supreme effort by which they eventually turned seemingly fatal defects into an ultimate victory of Rome. Centuries later, a morally drained Roman empire no longer could muster such determination, and helplessly watched the barbarians take over, bit by bit, the empire's territory and government. "You have the impression," Solzhenitsyn says to us, "that democracies can last. But you know nothing about it. Democracies are lost islands in the immense river of history. The water is always rising. . . . The existence of the civilization the West created is going to be at stake in the next years. I think it is not aware of this."

---

[1]Henri Frankfurt, *Before Philosophy* (Pelican paperback).
[2]Norman Cohn, *The Pursuit of the Millennium* (Harper Torchback).

# Foreign Policy and Morality: A Contemporary Perspective

NO HUMAN ACTION or activity can be separated wholly from the distinction between right and wrong. All the same, foreign politics does not stand in the same intimate connection to ethics as does government. The latter roots in morality through its foundations in habit, the accretion of common sense judgments and assessments of many generations, and in human nature, the philosophical yardstick for what is appropriate to the good life. Foreign policy lacks the direct reference to human nature, since it deals not with the relation between the particular man as citizen and the community of citizens as a whole, but rather relations between wholes who are not "natural" substances in the way each individual person is, and who have no center of normative experiences resembling the human soul. What is more, the immediate concern of foreign policy is not the citizens' good life, but rather the continued existence of an artifacted whole neither the size, nor the configuration, nor the duration of which are "given," as it were, "by nature." That does not mean that foreign policy is disinterested in the distinction between good and evil. The political entity as a whole is a world to its citizens, the traditional and normative order of their lives, and its existence, no matter how flawed, is valued as a good. The problem of what "existence" of a political entity means is not attended by standards of even the fuzzy recognizability as those of natural law: Nothing tells us how large or strong a state *ought* to be, and answers to such questions are sought by means of power contests rather than by judicial or philosophical statements. Thus in foreign

139

affairs, the problem of evil has traditionally been bracketed, placed in parentheses, on the assumption that the citizens' good life is properly the concern of each government and that external power or trade relations can and should be conducted as if in an atmosphere of moral neutrality. True, on occasion the internal order of countries would come to concern others. In sixteenth-century Europe, a country's religious affiliation often entered the foreign policy decisions of other countries. In the nineteenth century, European governments in their overseas policies concerned themselves with what they considered the judicial barbarism of non-Western governments. Both of these are cases of foreign policies being motivated by moral interests in other countries' internal affairs. After World War I, the problem of evil seemed to be discovered even at the heart of foreign affairs. Germany was charged with guilt in having caused the war and was subjected to punitive reparations and military restrictions. Then, in the framework of the "new order" supposedly created by the League of Nations, a concept of moral judgment became an attribute of foreign relations: "aggression," or "the aggressor." While it played some role in foreign policies it did not, however, permanently replace the traditional categories of power politics, the "politics of existence." One must assume, therefore, that in foreign affairs the moral element is, what it always has been, an outsider, an element of culture rather than politics.

ALL THE SAME we find that today the problem of evil is relevant to foreign policies, and that in an unprecedented way. In the past evil could be identified with the passions or self-seeking motives of particular individuals. Thus both Plato and Aristotle defined tyranny as the wielding of power by a person possessed by selfish passions. That definition, however, no longer serves us when murder is publicly legalized and justified by ideologies established as public orthodoxies and practiced by governing bodies and state institutions.

When the tyrant razed cities for his own greater glory, when the slave chained to the conqueror's chariot was dragged through the rejoicing streets, when enemies were thrown to the wild beasts in front of the assembled people, the mind did not reel before such unabashed crimes. . . . But slave camps under the flag of freedom, massacres justified by philanthropy or by a taste for the superhuman, in one sense cripple the judgment.[1]

In other words, we are today facing evil that issues not so much from passions and misdirected loves as rather from semi-rational idea systems and government planning.

The unprecedented character of evil in our time cannot be overemphasized. Human experience knows of evil as the result of private wills, recognized and judged by public authority and public conscience, in the light of the sacred and its representation by society. Evil in this century has come dressed in the mantle of apparent reason, the logic of history or the superman, or both, an ideology set up on the throne of public philosophy and enlisting conscience in the planned pattern of logical murder. The tyrant is no longer a personally lawless man but rather the demon of perverted political thinking. In his novel, *The Middle of the Journey*,[2] Lionel Trilling has contrasted the traditional experience of evil, in the person of John Laskell, with that of our days, in the person of Gifford Maxim. As they discuss the deed of a man who, when drunkenly slapping his daughter, killed her by the blow, Laskell places himself on a stool of semi-autonomous individuality:

> I didn't make myself and I don't dare cut my connection with all the things in the world that made me. I cannot hold myself free of these things. I will blame them when they injure and reduce me, as they do every moment of the day. And for that matter, I cannot avoid my gratitude to them.

Maxim replies:

> Like any bourgeois intellectual, you want to make the best of every possible world and every possible view. Anything to avoid a commitment, anything not to have to take a risk.

But for himself, Maxim says:

> My own heart is full of hatred and pity. Sometimes I cannot
> tell one from the other. When I feel the hatred I know it is
> generated by pity. And when I feel the pity I know it is
> generated by hatred. And when I do not feel either one or the
> other, then it is only emptiness, only emptiness. But when I
> feel anything at all, it is for all. All. We are all members of one
> another. Not in our suffering only, but in our cruelty as well. I
> have been in Spain, and I have seen Kermit Simpson shot and
> worse. . . . And I have helped. I have done it. You have
> helped. And even if I had not been there to see, I would know
> that I was involved. I am involved in the cruelties I have never
> seen and never will see. On both sides. You think only of what
> the other side must do to gain its ends and you feel separated
> from everything that is foul in them. But I know what "our"
> side must do, and not merely do; the doing would not be so
> terrible if we did not have to be what we do, and *I* know what
> we must be. (pp. 220, 271)

Gifford Maxim, one might add, speaks as a Communist who has
just broken with the Party. In fact, he is modelled on an historical
person, Whittaker Chambers. And this ex-Communist dismissed
Laskell's traditional point of view:

> You stand there now, thinking that you know us all, and
> disapprove of us all, and yet do not hate or despise us. You are
> being proud of that flexibility of mind. But it won't last, John,
> it's diminishing now. It is too late for that – the Renaissance is
> dead. (p. 304)

In other words, in the face of the logically structured public institution of evil, nobody has the right to take refuge in a merely private
world and let history go by. Evil that is a public design and murders
without a troubled conscience imposes on statesmen as well as
private citizens the obligation to take a stand.

Makers of foreign policy in our time have in fact acknowledged
that in the new situation foreign policy could no longer enjoy the
luxury of a morally neutral atmosphere. The Nazi-Fascist Axis and
Russia's Soviet Power were met with public expressions of moral

condemnation on the part of Western governments. The U.S.A. delayed its recognition of the Soviet regime for 16 years. Later it called on the world to put the Axis dictators "in quarantine." NATO, a defensive alliance triggered by the Communist takeover of Czechoslovakia, has acknowledged moral reasons for its existence. U.S. armaments have been maintained at high levels for the explicit purpose of defending the freedom that still remained outside the Communist orbit, and twice the U.S. sent its sons to war in this cause. Still, all this does not amount to a conversion of the "politics of existence" into "politics of justice." The distinction between foreign affairs and government has not been invalidated by the experience of evil in an unprecedented form. Insofar as foreign policy now includes a moral stance with regard to totalitarian regimes, this, first, is a selective rather than encompassing moralism, and, secondly, is a component element rather than the central purpose of foreign policy.

### Problems of Selective Moralism

THE INTRUSION of a selective moralism into foreign policy creates a number of new problems that have befuddled statesmanship in our time:

a) Policy makers find that the moral component does not provide answers for all questions of foreign policy. Many aspects of competitive power relations remain essentially the same as before. Foreign trade has a logic of its own that is largely impervious to moral considerations, and so does diplomatic representation. While much of foreign policy continues with the moral component in the same way as before the moral component, the latter is nevertheless not an arbitrary or deliberate embellishment; rather, it has forced itself on political minds and emotions with the persuasive power of the destiny of a culture. In spite of continuing permanent facts, then, there will be modifications of foreign policy by virtue of the moral component. That means, of course, that the limit and nature of the "moral" intrusion remains a somewhat open question admitting no single or easy answer. A largely phony concept presuming to supply an objective criterion for an answer is the notion that the Soviet Power has no ideological character but rather moves on a "two track" course, switching deliberately from ideology to Russian national interests and back. The notion is unrealistic, implausible, and begs the question. A foreign policy maker who has felt it necessary to allow moral considerations to color his judgments and influence his decisions is not a person with two minds and a switch in between, and neither are the Communist leaders. It is better to think of a tension in a single mind that encounters difficulties in discerning and heeding a moral obligation in the midst of somewhat amoral business.

b) A selective moralism is never a very satisfactory position. It will tend to expand into a universal moralism, i.e., a moralistic approach taking in all foreign policy decisions, and relations with all countries. This would require a central moral principle capable of serving as a guidepost and yardstick for all foreign policies. President Carter's "human rights" concern has been offered to fill this role. Earlier in the century, Wilsonianism made a stab in that direction. Today's tendency, however, should not be read as nostalgia for Wilsonianism but rather as a broadening out of the moral position implicit in anti-Communism.

c) If universal expansion fails or is not sought, then a selective moralism may become so repugnant to people that they would prefer to ban the moral consideration altogether and return to an amoral foreign policy which in its "realism" may appear more justifiable to them. This mood underlies the currently dominant assertion that the former "Communist threat" has been superseded by a "Soviet threat," i.e., that we have to deal with nothing else but a great power waxing too strong too fast.

d) A selectively moral element directed essentially against one nation may display a tendency to veer around and turn into moral self-condemnation. It will then become a self-destructive power, undermining the will to defense and even to existence as such. Vacillations and uncertainties of this kind probably account for more than one half of the confusions besetting the policies of non-Communist powers today. The remainder should probably be attributable to the equally mind-boggling conflict between fear of military inferiority and the fear of a nuclear war. Let us look at some of these problems in more depth.

## Questions Raised by Selective Moralism

AT THE CORE of the difficulties lies the selectivity of the moral component. It raises in people's minds such questions as, "Why condemn evil concentrated in one country rather than evil everywhere? Why make the moral condemnation of one country the burden of our foreign policy and the possible cause of a war? What title does one country, ours, have to judge others seeing that we, too, are far from perfection?" In view of such deficiencies in plausibility, is a selective moral condemnation, then, justifiable?

What is selectively condemned is the totalitarian rule of the Communist Party of the Soviet Union, manifested most tangibly in the Soviet concept of criminal guilt and the inhumanity of the Soviet penal system. What we see and observe in the Soviet Union differs radically from the flaws that have been found in sundry judicial systems and practices, over the centuries. Everywhere governments are held to be instituted for "the punishment of wickedness and vice," meaning that immoral personal actions are judged and punished by the yardstick of public laws and generalized human conscience, a pattern which one may call "immoral men – moral society." All human judicial institutions suffer from flaws, e.g., inordinate harshness, judicial errors, corruption in high places, but this does not usually give other governments reasons or rights to concern themselves with the mote in foreign countries' eyes. Public justice, even when flawed, then, has remained reserved to the internal relations between rulers and ruled, and out-of-bounds to the foreign policies of other states. Why should Soviet "justice" be an exception to this rule?

Traditionally public justice is founded on the standards of human nature and its proper limits. In the Soviet Union, however, the very concept of human nature is rejected. Criminal punishment is determined by standards not of human limits, based on experience, but of history, based on speculation. In the attribution of guilt, "abstraction, which belongs to the world of power and calculation, has replaced the real passions, which are in the domain of the flesh and the irrational." (Camus) Men are imprisoned, tortured, and executed because they are classified in some such category as "social origin," "racial origin," "wreckers," "cosmopolitans," the guilt being implied in the classification so that the accused bears the burden of proof of his innocence. Thus culpability has neither a factual nor a philosophical basis. The Soviet judicial system operates on the analogy of an army in combat: whoever fails to support the combat enterprise or is merely neutral is deemed an enemy. All the same, Soviet courts overtly use the language of courtrooms everywhere and refer to the measure of good and evil, except that they dissolve ethics into history, and that a history which has not yet happened. While it maintains order of a sort, this is done at the price of man himself. Indeed, the concept of man has disappeared from official thinking, and the Party's strategy has usurped the place of measure of everything.

> It has no reasonable basis but a *petitio principii*, which introduces into history . . . a value that is foreign to history, since that value is, at the same time, foreign to ethics, it is not, properly speaking, a value on which one can base one's conduct . . . . The end of history is not an exemplary or perfectionist value; it is an arbitrary and terroristic principle.[3]

> A living man can be enslaved and reduced to the historic condition of an object. But if he dies refusing to be enslaved, he reaffirms the existence of another kind of human nature which refuses to be classified as an object. That is why the accused is never produced and killed before the eyes of the world unless he consents to say that his death is just and unless he conforms to the Empire of objects. One must die dishonored or no longer exist—neither in life or in death. In the latter event, the victim does not die, he disappears.[4]

Thus in the Soviet Union, apart from cases of ordinary crimes, evil comes not in the form of transgressions of particular persons. Rather, it has taken the form of the entire Soviet system of power itself. The system as such consists in a transgression of the limits of human nature. The pattern can be described as "moral man—immoral regime." I do not say "moral man—immoral society" because in addition to the Communist regime there is a society, Russia, which as such is not the source of the evil. The immorality of the Communist regime is not the usual one—bad habits having gradually developed. Rather, it is the elaborate product of a fully articulated ideology. Nor does it stem from the root of lawless passions, unrestrained selfishness, or even endeavors to make an exception for oneself. Rather, it is evil resulting from a perversion of speculative reason, embodied in an official and all-pervasive plan, defended by no tradition but destructive beliefs that are daily renewed by the Communist Party. One need not assume that particular Party members sincerely believe in the Communist ideology. In all probability they do not. But the ideology has been woven into the entire fabric of Soviet power so that it can remain effective even without the support of spontaneous subjective conviction. Nor is the ideological quality of Soviet power incompatible with the empirical observation that power as such seems to be the chief Communist objective.

> The question of the twentieth century . . . has gradually been specified: How to live without grace and without justice? Only nihilism has spoken, returning once more to the theme of the romantic rebels: "Frenzy." Frenzy in terms of history is called power. The will to power came to take the place of the will to justice.[5]

Whether we want to call it the Communist threat, or the nihilist threat, or the threat of men without any inner measure of order and peace, the cultural reality has metamorphosed into a monster of inhumane power bent on limitless expansion. This is no parallel to Alexander's drive to extend political order to the limits of cultural geography. Rather, it is the peacelessness of demonism that comes from deliberately stepping out of the universe of reason, rejecting the premise that all men are members of one another and share the same condition, and thus remain impervious to persuasion. Nor is this still to be considered a matter of choice for them. If in tired hearts of particular Communists a yearning for quietude might stir, if they should grow weary of the irreconcilable hostility to which their ideology has doomed them, nothing avails but the path of defection. As long as they remain part of the system they will find that they no longer share with others the gift of peace.

We conclude: a) the fact and dynamics of Soviet Power cannot be accurately perceived if the underlying nihilism is not grasped; b) the terroristic practices of the Soviet regime differ not in degree but in kind from even the most defective system of justice based on the measure of God and the nature of man; c) therefore a selective moral stance singling out Soviet Power from all other regimes and all other kinds of corruption is fully justified. Indeed, an officially maintained moral indignation regarding the Soviet regime could not claim justification were it *not* selective: its selectivity testifies to its perceptiveness and discerning judgment. d) The selective moral condemnation of Soviet Power has become a necessary and enduring component of non-Communist governments inasmuch as any expansion of Soviet Power threatens not merely their national security but their culture. As far as the Christian civilizations are concerned, what is threatened is their concept of "man created, man fallen, man redeemed," to use the words of Alexander Schmemann. Moral opposition selectively concentrated on Communism is, indeed, an obligation for today's statesmen, and those who vigorously manifest it in word and action are entitled to a badge of honor.

It is necessary to extend these conclusions to an important addendum. In the present historical situation, a selective moralism is a fully justified element of foreign policy. On the other hand, the situation does not justify a universal moralism of foreign policies. There are several reasons for this. First, the burden of proof. Selective moralism is a reaction to the appearance of evil in an historically new form of massively evil power that knows no bounds. The evil manifests itself concretely and in self-evident patterns. If the facts are not deliberately ignored, the difference in kind between the unprecedented new evil and the evil of the personal-habitual type is clear enough so that the selective moralism can stand as an obviously proper reaction. If a universal moralism were embraced, however, the reference would not point to a new historical evil but to evil in general, which puts the government embracing this universal moralism in the position of either a universal avenger or a universal redeemer. That government would bear the burden of proof of its own virtue, a virtue entitling it to the role of such leadership. Secondly, a selective moralism as a component of foreign policy is obviously limited to fending off merely the intolerably worst fate. It is not committed to replacing the odious regime by any particular alternative, and, at any rate, it should not set up any kind of putative political perfection as the alternative. Universal moralism, by contrast, is inherently perfectionist and carries a millenarian tendency which is apt to develop its own totalitarian excesses of power. Its stance, moreover, is not one of self-defense but of global education. The third reason is that a government seeking to elevate virtue all over the world acts as if it stood to the peoples of the world in the relation of a whole to its parts, i.e., in the relation of a state to its citizens. In reality, however, it is not privileged to exercise the authority of a whole, nor does it possess power to make laws for others, nor does it dispose of a machinery to enforce laws it desires to make. The jurisdiction of its courts ends at its own boundaries. Thus in its endeavor to perfect the moral level of life in other states, it can use no other instrument but power pressure. In doing so, it will simply look like Don Quixote assailing the windmills.

All this is so obvious that exceptions to the inclusion of moral elements in foreign policy are practically unheard of. Thus even a selective, and defensive, moralism tends to become a very uncomfortable habit of mind in foreign offices, with a resulting tendency to evade the moral obligation altogether. In the nature of things as they are, any attempt in this direction must deny the relevant facts. We all know the various forms this denial has taken in our days, from the hope of Soviet "liberalization" to the "convergence" theory, to the assertion of an overriding "common interest" in peace. Since the facts have a way of persisting, however, one is driven to close one's official eyes to them, to bury them in the official silence of the media, or simply to harden one's heart. Moral cynicism in governments, however, cannot be practiced selectively. To turn one's back on the evidence of a particularly dangerous evil gives one the appearance of willingness to consort with it which amounts to a betrayal of the very foundation on which government rests.

Here, then, we have the extremes which are undesirable and unfeasible. Between them, a government practicing a selective moralism in foreign policy must seek to steer its course. It must never directly or indirectly deny its obligation to defend the culture against the evil of nihilism sitting on totalitarian blocks of power. It must avoid the reality as well as the appearance of a betrayal, watching even actions that are minimal in character but can be large in significance, as, e.g., the refusal to invite Solzhenitsyn to the White House, or the omission of Baryshnikov's defection from his biography issued by the White House on the occasion of his appearance there. On the other hand, the moral modification of foreign policy must remain within the limits in which a government disposes of means to influence another. In the nature of the case, this will mostly be the weapon of public opinion. Trade as a weapon does not carry much punch, because of its reciprocal character. Economic aid does have the leverage but cannot lend it to the purpose of pressure for long before it becomes politically unusable. Linking the moral condemnation with either military threats or armaments policy is not a credible endeavor, unless one can pretend to believe in the prospect of a moral evolution of the ideological mind, a pretense which presupposes an inordinate gullibility as a conversation partner.

In the very presence of the moral component, foreign policy still continues along its own path of logic. It is then useful to recall that negotiations have taken place, even in the midst of war, between belligerents; even nations fighting each other have carried on trade with each other, even bitter enemies have maintained diplomatic relations with each other, and the material ratio of armaments remains what it is regardless of moral components.

---

[1] Albert Camus, *The Rebel* (New York: Knopf, 1956), p. 4.

[2] *The Middle of the Journey* (New York: Avon Books, 1976).

[3] Camus, *op. cit.*, p. 224.

[4] *Ibid.*, p. 238.

[5] *Ibid.*, p. 225.

# Foreign Policy and America's Sense of Destiny

MANY COMPLAINTS have been heard that our country has not developed "an overall foreign policy," a course of action that would make evident sense and give consistency to our attitude with respect to other nations. In recent years the matter has both shifted and narrowed as people began to use the term "strategy," which, properly speaking a military term, connotes the "ordering of engagements to the end of victory." (Clausewitz) That term has entered our own language from the Soviet side; it belongs to Lenin, who saw world politics in the perspective of an ongoing class struggle that would have to culminate in the victory of the Soviet Union. Anyhow, whether "foreign policy" or "strategy," it is a fact that since the end of the Forties we have typically reacted to the initiatives of others, particularly the Soviet Union, rather than from our own sense of purpose. Since this applies to Democratic and Republican administrations and, among Republicans, both wings of the party, one surmises that there are causes deeper than the various political programs and ideologies contending for power in our country. I shall make an attempt to explain the character of our foreign policy by referring to something like a "jet stream," a causative current beyond the daily changes of wind and weather.

That causative orientation is found, in the case of nations, in their "civil theologies." Michael Henry, who first investigated the relation between civil theology and foreign policy of the US and the

USSR, distinguishes between "public philosophy," a "rationally perceived and implemented order," and on the other hand "civil theology," a "symbolically ordered expression of the society's desire for power and destiny."[1]

America's civil theology has its roots in the view the Puritans took of their "errand in the wilderness." It was first articulated in 1629 by John Winthrop, before departing England, as follows:

> Wee shall finde that the God of Israell is among us, when tenn of us shall be able to resist a thousand of our enemies, when hee shall make us a prayse and glory, that men shall say of succeeding plantacions: the lord make it like that of New England: for wee must Consider that wee shall be as a Citty upon a Hill, the eies of all people are uppon us.[2]

Their goal, he said, was "perfection in this world," warranted by the fact that all the people eligible for membership in the company were "visible saints" who emigrated in order to avoid the anticipated ruin of England and the pollution of the Old World, and also because these members had committed themselves to the "right" government of a "covenanted" relation between man and God as well as between man and man, under the authority of chosen magistrates and a governor. It followed that the Massachusetts Bay Company could not be compared to any "ordinary corporation." The Bible, not Parliament, was its ultimate authority, and its members swore allegiance not to the king but to "the government of (this body)."[3] Should they succeed, the place where they planted would become the hub of the universe.[4]

The concept of government by the saints lasted only until the revocation of the original charter in 1691 and the issuing of a new one in which qualification for membership was defined in terms not of saintliness but of property. Still, during the next century and right up to independence, Jonathan Edwards's theology continued to articulate the original notion of American destiny:

> [The world's rebirth] shall begin in some very remote part of the world, with which other parts have no communication but by navigation. [This new world was discovered so that] the new and most glorious state of God's church on earth might commence there; that God might begin in it a new world in a

spiritual respect, when he creates the *new heavens and new earth.*[5]

The church had been born east and moved westward, but the spiritual sun "will rise in the west, till it shines through the world like the sun in its meridian brightness."[6]

This symbolism surrounded the early years of John Adams, through whom America's public philosophy received its intellectual form. Americans, he said, "think that the Liberties of Mankind and the Glory of human Nature is in their keeping . . . , that America was designed by Providence for the theatre on which Man was to make his true figure. . . ."[7] From then on, it was the Constitution, fruit of the new political science, which made America an example for all to emulate. Others, as John Winthrop had already said, "did not establish a right form of government."

In the nineteenth century this religious sense of American destiny was expressed in secular terms. "Liberty is the cause, progenitor, preserver and protector of all the blessings we enjoy and impart to others. . . . Liberty is our place in history, our destiny, our ideal, the very soul of our existence."[8] In 1900 Senator A.J. Beveridge coined the slogan, "AMERICAN INSTITUTIONS FOLLOW THE AMERICAN FLAG."[9] Michael Henry draws this conclusion:

> Symbolically, then, the young empire of the West is not only the future redeemer of the world [but also] . . . the earthly order admired and even worshipped by the nations of the world, the nation whose very existence implies a restructuring of cosmic order."[10]

The use of the term "empire" in some of these formulations implies expansion not merely on the North American continent but possibly even beyond. If so, this empire was not to bring onerous domination but "the jubilee," as others came under the blessings of American institutions. In this way some notion of foreign policy might attach to the American sense of destiny. But the record shows that a movement of expansion was not envisaged as continuous and ubiquitous. Over long periods of American history the idea of expansion was dormant and remained unexpressed. In those times the sense of American destiny was entirely compatible with the idea that this country should redeem the world not by direct intervention but by example, as "the primitive and precious model of what it is to change the condition of man over the globe."[11] This in turn was compatible with the resolve to "avoid as much as possible entangling ourselves with their (European) wars or politics."[12]

Isolation as a political possibility ended with the two World Wars. The United States could not escape being drawn into both fighting and peace diplomacy. After the first war two astonishing events occurred. First, the peace treaty with the enemy was not much a matter of diplomacy: it was dictated under duress. But then followed a wholesale remaking of the political conditions, boundaries, governments, economics, and laws of half the world, America playing the role not of a partner among other nations but rather that of a demiurge. Wilson's Fourteen Points, something like the French Declaration of the Rights of Man, had set the stage for this event, even though they were largely ignored around the green table. Still, that global settlement bore the stamp of a "new epoch." Secondly, the American sense of destiny produced a vision of political perfection of world politics: the vision of "enduring peace," secured by world institutions. The plan envisaged sovereign nations automatically acting as good neighbors, nay, as good citizens, rushing to act collectively to the side of any one country against whom the crime of "aggression" had been perpetrated. The idea, it is true, was not new; it had been formulated by Immanuel Kant first in 1784 (*The Idea of a World History From a Cosmopolitan Point of View*), then in 1795 (*Perpetual Peace*). In its modern version, however, it came from the Puritan mind of Woodrow Wilson, erstwhile professor of political science at Princeton. As "Oliver Cromwell has been called 'God's Englishman' . . . , the title 'God's American' aptly describes Woodrow Wilson," said Richard Bishirjian.[13] Wilson's vision, though initially rejected by Americans, gradually took hold and came to exercise continuing influence on makers of this country's foreign policy, from Cordell Hull's "order under law," to Rusk's "lasting world peace" and Nixon's "peace in our time," – all of these being concepts of a "world condition" of security from war. Even though it no longer came in the forms of Puritan symbolism, it still was a notion of redemption, albeit one wrought by human activities.

The American sense of destiny, then, articulated itself not in one but two civil theologies, one pertaining to internal order, the other to foreign affairs. What our statesmen imagine or foresee, what they desire or fear, what language they use and concepts they coin, depend largely on these civil theologies. Before attempting to spell out the implications however, we should take a brief look at the Soviet Union.

The Soviet sense of destiny is certainly rooted in the ideology of the Communist Party of the Soviet Union, i.e., in Marxism-Leninism. The decisive difference of their civil theology from ours, though, can be narrowed down to their view of history, so that the rest of the ideology may be ignored. We think of history in terms of an "open" future, a future emerging from an indefinite number of possibilities in the midst of which men act with moral responsibility (or irresponsibility). In other words, we differ from the Soviets as well as from pagan antiquity in that the future appears to us as knowable or even controllable. We do foresee, at least in part, a few months or maybe even years, but not the course of mankind in its entirety. Our actions in history thus have the character of "a step at a time," while the course of history is left in the hands of divine Providence, the notion of Providence implying the ultimate mystery of history as a whole. All the same, "Providence" also contains human confidence in an ultimate intelligent purpose, without which there would be no history but merely a senseless jumble. This "openness" of the future gives to each human action the character of an ultimate responsibility, so that Aristotle can call them "particular ultimates," as distinct from "universal ultimates," the "particular" being ultimate in the sense that there "the buck" comes to a stop.

The Soviet view is diametrically opposed to this. It holds that history's ultimate goal is "scientifically" knowable, and that Marxism-Leninism is the science of that knowledge. This is the crux of Marx's legacy. One needs not go further into details of Communist ideology, or burn with revolutionary fervor, to embrace this notion of the future. Futurism is not even confined to Marx; it has numerous adherents in the contemporary West other than those indoctrinated by the Communist Party. On the other hand, once this view of history has come to be publicly entrenched and protected, as it has in the Soviet Union, it is well-nigh impossible to divest oneself of it. Any philosophy of history lies high above the daily concerns of ordinary men and women, so that only a few would have the incentive, and fewer still the conceptual tools, to criticize the official version of history. There being no alternative, this view slips into every public decision as a silent assumption, habitually unexamined and yet very efficacious, and far-reaching in its consequences.

There is much conjecture in leading circles that the Communist ideology in the Soviet Union is dead, and that our estimate of Soviet intentions should no longer take it into account. Often this conjecturing is based on somewhat literalist assumptions of how the ideology ever translated itself into Communist practice. Be that as it may, such a conjecture must extend to the conclusion that, instead of ideological motivations, Soviet policies are now generated by common-sense ideas. One thinks of "national interest," "economic expediency," and even motives of a "common world interest in peace." In other words, we believe that the Communists, having abandoned the artificiality and irrationality of ideological thinking, have fallen back on natural motives shared by all human beings. Even if this be so, under no circumstances can it apply to the sense of history, for there is nothing natural about the concept of history. If the Communist sense of history were to disappear, there would have to be another construction of history. The only alternative available today is the view ultimately stemming from Christian philosophy. Apart from those two views of history, there is nothing but the opposite of any history, namely, the myth of cyclical recurrence which derives from the paradigm of nature and its cycles. That, however, not only is not "history," but it also requires a correlative superstitious idea of "fate" to allow for any notion of destiny. There is no evidence that either this kind of cyclical myth or the ultimately Christian construction of history has any hold on Communist minds. We therefore must presume that the Hegel-Marxian idea of history prevails with undiminished vigor, whatever may have befallen the rest of the Communist ideology.

Mention was made before of the far-reaching consequences of this perspective. With the future foreknown, the deliberating consciousness is structured by an ultimate given end. It thus resembles the consciousness of an army during war, when together with the war there is also given its end, victory. Once the ultimate end appears as given, all immediate decisions are seen as parts of the movement toward that end point. This is why the term "strategy" comes readily to the Soviet mind. The mind functions in terms of action within a larger and all-embracing dynamism. This sense of movement allows of no present as a kind of dwelling place; the present, rather, is nothing but a "stage of transition." It becomes impossible to refer "particular ultimates" to "universal ultimates," i.e., to principles.[14] The result is a restless activism which does envisage an ultimate but faraway "peace," which is attainable only through victory, also faraway, so that the intermediary future, of indefinite length, appears as nothing but "struggle." Not only in the short run but also in the long, all things remain in motion and therefore relative except "the struggle," which is absolute. We are not concerned here with debating the truth of this outlook. The fact that this type of consciousness prevails in Soviet minds, however, is indeed truly known.

What about foreign policy in this context? Immediately after their revolution, the Communists saw no possibility of any foreign policy in the new world they believed they had ushered in. They did not even set up a foreign ministry. This came later, when they had lost the war against Poland but won their own civil war and accepted "Socialism in one country" as a continuing situation. Lenin's *Imperialism*, meanwhile, had applied Marx's class struggle to all world politics, even to the point of envisaging the "last battle" of the class struggle as an international war. From then on they began to develop a world revolutionary strategy as Russia's foreign policy, formulated in Stalin's *Foundations of Leninism* (1924), *Problems of Leninism* (1926) and in the *Program* of the CPSU of 1961. The characteristic of this world strategy has been the quest of new theaters for the Soviet global attack on "imperialism." This has been accompanied by a continuous propaganda campaign of an equally global character, largely centering on the peace theme, and aiming at the loosening and eventual dissolution of the Western alliances. Khrushchev began to link this propaganda campaign to the vision of a "peaceful transition from capitalism to socialism.' One perceives that the Soviets never feel lacking in purpose or motive for action; there is always plenty of material for conceiving political initiatives. This does not mean that they have not on occasion vacillated and at times retreated. There seems to be a limit to their willingness to retreat: Their own country, the chief instrument of the world strategy, must be preserved as a power base; in addition the reversion to capitalism of any country in which socialism has been established has turned out to be unacceptable to the Soviets, presumably because this would run counter to the direction of history.

Explaining American foreign policy through its civil theology is more difficult. The record says that the United States has made foreign-policy decisions largely by way of reacting to Soviet initiatives. It also reveals in these reactions a pattern of lowering rather than raising the ante. Let us begin by driving the myth of "a city upon a hill" to its logical conclusion: A nation considering itself as the definitive model and the destiny of all mankind cannot really have a foreign policy, chiefly because it places itself in a class of one, distinct from all other nations. Its stance must be one of pointing to itself as a self-explanatory message. Before the Carter administration, the building of the United States Information Agency had engraved over its portals the motto: TELLING AMERICA'S STORY ABROAD. This motto is a symbol of our self-understanding. To gauge it rightly, let us check our impression were we to hear something like it from other countries: "Telling Great Britain's story abroad"; "Telling Italy's story abroad." Those mottoes strike us as ill-fitting because we do not conceive, let us say, Great Britain as having a story to tell. Great Britain, however, is known for her remarkably shrewd foreign policies, her correct judgments of possibilities, desirabilities and threats in the pattern of other nations' intentions and capabilities. It may not be exaggerated to generalize that the United States does not typically see foreign problems in this manner. Great Britain's foreign policies have often appeared to Americans as precisely the kind of dangerous games breeding wars from which this country desired to escape once and for all.

Only two types of foreign policy are compatible with this self-understanding: Isolationism (no so-called entangling alliances) and wars in the spirit of a crusade ("to make the world safe for democracy"). Insofar as they are given to this attitude, American leaders are simply not in the habit of looking for factors and developments likely to lead to war, in view of the power and aspirations of diverse nations. Clearly, in a system composed of particular entities accidents are bound to happen, as Hegel said in #324 of his *Philosophy of Right*. This reality is ignored by American thinking which does not embrace war as a recurrent possibility. Rather, it moves in concepts of good and evil, ideal government and enduring peace. Specific exceptions to these generalizations are not infrequent. All the same, it seems that the generalization is capable of grasping a fundamental difference between foreign policy of the United States and foreign policies of other powers, outside of Communist regimes. The American government seems always to be taken by surprise when the Soviet Union opens up another theater or incorporates another country into the socialist system. "Taken by surprise" here does not mean having faulty intelligence. It means that activity about national interest begins only with a detrimental event's occurrence, and not before. As for wars of nations other than Communist regimes, the typical American reaction resembles that of the King of Saxony when it was reported to him that a revolution was under way: "But, are they allowed to do that?"

Michael Henry sees the Soviets' civil theology as an appropriation of the Christian myth, and America's as another version of the same myth. Something can be said for this thesis. Both are indeed oriented toward ideal perfection in history. All the same, there are basic differences. Soviet thinking is cast in terms of "coming-to-be," the future as a foreknown yet dynamic necessity. America's self-understanding expresses itself in terms of symbols of "being," above all this country's "being" as the hope of the world. The Soviets' vision leads them to unceasing and energetic action; America's image induces an optimistic self-advertisement. The Soviets think of the all-perfect future as requiring the previous destruction of "everything that exists" (Marx). Hence it is the process of destructive struggle that occupies their imagination, rather than the future society whose coming will take care of itself once the old structures and habits have been removed. We believe that, if only the Russians (or whosoever wills us ill) really knew us, they would surely change their minds. Hence our need for "TELLING AMERICA'S STORY ABROAD." Hence the ever-cocked ear to sounds of the other side's returning openness. Hence our predilection for gestures. All this makes sense only on the assumption that John Winthrop's image of the city upon a hill is still with us.

What about America's other myth, the world-without-war? We see it as an instituted peace among sovereign nations, a covenant binding all nations to instant solidarity against any so-called aggressor and imposing on every government one single interest common to them all – world peace. Such a covenant must render all armaments and alliances anachronistic. Aggression, an atavism, is automatically stamped as a crime against humanity. The time is considered ripe for spears to be beaten into ploughshares, and for the end of diplomacy. This, too, may be considered as something "coming-to-be." However, with the League of Nations, the Briand-Kellogg Pact "outlawing war," and the subsequent alliance between the Soviet Union and its supposed class enemy, we fell into the illusion that "world peace" is already here, even though still imperfectly acknowledged. So, again, it was a matter of showing forth something "in being," rather than the process of "coming-to-be." The logic of this assumption caused us not to conduct foreign policy on the premise that peace between particular nations is a concrete as well as a frail and vulnerable growth requiring diligent cultivation. Our rhetoric has preferred to speak of peace as "enduring," "lasting," "just" and "global," thereby proclaiming that in our eyes there is only *one* universal peace for all, which is tantamount to declaring that we already live in a world in which war is no longer licit. The practical disappointment with the League of Nations did not prevent us from setting up the UN as a sequel. When the UN proved even more of a failure, the "lasting peace" slogan continued all the same, as did the concept of aggression as a criminal trespass. Most important, though, was the idea of "pacts" – the old idea of covenants – as a universal formula for peaceful solution in lieu of war.

In the light of this idea, all conflicts are deemed alike; all consist of differences which are equally amenable to being composed. The solution lies invariably in the mechanical middle, a concept having nothing of the metaphysical character of Aristotle's mean. Thus our diplomats are typically lusting for pacts, if one may be allowed an analogy to Augustine's *libido dominandi*. Pacts are not to be examined critically for their political effects or consequences. They are valued as if they were ends in themselves. In this sense U.S.

policy may be said to incline to satisfaction with promises of expectations in the place of tangibilities. Promises are taken for realities in the perspective of progress. Sometimes it appears as if all our foreign policy were conceived in terms of psychological states, something like "relaxation," "growing trust," or the like, failing which we are willing to settle for simply pointing out, again, the other side's "orneriness."

Another aspect of a world without war tends to substitute economic for military means of pressure. This idea also is ancient; it comes from Saint-Simon, who saw the new world as consisting of "industrial states" taking the place of the former "military states." At times, for instance after the universal devastation of World War II, the Marshall Plan made eminent sense. Since then, however, U.S. foreign policy has looked on economic aid and economic sanctions as prime instruments of foreign policy *par excellence*. Again, the means tend to be seen as if they were ends. At any rate, we are not really curious about their precise effects and long-range utility; economic means are simply judged morally superior to military or political ones, in this new world without war.

"World peace" is a concept which the Soviet Union seems to share with us, from which arises the illusion of a good common to both countries. One easily concludes, then, that a commonly agreed conduct is morally possible. If the Soviet Union derived its moral notions directly from its utopian vision of a perfectly harmonious society, there might be something to this expectation. In fact, however, the Soviet mind does not project the envisaged good of the future into the present, in any shape or form. In other words, their present practice in no ways reflects the anticipated classless, stateless and crimeless society. As was already mentioned, before that society can arise, a wholesale destruction of the present-day society must be effected by means of a protracted revolutionary struggle which, among all the relativized bits of morality, ranks as the sole "absolute" (Lenin, *On Dialectics*). In this perspective, the practice of life can be nothing else but irreconcilable class struggle, and its requirements the sole norm of conduct. By contrast, we do pull the moral norms of a world without war into the present. This is no mere psychological inclination. The entire project of "perpetual peace" provides an approximation to the ideal by the effort of pretending that universal peace is already a present reality.

Thus we do derive criteria of government conduct from our utopia. In a sense, both sets of norms can be called irrational. But the Soviets, in spite of the irrationality of their myth, appear to be operating on the solid ground of realities, while we, the Kantian rationality notwithstanding, appear to be busy with manipulating the clouds.

Against this appraisal the following objections may be raised: a) it does not do justice to those aspects of American foreign policy that seem to have a clearly realistic character, e.g., our military strength and deployment; b) it criticizes without pointing to alternatives. To the first objection I reply that our military stance has indeed been the most realistic aspect of our foreign policy, so much so that many thinkers about these problems have come to look on military strategy as the whole of American policy. They set aside, however, Clausewitz's insight that the national purpose is political in war no less than in peace, so that a military purpose in the absence of a clearly political purpose tends to spin on itself and can finally be reduced to absurdity, which is what left-wing demonstrators are engaged in doing.

The second objection deserves to be answered at greater length. I have submitted a criticism of American foreign-affairs thinking as vitiated by a false sense of goodness. This criticism applies to the two civil theologies mentioned here: the first being pretentious claims that America is the ultimate flower of political culture as well as the realization of God's kingdom on earth; the other being the illusion that a covenanted "world peace" could be as secure as peace within legitimately established systems of government. In practice, both these notions project onto international relations the kind of common good that pertains to government alone. The misplaced values are lacking in ontological reality. International relations occur between communities each of which has realized a particular common good and, yet, in that they all are devoted to the common good, they are all members of the same class. This class, however, has no institutional, legal or existential unity. Goodness in international relations pertains to reciprocity rather than to community. Reciprocity, in turn, occurs in a variety of fields: pragmatic reciprocity, reciprocity of diplomatic intercourse, economic reciprocity, military reciprocity, reciprocity regarding limits of power that do not stand under the judgment of equality, reciprocity even in combat. Reciprocity flows from the realization that nations great and small are all alike insecure, dependent on one another and yet legally independent. This premise can be compared to that other premise of all human forebearance, that we all are creatures, that no one among us can rationally claim divinity. From this premise came the flower of the "balance of power," a system without institutions or sanctions, which is thoroughly misunderstood if one thinks of it as an equilibrium of mutual distrust and hostility. It does evoke the notion of equilibrium, yet not of things, not even of power, but of intentions, as expressed in the eighteenth-century norm that nations should "do each other the greatest possible good in peace, and the least possible harm in war." National interests evolve in the perceptions of reciprocity but, since there is a multitude of particular common goods, accidents may always happen and must be counted with at all times. No instituted security of sovereign nations is possible, not even with the best of all possible intentions.

The endemic insecurity of a system of independent nations stems not merely from the particularity of the common good, but also from the irremediable inequality of their power, rooted in accidents of geography, demography, culture and technology. Individual human beings, as Hobbes has observed, have a roughly equal status in that physical brawn and capacity of brain tend to cancel each other out. Still, individual persons are clearly unequal in their natural equipment and potentialities. States, however, are not only much more unequal but also have no natural limits to their size and strength. All the same, a balance of power has under favorable circumstances been effective, in that the greater power of some states either was made or turned out to be not unacceptable to their weaker neighbors. This pattern of relationship, however, must exclude nations "so preeminently superior in goodness that there can be no comparison between (its goodness) and what is shown by the rest."[15] Like Aristotle's preeminent individual who "can no longer be treated as part of a state," they can not properly function as part of a pattern of international relations. China of old so interpreted itself, as the "Kingdom of the Middle," i.e., of the center of the cosmos, surrounded by inferior barbarians. Fortunately, China committed itself only for a limited time to a policy of imperialism, after which a coexistence between the Kingdom of the Middle and the rest of the world was predicated on each keeping a great and safe distance from the other. The Soviet Union, also claiming "preeminent goodness" by virtue of its vision for the future of mankind, has committed itself to a limitless imperialism which can be frustrated only by internal weakness. Otherwise, the Soviets must count on a continuing front of resistance against their aspirations, unless they succeed in dismantling the Western alliance and begin to overpower the rest of the nations one after the other.

It cannot be gainsaid that a similar wall of resistance is building up against the United States. We attribute this anti-Americanism either to envy or to ignorance, at any rate to accidental psychological causes. I am not persuaded that anti-Americanism does not follow necessarily from our continued claim that our being is a model for all. This claim could be maintained with some justice as long as America showed forth a government under God and obedient to God; it elicited no ill-will when based on the kind of constitution we had achieved, while keeping to ourselves in international relations. Once we entered the world scene as either a giant or a demiurge, the pretentiousness of the claim precluded its acceptance by others. This country is not by design imperialistic. That fact, however, cannot become clear to the world unless we develop leaders of our foreign policy who abandon pretensions – without thereby betraying their country – and who learn to conduct our foreign policy with a basic commitment to a sober reciprocity.

---

[1]Michael Henry, *The Intoxication of Power, Sovetica* vol. 43 (Dordrecht: D. Reidel, 1979), p. 18. See also the excellent Introduction of Richard J. Bishirjian to his *A Public Philosophy Reader* (New Rochelle: Arlington House, 1978). Further Michael Novak, *Choosing Our King: Powerful Symbols in Presidential Politics* (New York: Macmillan, 1974) and Robert N. Bellah, *The Broken Covenant* (New York: Seabury, 1975).

[2]John Winthrop, *Papers* II, p. 295, quoted in Loren Baritz, *City on a Hill* (New York: John Wiley and Sons, 1964), p. 17.

[3]*Ibid.*, p. 40.

[4]*Ibid.*, p. 17.

[5]*The Works of President Edwards* (New York, 1830), quoted by Baritz, *City*, p. 64.

[6]*Ibid.*, p. 65.

[7]John Adams, *Diary and Autobiography*, ed. H.L. Butterfield et al., 1961, quoted by Baritz, *City*, pp. 109 f.

[8]Issac Wise in 1869, quoted by Michael Henry, *Power*, p. 85.

[9]*Ibid.*, p. 92.

[10]*Ibid.*, p. 90.

[11]Thomas Jefferson, quoted by Baritz, *City*, p. 98.

[12]John Adams, quoted by Baritz, *City*, p. 126.

[13]*Philosophy Reader*, p. 60.

[14]See Aristotle, *Nicomachean Ethics*, 1142a 13-30.

[15]*Ibid.*, *Politics*, 1284a 3-8.

# Part II
# The Recovery
# of Order

# Eric Voegelin's Philosophy and the Drama of Mankind

NEARLY TWO DECADES AGO there appeared the first three volumes of Eric Voegelin's exemplary quest for a theoretically intelligible order of history (Vol. I, *Israel and Revelation;* Vol. II, *The World of the Polis;* Vol. III, *Plato and Aristotle*). The plan projected three more volumes: Empire and Christianity, The Protestant Centuries, and The Crisis of Western Civilization. When the fourth volume was actually published in 1974, its title, *The Ecumenic Age*, indicated that the author's ideas had undergone a considerable change during the intervening years. In the Introduction Voegelin announces not only "a break with the program" of *Order and History*, but also the partial abandonment of his former views on the course of history, although the revised concept still issues from the rigorous application of the original principle guiding the entire work: "The order of history is the history of order." That work seems to have attained its climax in *The Ecumenic Age*, since volume V, under the title *In Search of Order*, will conclude the project with a presentation of studies of contemporary problems that led to the whole undertaking.

The turn which Eric Voegelin's thought has taken between 1957 and 1974 was unexpected. Let us see what the first three volumes induced his readers to anticipate and what actually came forth. A word of caution first: no overview of Voegelin's work can possibly claim completeness, for Eric Voegelin has not developed anything like an abstract and logically closed system. From the beginning, he has set out to "find what he could find," and to grasp the problems of order through its manifold of historical manifestations, each of them in its own terms. Thus his pages are packed with the analyses of cultures, situations, texts, symbols, and underlying experiences of which each has shed much light on particulars, so much so that some of these "particulars" have appeared as separate books and others, in the form of articles, are eagerly consulted for references. Eric Voegelin has always maintained that he has proceeded empirically, i.e., in deference to what actually has occurred in history. He has analyzed those occurrences so thoroughly, however, that one cannot possibly report on the quantity and quality of these analyses short of encyclopedic form. Comprehension of these materials could be accomplished only through theoretical principles, some of which must have antedated the work on particulars. On the other hand, the work of sympathetically understanding historical manifestations of order yielded theoretical insights, one is almost tempted to say, *a posteriori*, and the perception of a context of history as a whole, in which these manifestations occur or rather, group themselves, was also a purely theoretical achievement. There is, then, an encyclopedic as well as a philosophical aspect to Eric Voegelin's work, so that the reader seeking to grasp Eric Voegelin's philosophy finds himself again and again distracted, or rather attracted, by the many fascinating excursions into hitherto little known terrain, except that these really are no excurions but the main path of the quest. So follow him one must, carefully trying to keep hold of the philosophical structure of the inquiry even while being astonished by the wealth of new facts.

Turning to the first three volumes: what, after reading them appeared to have been "the history of order"? It is seen as a process of tension, and even progression, between two types of order, the original and ubiquitous "cosmological empire," and the order emerging from what Voegelin has called "the leap in being." Cosmological order, represented in the ancient Near East by Egypt and Mesopotamia, understood itself as a compact unit of gods, men, nature, and society. The king, either himself divine or divinely commissioned, secured the tie between the gods ruling the natural forces of regenerative fertility and men, through the order of society as part of the cosmic order. A tight package of symbols, each integrated with all the others, all together bespeaking the oneness of being and order. Between 800 and 300 B.C., however, there occurred a number of "spiritual outbursts" which led to a break with the cosmological order and the perception of a higher and "truer" way of life. Voegelin mentions four of these "leaps." First came that of Israel, through Moses and the prophets; next that of Greece, through the great philosophers from Parmenides to Aristotle; then India, through the Buddha and Mahavira; finally China, through Confucius and Lao-tzu. Voegelin showed the two latter leaps to have remained somewhat incomplete and focusses his attention on Israel and Greece, the analysis of which in his first three volumes is itself a breakthrough in historical scholarship. While the cosmological order understands men as living in a natural and social cosmos that is "full of gods," the "spiritual outburst" consists in a human experience of participation in a transcendent divinity beyond both the natural and social tangible existence. The experience has the character of a discovery, not only of the transcendent god but also of that in man which can respond to and participate in, the divine. The discovery results in a depreciation of the cosmological symbols of order and the perception and practice of a "new life," which appears as a "leap" in being, rising above what went before. In his *Programmschrift, The New Science of Politics* (1952), Eric Voegelin points out that any society understands itself as representative of transcendental truth, and he distinguishes between "cosmological," "anthropological," and "soteriological" truth. Quoting Clement of Alexandria to the effect that Christianity has "two Old Testaments," that of the Hebrew and that of the Greek tradition, he leaves a hint that in the Christian "leap" the two former leaps of being have converged.

On the basis of the first three volumes, then, the history of order appears as a single "course," a line which at one point, that of the two parallel leaps, shows something like a bulge but then again narrows to a single line. How could the reader, at this point, picture to himself the completion of the project? On the encyclopedic side, Voegelin had covered the ancient Near East, Greece, and, in his *New Science*, a crucial segment of Roman history. In the same book and in his *Science, Politics, and Gnosticism* (German 1959, English 1968), he had dealt with modern times. The great gap was obviously the Middle Ages and the Renaissance. Regarding the philosophical aspect, Voegelin had characterized the "leaps" as something higher and better than what went before. What was it that made the difference? Voegelin called it "differentiation," newly gained deeper insight into aspects of order not clearly distinguished in an earlier compactness of symbols. Israel differentiated righteousness from fertility and security, the people understanding themselves as standing over against a God whose will is righteousness. In the case of Greece, the differentiation was the discovery of the soul as the "sensorium of transcendence," so that in the depth of the soul Socrates and Plato could recollect a higher vision of being, conversion to which amounted to a new life. Here, surely, were philosophical judgments. On the other hand, Voegelin's view of modern times is contained in the chapter title, "Gnosticism – The Nature of Modernity." Gnosticism here functions as a pejorative term, following modern scholarship which had shown the Gnostic religions of the second to fourth centuries to have distorted already existing symbols of order and to have perverted the entire notion of "knowledge."

Finding in modern ideologies a pattern similar to ancient Gnosticism, Voegelin came to speak of the "deformation" that had taken place in modern times, and of "ideologies" as the abandonment of reason. Thus, both with regard to the leaps in being and to modern times Voegelin arrived at judgments about the contents of beliefs. Nor were these judgments emotionally pronounced. On the contrary, they emerged from the most rigorous scholarly treatment of the problems involved, the most precise definition of categories, an attitude of the strictest personal detachment. The great excitement generated by the publication of Voegelin's works must be seen chiefly as caused by his demonstration that values can be treated scientifically. Both "scientific" and "values" should here be put in quotation marks, because Voegelin used science in the classical sense and not in the reductionist meaning imposed by the Positivists; he also would never speak of "values" since that term, of Positivist coinage, had come to denote the utter relativity of wholly subjective "preferences," so that it seemed to make sense to speak of "the values of a dope-peddler." It is precisely because Voegelin sees the ontological context of the good that he had found again the mode in which a scholar could, in the strictest discipline, make distinctions and arrive at judgments about the quality of beliefs. Since Voegelin had formed concepts of "lower" and "higher" being, since he had contrasted rationality with "deformation" and philosophy with "ideology," and had compared historical types of existence in terms of good, he obviously had developed his philosophy, of which the reader could expect to see a fuller and more explicit statement. Voegelin's *Anamnesis* (in German, 1966) may be considered a start in that direction. That book, however, was never translated, possibly meaning that the author looked on it as an interim station. On the other hand, volume IV, when it finally appeared, continued the whole work along wholly unexpected lines.

First, on the plane of pragmatic events, *The Ecumenic Age* moves not forward from Greece and Rome, but rather turns back, covering to some extent the same ground as before. The motive came partly from Voegelin's discovery of a new configuration in history, a new "age." Karl Jaspers had proposed calling the period from 800 to 200 B.C. "the Axis Time," a concept which Voegelin had rejected since it focussed on "spiritual outbursts" like Zoroaster, Parmenides, and Socrates, but excluded Jesus Christ and St. Paul. Nor did Toynbee's outline of twenty-one civilizations, rising and falling from time immemorial, seem to him to fit the facts. He found, on the basis of ubiquitous records, that the ecumenic empires were structures *sui generis* transcending the boundaries of civilizations, and that they would entail the kind of spiritual outbursts that occurred. He showed that after the decline of the ecumenic empires there ensued, from their ruins, the generation of the civilizations we know, so that civilizations are of far more recent origin than Toynbee assumed.

The ecumenic age began with Cyrus' conquest of Media in 550 B.C., rapidly followed by that of Lydia and that of Babylon, and ended around 546 A.D. with the decline of the Roman empire, so that it comprised the Achaemenian, Macedonian, Maurya, Seleucid, and Roman empires. Voegelin's volume thus covers a period of roughly 1100 years. While the reader's eager hope to read all about the Middle Ages is disappointed, in other respects he may find what he was looking for, although again in unexpected form. Voegelin does finally turn to Christianity, but only through an analysis of St. Paul's "vision of the Resurrected." Voegelin's own philosophy also moves toward fuller and more complete articulation, but does this still through the treatment of historical materials. The lengthy and very meaty Introduction, the central chapters on "The Process of History" and "Conquest and Exodus," and the concluding chapter, "Universal Humanity," are chiefly philosophical. Even here, however, Voegelin philosophizes not by himself but with the help and in the company of the privileged individuals to whom, in the course of centuries, epochal insights have been granted. Thus the reader will now have to give up his expectation of seeing the centuries of Christian culture included in *Order and History*, since volume V is not intended to deal with them. On the other hand, he can begin, as we shall do a little later, to put together the chief elements of Voegelin's philosophy. Finally, he will note the revision of Voegelin's former concept of the "course of history." Indeed, the revision of this view and the articulation of Voegelin's own philosophy are one and the same process.

The reader becomes aware of this mixture in the first chapter, "Historiogenesis." This is Voegelin's term for the kind of symbolic speculation that traces the background of a society's present *res gestae* to the ultimate ground and beginning of all things. As a type of speculation it has largely escaped attention, and Voegelin is the first one to give it a name. Voegelin places it in the same class with theogony, anthropogony, and cosmogony, together with which it forms an aggregate covering the whole field of being, with historiogenesis obviously constituting the time dimension. Voegelin notes that there is something like an equivalence between historiogenetic, cosmogonic, anthropogonic, and theogonic speculations; indeed, they all borrow from each other. He also finds that historiogenetic speculations of the Sumerians are an equivalent of the structurally similar speculations of Hegel, so that historiogenesis is "virtually omnipresent" and not characteristic merely of archaic man. It is findings like these, scattered around his chapters, that induce Voegelin to abandon the contradistinctions of periods and types of order that dominated the first three volumes:

> The constancies and equivalences adumbrated work havoc with such settled topical blocks as myth and philosophy, natural reason and revelation, philosophy and religion, or the Orient with its cyclical time and Christianity with its linear history. And what is modern about the modern mind, one may ask, if Hegel, Comte, or Marx, in order to create an image of history that will support their ideological imperialism, still use the same techniques for distorting the reality of history as their Sumerian predecessors? (p. 68)

Voegelin is obviously beginning to work with "constants" of consciousness which seem to appear in culturally different but structurally similar "equivalents." Nor does he find a sharp line
separating historiogenesis and speculations about the cosmos in
which things exist and perish. "The cosmos," in turn, "is not a thing
among others; it is the background of reality against which all existing things exist; it has reality in the mode of non-existence," (p.
72) a "fundamental experience in early societies just as much as in
later ones." The answers to this tension produced at various times
in various cultures are, again, equivalents of each other,

> for the answers make sense only in relation to the questions
> which they answer; the questions, furthermore, make sense
> only in relation to the concrete experiences of reality from
> which they have arisen; and the concrete experiences,
> together with their linguistic articulation, finally make sense
> only in the cultural context which sets limits to both the direc-
> tion and range of intelligible differentiation. Only the complex
> of experience-question-answer as a whole is a constant of con-
> sciousness. . . . No answer, thus, is the ultimate truth in
> whose possession mankind could live happily forever after,
> because no answer can abolish the historical process of con-
> sciousness from which it has emerged. (p. 75)

Here is historical relativity but no relativism, insistence on ontic
constants but no essentialism, a notion of history that consists not
of the series of factual events in time, a concept of consciousness as
concretely conditioned but yet pertaining to universal mankind.

These assumptions established, Voegelin now outlines the age he
has termed "ecumenic," since the word "ecumene," meaning the
humanly inhabited globe, played a key role in the self-
understanding of men living in that time. "Ecumene" occurs in two
different contexts. First, it means the object of actual or potential
unification by conquest, as in Polybius; second, it means the potential range of desired unification by the same spiritual conversion, as
in St. Paul. Voegelin speaks of these as the "pragmatic" and the
"spiritual" ecumene, the two being in intricate and complex relationship with each other. The great conquests overran and upset
many ethnic societies whose members' existence was threatened by

senselessness through the destruction of their political and religious order. They were not the only ones to have problems, though. The conquerors, pushing toward the mythical "horizon," the end of the world, did not know in concrete terms how far to expand their rule, nor did they know what it was they were eventually ruling, so that they were threatened by the specter of a huge power organization without spiritual meaning. On the other hand, the uprooted population of many places, deprived of the meaning of their small ethnic societies, partly responded by outbursts of universal spirituality which in turn formed movements in search of a people whose order they could become. "This millennial process of dissociation of order, its vicissitudes to the end in the rise of orthodox imperical civilizations, is what we have called the Ecumenic Age." (p. 145)

Voegelin's decision to focus his studies on antiquity, leaving out not only the ecumenic empires of Genghis Khan, Tamerlane, the Ottomans, and the Hapsburgs, but also the entire Christian culture of the Latin West and the Greek-Russian East, must remain a puzzlement. All he reveals about his motive is contained in the statement that "the men living in the Ecumenic Age were forced by the events into reflections on the meaning of their course," and thus raised "the issues of a philosophy of history." (p. 171) Voegelin the philosopher, we remember, relies on the exegesis of texts reflecting historical but paradigmatic experiences. He may have considered the 1100 years straddling Christ's birth richer soil for such kinds of finds. That means, however, that he reflected on history through the mind of Plato rather than through that of Augustine, and on being through Parmenides rather than Thomas Aquinas. The gap of Christianity will remain permanent in his work, because the "reflections" of the Ecumenic Age struck him as more significant. One of the issues close to his interest is that of identity. A mighty historical process was going on, but who or what was its subject? It was not a process of "Babylon or Egypt, of Persia, Macedonia, or Rome, of the Greek or Phoenician city states, of the Maurya or Parthian empires, of Israel or the Bactrian kingdoms, though all of these societies were somehow involved in it." (p. 171) It might be that "the ecumene" was the hitherto unsuspected subject of the historical process," but the ecumene was not anything like a given entity; rather it was a *telos*, an aspiration.

The problem once identified, Voegelin follows the speculations of Herodotus, Thucydides, Plato, and Aristotle, all of whom he sees as depending and centering on the basic insight formulated by Anaximander:

> The origin (*arche*) of things is the Apeiron. . . . It is necessary for things to perish into that from which they were born; for they pay one another penalty for their injustice (*adikia*) according to the ordinance of Time. (p. 174)

Behind the up-and-down of existing things Anaximander saw the One which he called "the Boundless." One notices the equivalence of this concept to Voegelin's "non-existence." "The process" is the coming of "things" from the Boundless and their going back again, a process of necessity "according to the ordinance of Time." The great thinkers who reflected on the meaning of the historical process formed part of a "field of noetic consciousness" in which the thinkers could toss each other their discoveries in full awareness that they all were talking about the same reality that Anaximander had identified. Herodotus sees that

> "the thing" called man does not participate in (the process) with the whole of his existence. A part of man has been exempted. For man has split into a power-self that is his own and another part of his self that cannot escape participation, though its participation is experienced as victimization by the process. (p. 180)

He also found that "conquest is exodus, for one must leave behind what one has in order to conquer." (p. 181) It was Plato, however, who achieved the most important development of Anaximander's insight, in *Philebus* 16c-17a, noting that all things have their being "from the One and Many, and conjoin in themselves Limited (*peras*) and Unlimited (*apeirian*)," so that the domain of human knowledge is "in-between" the One and the Unlimited. The Greek word for in-between is *metaxy* which in Voegelin's vocabulary becomes a noun, the Metaxy, invoking something like a space but also serving as something like a synonym for both the *condicio humana* and "human nature." The "dialogue of mankind" is carried on in the language characteristic of the "noetic consciousness" which in the philosophers supplanted the imagery of the cosmological myth, as it discovered the mind as a movement of the soul toward the transcendence; also "discovered the discovery to have meaning as an event in history."

This "noetic consciousness," the discovery of the mind," as Bruno Snell has called it, occupies Voegelin throughout the central chapters of volume IV. On the one hand, it remains anchored in the basic insight of Anaximander and thus remains aware that "man can neither conquer reality nor walk out of it," that "no imperial expansion can reach the receding horizon; no exodus from bondage is an exodus from the *condicio humana*; no turning away from the Apeiron, or turning against it, can prevent the return to it through death." (p. 215) In one respect, "things" remain what they have always been. But human consciousness changes, and discovers its own movements as events in history. Voegelin analyzes what actually happens:

> Participation in the noetic movement is not an autonomous project of action but the response to a theophanic event . . . or its persuasive communication. To this revelatory movement . . . from the divine ground, man can respond by his questioning and searching, but the theophanic event itself is not at his command. (p. 217)

"Noesis," from the Greek *nous* which, although usually translated as "mind," is defined by Aristotle as "itself divine or the most divine thing in us," (*Nic. Ethics* 1177a15) thus must be understood as the openness of consciousness toward that "eminent" reality which is "more real" than things. In this openness the world with its "things" becomes intelligible. "The life of reason," concludes Voegelin, "is thus firmly rooted in a revelation." (p. 228) The revelation, or "theophany," however, has also an unbalancing effect in that its experience as a dynamic movement of consciousness has a way of opening up the expectation of "an ultimate transfiguration of reality," i.e. a "new world" in which "things" would no longer be what they have been so far. "The philosopher has to cope with the paradox of a recognizably structured process that is recognizably moving beyond its structure." (p. 227) In a poignant summary of his findings about the noetic consciousness as a movement forming "part of the structure" Voegelin states: "The history of revelation reveals the Beyond of history and revelation," in the sense that the theophanic event is a "response to an irruption of the divine in the psyche," which in each case has a specific content but will continue as a movement "if the phase of the response that has reached the stage of symbolization is sensed to be no more than penultimate." (p. 223) The "divine irruption" and the "human responses" are again constants, while the "content" of the revelation and of the responses varies in time and space. Voegelin sees the variety of revelations as equivalents: "The God who appeared to the philosophers and who elicited from Parmenides the exclamation 'Is!,' was the same God who revealed himself to Moses as the 'I am who [or what] I am,' as the god who is what he is in the concrete theophany to which man responds." (p. 229) With a view to the danger of losing, from the unbalancing effect of the theophany, the primary experience of the cosmos represented by Anaximander's dictum, Voegelin proclaims "the postulate of balance" which, he says, is "the task incumbent on the philosopher." (p. 228) The entire discussion of the noetic consciousness as a movement incited by theophanies and accompanied by the perennial danger of losing out of sight the world of things over its vision of the Beyond, is Voegelin's description of "the process of history." Here is the core of Voegelin's thought.

At this point, the reader's patient waiting is rewarded, for now Voegelin turns to Christianity, if only in a chapter of thirty-three pages rather than a whole book, and only to "the Pauline Vision of the Resurrected." Since many of Voegelin's readers will be Christians let it be clear that to this writer, who considers himself a Christian, the chapter was deeply disappointing. The treatment is dominated by the notion of equivalences: St. Paul, on the one hand, is put into the same category with Plato, with St. Paul's performance receiving a grade of "superior," and on the other hand with Hegel, who comes out worst. Paul's vision is analyzed in the terms of "noetic consciousness," even though Voegelin concedes to St. Paul the discovery of "pneumatic consciousness." The dynamic has shifted from the paradox of reality to the abolition of the paradox, i.e. toward the vision of a reality in which both disorder and mortality are vanquished by God. Similarly, the dynamic has shifted "from the human search to the divine gift, from man's ascent toward God through the tension of Eros to God's descent toward man through the tension of the Agape." (p. 246) Paul's construction is called "a myth," the story of the fall from and the return to, the imperishable state of creation intended by divine creativity. Thus St. Paul, for the first time, brings into sight the eventual end of the movement thereby revealing its full meaning, which is why "the Pauline myth is distinguished by its superior degree of differentiation" over Plato. (p. 250) So now we learn about the advantage of this superior differentiation in the series of philosophical equivalents. "What becomes visible in the new luminosity . . . is not only the structure of consciousness itself (in classical language: the nature of man), but also the structure of 'an advance' in the process of reality," which enables us to draw the conclusion that " 'history' in the sense of an area in reality in which the insight into the meaning of existence advances is the history of theophany." (p. 252) Paul excels in this series because through him

> the transcosmic God and his Agape were revealed as the mover in the theophanic events which constitute meaning in history. . . . Paul, furthermore, differentiated fully the experience of the directional movement by articulating its goal. . . . Finally, Paul has fully differentiated the experience of man as the site where the movement of reality becomes luminous in its actual occurrence. In Paul's myth, God emerges victorious, because his protagonist is man. He is the creature in whom God can incarnate himself with the fullness of his divinity, transfiguring man into the God-man. (p. 251)

The treatment strikes me as unsatisfactory on a number of counts. The title is misleading, since "the vision" is the entire "speculation" of St. Paul as analyzed by Voegelin, leaving out of consideration the single, brief vision on the road to Damascus which was Paul's encounter with the person of Jesus Christ. St. Paul knew Jesus to have been a contemporary person who was born, lived, preached, performed miracles, "suffered under Pontius Pilate, was crucified, dead, and buried." Apart from the problems of the "historical Jesus," the facticity of Jesus himself separates Christian theology as a type from all myths and philosophical speculations. Since Voegelin points out that Plato's myth was an *alethinos logos*, a true story, he should have allowed a special

category also for St. Paul's story. Myths and philosophical speculations are induced by the ubiquitous "mystery of meaning" which
Eric Voegelin has done more than anyone else to illuminate. In that
respect it is true that they are equivalents of one another. Christianity, however, was born from amazement about a particular person Jesus, his deeds, teachings, and such claims as that men in
order to gain their lives must lose them for his sake, that it will be
he whom men will face in the ultimate judgment, that there will be
a new covenant with God in his blood, that he would die to free
humanity from sin, that he alone had full knowledge of the Father.
Christian theology, then, stems not from a sense of general
wonderment about the world of things and the Boundless, which
probably would not have been very sophisticated in simple
fishermen, but rather from the question which Jesus himself put:
"Who do you say I am?" That question, perennially with us, was
answered in the first century not only by St. Paul but also by the
synoptic Evangelists, St. John, and the author of the Letter to the
Hebrews, of whose reports Voegelin makes no use. What is more,
Voegelin's exegesis of St. Paul would not have to be changed if one
removed Jesus Christ from it altogether. Voegelin allows that Paul
shows that man is a creature in whom God can incarnate himself.
St. Paul, however, reflects on what it means that God did incarnate
himself in one particular man at one particular time. His speculations are about the consequences of this "mighty deed" of God, not
about the processes of consciousness, which is why general speculations and myths about "Heaven and Earth" are assimilable to
Christian dogma, but the reverse is not true.

If Voegelin's chapter on the Pauline Vision of the Resurrected
had been adopted as the early Christian theology, the Apostolic
Creed might have read: "I believe in God the Father Almighty,
Maker of Heaven and Earth: and in St. Paul his prophet, mighty in
vision, and in the Spirit of Freedom which he proclaimed." It seems
that, for once, Voegelin has approached a great spiritual reality
from a standpoint extraneous to it. Noting that he defines "the
Resurrection" as "St. Paul's vision of the Resurrected," we may infer that that standpoint is the same characterized by St. Paul when
he saw that the gospel of Jesus Christ must be "a foolishness to the
Greeks." If the shoe be fitting, Eric Voegelin would have to concede
the application to himself of his own remarks that "critical doubts"

about the life, death, and resurrection of Jesus Christ "would mean that the critic knows how God has a right to let himself be seen" (p. 243, where the middle part of the sentence reads: "about the vision of the Resurrected").

The reader will be astonished by the title of the following chapter, "The Chinese Ecumene," but may be assured that it is a necessary part of the whole argument. The ecumene, at first an expression for the place of human habitation within its horizon of divine mystery, was deprived of mystery when conquests and explorations uncovered "an unmysterious geographical expanse." At this point there resulted a conflict with the structure of existence which could be mended only "when the concupiscential associates with a spiritual exodus, when the empire associates with a spiritual movement." (p. 273) This process, which Voegelin has traced in the Near East and the Mediterranean, "is paralleled in China by an equivalent process." Inevitable questions arise: "Are there two mankinds who independently go through the same process? If not, what justifies the language of the one mankind in whose history both the Western and the Eastern Ecumenic Ages occur . . . ?" Voegelin allows for the differences: In the West, a radical break with the cosmological form through Israel and Hellas, giving rise to the "new symbolisms of revelation and philosophy"; in the East this kind of thing "has a habit of never emerging completely." In the West, the drama of mankind is "enacted by a society of societies, in China . . . in a single society," which, moreover, is "singularly devoid of associations with imperial conquest." Still, the fact remains that "the ecumenic ages occur in the plural." (p. 300) The concluding chapter, "Universal Humanity," opens with the provisional formula of an answer to this question. The "differentiations" in consciousness, succeeding each other, "advance man's insight into the constitution of his humanity beyond man's personal existence in society." (p. 304) As the process tends toward a reality beyond the social reality, the "structure of history is eschatological," and history is not a "merely human but a divine-human process." And now he presses toward the conclusion:

The mankind whose humanity unfolds in the flux of presence
is universal mankind. The universality of mankind is constituted by the divine presence in the Metaxy.

As always, Voegelin raises doubts about his own findings. In this case, they are three:

1. Why should there be epochs of advancing insight at all? Why is the structure of reality not known in differentiated form at all times?
2. Why must the insights be discovered by such rare individuals as prophets, philosophers, and saints? Why is not every man the recipient of the insights?
3. Why when the insights are gained, are they not generally accepted? Why must the epochal truth go through the historical torment of imperfect articulation, evasion, skepticism, disbelief, rejection, deformation, and of renaissances, renovations, rediscoveries, rearticulations, and further differentiations? (p. 316)

These questions, Voegelin tells us, are not to be answered; they "symbolize the mystery in the structure of history by their unanswerability." He calls the symbolism simply "the Question," which is "a structure inherent to the experience of reality." He shows through a series of analyses that the Question is a constant in various modes of experience, raising particular questions in regard to

a) the existence of the cosmos,
b) the hierarchy and diversification of being,
c) the experience of questioning as the constituent of humanity,
d) the leap of existential truth through noetic and pneumatic illuminations of consciousness,
e) the process of history in which the differentiations of questioning consciousness and the leaps in truth occur, and
f) the eschatological movement in the process beyond its structure. (p. 326)

This process, occurring "in the consciousness of concrete human beings in concrete bodies on the concrete earth in the concrete universe" (p. 333) is the drama of mankind. There is no "length of time" in which things happen, there is only "the reality of things which has a time dimension." Similarly, things "do not happen in the astrophysical universe; the universe, together with all things founded in it, happens in God." (p. 334)

How does Voegelin come by his findings? There are two kinds of findings: first the exegeses of thinkers, texts, myths; second the fitting together of these findings in Voegelin's own philosophy. Both are involved in the philosophical structure of linguistic symbols. We remember the experience-question-answer complex which he pointed out as a "constant" of consciousness. Unlike McLuhan, he would say, "the language is the message," but "only when read in the light of the underlying experience." If Voegelin has shed new light even on thinkers whom most people believed they knew well, it is because of his supreme skill in discovering in the texts language symbols that reveal the crucial experiences. Speaking of Aristotle, in his article "Reason: The Classic Experience" (*Southern Review*, Spring, 1974), he groups two clusters of symbols, first those of "restless wondering": "wondering, seeking, searching, search, questioning"; then those of the desire to escape ignorance: "ignorance, flight from ignorance, turning around, knowledge," each with the original Greek term. These he calls the experiential "infra-structure for the noetic insights proper." To identify and understand the insight proper one further requires an analysis of the "movement of consciousness," which in turn demands a thorough knowledge of the background of other philosophers, myths, and external circumstances. It also requires a sensitivity for the theophany. Eventually, then, the analysis progresses to the point where it is possible to formulate findings such as the one in the above quoted article:

> There is both a human and a divine Nous, signifying the human and divine poles of the tension; there is a *noesis* and a *noeton* to signify the poles of the cognitive act intending the ground; and there is generally the verb *noein* to signify the phases of the movement that leads from the questioning unrest to the knowledge of the ground as the Nous.

Thus the new understanding of Plato and Aristotle, Anaximander and Heraclitus, Cicero and Philo, hinges on the special vocabulary of each that Voegelin discovers as their personal creation and the key to their meaning.

In the course of his many years of work, his own philosophy likewise became more articulate through the building of his own vocabulary, of which the following are a few representative examples: *reality, structure of reality, process of reality*–that which is there not by human making, that which men are born into and leave behind when they die, also that from which they have experiences; *primary experience*–the original, unselfconscious experience of the fullness and totality of that reality, before reflection would analytically separate the various aspects, the *primary experience* being adequately represented by the cosmic myth or also such mytho-philosophical statements as Anaximander's; *noetic consciousness*–the consciousness originating in the experience of the *nous* (roughly: the mind) as the divine ground in which men participate through that in them which also has the character of *nous*; *the Metaxy*–Voegelin's noun signifying the in-between situation of "the spirit" and human knowledge, a term derived from Plato where it means at one point "in between divine fullness and human need," and at another "in between the One and the Unlimited"; *exodus*–the movement of both human knowledge and spirit outward and upward, leaving behind "what one has," i.e. country, security, formulas of certainty, a symbol coined by St. Augustine's phrase *incipit exire qui incipit amare* (he begins the exodus who begins to love); *differentiate*–a process or refinement, distinction, as well as deepening of man's understanding of reality through which certain aspects become *luminous* that were not so before and which thus has the character of a discovery and the awareness of the discovery as the process; *tension toward*–a Voegelinian neologism that combines "tension" in the form of unrest, inadequacy, wondering, sense of incongruence with a factor of "direction" which Voegelin sees as the constant "perspective" of consciousness, it being "consciousness of something"; *derailment*–the historical mishap of literalist misinterpretation of language that has meaning only as a symbol of theophanic experience but is eventually read as if it were the description of objects called "the truth." The list is long enough and will have served its purpose, to alert the reader to the same kind of attention to his vocabulary that Voegelin bestows on the materials of past symbolizations.

A brief summarizing assessment of Voegelin's philosophy cannot possibly succeed, first because Voegelin's insights have come through his work on concrete materials of the past rather than through system-building logic, and, second, because now as before Voegelin's mind is still open, his philosophy still deepening and widening, so that he would positively refuse to say: "Here it is; this is my last word." Provisionally, however, one may say the following: as already mentioned a philosophy of consciousness is at the core of his thought. "Consciousness" must not be understood as an idealist or even sensationalist concept. There is a reality apart from the mind and it can be known. Reality is both a structure and a process. It also appears in knowledge as hierarchical, from which stems man's urge to link himself to "more eminent" reality. In the structure of reality there is an everlasting sameness, most emphatically in the "things" and their coming and going. Man, insofar as he, too, is a "thing" remains subject to this sameness. But man, a thing that has consciousness, also participates in reality as a process.

At this point it might appear that Voegelin combines a philosophy of structure with a philosophy of process. The "process" of which he is talking, however, has not the character of evolution or progress, i.e. a steady automatic change resulting from impersonal forces. The process is history, and history occurs in and through the changes of human consciousness and the order resulting therefrom. Again, it would be a mistake to confuse this with Marx's dictum: "Men make their own history." History occurs in and by the tension between God and man, through theophanies over the time, place, and character of which men have no control, and through responses by concrete people in concrete cultures, under concrete circumstances. In this sense, while one may speak of one aspect of reality as a process, one must speak of history as a drama. It is dramatic in its key experiences and movements, its strong impressions of "before" and "after," as well as in its occasional "deformations" to the point of a "loss of reality" through the "closing" of the soul to the transcendent divine. Man's existence thus is necessarily historical, but there is no such thing as "history" as a series of pragmatic events strung up on a time line and conceived as that "in which" things happen. History conceived as a whole becomes the new "horizon of divine mystery" replacing the ancient geographic horizon of Okeanos which fell a victim to conquests and explorations. The theophanic events, together with the human responses, constitute history. The drama of mankind occurs in various places, sometimes simultaneously, sometimes independently from each other, as a drama that has a constant structure but a variety of contents, and an overall unity only because it is a human drama under God. As far as reality is concerned, it includes elements of sameness but also man, and thus is "a structure which moves beyond itself." More precisely, however, this movement is represented by St. Paul's insight that "transfiguration is in process in untransfigured history." (p. 302) In other words, there remains a world which becomes intelligible through the question of "the Beginning," in which there occurs a dramatic movement towards "the Beyond." It is obvious that the conventional categories of being, becoming, nature, human nature, process, epistemology, metaphysics have no application in Voegelin's philosophy. It is philosophy inseparable from history, both the historical past as the genesis of crucial insights and the historical process as the drama of existence; it is also inseparable from the experience of a reality intelligible only through its divine ground; it is inseparable finally from the experience of human participation in the divine through revelation.

A few queries remain. Voegelin has made very good use of the concept of "equivalences," but one wonders also about its inherent dangers. One envisages all experiences, symbolizations, spiritual outbursts, new insights of history lined up in a complete series and surveyed by an even more perfectly encyclopedic Voegelin. In the process of this conceivable survey, where will Voegelin stand? If he were looking at all the moments of "differentiating consciousness" that "constitute history" (p. 332) from where will he look at them? He himself has seen the problem very well:

> To accept the process of differentiation as the exclusive source of knowledge means, negatively, to renounce all pretense to an observer's position outside of the process. Positively, it means to encounter the process and to participate both in its formal structure and the concrete tasks imposed on the thinker by his situation in it. (p. 314)

If he "participates in the formal structure of the process" can he do so without participating in the divine ground concretely, through one of the theophanies by which men order their lives? If participating, in which one? If not – can he have a human habitat? He himself disclaims that there is anything like a sum of all truths, or a truth beyond all truths.

The problem becomes more acute when the encyclopedic surveyor of all "equivalents" proceeds to judgment and finds that there has been a "loss of balance," and later a "deformation." The potential task of therapy begins to appear utopian, however, when Voegelin goes further to say: "none of the several eruptions expands the exegesis of the theophanic event into a fully balanced symbolization of order that would cover the whole area of man's existence in society and history." (p. 301) The task here appears as not merely restorative but one of original achievement of what none of the "concrete men in concrete bodies in concrete societies" have achieved. A human being, even when he contemplates millennia, cultures, prophets, philosophers, saints, and the "process" as a whole, must be somewhere, and he can be anywhere only by commitment.

Finally, Voegelin's discovery of the "Ecumenic Age" suggests both a similarity and decisive difference to the age in which we live and which one may call the "Mimetic Age," having many of the problems identified with conquest. I would propose the experience of the Russian Chaadaev (1794-1856) as representative. In 1829, Chaadaev published his first *Philosophical Letter* which complained that Russia, compared with the West, was nothing.

> We have never marched alongside other peoples; we belong to none of the great families of the human race . . . we have not been touched by the universal education of the human race . . . a certain intellectual method, a certain logic is lacking in all of us.

It is an experience that later befell Mustapha Kemal, the father of "modern" Turkey, and Nehru, the leader of India's "moddernization." Moved by this experience, strong groups within a number of countries set out to import the West and at the same time to deculture their own people, by supressing its tradition and religion. From the resulting dissociation and confusion, one would expect eventually spiritual outbursts, and indeed we are witnessing

the first one, in the prophetic figure of Solzhenitsyn. One would imagine that his Mimetic Age, with its peculiar dislocations and
disorientations, might deserve a special chapter in the forthcoming
last volume.

# Conservatism and the
# New Political Theory *

IN HIS NOVEL, *The Eustace Diamonds*, Anthony Trollope has
sketched this portrait of England's Conservatives:

> They feel among themselves that everything that is being
> done is bad, – even though that everything is done by their
> own party. It was bad to interfere with Charles, bad to endure
> Cromwell, bad to banish James, bad to put up with William.
> The House of Hanover was bad. All interference with
> prerogative has been bad. The Reform bill was very bad. En-
> croachment on the estates of bishops was bad. Emancipation
> of Roman Catholics was the worst of all. Abolition of corn-
> laws, church-rates, and oaths and tests were all bad. The med-
> dling with the Universities has been grievous. The treatment
> of the Irish Church has been satanic. The overhauling of
> schools is most injurious to English education. Education bills
> and Irish land bills were all bad. Every step taken has been
> bad. And yet to them old England is of all countries in the
> world the best to live in, and is not at all the less comfortable
> because of the changes that have been made. These people are
> ready to grumble at every boon conferred on them, and yet to
> enjoy every boon. They know too their privileges, and, after a
> fashion, understand their position. It is picturesque, and it
> pleases them. To have been always in the right and yet always
> on the losing side; always being ruined, always under persecu-
> tion from a wild spirit of republican-demagogism – and yet
> never to lose anything, not even position or public esteem, is
> pleasant enough. A huge, living, daily increasing grievance
> that does one no palpable harm, is the happiest possession
> that a man can have. There is a large body of such men in

191

England, and, personally, they are the very salt of the nation. He who said that all Conservatives are stupid did not know them. Stupid Conservatives there may be, – and there certainly are very stupid Radicals. The well-educated, widely-read Conservative, who is well assured that all good things are gradually being brought to an end by the voice of the people, is generally the pleasantest man to be met.

We all recognize the likeness. We feel the kinship and congeniality. And yet, all of us know that this portrait does not apply to American conservatives of the mid-twentieth century. For American conservatives of the last quarter of a century have been a forward-driving force, an innovating force, one might even be tempted to say, an up-turning force. They have not been disposed to spend their time lamenting a status quo of this or the last century. Rather, they have mounted attack after attack against the status quo. For the status quo in America has been the liberal Establishment. That remark is not quite accurate. To be correct, it would be necessary to distinguish a social status quo from an intellectual status quo. The social status quo, an America of middle-class people, predominantly still individualist, predominantly still committed to free enterprise, predominantly still believing in God, the forgiveness of sins, and life eternal, has by and large pleased our conservatives. Their quarrel has been with the intelligentsia who have both alienated themselves from the traditional order of this country and have woven over it a network of institutions where "un-American" ideas are nurtured by academic deans, socialist press publishers, juridical sociologists, with-it theologians, and ideological bureaucrats. Even though no more than a thin top layer, it must be called the Establishment, for all through the institutions of this country which are concerned with meaning, goals, information, education, and moral correction there prevails, by tacit agreement, what has been called the second religion of the intellectuals, an amalgam of socialism, positivism, progressivism, and anti-Christian humanism. The intellectuals do not explicitly postulate this their religion, rather they take it for granted; yet nobody who "deviates in the slightest" from these beliefs will slip by the watchdogs of the academy, the press, the media, and the judiciary.

Today's intellectual Establishment is a composite of yesteryear's revolutionary ideologies. If they still speak the language of opposition they know how to mute and conceal it. The public hears their voice not as coming from the basement but as if from the seats of authority, the cathedra, the editorial, the textbook, the bench, and the regulatory office. They have been in undisputed possession of the commanding heights for so long that nobody can still recall ever having heard another message of direction. Particularly for those who seek and impart education, the thing to do, the way to prove their decency, is to conform to this message. The sole effective rebellion against this Establishment comes from yesteryear's anti-revolutionaries, the conservatives. It is they who now, rather than standing pat, take the bold step forward, voice the daring alternative.

Since our topic is the reconstruction of political theory, let us look at one of the most original, furthest advanced political theorists, Eric Voegelin. Since we are speaking of the public difference made by the thinking of conservatives, we shall not consider the whole work of Eric Voegelin – who in many ways is a professors' professor – but chiefly the two works that have been most widely read and discussed, *The New Science of Politics*, and *Science, Politics, and Gnosticism*.

## II

VOEGELIN'S restoration of political theory can be gauged if we consider what political science was unable to do at the time when Voegelin was a young academic teacher in Vienna. It was the time when fascism had possession of Italy, and Hitler clamped the iron heel of his stormtroopers on Germany. As he himself described the situation:

> Europe had no conceptual tools with which to grasp the horror that was upon her. There was a scholarly study of the Christian churches and sects; there was a science of government, cast in the categories of the sovereign nation-state and its institutions; there were the beginnings of a sociology of power and political authority; but there was no science of the non-Christian, non-national intellectual and mass movements

into which the Europe of Christian nation-states was in the process of breaking up. (*Science Politics, and Gnosticism,* 1968, p. 5)

The inadequacy of positivist political science when confronted with a novel phenomenon like totalitarianism can be gauged by the work of a leading scholar, Herman Finer's *Mussolini's Italy*. Painstakingly accurate in its facts, the book utterly failed to comprehend the spirit of evil in fascism. Its incomprehension was a fitting foil to Neville Chamberlain's illusion that Hitler was nothing more than a zealous German patriot who merely desired to unite all ethnic Germans and who could be appeased by offering him the German-speaking part of Czechoslovakia. Similarly, the educated classes of Germany, used to keep up with philosophy and sociology, could not find there any conceptual tools that would lead to an understanding of Hitler's movement and regime. With intellectually innocent eyes, they went forward to their disaster. On this side of the Atlantic, the positivistic "taboo on theory" had actually barred people from imagining that there could be any such thing as a distinction between a good and a bad government, or between irrational mass movements and *bona fide* political parties.

The experience of this intellectual helplessness in a dark hour of human history was the motive that spurred Eric Voegelin's forward moves into political theory. Roughly, the new terrain which he opened and secured can be characterized as follows:

a) Totalitarian mass movements result from underlying idea systems that must be understood as "variants of theologizing," as they converted religious symbols into mundane ones, thereby creating political "religion substitutes." To analyze this, Voegelin had to discover the distinctions between theologies rational and irrational, and religious experiences high and low. As he plowed into such questions, Voegelin noted that half a century earlier it would have been impossible to establish any answers in terms of scientific discipline. The task had become feasible since "for two generations, now, the sciences of man and society are engaged in a process of re-theoretization. The new development, slow at first, gained momentum after the First World War, and today it is moving at breathtaking speed." (*The New Science of Politics,* 1952, p. 3) In philosophy, classics, orientology, biblical studies, and comparative religion eminent scholars had done work that deliberately broke out of the shell of positivist limitations. This was the development that permitted Eric Voegelin to call his own book: "the new science of politics," a title that in no ways implied a claim of unprecedented invention.

   b) Using analytical tools developed through these scholarly advances, Eric Voegelin began to do new work in political theory, as he developed an in-depth understanding of totalitarian movements and their intellectual foundations. If one may be allowed to reduce this work to a brief formula, he showed that the totalitarian thought pattern had "immanentized the transcendence." Transcendence here is shorthand for the ensemble of historical symbols and concepts through which man had comprehended the divine in contrast to the "things of this world." Since the event of philosophy, the concepts of these two realms had been kept separate, acknowledging a tension between immanence and transcendence that is characteristic of the human condition. The totalitarian idea systems had attributed the absolute character of symbols of transcendence to forces and entities of this world. This amounted to a deification of something that ought not be deified because it could in no ways claim to be god. In other words, the divine transcendence was conceptually pulled into history and identified with political enterprises so that, as Camus remarked, "politics became religion" and "logical murder" was legalized.

   c) Further, Voegelin called attention to the character of these idea patterns as a closed "system" the internal logic of which was tyrannically used to displace human experience and the exploration of reality. He showed that Comte and Marx "prohibited any questioning" that might endanger their systems, so that the system itself was substituted for reality and became a false "second reality." (Musil) To use Maritain's words, "they impugn from the outset . . . the reality to be known and understood, which *is here*, seen, touched by the senses, and with which an intellect which belongs to a man, not an angel, has directly to deal: the reality *about which and starting with which* a philosopher is born to question himself: if he misses the start he is nothing." (*The Peasant of the Garonne*, 1968, p. 100) This givenness of being was removed in totalitarian thinking, the "start" of which is rather his will to power, first manifested as the power of manipulated concepts, then as the power to change, destroy, and manipulate being, which in turn requires intellectual control of the divine ground of being. As a result of ideological thinking politics, which Aristotle had recognized as belonging to the realm of "acting," i.e. human choices made in view of a given reality, now shifted to the realm of "making." Or, to use again Musil's language, politics, which had been understood as action within the limits of "real possibilities" was now being looked at as the "impossible dream," the creation of "possible realities."

### III

IN THESE analytical efforts, Voegelin developed a number of more general concepts of political theory which were first brought together in his two chapters on the problem of political representation, in *The New Science of Politics*. Representation, he pointed out, is not agency, political representation is governed by man's understanding of the society in which he lives as a "cosmion," a little world, so that it essentially represents the truth of being. This he proved to be an empirical finding applicable to all civilizations and all ages. Society is an integral part of man's self-understanding, for in political association man participates in the order of being which includes of necessity the divine ground of being. Thus the problem of God in political existence is not abitrary. It cannot be escaped.

Voegelin's thinking here has been called "theological." It is not. It is strictly anthropological – anthropology understood, of course, philosophically. Voegelin's anthropology is new in language and conceptual categories but in substance it draws on thousands of years of thinking fed by experience. Indeed, Voegelin characteristically has developed his concepts through an exegesis of texts of political thought from all ages and many cultures, not only of the philosophers but also of the cosmological myths. Historically speaking, his anthropology, while deeply rooted in the past, is also "new" because it is a restoration achieved against a background of two hundred years of the "contracted self," a concept of man willfully reduced to a fragment of human experiences and involvements. In contrast to his artificially reduced human reality, Voegelin has regained the full dimension of man's concerns, questions, experiences, symbolizations, and participations. The fact that this reality includes God does not stem from an intent to proselytize but rather from an empirical recognition of the full dimension of reality which humans have embraced in their endeavor at self-understanding.

a) In addition, we find in Voegelin's work the new distinction between ideology and philosophy. Ever since Napoleon had ridiculed Destutt de Tracy by using "ideologists" in a snarling tone, the concept has been used pejoratively. Marx used it to characterize what he termed the "false consciousness" of the bourgeoisie, Max Weber took the pejorative color of the term for granted, and so did Karl Mannheim. What was new was not the element of deprecation but Voegelin's contradistinction between ideology and philosophy which implied a scientifically elaborated dichotomy between rationality and irrationality. This was possible only after a painstaking reinterpretation of philosophy attained by a profound rereading of the texts, chiefly of Plato and Aristotle.

Voegelin disclaimed any attention to "return to the specific content of an earlier attempt" of political science. He does want, however, to return to "the consciousness of principles." This meant, above all, that one had to rid oneself of the modern notion of philosophy as an academic field consisting in a survey of a great variety of philosophies, like a survey of various opinions. The discovery of philosophy was an historical event in which there emerged a new mode of human participation in the order of being, a mode in which the mind and its workings became itself a basic experience of the soul. One cannot simply change the meaning of philosophy that was shaped in this event. There are no philosophies, there only is philosophy, a way of life rooted in experiences and articulating new and differentiated symbols of order.

Voegelin describes this event of man-becoming-conscious in the following terms:

Man is not a self-created, autonomous being carrying the origin and meaning of his existence within himself. He is not a divine *causa sui*; from the experience of his life in precarious existence within the limits of birth and death there rather rises the wondering question about the ultimate ground . . . of all reality and specifically his own. The question is inherent in the experience from which it rises: the (rational animal) that experiences itself as a living being is at the same time conscious of the questionable character attaching to this status. Man, when he experiences himself as existent, discovers his specific humanity as that of the questioner for the where-from and the where-to, for the ground and the sense of his existence. . . . The adequate articulation and symbolization of the questioning consciousness as the constituent of humanity is . . . the epochal feat of the philosophers. ("Reason: The Classic Experience," *Southern Review*, p. 241)

It was the new, philosophic mode of human participation which made the science of political order possible. But the concepts and symbols developed by the philosophers could not have any meaning apart from the motivating experiences. As Voegelin put it:

[The] Platonic-Aristotelian analysis did not in the least begin with speculations about its own possibility, but with the actual insight into being which motivated the analytical process. The decisive event in the establishment of (political science) was the specifically philosophical realization that the levels of being discernible within the world are surmounted by a transcendent source of being and its order. And this insight was itself rooted in the real movements of the human spiritual soul toward divine being experienced as transcendent. In the experiences of love for the world-transcendent origin of being, in *philia* toward the *sophon* (the wise), in *eros* toward the *agathon* (the good) and the *kalon* (the beautiful), man became philosopher. From these experiences arose the image of the order of being. (*Science, Politics, and Gnosticism*, 1968, p. 18)

From this analysis follows the criterion of rationality in existential terms:

Thus, the reality expressed by the Nous symbols is the structure in the psyche of a man who is attuned to the divine order in the cosmos, not of a man who is in revolt against it; Reason has the definite existential content of openness toward reality in the sense in which Bergson speaks of (the open soul). If this context of the classic analysis is ignored and the symbols Nous or Reason are treated as if they referred to some human faculty independent from the tension toward the ground, the empirical basis from which the symbols derive their validity is lost; they become abstracts from nothing, and the vacuum of pseudo-abstracts is ready to be filled with various non-rational contents. ("Reason: The Classic Experience," X *Southern Review*, p. 246)

The characteristic of philosophy is therefore the attitude of spiritual openness which Bergson has named "the open soul" as well as the intellectual openness which is the opposite of ideological reductionism, the willful excision of questions and of factual evidence from the record. And the philosophical science of political order is, like all science, firmly based on experience and ceases to be science as soon as the experimental basis is removed or ignored.

b) Philosophy was an historical event of the first magnitude and must be recalled as that. This insight served as the pivot of Voegelin's construction of history. An irrational concept of history has played the decisive role in the intellectual and social disorders of our time. Contemporary ideologies are all futurist. The future is given the place of eminent and absolute reality; this means, as Camus put it, that "no one is virtuous, but everyone will be." Ethics gives way to an absolute imperative to act, for the sake of history. "To choose history, and history alone, is to choose nihilism. . . . Those who rush blindly to history in the name of the irrational, proclaiming that it is meaningless, encounter servitude and terror and finally emerge into the universe of concentration camps. Those who launch themselves into it preaching its absolute rationality encounter servitude and terror and emerge into the universe of the concentration camps." (A. Camus, *The Rebel*, 1956, p. 246) It was in the name of "philosophy of history," an eighteenth century enterprise that sought to establish a science of history on the basis of an exclusion of the divine and the assumption of man's autonomy, which had set up the usurpation of divine rank by the historical future and the forces working for it. Unless one could find an intelligible construction of history as an alternative, there could be no escape from terror, concentration camps and legalized murder.

Voegelin's brief formula for an alternative construction is that "the order of history is the history of order." The mere sequence of actions and events, kingdoms and wars, rulers and dynasties has no meaning. Meaning is experienced when one mode of human participation in the order of being replaces another. This may happen as the result of the experiences and articulations of a few concrete persons, and within the limits of a small people, but insofar as what happens this way is seen as universally human, the concrete persons or small people are functioning as representatives of mankind. Nor are such experiences and articulations events in a separate sphere of the mind. They result in a new outlook on life, hence in a new mode of living. Borrowing a term of Bergson's, Voegelin has called them "leaps in being." A leap in being occurs when experience and insight rush in on established traditions with the effect of something like a "new truth," so that people, looking at their own past, begin to separate the "before" from the "after." Thus history, too, is an order of time stemming from typical experiences that result in ordering symbols. The symbols, reflecting the reality of experience, shed light not only on a particular "leap in being" but on the whole of human existence in time. Voegelin's work first concentrated on two such leaps, the first identified with the experience and insights of the Hebrew prophets, the other with the advent of Greek philosophy.

In *The New Science of Politics* he hinted, under the name of "soteriological truth," at a third leap identified with the experience of Jesus of Nazareth. The order of history, thus constructed, is no story of inevitable progress. A "leap in being" is indeed something like progress, but, first of all, any such leap always encounters also resistance, and, secondly, there is no guarantee of its permanence. True, once it has occurred it cannot be made undone or even neglected. It becomes a fixture in historical memory. But there is also the possibility of deliberate revolt against that memory. Even though it turns out impossible simply to fall back on the *status quo ante*, the revolt will result in a fall from being, a "loss of reality." What happens in such cases can be grasped only in the light of that order of understanding against which the revolt is aimed. In this sense, Voegelin is probably the one political theorist who has shed most light on the character of our time, as when he coined the formula "Gnosticism – the nature of modernity."

The use of the name of an heretical religion of the early Christian centuries was analogical. Voegelin showed that an analysis of ancient gnosticism helped us to understand the ideas and symbols that have played a major role in the shaping of the modern outlook.

In that context he also coined the phrase that has been so widely noted, of the fallacious "immanentization of the Christian eschaton," which pinpoints the chief source of political irrationality today. Voegelin's analysis of our time takes up the last three chapters of *The Science of Politics* and all of *Science, Politics, and Gnosticism*. It induced *Time* magazine to give a major review to his work, in 1953, and to commit itself to Voegelin's ideas for at least the following ten years. One may say, however, that it is regrettable that Voegelin's deprecatory judgment of our time should have occupied the attention particularly of young people, to the exclusion of his constructive philosophy, particularly of history.

The term "gnostic" has thereby lost its usefulness as a heuristic tool as it became an epithet, a means by which people excuse themselves from thinking as they gain in one-upmanship. In view of this regrettable selectiveness, it may be in order to quote here a passage from Voegelin's last major work, the fourth volume of his *Order and History*: "This ultimate mode of lastingness to which as a measure we refer the lasting of all other things, is not a 'time' in which things happen, but the time dimension of a thing within the whole that also comprises the divine reality, whose lastingness we express by such symbols as 'eternity.' Things do not happen in the astrophysical universe; the universe, together with all things founded in in it, happen in God." (p. 334)

## IV

AT THIS POINT we return to Trollope's portrait of English conservatives in order to find out something about ourselves. We have seen that that portrait is not our own likeness. That means, we have inherited a name but not the content to which this name referred when it arose. In other words, it does not make sense today to raise the question: "What is a conservative?" as we could not possibly answer that question in any way like Trollope did, by means of a portrait. Nor can we answer it by defining something like a party line. That is a political vice reserved to such modern movements as have crystallized around an ideology. There is a small group of Americans calling themselves conservative who feel collectively bound to a party line: the assertion that there is only a single kind of human order, the order of the market tending to equilibrium. That belief, however, does not even extend to all who are otherwise also known as libertarians; nor is insistence on market prices alien to those others who may refer to themselves by the awkward and ill-fitting name of traditionalists. The fact is that a name without a content, conservatism, has been arbitrarily thrown into the modern political scene and has stuck on us. But to whom do we refer as "we," then?

By the *via negativa* we can indeed group together all citizens who oppose and abhor the politics of futurist, revolutionary, progressivist ideologies which confuse civilization or revolution with works of human salvation. That problem first became a test of political judgment through the phenomenon of fascist and communist totalitarianism and legal murder. Having learned to recognize the spirit of political irrationality on that large scale, we were able to discover it in the politics of liberal welfarism too. Finally we came to discern the intellectual and spiritual elements of such perversion in religion, philosophy, literature, art, and the sciences of man. "We," then, are primarily those who feel they must say "no" to these tendencies and movements. But what is it to which we say "yes"? Basically, and in one word, to common sense. That is our affirmation in the realm of politics. Political common sense, however, is not to be had for the asking, in our time.

The *Politics* of Aristotle is largely common sense, but it is informed by fully adequate concepts of God, nature, society, and man. Today such concepts must be regained by a deliberate effort, for the wares available on the intellectual market are defective, broken, distorted, and phony. Thus whoever holds a view of man that reduces the human person to a fraction of his full reality cannot see man for what he is, and thereby bars himself effectively from common sense. Whoever entertains a view of history that destroys the present and past and locates all values exclusively in some human future, is also barred from common sense. Whoever acts under the illusion that man can create a new man, a new world, or a new society lives in a dream-world and is barred from common sense. Whoever looks on particular social forces, political movements, or policies as something like a hallowed cause that implies full justification, is divinizing human action and is thereby barred from common sense. Common sense is political sobriety that is fully aware of human limits inherent in the human condition.

Thus there is a philosophical and cultural patrimony to which "conservatives" are committed by their affirmation of common sense. In the face of modern reductions and distortions, they press toward a restoration of the human image in the fullness of its dimensions. That prohibits a willful exclusion of the transcendence, which exclusion is nothing but an ideological choice. They reject the false certainty of closed idea-systems because our experience of life is not systematically closed. They reject the false dichotomy of fact and value, the illicit tyranny of the methods of physical science over the knowledge of man. They disdain the ideology-ridden fragmentation of life and the human person in literature and art.

In all of this, conservatives are very far from something resembling *nostalgia*. Since modern thinkers and modern scholarship have already blazed trails of rediscovery, we simply decide to live and think *à la hauteur des principes*. We thereby know that in our time not all roads lead downwards. Left politics characterize the Establishment, but already are going from defeat to defeat. This may not be cause for celebration, since we are tied up with liberals in historical existence. But we rejoice in all signs of recurring sanity. Thus, with Whitaker Chambers we fully realize the grim significance of our fight against the assault on the human mind. But with Maritain we can also see, in the midst of much darkness, the stars weakly glimmering.

*This article is based on an address presented at the ISI National Friends and Alumni Conference in April of 1978, held in Washington, D.C. The theme of the Conference was: "The Consequences of 25 Years of Conservative Thought."

# Greatness in Political Science: Eric Voegelin (1901-1985)

ERIC VOEGELIN, one of the greatest minds of our times, died on January 19, 1985. We stand in awe, admiration, and affection as we now try to obtain an overview of his achievement. Even a summary is not quite possible at this time. Volume V of *Order and History*[1] will be published posthumously. In addition, a number of papers may still be released by the estate. It could be years before the final line can be drawn under Voegelin's publications. Meanwhile, following his tip toward understanding ideas by penetrating to the motivating experience, we may begin with the experience that motivated Voegelin. He himself described it as a double-pronged frustration with the philosophical ambience of his student years. Like Faust he sighed: Now I have studied "the neo-Kantianism of the Marburg School, the value-philosophy of the South-West German school, the value-free science of Max Weber, the positivism of the Viennese school, of Wittgenstein, and of Bertrand Russell, the legal positivism of Kelsen's Pure Theory of Law, the phenomenology of Husserl, and, of course, Marx and Freud," all of these leaving the uneasy feeling that they "imprison themselves in their restricted horizon and dogmatize their prison reality as the universal truth."[2] As a political scientist, he felt obligated to comprehend the nature of the ideological mass movements which, armed to the teeth, threatened the world with terror. In this task he received no help at all from his philosophical equipment. He concluded, even then, that "the center of a philosophy of politics had to be a theory of consciousness."

His contemporaries, at that time, enclosed consciousness wholly in "subjectivity," so that any consciousness relevant to political order had to be seen as "intersubjective." Voegelin experienced by himself an uneasiness with restricted horizons, which made him realize the source of this uneasiness as "a consciousness with a larger horizon"–his own.[3] From this one had to infer that a philosophy of consciousness required investigating "consciousness in the concrete, in the personal, social and historical existence of man, as the specifically human mode of participation in reality." From the outset Voegelin could see this investigation only as a philosophy of history. If he started his work with Plato and Aristotle, this was not a matter of accidental convenience since "the story of the quest can be a true story only if the questioner participates in the comprehending story." In other words, "the story cannot begin unless it starts in the middle."[4]

The temporal "middle" is, in a spatial sense, the symbolism of Plato's *metaxy*, the "halfway between god and man."[5] Plato applied this term to love, the "neither mortal or immortal messenger." Voegelin broadened the context: "The play of order is always enacted, not before the future but before God: the order of human existence is in the present under God" at all times.[6] "In the middle" also characterizes the human experience of finding oneself in a "stream of being" already going on and sure to continue after us. It indicates that human consciousness both inclines and has power to transcend its particular existence and the particular society, things, and times: it is "capable of infinity" even though dependent on a particular human body.

With this we have also arrived "in the middle" of Voegelin's philosophy. He began with Greek philosophy, a "phenomenon in history" but also "a constituent of history," no less than "history is a constituent of philosophy" as well as "a field of phenomena for philosophical investigation."[7] As a "phenomenon in history" philosophy is preceded, all over the globe, by the order of the myth, so that part of Plato's symbols concern his experience of an epochal newness of life that is philosophically lived. Plato and Aristotle are succeeded, on the other hand, by schools formed in their names through which occurs a hardening of this way of life into prepositional doctrines while philosophy sinks to the level of a contest between academics. Along this outline, then, Voegelin turned to a study of the order of the myth, the "cosmological empires," and to parallel breaks with the myth, primarily that of Israel. The vast scene of Voegelin's research is beginning to open before our eyes. If one may distinguish in his work the aspects of philosophy, symbolization, history, and gnosticism, none of these should be separated from the others.

The order preceding philosophy was characterized not only by the symbolism of the myth, but also by the fact that society as a whole was the lone source of order. The myth was effective chiefly as social ritual. Societies clustered around their myths so that different myths, or different gods, ruled in great variety. The break with this condition came as there arose, in various places, solitary figures of authority *vis-á-vis* society: Greek philosophers, Hebrew prophets, Chinese sages, the Indian Buddha. Now the question of truth came to the fore: the private person who was not "one of the scribes" and who held no official position, spoke "with authority" as he communicated the truth mystically experienced in his soul. At the same time the solitary persons of authority could not institute social ritual; they had to communicate truth personally, by means available to a solitary person. The imagery of the Hebrew prophets differed from the imagery of a myth. The Greek philosopher used the help of the disciplines of logic and argument. The philosopher's communication, moreover, did not convey stories about gods, but rather insight into the deepest movements of the soul, where the "order of being" revealed itself in the experiences of the "tension between God and man." Such experiences as *thanatos* (death), *eros* (love), *dike* (justice) were universally acknowledged and therefore amounted to an empirical control over the private thinker's subjectivity. Consciousness is not something enclosed between the walls of one's skull, it is "consciousness of something," the eminent reality of being, which "all men by nature desire to know."[8] The eminently new experience of the philosopher was of the *nous*, the mind which could reflect on ignorance as a movement and mystery as an "object." He found himself being "moved by some unknown force to ask the questions, he feels himself drawn into the search."[9] The *nous* was experienced not as if it were an instrument, but rather as "divine or the most divine element within us."[10] "Wondering, searching, questioning" became core concepts of a cluster of symbols "bringing forcefully home the philosopher's understanding of the process in the soul as a distinct area of reality with an order of its own."[11]

Voegelin's approach to Greek philosophy is powerfully innovative, not in that its elements cannot be found in the works of
other scholars, but in that he does not allow Greek philosophy to
sink to the level of a chapter in a "history of ideas." Nor do Greek
philosophers interest him as representing "schools," or even
Athens, seeing that they speak in the name of the constancy of
human nature. The history in which he meets them is not a chain of
ideas but the historically moving order of human existence. That
history is not future-determined. It should be seen in all its dimensions as the "flowing presence of God." This entails, for us, "the
obligation to communicate and to listen," for "the revelation comes
to one man for all men, and in his response he is the representative
of mankind."[12]

In the loving reunion with Greek philosophy Voegelin found, not
so much a number of concepts – although these he found, too – but
through the exegesis of the texts a mystical unity of souls past and
present in the quest for order. All human order originates in the
*metaxy*, "in-between God and man." The philosopher's wonderment, his "serious" search, his experience of being "drawn," his exploration of the soul and the *nous* resulted in the higher insights
that bear the mark of philosophy. The Hebrew prophets, approximately contemporaneous with Greek philosophers, experienced
the tension between God and man with a stronger emphasis on the
irruption of the divine into the human, that is, "revelation." Both
occur with "a temporal flow" of experience in which eternity is present. "This flow cannot be dissected into past, present, and future
. . . rather, it is the permanent presence of the tension toward eternal being, related to worldly time."[13] The tension is personally
experienced, but the experience is not an idiosyncrasy. He who experiences this tension represents mankind and knows that the experience must be communicated as authoritative. If one wonders
why important insights into order are allowed to arise in the soul of
one man rather than all men, one must likewise wonder why such
events as Hebrew prophecy and Greek philosophy are allowed to
occur in small and powerless peoples rather than under the canopy
of world-spanning imperial power. In Volume IV of *Order and
History* Voegelin gives full attention to these problems. Before, in
"Immortality: Experience and Symbol,"[14] he had met and analyzed
the other objection: "the experience is an illusion," leaving it in

shreds after a few very precise arguments. Now he turned to three fundamental questions:

1) Why should there be epochs of advancing insight at all? Why is the structure of reality not known in differentiated form at all times?

2) Why must the insights be discovered by such rare individuals as prophets, philosophers, and saints? Why is not every man the recipient of the insights?

3) Why when the insights are gained, are they not generally accepted? Why must the epochal truth go through the historical torment of imperfect articulation, evasion, skepticism, disbelief, rejection, deformation, and of renaissances, renovations, rediscoveries, rearticulations, and further differentiations?[15]

To these questions there is no answer, just as little as there is an answer to the question, "why is there something rather than nothing?" In Voegelin's words, "The questions symbolize the mystery in the structure of history by their unanswerability." The Question, as he calls it from there, is a "symbolism *sui generis*" and must be seen "as a constant structure in the experience of reality."[16] "To face the Mystery of Reality means to live in the faith that is the substance of things hoped for and the proof of things unseen (Heb. 11:1)." The questioning mind essays something like "adequate" answers concerning things and events in the cosmos, answers that should be seen as "equivalents" in history: the myth, the *noesis* of philosophers, the revelation of saints.

> The physical universe as the ultimate foundation for the higher strata in the hierarchy of being cannot be identified as the ultimate reality of the Whole, because in the stratum of consciousness we experience the presence of divine reality as the constituent of humanity. . . . Things do not happen in the astro-physical universe; the universe, together with all things founded in it, happens in God.[17]

Volume IV of *Order and History* begins with this incisive statement: "The present volume, *The Ecumenic Age*, breaks with the program I have developed for *Order and History* in the Preface to

Volume I of the series." With what did Voegelin break, and for what reason?

We have seen that his emphasis on the "concrete consciousness" as a source of "objectivity" introduced, from the outset, into consciousness the dimension of history. By virtue of its concreteness it is an historical event; history, therefore, is a dimension which it desires to interpret in its quest for knowledge. The intertwining of consciousness and history, as being constituted and as constituting, as participating and yet ignorant of the terms of participation, caused Voegelin to develop his philosophy of consciousness through historical materials, in consequent conjunction with a philosophy of history. In Plato he found a strong "epochal" sense, a sharp separation of the "before" from the "after," – the "before" seen as the "falsehood" of the poets creating the myth, the "after" seen as the truth of the *nous* and the philosophical symbols arranged in disciplined order. Voegelin called this event a "leap in being," since philosophers understood themselves not as inventors of new ideas but as discoverers of a "new life." The structural similarities between this particular "leap in being" and the one in Israel, and yet also a third, in Christianity, suggested to Voegelin a progressive succession from the cosmological order of myth and the political form of the "cosmological empire" (Egypt, Assyria, Babylon), through a process of "differentiation" to a higher type of human existence. The "differentiation" happened to the compactness of ordering symbols in the cosmological myth, from which the Hebrew differentiated the element of righteousness and Greek philosophers the element of the soul. This did not commit Voegelin to a progressivist view of history, since he also saw clearly the potentiality and actual occurrence of retrogression, as well as a "fall" from the new and higher order.

This first scheme – "cosmological empire" to "leap in being" to new order of human existence – became possible through the insight that the experiences and symbolisms of a Plato concerned neither philosophers nor Greeks alone but all mankind, which also applied to Israel. When dealing with the content of truth in political representation, Voegelin at first distinguished three "types of truth": "cosmological truth, anthropological truth, and soteriological truth,"[18] in each case "the truth of man and the truth of God" being inseparable, each authoritative, and each forming

human character.[19] No relativism follows from this listing of three
"types of truth." The "differentiated" truth is higher, and the
philosopher is not permitted to retrogress "from the maximum of
differentiation."[20] "The opening of the soul was an epochal event in
the history of mankind because, with the differentiation of the soul
as the sensorium of transcendence, the critical, theoretical standards for the interpretation of human existence in society, as well
as the source of their authority, came into view."[21] This remark
enables us to understand Voegelin's "giant cycle, transcending the
cycles of the single civilizations: . . . the pre-Christian high civilizations would form its ascending branch; modern, Gnostic civilization
would form its descending branch."[22] Thus cosmological empires,
leap in being, maximum of differentiation, Gnostic fall from truth
could be fitted together into something like a form of history, insofar as it could be known. That plan, which called for three more
volumes of *Order and History* to deal with the "descending
branch," was abandoned.

The reasons were, on the one hand, new discoveries of ar-
chaeologists and the historical sciences, and, on the other hand,
new discoveries of categories, experiences, and problems on the
part of Voegelin. Among the former figure discoveries of civilizations older than Egypt, and of early symbols in places where one
would not have expected to find them. Among the latter there is
the growing importance of cosmogony ("the Beginning") in its relation to "the Beyond," the awareness of linear constructions of
history long before the Greeks and of cyclical constructions right
down to the present. Two difficulties resulted: the impossibility of
accommodating the new materials and insights in the limit of three
volumes when even five additional ones would not suffice; "the impossibility of aligning the empirical types in any time sequence at
all that would permit the structures actually found to emerge from
a history conceived as a 'course.' "[23] Abandoning the overall form of
successive historical structures did not require the abandonment of
the principle on which Voegelin's work was based. On the contrary,
it was the consistent and persistent application of these principles
that had led to the two "impossibilities." Thus, in both the first
scheme of history and in the new one, the order of human existence
has a history. Advances, which result from "spiritual outbursts,"
produce sharp distinctions of "before" and "after," so that "the

order of history" is still "the history of order." By contrast, however, the new materials and insights required that "the analysis had to move backward and forward and sideways, in order to follow empirically the pattern of meanings as they revealed themselves."[24] New problems emerged as Voegelin's research focused on the type he called "ecumenic empire," or multi-civilizational empire, occasioned both by the conqueror's need for a trans-civilizational truth of his imperial, representative position, and spiritual outbursts of subjected peoples as a response to their experiences of anxiety and disorder. In any case, "the form which a philosophy of history has to assume in the present historical situation . . . is definitely not a story of meaningful events to be arranged on a time line." "Lines of meaning" can be found in history, but not a "meaning of history."

Voegelin has given us a new, deeper, and more accurate reading of Plato and Aristotle; he has rediscovered and restored the science of politics on the basis of "critical, theoretical standards for the interpretation of human existence," thereby enabling us once again to make value distinctions regarding political order not as a matter of sheer opinion but of strictly disciplined theory. Of these standards Voegelin's evaluation of modernity is the most important application. Had he not said, "the validity of the standards . . . depends on the conception of a man who can be the measure of society because God is the measure of his soul"?[25] Political science, centering on philosophy, is under obligation to abide on the level of differentiation attained by Christianity.

> Whenever in modern history a revolt against the maximum of differentiation was undertaken systematically, the result was the fall into anti-Christian nihilism, into the idea of superman in one of the order of its variants – be it the progressive superman of Condorcet, the positivistic superman of Comte, the materialistic superman of Marx, or the Dionysiac superman of Nietzsche.[26]

Voegelin did not engage in vague accusations: he traced fatal intellectual and spiritual mistakes in precise detail. The ideologists of our time are indeed aware of the poles of inner tension between God and man in which man has found his order of existence. Marx, for instance, admitted that the question of God was urged on man by "everything palpable in life,"[27] yet Marx proceeded to forbid this question to "socialists." The ideologists perceived, as did others, the dimensions of the Beyond, the Transcendence. They did not discard this dimension, but they perverted it by drawing the transcendence into the historical immanence, thereby endowing something human with the character of divinity. Similarly, they were aware of the eschatological element at the center of the Christian view of order, but they played false with the eschaton by misplacing it *in* history. This is the famous "immanentization of the eschaton."[28] The mystery of history is a part of the ideologists' experience as much as that of normal men, yet they manifested their disrespect by devising idea systems around a "stop-history" concept, the stop to occur either in the present or in the future. Such fallacies should not be dismissed as *jeux d'esprit*, diversions of an idle mind, for they have entered public life and given social dominance to "falsehood."[29] There resulted the phenomenon of the "second reality" where the spiderweb of thought replaces a commonsense perception of reality.

In assessing modernity Voegelin, like Hans Jonas, Gilles Quispel, H-C. Puëch, H.U. von Balthasar, made use of modern research on Gnosticism, a religion that was the great rival of Christianity in the first five centuries of our era. His achievement was to have shown conclusively that gnostic thought, while formulated with the strongest symbolic apparatus in antiquity, has continued as a destructive force in civilization and as an abiding potentiality of breaking with the spiritual order of faith. The ancient gnostic saw himself "thrown" into a diabolically created cosmos by the fault of a radically transcendent divinity. Man, who now could repair that original mistake and save the divinity, felt himself infinitely superior over both cosmos and God. Voegelin points to the contemporary actuality of this experience:

Whether the addiction assumes the forms of libertarianism and asceticism preferred in antiquity, or the modern form of constructing systems which contain the ultimate truth and must be imposed on recalcitrant reality by means of violence, concentration camps, and mass murder, the addict is dispensed from the responsibilities of existence in the cosmos. Since Gnosticism surrounds the *libido dominandi* in man with a halo of spiritualism or idealism, and can always nourish its righteousness by pointing to the evil in the world, no historical end to the attraction is predictable once magic pneumatism has entered history as a mode of existence."[30]

On the margin of that human order which has accepted the mystery of the cosmos, Gnosticism has continued as a rebellious will to "change reality."[31] Thus "the *gnosis* of the gnostic is *agnoia*, ignorance of the truth. But it is not innocent ignorance: he *wills* the untruth, although he *knows* the truth."[32] On the basis of the texts, Voegelin has repeatedly unmasked this will to untruth.[33] Again, on the basis of documentary evidence, modernity has been aptly defined as the rise of a variety of Gnostic movements and their doctrines to social dominance, resulting in profound disorder of spirit, mind, and practice. Eric Voegelin has guided us to an understanding of what is the character of our time, through his clear distinction between ideology and philosophy, Gnosticism and order.

[1] Eric Voegelin's works are quoted under the following abbreviations: *AE* [*Anamnesis*, trans. and ed. by Gerhart Niemeyer (Notre Dame and London, 1978)]; *NS* [*The New Science of Politics* (Chicago, 1952)]; *OH*, I [*Order and History*, vol. I: *Israel and Revelation* (Baton Rouge, La., 1956)]; *OH*, II [*Order and History*, vol. II: *The World of the Polis* (Baton Rouge, La., 1956)]; *OH*, III [*Order and History*, vol. III: *Plato and Aristotle* (Baton Rouge, La., 1957)]; *OH*, IV [*Order and History*, vol. IV: *The Ecumenic Age* (Baton Rouge, La., 1974)]; *SPG* [*Science, Politics and Gnosticism*, trans. William Fitzpatrick (Chicago, 1968)].

[2] *AE*, p. 3.

[3] *AE*, p. 4.

[4] "The Beginning of the Beginning," unpublished ms. (1975), p. 22.

[5] *Symposium*, # 202.

[6] *OH*, II, p. 5.

[7] *AE*, p. 117 f.

[8] Aristotle, *Metaphysics*, # 980.

[9] *AE*, p. 93.

[10] Aristotle, *Nicomachean Ethics*, # 1177a.

[11] *AE*, p. 97.

[12] *OH*, II, p. 6.

[13] *AE*, p. 133.

[14] *Harvard Theological Review*, 60 (1967), p. 251 ff.

[15] *OH*, IV, p. 316.

[16] *OH*, IV, p. 326.

[17] *OH*, IV, p. 334.

[18] *NS*, p. 76 f.

[19] *NS*, p. 67 ff.

[20] *NS*, p. 79.

[21] *NS*, p. 156.

[22] *NS*, p. 164.

[23] *OH*, IV, p. 2.

[24] *OH*, IV, p. 57.

[25] *NS*, p. 70.

[26] *NS*, p. 80.

[27] *Economic and Philosophical Manuscripts of 1844* (Moscow, 1961), p. 112 f.

[28] *NS*, p. 29.

[29] Solzhenitsyn writes: "Our present system is unique in world history, because over and above its physical and economic constraints, it demands of us total surrender of our souls, continuous and active participation in the general, conscious lie." *From Under the Rubble* (Boston and Toronto, 1974), p. 24.

[30] *OH*, IV, p. 28.

[31] Karl Marx, *Theses on Feuerbach*. Thesis # 11 says, "The philosophers have only interpreted the world in various ways; the point is, to *change* it."

[32] Gregor Sebba, "History, Modernity, and Gnosticism," in *The Philosophy of Order: Essays on History, Consciousness, and Politics*, ed. Peter J. Opitz and Gregor Sebba (Stuttgart, 1980), p. 241.

[33] Cf. his discussion of Nietzsche, *SPG*, pp. 28-34. Henri de Lubac, in his *Drama of Atheist Humanism* (Cleveland and New York, 1963), emphasizes the same element of negative will as the core motive of Feuerbach, Marx, Nietzsche, and Comte.

# Ideas Have Also Roots

ON JULY 17, 1980, the *Wall Street Journal* carried Irving Kristol's article, "The New Republican Party," which called for the articulation of a Republican "ideology." In an age of "organized opinion," – Kristol's synonym for "ideology" – the Republican's distaste for anything ideological has become anachronistic, he said. One cannot fight ideologies with nothing. Instead of at least sketching the outlines of a Republican official opinion, however, Kristol went on to describe the four elements which now make up the Republican Party, which description did not advance his purpose. This paper is meant as an attempt to respond to Kristol's call. I shall begin, though, pleading with Mr. Kristol to drop the term "ideology" in this context. Precisely because we do live in an age of ideologies, we need to keep this most useful concept which, as it has been employed in a pejorative sense throughout its history, helps us to distinguish between irrational political thought on the one side, and philosophy as well as common sense on the other. Having stated my one reservation, though, I emphatically agree with Kristol's thesis that you "cannot fight something with nothing." With the exception of Mr. Carter's somewhat wobbly sally onto the glacis of human rights, we have fought the battle of ideas exclusively with gestures which frequently missed the point and were also based on mistaken assumptions. The recent elections have assured conservative intellectuals, meaning all those capable of articulating the conservative persuasion, of a hearing. We will be heard with genuine attention, if for no other reason than curiosity, but maybe for not more than two or three years. Still, our situation reminds one of that of Edmund Burke to whom, in the 1780s, hardly anybody paid attention. Then came the French Revolution which

217

gave him his chance, and his intellectual response to it turned into words ringing down the centuries.

It is a response to our historical situation which we are called to formulate. That means we must avoid anything resembling Madison Avenue's approach like the devil himself. Nor is it incumbent on us to create a self-image. The plight of our age is too serious for such frivolities. Mr. Kristol is right in pointing out that we are beset, on the right and the left, with deeply irrational ideologies. "It is incumbent on us, at all events, to give a definite answer to the question implicit in the blood and strife of this century. . . . Ideology today is concerned only with the denial of other human beings, who alone bear the responsibility of deceit. It is then that we kill. Each day, at dawn, assassins in judge's robes slip into some cell: murder is the problem today." (Camus, *The Rebel*, Vintage Book 1956, p. 4f) Vis-à-vis this frenzy we must find terms for the mode of reason. Fortunately, the groundwork has been done admirably by great political theorists and philosophers of the last two generations. We are now in a position to distinguish clearly between activist ideology (the Fascists, Communists, National Socialists, Anarchists, and a great variety of terrorists operating today in small groups), and the "soft" intellectual irrationality that indulges itself in a dreamworld of such visions as "a world safe for democracy," "war on poverty," "world law," and so on. In all cases, though, we cannot simply come forth with rational alternatives: we must travel the negative way which moves to rationality through an analysis of concrete forms of irrationality. I shall make five points: two about sources of irrationality, three about their results.

1. The activist irrationality of our days is the kind of politics that presumes the character of an absolute, the absolute which in all tradition has belonged to the divine, the transcendent, the sacred. I am not referring to the kind of politics which takes sword in hand to the end of forcible conversion or the enforcement of conformity. That is bad enough. What troubles us today, however, goes further. It is a politics which sees itself as the absolute, to the exclusion of any religious authority. Marx may serve as an example. He disdained political reforms which he called "political emancipation." Instead, he called for "human emancipation." What he rejected was civil rights; what he embraced was the creation of a new man in a new world. He went on to claim that the self-emancipation of the

proletariat from the dominion of capital, by means of violent revolution, would realize that "human emancipation" not merely for the proletariat but for all men. Thus a revolutionary enterprise was lifted from, or above, politics and endowed with the character of an absolute good, which pushed its opponents into the role of absolute evil. Hence the drive for total power which alone could assure victory. Meanwhile, the enterprise itself is claimant, judge, and normative standard, all in one. It moves not toward a concrete objective, which is rather characteristic of normal politics, but toward an ever-expanding and ever-intensifying power, limitless because no particular object will satisfy it and no normative standard is allowed to restrict it. The concept of peace is alien to this kind of politics, as is the idea of the balance of power. Marx proclaimed the principle of "permanent revolution" in 1850, and Lenin gave it a new name, "protracted struggle," in 1920. Both men issued repeated and insistent warnings against the temptation to consider the revolutionary movement accomplished at any particular time. Neither peace nor its attendant, law, nor a notion of live and let live, nor even the axiom of a common human condition ties the leaders of such an enterprise to the rest of the world.

This is what Camus has called "politics (become) religion." His remark referred, strictly speaking, to the activist ideologies of our time. His analysis, however, has a wider scope, which will occupy us presently. For the moment, however, we must stop to make clear that we are not looking at the problem of politics and religion in the institutional sense. Religious establishment is not the trouble of our century. Rather, we are tossed about by irrationality flooding in through an intellectual breach in the divider between the natural and the supernatural. The kind of thinking which gives the character of salvation from all evil to progress, or to the wholesale solving of "problems," or the basic transformation expected from revolution, constitutes an illicit pulling of divinity into the historical immanence, and a fallacious deification of political forces and political mission, from which stem the polarization of humanity into two essentially unequal elements, and the justification of total power ("murder," Camus would say) of one over the other.

In belaboring what must by now be obvious, I am really making an argument relevant to the problem of fusion among the two conservative movements. For conservatives cannot make a recommendation in public that one must keep away from such dangerous merging of relative politics with the absolute of religion, unless we as conservatives recognize a religious absolute that must not be thus abused. It is the liberals' disregard for the religious absolute that explains their failure to see Soviet communism for what it is—a fallacious and perverted religion—and this failure in turn engenders the liberal disposition to expect an imminent turn of the Communist mind to rationality, in spite of consistently recurring evidence to the contrary, and their persistent attempt to reconcile what is irreconcilable. These are illusions that come naturally to an agnostic mind. Not that all religious believers are immune from it. Nor can one say all agnostics necessarily must be deceived about the Soviet mind. The point is that, when conservatives address the nation, the problem of mistaken politics toward the Soviet Union must be explained in its intellectual origins and that cannot be done if man's spiritual dimension is neglected as irrelevant. Conservatives, speaking publicly about totalitarianism must take into account the religious dimension of human experience.

2. Ideology is not confined to communists and fascists. We, too, have our share of it, and it shows in our policies. All modern ideologies have the same irrational root: the permeation of politics with millenarian ideas of pseudo-religious character. The result is a dreamworld. Woodrow Wilson dreamed both of "a world safe for democracy," and of "enduring peace," a "world safe from war." More recently, our national leaders have talked about "creating" a new society, a "Great Society," and to that end making "war against poverty," "war against hunger," "creating new men," "making the world new as at the beginning," building "a city shining on a hill." All these presume that man could create himself, implying that he is not a creature, dependent on God, but the master of his own soul and destiny. Civilizational activities are given the character of salvation and thus stamped with a label of sacredness.

In foreign policy, the decision-makers themselves talk to each other in ideological jargon. Eric Voegelin has described their situation:

> The identification of dream and reality as a matter of principle has practical results which may appear strange but can

hardly be considered surprising. . . . Gnostic societies and their leaders will recognize dangers to their existence when they develop, but such dangers will not be met by appropriate actions in the world of reality. They will rather be met by magic operations in the dreamworld, such as disapproval, moral condemnation, declarations of intention, resolutions, appeals to the opinion of mankind, branding of enemies as aggressors, outlawing of war, propaganda for world peace and world government, etc. If a war has a purpose at all, it is the restoration of a balance of forces and not the aggravation of disturbance. . . . Instead the Gnostic politicians have put a Soviet army on the Elbe, surrendered China to the Communists, at the same time demilitarized Germany and Japan, and in addition demilitarized our own army. The facts are trite, and yet it is perhaps not sufficiently realized that never before in the history of mankind has a world power used a victory deliberately for the purpose of creating a power vacuum to its own disadvantage. (*The New Science of Politics*, 1952, pp. 170, 172)

Voegelin wrote thirty years ago, but today our policies toward the Soviet Union, the Salt treaties, détente, our mistaking condemnation of the invasion of Afghanistan for action, our persistent use of the term "aggressor" as if it were an efficient weapon, the "banning" of certain means of power, for instance, poison gas, the constantly reiterated expectation of "peace in our time," or "enduring peace," all these testify to a besetting lack of a sense of reality in our foreign policies. We introduced "human rights" into our foreign policy not as a weapon of propaganda, which it properly is, but rather as a pretension on our part to play the role of a kind of world supervisor, a global governess, chiefly in dealing out punishment to our own friends. We set up the United Nations with the implicit expectation that it could and would function as a kind of embryonic world government, and we still acknowledge that pretension even in the face of ridiculously unrealistic results. Sobriety in foreign as well as domestic policies cannot be restored unless we, the conservative element in our nation, are united in recognizing that in all these cases the "dreamworld" stems from the illicit mixture of pragmatic politics with misplaced religious expectations, which in turn requires us to acknowledge the right place of religious expectations. One need not be a believer in order to treat man's religious hopes with the seriousness they deserve. The problem of our time is a Western intellect disoriented by inadequate religion.

3. If our domestic policies suffer from a touch of millenarian illusion, they suffer even more from the loss of a concept of man. The evidence is all around us: Modern novels and stories are filled not with living characters but rather with ciphers which represent an aspect of ideological abstraction, or else an abstractly presented "problem." The theater and the screen are served by writers who have difficulty in finding plots, i.e. stories of the drama of human souls. So they invent either unreal happenings or else make "stories" out of technical problems, reminding one of the theatrical fare of the Soviet Union which invariably turns on the problems of the factory or collective farm, or at most the armed forces. But the loss of a concept of man is manifest in other fields. Philosophers no longer talk about man, but only about the meaning of words. In jurisprudence they do not consider moral responsibility but rather circumstantial influences, or sickness. In education man is seen as completely malleable, an object for conditioning. Welfare work operates on the notion of social objectives which no longer have anything to do with persons. The list could go on.

The concept of man was not lost all at once but over a long period. It is impossible to tell or even sketch the story here. By way of example, let us merely quote a remark by Henri de Lubac, in his analysis of the positivism of Auguste Comte, embodied in Comte's writings of the 1830s and '40s. Comte was determined to "do without God," and envisaged a universe of nothing but phenomena which could be fully known by the methods of the natural sciences. Positive sciences, as he called them, did not admit of any doubt and did not allow any disobedience or even variance of opinion. Comte postulated a social order dominated by "sociology," a science which had made morality a matter of scientific knowledge that was undisputable. "Thus," says Lubac, "if man, in his moral being, is crushed by society, it is because, in his essence, he is first crushed by the universe. The positivist order is an acceptance of Inevitability. There is nothing in man that escapes its blind face." (*The Drama of Atheist Humanism*, Meridian Books, 1963, p. 157)

Reductionism also loses the whole man. Marx sees nothing but the economic aspects of human life, treating everything that pertains to human consciousness as secondary and derived. Man's economic activities and relations alone are counted as real, as far as society and history are concerned. Values are merely subjective and therefore unreal. Similarly Freud also reduces man to a fragment, the hidden but ultimate reality of the unconscious. Freud does acknowledge the governing function of reason but finds that its result, civilization, is always beset by endemic discontents, because the "real" man is located elsewhere. Hence psychology as a science knows, on the whole, only the neurotic man, the sick man, mistaking him for the whole of human reality. Again this inadequate concept of man is amply manifested in our literature.

The story of this loss of the fullness of man is a long one, but it is intrinsically bound up with the rebellion against Christianity. One can recognize and deplore the problem without being able to name a remedy. I am convinced that one cannot merely wish for a concept of man and obtain it instantly, as from a fairy. There is such a thing as an area of intellectual destruction where no growth is possible. The destruction began with the Enlightenment and was continued by Romanticism, so that now there is a "Wasteland." As our libertarians manifestly are heirs to the Enlightenment it would simply not do to address to them an urgent appeal to restore the concept of man. But there are those who have not left the ground of the Christian tradition and who are still capable to envisage the concept of man which Alexander Schmemann tersely defines: "Man – created; fallen; redeemed." "Created" – therefore having a recognizable nature; "fallen" – that nature vitiated by sin and thus given to evil; "redeemed" – in a renewed relation with the God of goodness. There were outstanding thinkers in the past, who, in spite of not being Christian, essentially accepted this concept of man: Montaigne, Montesquieu, Tocqueville, Jacob Burckhardt. These men represent the Enlightenment without having severed the link between themselves and the Christian tradition.

I should like to put these four up as my leading paradigms for the possibility of conservative "fusion," for they were men who, though unable to believe in God, did not worship an inferior substitute. In our time, one can turn to some great literature in which there are still living human characters, because the authors can still imagine the fullnes of man's experiences: William Faulkner, Walker Percy, Flannery O'Connor, Wyndham Lewis, François Mauriac, Georges

Bernanos, Robert Musil, Alexander Solzhenitsyn. Thus some islands are sticking out of the flood of devastation. Could we possibly agree to meet on these places? Russell Kirk, in his article, "Criminal Character and Mercy" (*Modern Age*, Fall 1980) resorts to factual reporting with a minimum of symbolism and a maximum appeal to universal experiences. Could that be acceptable as a mode of communication between two elements of our civilization who have lost the community of symbols as regards man? This method would be slow and tedious, but it might offer a way out.

4. We shall now move a little faster, as we turn to the loss of the notion of evil. In the Christian tradition evil was conceived as not having autonomous being of its own (rather, as a deprivation of good), and accounted for by the myth of the fall and the idea of original sin. The great wave of profanization in the seventeenth and eighteenth century swept this kind of thinking away. Human reason raised the claim that it is capable of knowing all, that no divine mystery would be left, and no mystery of man either. Hence the eighteenth-century explanation of evil as resulting from institutions that had grown in history instead of being established on the basis of rational knowledge. It followed that evil could be removed through new and rational institutions. The next and logical step was Rousseau's teaching that man is good in himself, as witnessed by the happy and noble savage. All that is needed is a return to nature. The nineteenth century then was full of programs of freedom conceived as releasing or restoring this basic goodness. There could be no more evil "if only the will of the people were to prevail," or "if there were no more private property," or "if the market forces were allowed to work freely," or "if authority were eliminated," or "if the unconscious were adequately recognized," or "if all restraints and rules were abolished." In our century, finally, there is no more concept of evil, in the minds of many, if not most, educated people. There may be grievances, disease, frustrations, but all these are causes that can be remedied with assurance of success. At any rate, evil is located in the environment rather than in the human heart.

If I said that this is the assumption in the minds of many people, I should have further qualified it by saying, "in most cases." For while evil had indeed disappeared from our thinking about man, it is still attributed to some men. Hitler, and Nazi Germany, are undoubtedly something like the incarnation of evil, in liberal eyes. Likewise, they think of Nixon as evil in himself, rather than as a victim of circumstances. From these exceptions results a residue of gnawing doubt that there may be real evil, after all. I would submit that these residual doubts all have been heaped on the back of what is now called, somewhat imprecisely, "Fascism," and that this service of Fascism as a scapegoat has something to do with the fact that Fascism is now dead and gone. For while Hitler was alive and Nazi Germany was strong, a good many liberals were quite prepared to look upon the phenomenon as basically rational and good, but distorted by removable frustrations. Thus Neville Chamberlain saw in Hitler only a passionate and somewhat excessive German nationalist. But now that Nazism has been smashed it seems safe to identify it, a present unreality, with evil, the perennial unreality, thus freeing the modern liberal mind from all residues of the Christian traditional view of evil.

One would think that banning ideas of evil from one's mind would bring about an atmosphere of unqualified goodness. Not so. The result, rather, has been a generally amoral atmosphere. Together with the awareness of evil the awareness of a definable goodness also vanished. If there is no more rationale of punishment, neither can there be any rationale of discipline. Again, our age is by no means consistent in that respect. For while dismantling the structure of norms that was acknowledged in the hearts of men, it is building up an external one, e.g., in the forms of "codes of ethics," codes which become necessary when ethics are no longer habitual. But there is no code of ethics available for criminals, and we are appalled at the ease with which people today commit crimes on any slight impulse. The liberal assumption of recognizable influences of the environment goes overboard when the motive of crime is often a shoulder-shrugging "why not?" Here modern anitnomianism becomes visible to the casual observer, as it also becomes visible in the rapid waning of sexual morality, and the directionless drifting of foreign policy. "The center cannot hold" is no longer merely a poet's metaphor but a horrible everyday experience.

5. Finally, let us turn to what I should like to call the "loss of the concept of politics." We shall examine this intellectual process in the context of two other concepts, history and nature. History, not a discipline merely analyzing the past, but the vision of meaning in

the succession of all that is remembered and all that is yet to come, has been at the core of Western civilization since Augustine. The Enlightenment made its cut of separation here, too, as it came up with the idea of progress which was embedded in a newfangled "philosophy of history." "The infinite perfectibility of man," Condorcet called this view of history. The movement is not only forward in time, but also steadily higher in value. In this perspective history began to appear as a process with the character of salvation, salvation consisting in the climbing and struggling of man rather than the saving grace of God. The resulting futurism, however, began to destroy the past as something that needs to be overcome, or to be combatted. Hence the utterly sneering and contemptuous tone with which the word "reactionary" is uttered. To be in continuity with the past is seen as something unspeakably vile. The modern man has cast his anchor into the future alone. There is his true home, there only are values to be found. "The movement which starts with Hegel, and which is triumphant today, presumes . . . that no one is virtuous but that everyone will be." (Camus) As modern man decided to live exclusively in history, i.e. in the anticipated future, he sacrificed the concept of nature, i.e. of an inherent order of being. With the concept of nature he lost the standard of normativity. "That which has no nature has no norm." (Hans Jonas) History, which has wholly displaced nature, cannot provide any standard of action other than the expediency of action itself. A last and feeble residue of the concept of nature is the concept of equilibrium originally underlying all economics, though now dismissed by economists. It still functions as an unspoken assumption, playing the part of the "mother" to whom man can return when at the end of his tether.

This leads us to the loss of the concept of politics. Politics, government, used to be based on an autonomy of meaning which now is being swallowed by millenarian history on one side, and the direction of economic processes on the other. Politics in the traditional sense had its clearly limited functions. This autonomous political function was established in theory by Plato and Aristotle, but it is also explicitly acknowledged by the Bible, the *doctrina Christiana*, and the Christian liturgy. By way of example, we find the limitation expressed in the Anglican intercession for "all Christian rulers, that they may truly and impartially administer justice, to the punishment of wickedness and vice, and to the maintenance of thy true religion, and virtue." If history, however, takes on the character of a process of salvation, with salvation to be attained in this world and by political power all limits vanish. Government then functions to "make new men," "create a new society," combat "the terrible force of habit," and in general to have everyone and everything "become what so far they are not." This, as Rousseau put it, "is a task for gods *not men*," which did not prevent him from assuming precisely this divine role and passing the idea on to Hegel, Marx, and Lenin. When totalitarian groups assume power, they are no longer in the political business of governing. Totalitarianism is irrational precisely because it is metapolitical. Camus' term "assassins in judges' robes" metaphorically grasps the phenomenon of men occupying seats of traditional power while being engaged in the untraditional task of making a new world. Mr. Reagan's habit of quoting Tom Paine to the effect that we are now in a position to make the world anew proves that conservatives are by no means immune to the heady notion of human self-creation.

The other direction in which government tends to lose its political character is economic *dirigisme*. Burke strongly emphasized the political quality of government: "the state ought not to be considered as nothing better than a partnership agreement in a trade of pepper and coffee, calico or tobacco . . . to be taken up for a little temporary interest." These words reflect Aristotle's original insight:

> The end of the state is not mere life: it is, rather, the good quality of life. . . . Similarly, it is not the end of the state to provide an alliance for mutual defense against all injury, or to exchange and promote economic intercourse . . . it is the cardinal issue of goodness or badness in the life of the polis which always engages the attention of any state that concerns itself to secure a system of good laws well obeyed. [The state] must devote itself to the end of encouraging goodness. Otherwise, a political association sinks into a mere alliance. . . . Otherwise, too, law becomes a mere covenant – or 'a guarantor of men's rights against one another' – instead of being, as it should be, a rule of life such as will make the members of the polis good and just." (Pol. III, p. 9)

Today, however, governments are judged almost exclusively in terms of trade balances, interest rates, labor's wages, profits, or welfare incomes. The ultimate of this development is socialism where the functions of economic production are fully merged with those of government, government then confining itself to adding courts, police forces, and jails to the means of production. Even "free" societies, though, move in this direction, e.g., when defining the task of government in terms of "monetary" or "fiscal" policies. As political obligation is replaced by economic utility, the bonds of allegiance are fatally weakened. Under the circumstances, wars become inconceivable, not only on the grounds of atomic destruction, but because peoples see themselves less and less as citizens and more and more as "coupon clippers." As a result, the government's mere possession of armaments is regarded by many as an obscenity, and the government's police are called "pigs." Society begins to crumble at its political center.

In this situation we, the two branches of what is called "conservatism," confer to the end of finding a ground for unity, a quest in which nations, and our entire civilization should likewise engage. We find, however, that unity cannot be attained by mere shoulder-slapping cordiality, nor by agreeing on wishful slogans. Let us remember the lesson learned by many of our intellectuals when the horror of the Nazi regime came upon them. They found that their mental equipment was simply inadequate to the task of grasping this new demonism. One had to delve deep down and rethink the very bases of our cultural and historical existence. To this end, one had to trace, with a new and more penetrating analysis, the intellectual history of the past centuries. Some went back to the French Revolution and the Enlightenment, others to the Middle Ages, still others to the first centuries of our era. Only in making this intellectual effort could they come up with concepts adequate to deal with the contemporary situation.

We do not face a new Nazism, and Communism has almost become an old hat for us. Our crisis, though, is fully as deep as Europe's was in 1933. Thus we, too, must begin to think new thoughts gained by retracing our intellectual history. Richard Weaver taught us that "ideas have consequences." We must tell each other now that ideas have also roots, and learn how to think by going to the *radix*, the root of our disunities. One byproduct of that kind of effort is that we learn not to blame others, as we come to see ourselves as part of the problem.

I am trying to say that, as we endeavor to find a united voice of conservatives, we must go the way of political theory, philosophy, and comparative religion, for in our time the choice is no longer between faith and agnosticism, but between a God of reality and self-deifying humanism. That does not exclude a discussion of policies or even programs. But policies and programs must appear arbitrary if they are not undergirded by common assumptions, convictions, and principles, and these cannot be just picked up on the street, as it were. One reason why that is impossible is the ubiquitous presence of positivism dominating the social sciences and to some extent also the humanities. Positivism, a late-blooming flower on the stem of Cartesian philosophy, bans all rational consideration of values, indulges in a fetishistic adoration of facts (all facts being alike), and engenders a fateful insensibility to all transcendence. Most contemporary higher institutions of learning impose on their students the positivistic "taboo on theory," meaning on a philosophical inquiry into the things of human order. Thus in this respect, too, we have to move forward by first going back in our own history, unravelling the strands that became knotted.

Implementing this approach, we could think of issuing a series of "notebooks," to which we might even give such a name as "Signposts." The *Federalist* model, however, is not useful insofar as the publication of articles by three authors under a common *nom de plume* was possible then because there was still a political theory accepted by all educated people. This is no longer our advantage. Hence our need to dig deeper, deeper into theory, and deeper into history. The particular issues of this series of studies, therefore, should each be written by one author, even though there may be several contributors. The entire series also ought to have one editor. It will not do to indulge in the practices of "pluralism" when what we are seeking is unity. The time is ripe for such an enterprise. More in this country than in any other Western country, the intellectual resources are at hand. Attainment is by no means impossible. But if it is unity that we endeavor, we need to begin with the united resolve to go on this quest.

# Reason and Faith:
# The Fallacious Antithesis

ALFRED NORTH WHITEHEAD somewhere described evil as "the brute motive force of fragmentary purpose." If one wonders about "purpose," one would hardly go wrong to impute to Whitehead a concept which, like Augustine's concept of will, embraces effect, imagination and memory, with striving. If this be valid, "fragmentary purpose" would be an aspect of "fragmentary reality." The antonym of "fragmentary purpose" we take to be something like "wholeness of purpose," or "wholeness of reality." One is reminded of a similar description of heresy which also centers on the fragmentary kind of heretical belief: "Nearly every heresy is a one-sided and exaggerated expression of some truth. The heretic sees one side of truth very clearly indeed, and refuses to believe that there are other sides. He takes a statement which is symbolic, treats it as if it were a literal fact, and proceeds to build an argument about it, as if he knew all about it."[1]

These remarks are made so that I may enter, at one particular point, into a fragmentary discussion of a huge subject that properly requires treatises merely for the definition of its terms: faith and reason. The difficulty of definition is augmented in this essay, as I shall argue, by an antithetical separation of the two, yet one must make a distinction. Do we call reason that which "the human mind, left to itself" spells out to explain to itself the world? Defined that way, the works of the human mind would necessarily include those of the "myth-making faculty," and thus all but the few "higher" religions. It also would include the "natural theology" of the philosophers or philosophical systems, not only Plato and the Stoa, but also Plotinus. Thus it becomes impossible to draw a line between reason and faith along the boundary between the natural and the supernatural. Hence, if we insist on starting out from a sharply antithetical notion of reason vs. faith, we find ourselves compelled to locate it in the positivistic fact-value dichotomy with its initial decision "to do without God," and "to submit to the object." In other words, the antithesis as such is very recent, and very, very young indeed. To reason, defined as "objectivism," faith would necessarily stand opposed as nothing but a subjective "preference." We recognize in these terms a modern jargon signalling to us that we are on familiar, but also dangerously treacherous ground.

Instead of making an argument in abstraction, I shall focus this essay primarily on two thinkers, Augustine and Richard Hooker. Augustine is selected because he, first trained in Greek philosophy, and then "by Christ" in Scripture, is the first thinker in whom we can clearly trace what happens when one refuses to say "either-or" and dares say "both-and"; Richard Hooker, because he is the first thinker to recognize, and analyze as "fragmentary" an argument from faith alone that will not stand the test of reason. Augustine's thought can be dubbed "meta-critical," Hooker's "anti-ideological." Both thinkers can be said to achieve a wholeness of "purpose," or of consciousness, in keeping with Whitehead's dictum. Neither is presented here by way of a contribution to specialist studies of these thinkers.

I

A GENERALLY accepted assumption about Augustine is that he was strongly influenced by Neo-Platonism and that he Christianized it as he worked it into his intellectual building. I prefer to take my *point d'appui* with Rudolf Schneider, who in the course of an intensive effort extending over a quarter of a century,[2] has definitively established: (a) that Augustine's entire thought is shot through and through with ontology even though he never established a system of ontology, and (b) that Augustine's ontology is wholly Aristotelian. It seems that Augustine, who of Aristotle's works read only *The Categories*, obtained his knowledge of Aristotelian philosophy in the schools of Carthage, and from his reading of Cicero. At any rate, all of Aristotle's important ontological concepts can be found in Augustine's *de trinitate, de civitate Dei, de genesi ad litteram,* and in his controversy with Julian of Eclanum, not to speak of many other works. Schneider's later book focuses on the soul, a topic in which all important ontological concepts play a key role. Schneider shows that the following conceptual elements of ontology are common to Aristotle and Augustine:

The *analogia entis*, by virtue of which both thinkers distinguish between hierarchical levels of being;

*potency and act*, by virtue of which both agree that a being having active and passive potency cannot be pure act and thus cannot exist by itself;

the *categories*;

the *transcendental qualities*, for example, the concept of oneness (*unum*) used virtually as a synonym for a being composed of form and matter;

the *inner sense* that apperceives the situation of being, the norm, and the appropriate action;

the *ground* (*aitia*), entering into the ontological structure of the soul as form, end, and movement, and into the general notion of composite beings;

the *soteria tou einai*, which Augustine translates as both *salus* and *esse conservare*, and which we may render as *renewal of being* or *preservation of being* although *salvation of being* would be literal;

the *concept of nature*, comprising the principles of movement, essence, and essence-end-movement.

This list, while not full, suffices as a foil for pointing out Augustine's further developments by means of Scripture.

We shall emphasize here chiefly the differences between Augustine's and Aristotle's anthropology and theology, always keeping in mind the basic concepts shared between the two. Aristotle's anthropology centers on the insight that man, composed of body and soul, form and matter, depends on other beings for the renewal and preservation of his being. He needs food to sustain the growth of his form, and, after completion of the growth, to sustain the continued existence of the developed form. Thus in order to be happy, man requires external goods as well as goods of the body. As he also needs goods of the soul, he is dependent on the fellowship with other human beings to enjoy them. Still, Aristotle is aware that the combination of form and matter cannot be secured indefinitely. While the form is the ruling element, matter retains a certain autonomy by virtue of which it outlasts the destruction of the form. Hence man, to save his being, must rely on procreation, saving human beings through the species. Also man requires for his well-being a political association so that he may attain to the "good life" in which rulers and ruled combined seek to save their being in association. To his gnawing concern with man's propensity to destruction, Aristotle provides two ultimate answers: (a) in a virtuous political order which fully develops the potency of the human soul, in company with others, man can attain what Aristotle calls "self-sufficiency," i.e. a deliverance from his ontic precariousness; and (b) even beyond this, man, striving to "immortalize," may lift his mind to the contemplation of the *aitia*, the eternal things, in pure *theoria*, in which his human concerns with external goods and goods of the body recede in importance, so that the threat of changes and misfortunes seems forgotten. These two constitute Aristotle's attempt to find "solutions" to the problem of man's ontic instability and dependence, solutions that seem to lie within human powers of attainment.

At this point Augustine carries Aristotle's ontological insights consistently further, beyond Aristotle's psychological conclusions and practical remedies. He does this by introducing the concept of man's "mutable" being, mutable as contrasted with the *actus purus* of God. "Mutability" means, on the one hand, that man is the one created being that also can conduct itself so as to change its nature for the worse. Thus, where Aristotle sees mainly the propensity of circumstances to changes, and the likely turns of "fortune's wheel," Augustine sees human life more profoundly insecure than that. To use the modern words of Romano Guardini instead of Augustine's: ". . . the existing order of things, indeed of life itself seems but loosely, precariously balanced across the chaos of existence and its uncontrollable forces. All rules seem temporary, and threaten to give way at any moment. Things themselves appear now shadowy, now ominous. Reality is by no means as substantial as it may seem, and personal existence, like all existence, is surrounded by and suspended over the powerful and perilous void. . . ."[3] With all his closeness to Aristotelian categories and conceptual structures, Augustine draws from them a view that is worlds beyond the sunlit cosmos of the Stagirite. Sharing Aristotle's insight that the renewal and preservation of being entail dependence on other beings (things and creatures), Augustine translates this into a general law of created being (*"esse cum"*) and logically extends it to essential dependence on the immutable being of God. It follows that, speaking ontologically, the *salus*, the salvation of man's precarious being, ultimately cannot be attained in this world of mutability. Aristotle's "self-sufficiency" can be realized not in the *polis*, but only in a new life of union with God. Likewise, Augustine replaces Aristotle's contemplation (*theoria*), the forgetting of life's care over the vision of the *aitia*, with man's *peregrinatio*, his pilgrimage to God. This implies more than a shift from a solution in the mind to a solution in the whole of life. It also means a shift from a static to an historical and dynamic principle.

> Yet those doubtless judge better who prefer to that knowledge the knowledge of themselves: and that mind is more praiseworthy which knows even its own weakness . . . for he has preferred knowledge to knowledge, he has preferred to know his own weakness, rather than to know the walls of the world, the foundations of the earth, and the pinnacles of heaven. And by obtaining this knowledge, he has obtained also sorrow (*dolor*); but sorrow for straying away from the desire of reaching his own proper country, and the Creator of it. . . . Visions have been sent to us from heaven suitable to our state of pilgrimage, in order to remind us that what we seek is not here, but that from this pilgrimage we must return thither, whence unless we originated we should not here seek these things.[4]

Augustine does not discard the treasure of Aristotle's contemplation, but realizes that pure contemplation will begin only at the end of that pilgrimage, where being is ultimately delivered from any threat of nothingness. Here roots Augustine's psychology, here his concept of will prominently involving the affects, memory and imagination, here also roots ultimately his Christology, all ontologically founded. "Augustine has established the prevalence of ontology in Christian theology!"[5]

Theology is Augustine's other great improvement over Aristotle. Both Plato and Aristotle, and not only they but Stoics and Neo-Platonists as well, had developed, a more or less philosophical (natural) theology. Aristotle's was confined to a few bare outlines. His God is *actus purus* and thus self-subsistent, and prime origin of all movement. Plato, Aristotle's teacher, had known more. He had more than once given profound and convincing accounts of noetical, mystical experiences of the Beyond. Apart from psychology, however, Aristotle's God is even ontologically inadequate. "Aristotle does not see that, when he understands God as a being existing in himself, everything outside God must in its existence and essence depend on God, if the concept of God is not to be made meaningless."[6] That leads to the following appraisal of Augustine as compared with Aristotle: "Aristotle has failed to carry through his ontological insights in the other disciplines, systematically and consistently. Augustine has proceeded much more systematically and consistently."[7] The reason for Augustine's greater power of unity and principle lies in his biblical faith. That faith, of course, did not come to him as the fruit of analysis and contemplation. All the same, he accepted it and committed himself on the ground of reasonableness as well as authority.

Thus Augustine's conversion must have had not only that deeply liberating personal effect of which he tells us in the *Confessions*, but also the effect of supplying for his philosophy "the other half," hitherto missing. Beginning with Aristotle's prime mover, he now sees further that God is creator of everything, the origin of all existence because he *is* existence itself, the maker of all essences, a good God whose created things are all good, a God who annihilates nothing but cares for, and saves, being. Thus to the total ancient philosophy Augustine adds a) the personal God, b) the goodness of God and of all created natures, c) the Christian faith in the recovery of the original goodness of creation by grace, beyond temporal-spatial existence. Further, Augustine had learned through his own experience "that the situation of being, the *unum*, must first be changed if one is to attain to the knowledge of the *verum*. Augustine's great achievement in ontology is his insight that the oneness of being has primacy before knowledge and will – an insight which in general theory was already available before him."[8]

Even though Augustine boasts that he was "taught by Christ and not by Aristotle and Chrysippus," he has no practical difficulty with assimilating one to the other. Christian faith provided insights that could not be attained by philosophers on their own, but fitted harmoniously with philosophically secured truth. Mortimer Adler has said: "Philosophy produces a shell into which faith can be poured."

It may be more accurate that philosophy provides a structure in which faith finds confirmation of its reasonableness, in turn providing that structure with depth and height in which consciousness attains wholeness. Whitehead's wholeness of purpose certainly must include concern with vision of eternal things capable of overcoming man's exclusive preoccupation with short-range temporal purposes. The problem of faith and reason, however, is not located at this point. The problem is found in the way in which the philosopher arrives at the idea of God by way of inferring strong probabilities from his observation of things seen and unseen. "There *must be . . .*" is what he says. There must be a prime mover, an ultimate One, a workman-creator, a divinity *beyond* the gods of our fathers, and so on. God is a product of philosophic intuitive speculation. This is essentially belief. Belief also figures in religion, but religion moves beyond belief to commitment, reliance, trust, and submission. Thus Augustine, in filling his works with scriptural quotations (even though his thought merged them with philosophical structures) created for his readers the difficulty that they could not accept the authority of Scripture except by a "leap of faith," a personal risk which to them might appear a betrayal of reason. Reason was taken for something all men had in common, but faith as something common only to those who had personally committed themselves, and thus as something "subjective." Augustine himself made clear that "praise of God" is a requirement for that kind of knowledge which he had added to ancient philosophy. Faith and love, thanksgiving and praise, are personal as well as corporate acts, which, to those who for some reason will not or cannot join, appear as illegitimate intruders in the impersonal universe of philosophical reasoning, and present a false note in the philosophical ideal of practical life according to Aristotle's formula, "deliberation without passion." Reason vs. faith, then, is a conflict not between two varieties of belief, but rather between an intelligible universe that opens up only as an individual submits to it with praise and thanksgiving, and one whose access risks no more than the acceptance of its axioms.

Two remarks can be made about this. The first rests on the findings of a modern book, that the supposed risklessness of philosophical and scientific thinking is an illusion, an illusion erected into a dogma by "objectivism" in our modern age.[9] Polanyi

proves in countless ways that there is no such thing as the impersonal action of the object on the human mind, so that "objectivism"
itself is a belief, and an unreasonable one at that. Rather, says
Polanyi, all knowledge involves an element of intellectual passion,
a tacit component of previous beliefs, as well as a personal commitment.

> Like the tool, the sign or the symbol can be conceived as such
> only in the eyes of a person who *relies on them* to achieve or
> signify something. *This reliance is a personal commitment*
> *which is involved in all acts of intelligence by which we in-*
> *tegrate some things subsidiarily to the centre of our focal atten-*
> *tion.* Every act of personal assimilation by which we make a
> thing form an extension of ourselves through our subsidiary
> awareness of it, is a commitment of ourselves. . . .[10]

This "personal" element, however, must not be confused with "subjectivism."

> . . . personal knowledge in science is not made but discovered,
> and as such claims to establish contact with reality beyond the
> clues on which it relies. It commits us, passionately and far
> beyond our comprehension, to a vision of reality. Of this
> responsibility we cannot divest ourselves by setting up objec-
> tive criteria of verifiability – or falsifiability, or testability, or
> what you will. For we live in it as in the garment of our own
> skin. Like love, to which it is akin, this commitment is a "shirt
> of flame," blazing with passion, and, also like love, consumed
> by a devotion to a universal demand.[11]
>     This personal coefficient, which shapes all factual
> knowledge, bridges in doing so the disjunction between sub-
> jectivity and objectivity.[12]

For myself, I wish that Polanyi had chosen another term in lieu of
"passion." Henri Bergson, philosophizing in a similar vein, points to
"emotion" as the source of all creation. Augustine's wide-spanning
concept of "love" comes to mind; and a modern writer might well
speak of "the affects." All these amount to what Polanyi means. Going beyond a mere analysis of the process of knowledge, Polanyi
severely criticizes "the principle of moral and religious indifference

which prevails throughout modern science"[13] and insists "that
science can then no longer hope to survive on an island of positive
facts, around which the rest of man's intellectual heritage sinks to
the status of subjective emotionalism."[14]

The other remark must question the subjectivism attributed to
Augustine by those who find his Scriptural dependence one which
is invalid because they cannot personally share it. "Augustine,"
says Rudolf Schneider, "does not insist exclusively on the world of
his own experiences, but believes firmly in the existence of real, external being beyond all experiences. Because there is being, there
can be experience. Because there is reality, there can be subjec-
tiveness. . . ."[15] To put it differently, Augustine believes in, and
speaks of, the same reality as the philosophers. He might have invoked Bergson's distinction between the knowledge "of the object
. . . a knowledge attained by the intellect . . . that is sought for its
utility to man, and which enables him to manipulate matter, and
thereby, to control it and act upon it," and "absolute knowledge"
which does not "move around its object but enters into it" and
which "attains the absolute" but, in order to do so, must be "in sympathy with reality without any thought of relation or comparison."
Thus reality has dimensions into which one must enter with faith,
praise, and worship if one is to understand at all. "Believe that you
may understand; understand that you may believe."[16] There are
dimensions of reality which must remain not only unintelligible but
even unimaginable to the closed soul. The open soul, however, loving and praising, while disciplined in virtue, will attain a width of
vision in which its knowledge of objects is not denied but finally
placed in the fullness of context.

On the other hand, nobody can deny that Augustine's *Confessions*
is a most subjective work. It has been called the first
autobiography – wrongly, I believe, for the modern autobiography,
on the model of Rousseau, penetrates into the self in isolation from
the world, indeed, in hostility against all that exists. By contrast, in
his *Confessions*, Augustine "describes the mutation of his subjectivity to God."[17] The proof is that he, through divine grace,
rediscovered an interest in the things of this world. "The path to
this point goes through the awareness and experience of the
fallibility of external things and of virtue. Along this path the interest in things is diminished until it is completely destroyed by

despair so that there is left only the knowledge of the hopeless *in-firmitas*. Through grace a new interest in things is kindled and they are seen in the way in which they are from God. The relation of God as *actus purus* to the mutable world becomes the central theme and the new vision of man renewed by grace."[18] One must distinguish here between the personal elements of religion and its public aspects. Augustine has portrayed his personal conversion and salvation. What he communicated publicly, however, was the *doctrina christiana*, which results in general assumptions common-ly held, entering into any human endeavor and awareness. This is what one may call Christian culture, a pattern largely independent of personal religious events, even though such events continuously feed and develop it. Christian culture is not the same as the Church. The Church, in turn, exists as a public community of praise and worship, of faith and love, independent of whether every single one of its members is or is not a believing Christian. In the same way, Christian culture will long survive the Christian convictions of in-dividual members. Its basic assumptions will continue to govern much of human thinking, feeling, knowing and acting even when Christianity itself, within the culture, may have come under severe attack and indeed, disdain.

One must expect, then, that Augustine's ability to penetrate, with the love of the open soul, into aspects of reality barred to the critically closed soul, would bring about a net increase of rationality in the total world view. Let us corroborate this expectation by means of three samples: Augustine's view of human nature, his concept of history, and his idea of the state.

## II

SINCE PLATO AND ARISTOTLE, the concept of nature, and especially that of human nature, has provided the chief norm for the order of human life. Essence was taken as the ultimate ground of inner possibility, so that man's essence rules his movement, i.e., his coming-to-be what he is. Reliance on nature as norm, however, led Plato to remark that a city in accordance with human nature was not to be found on earth, but was laid up in heaven; while Aristotle despaired of finding a city with a hundred fully developed, mature men (*spoudaioi*) in it. Both Plato and Aristotle (the former in *The*

*Laws*, the latter in Books IV-VI of the *Politics*) were compelled to
speak of order in the midst of perversion, where nature appeared
as a concept of scant relevance. Augustine, by contrast, developed
two concepts of human nature. The first describes human nature
"as it is from God," good in the proportion and hierarchical order of
all its parts, and meant to cleave to God for the security of its being. The second concept is that of human nature as vitiated by the
sin of defection from God. Augustine saw man as the only creature
capable of changing its nature, or rather, corrupting it, which
would not be possible if its nature were not originally good. The
result is a perverted nature, subject to inferior forces, bad habits,
and inner disunity. Fallen man is endemically disobedient not only
to God, but also to himself. The vitiated nature, however, still has
the endurance of a form, albeit a form defective in its false loves
and bad dispositions. Augustine's two concepts enable him to account for the irrationalities of social and political life on this earth,
for the "discontents" besetting all civilization. He can also refer the
problem of inescapable failure of even our best efforts to the
perfection awaiting those who cleave to God, without thereby com-
mitting himself to a gnostic declaration of war on the world of
created things around us.

Augustine's concept of history was perhaps his most incisive
break with ancient philosophy and culture. He perceived "the con-
tingency of the universe" and thereby opened the gate for science.[19]
For the ancients, who looked to nature for final ends, history was
without meaning or order. On the other hand, they considered the
future predictable, since augury and oracle contained keys to its
knowledge. Men relying on this knowledge, however, again and
again found themselves misled, so that precisely where they looked
for certainty, they reaped a besetting insecurity. *Tyche* and *For-
tuna* were powerful deities, but also notoriously capricious. Man's
well-being in this world was subject to radical and lightning-fast
turns of "the wheel of history." Worse yet, the quest for the "good
state" or "the best state" seemed almost quixotic. In the words of
Frederick D. Wilhelmsen:

> Given a polity firmly based on an understanding of the struc-
> ture of reality; given a compact nucleus of virtuous men
> heading this society and governing it according to good laws;

given the ideal of virtue as a public goal acting as a leaven throughout the whole community making good men better, indifferent men good, and bad men ashamed; given the material power and technology necessary to maintain itself against all internal and external enemies; given a level of civilization incomparably superior to that of the rest of the world; given all these things, and then add to them failure, not a failure unforeseen but one first adumbrated as the most remote and trivial of possibilities and later sensed as a real menace which ought to be rejected as absurd and even inde-cent, and then add again a failure now accepted as an in-evitable fatality whose sentence of death can only be post-poned by rear guard tactics; given all this, and we are given a polity confronted crudely and inexorably with the powers of unintelligibility, the vacant stare of the absurd.[20]

This is a conclusion which Marcus Tullius Cicero, falling under the murderer's steel, had to acknowledge with his last breath. It also would have been the conclusion to which Rome's sack by the barbarians, in 410, would have driven a pagan philosopher. For Augustine, however, the death of Jesus Christ on the cross, and his resurrection to eternal life, were the great light planted at the very center of apparent absurdity. Moved by his faith in the revealed meaning of God's death, Augustine could see history as the great movement from the corruption of man's being to its ultimate salva-tion, to man's deification in union with God. This also made possible a concept of Providence, the humanly unknowable but purposeful dispositions of a good creator and redeemer God. History's im-penetrable irrationality thus vanished. A new sense of freedom resulted. "The stars, in their unalterable courses, did not, after all, implacably control our destinies. Man, every man, no matter who, had a direct link with the Creator, the Ruler of the stars themselves. . . . It was no longer a small and select company which, thanks to some secret means of escape, could break the charmed circle: it was mankind as a whole which found its night suddenly il-luminated. . . . No more circle! No more blind hazard! No more Fate! Transcendent God, God the friend of men, revealed in Jesus, opened for all a way which nothing would ever bar again."[21] The future, once considered predictable by magic and deceptive means, now appeared open, its possibilities a human responsibility, its ultimate outcome in the hands of a God of Love. "The future is open, and it is God's." Nor was any speculation on the basis of a scriptural numbers game allowed to take the place of faith and Christian patience. The whole of history is intelligible because it moves toward an ultimate eschatological goal of divine justice and fulfillment.

Augustine's idea of the state ranks with his double concept of human nature as one of the greatest achievements ever in political thought. A radical Christian other-worldliness would have echoed Tertullian's view: "Thus there is nothing more alien to us than public affairs." A superficial reading may suggest that this was also Augustine's view. For he distinguished between two principles of human association: ". . . two cities have been formed by two loves: the earthly by the love of self, even to the contempt of God; the heavenly by the love of God, even to the contempt of self. The former, in a word, glories in itself, the latter in the Lord." The earthly city is not identical with the state, however, nor the heavenly with the Church. They are what in modern jargon are called "life-styles," diametrically opposed. Their mutual exclusiveness, however, does not spell civil war. The state is instituted to keep a peace and an order that is commonly good for both of these group-ings. The state, then, is homogeneous neither in religious nor in moral terms. The faithful of God cannot dictate terms of highest virtue, nor can the mass of egotists write their vices into law. This means that under no circumstances can the state be a paradigm of perfection, not even in theory.

On the other hand, it cannot be considered a matter of indif-ference by Christians. As a framework of peace, it constitutes the highest common good "on this earth." As composite as each in-dividual person, the state has no power to exist in itself. It remains beset by tendencies toward failure and nothingness. But even in the wretchedness of "alienation from God," Augustine finds the possibility of "peace," i.e., order and justice. Just as human nature, vitiated by sin, still manifests an order, even in perversionbso the state, populated by good and evil at the same time, operates under a law of order which Augustine spells out in the great chapters 12-17, and 24, of Book XIX of the *City of God*. Substituting for Cicero's unduly idealizing concept of a people ("an assembly of ra-tional beings where concepts of true justice are acknowledged") a better, because it is a more empirical concept ("an assemblage of reasonable beings bound together by a common agreement on the objects of their love"), Augustine likewise moves the concept of the state to the ground of realism. The state, in keeping peace and order, is the most important worldly institution in which all Christians should fully cooperate. Not being born from a community of the highest virtues nor even from one of the highest aspirations, the state, in keeping peace and order, is not performing a task of salvation. The highest destiny of man lies beyond the state, because it cannot be attained in space or time, or even by human powers alone. It will come by God's grace, beyond history and death. In his political theory, then, Augustine is not writing with the pen of theology. Cast in wholly ontological terms which are adapted to this-worldly realism by introducing the concept of original sin, Augustine's political order speaks to all, believers and non-believers alike. Realizing that the state, comprising within itself morally mixed company, can never amount to human perfection, Augustine has created the concept of the *limited* state, which has remained a hallmark of Western civilization.

## III

AUGUSTINE WAS the first philosopher to succeed in combining knowledge attained by virtue of faith in revelation with knowledge attained by the critical discipline of philosophical intellect. Even though critical philosophy as we know it came into existence only in modern times, one may well call Augustine the first post-critical thinker, who methodically and deliberately explored the relation between faith and reason in the wholeness of consciousness. If we now turn to Richard Hooker, we do so because we find in him another kind of discovery regarding that relation. His writing was prompted by finding in the 16th century English Puritans (and their *"Admonition to Parliament"* of 1572) a kind of consciousness that was feeding on faith while disregarding or even abandoning the bond of reason. It was Hooker's achievement to have recognized and analyzed this as a type of "fragmentary consciousness," an awareness which should have, but did not, come from the authorities of the Church of England. Hooker, a relatively obscure priest, wrote *The Laws of Ecclesiastical Polity* "though for no other cause but for this; that posterity may know we have not loosely through silence permitted things to pass away as in a dream . . ."—surely one of the most memorable opening sentences of any book. The Puritans' *Admonition* had demanded that the laws of England, particularly those pertaining to the Established Church, should be replaced by laws exclusively derived from the Bible, selected by Calvinist interpretation.

In his *Preface*, Hooker directly addresses the Puritans: "Surely the present form of church-government which the laws of this land have established is such, as *no law of God nor reason of man* hath hitherto been alleged of force sufficient to prove they do ill, who to the uttermost of their power withstand the alteration thereof." (emphasis supplied) Contrariwise: "The other, which instead of it we are required to accept, is only by error and misconceit named the ordinance of Jesus Christ, no one proof as yet brought forth whereby it may clearly appear to be so in very deed."[22] Hooker's criticism from the first invokes his own belief: ". . . there are but two ways whereby the Spirit leadeth men into all truth; the one extraordinary, the other common; the one belonging but unto some few, the other extending itself unto all that are of God; the one, that which we call by a special divine excellency Revelation, the other Reason."[23]

The Puritans held their belief not in conjunction with their reason, but separate from it, so that they adamantly refused to enter into any discursive "conference." This led Hooker to probe for the defects of such a consciousness—defects he located through the following symptoms: a) self-justification ("a singular goodness") based indirectly on the radical nature of their total critique of England's ecclesiastical order; b) tracing all the world's evil to the extant institutions of ecclesiastical government; c) asserting that the proposed Puritan institutions will be "the sovereign remedy of all evil,"; d) a reductionism that finds in Scripture only evidence supporting the Puritan demands; e) the resulting "high terms of separation between such and the rest of the world." In his own summary of this attack, Hooker attributes to the Puritans: "A custom of inuring your ears with reproof of faults especially in your governors; an use to attribute those faults to the kind of spiritual regiment under which you live; boldness in warranting the force of their discipline for the cure of all such evils; a slight of framing your conceits to imagine that Scripture every where favoureth that discipline; persuasion that the cause why ye find it in Scripture is a seal unto you of your nearness to God."[24] He accuses the Puritans of having formed "a cause," using the term precisely as we do today, when speaking of someone as "*engagé*." The "cause" is a world apart, not merely distinct from the world in which all men live together, but antithetical to it, and thus claiming for itself a singular, indeed, an ontic merit compared with which the rest of the world appears as mere refuse. The members of "the cause" are distinguished by a special knowledge, that stems from their "nearness to the Spirit," or the possession of Marxism-Leninism—to whatever source of truth from which all others are barred. Such faith is neither proclaimed to others with a view to sharing it, nor defended by argument. It is used as a title of certainty about which one cannot communicate, and which admits between "the cause" and the rest of men only the relation of conquest and submission.

This led Hooker to reflect deeply on the relation between faith and reason. "The general and perpetual voice of men is as the sentence of God himself. For that which all men have at all times learned, Nature herself must needs have taught; and God being the author of Nature, her voice is but his instrument."[25] In a sentence that recalls the famous dictum of the great Muslim mystic, Ghazali, "reason is God's scale on earth," Hooker states, "Wherefore the natural measure whereby to judge our doings, is the sentence of Reason determining and setting down what is good to be done."[26] And, with reference to the laws of ecclesiastical policy, he remarks: ". . . those Laws are investigable by Reason, without the help of Revelation supernatural and divine."[27] Finally, Hooker's teaching is thus summed up: "It sufficeth therefore that Nature and Scripture do serve in such full sort, that they both jointly and not severally either of them be so complete, that unto everlasting felicity we need not the knowledge of any thing more than these two may easily furnish our minds with on all sides. . . ."[28] The general idea can already be found in Thomas Aquinas. Hooker's specific achievement is the analysis of a Scripture-based political movement as one whose pretended godliness is spurious because its message denies and evades the common bond of reason that is valid for the relations of men with men. In a somewhat similar vein, the Muslim mystic Quchairi, speaking on the subject of "intuitions," states that they may come from angels, Satan, the natural man, or from God himself. "These," he says, "can be recognized in the following way: an intuition from an angel will be in conformity with reason and will lead to good works; an intuition from Satan will lead to sin, while an intuition from Nature will lead one to follow one's natural propensities, particularly pride and lust. . . ."[29]

## IV

IT SHOULD BE CLEAR by now that we have not attempted anything general about the topic of faith and reason, but have touched only on two particular points suggested by Whitehead's concept of "fragmentary purpose." Purpose, which flows from imagery, memory, love, and striving, can be fragmentary in terms of a reality that is nothing but natural. The central thesis of Michael Polanyi's book, *Personal Knowledge*, is that there is no such thing as a purely "objectivist" science, and that fanatical adherence to that fallacious concept can only destroy science. "The science of today," he says,

> serves as a heuristic guide for its own further development. It conveys a conception about the nature of things which suggests to the enquiring mind an inexhaustible range of surmises. The experience of Columbus, who so fatefully misjudged his own discovery, is inherent to some extent in all discovery. . . . An empirical statement is true to the extent to which it reveals an aspect of reality, a reality largely hidden to us, and *existing therefore independently of our knowing it.* By trying to say something that is true about a reality believed to be existing independently of our knowing it, all assertions of fact necessarily carry universal intent. . . . The enquiring scientist's intimations of a hidden reality are personal. They are his own beliefs which – owing to his originality – as yet he alone holds. Yet they are not a subjective state of mind, but convictions held with universal intent, and heavy with arduous projects. . . . He has reached responsible beliefs, born of necessity, and not changeable at will. In a heuristic commitment, affirmation, surrender and legislation are fused into a single thought, bearing on a hidden reality.[30]

This result, which Polanyi reached through a number of distinct partial analyses, finally enables him to group "the conception of religious worship as a heuristic vision and align religion in turn also with the great intellectual systems, such as mathematics, fiction and the fine arts, which are validated by becoming happy dwelling places of the human mind."[31] And finally:

> The enquiry into the nature and justification of personal knowledge . . . has led to the acceptance of our calling – for which we are not responsible – as a condition for the exercise of a responsible judgment with universal intent. . . . Calling; personal judgment involving responsibility; self-compulsion and independence of conscience; universal standards; all these were shown to exist only in their relation to each other within a commitment. They dissolve if looked upon non-committedly. We may call this the ontology of commitment. . . . The paradox of self-set standards and the solution of this paradox are thus generalized to include the standards which we set ourselves in appraising other organisms and attribute to them as proper to them. We may say that this generalization of the universal pole of commitment acknowledges the whole range of being which we attribute to organisms at ascending levels.[32]

Augustine's reality was less fragmentary than that of ancient philosophy because it took in "the whole range of being which we attribute to organisms at ascending levels." It also turned out to be a heuristic vision of the most productive kind which, among other things, produced a rational concept of the whole of history of which no previous thinker had been capable. The close linkage of faith and reason, even though the one is acritical and the other critical, turns out to be ontologically founded rather than being merely a pious wish to include everything. Hooker taught us the sober alertness required to hold these two dimensions in the necessary balance and mutual tension of consciousness. Their linkage can be immensely productive but contains also destructive potentialities. Where faith is mistaken for critical knowledge, and critical knowledge allowed to play the part of faith, a fall into an abyss of inhumanity may result. Occurrences of this kind are too numerous in our memory to make the above finding with a sense of triumphant comfort. The radical "scientist" objectivism that has crippled modernity comes from a deep fear with which one can sympathize, although emotional sympathy must not be allowed to seduce us into a philosophical endorsement. We find, once again, that being human is a risky business, beset on all sides with insecurities and pitfalls. Vigilance is the price not only of freedom, but also of truth and "responsible" personal commitment.

[1] Claude B. Moss, *The Christian Faith* (London: S.P.C.K., 1965), p. 48 f.

[2] Rudolf Schneider, *Das wandelbare Sein* (Frankfurt: Klostermann, 1938); *idem, Seele und Sein, Ontologie bei Augustin und Aristoteles* (Stuttgart: Kohlhammer, 1957).

[3] Romano Guardini, *Meditations before Mass* (Westminster, Md.: Newman Press, 1955), p. 192.

[4] St. Augustine, *De Trinitate* IV. 1-2.

[5] Schneider, *Seele und Sein*, p. 31.

[6] *Ibid.*, p. 30.

[7] *Ibid.*, p. 31.

[8] *Ibid.*, p. 21.

[9] Michael Polanyi, *Personal Knowledge* (Chicago: University of Chicago Press, 1962).

[10] *Ibid.*, p. 61.

[11] *Ibid.*, p. 64.

[12] *Ibid.*, p. 17.

[13] *Ibid.*, p. 153.

[14] *Ibid.*, p. 134.

[15] Schneider, *op. cit.*, p. 27.

[16] Augustine, *Sermo* 43. 7. 9; 118. 1.

[17] Schneider, *loc. cit.*, p. 20.

[18] *Ibid.*, p. 48.

[19] Stanley L. Jaki characteristically uses this expression in his books and lectures to distinguish a universe that has issued from divine creation and thus might not have been from a universe that is supposed to exist in timeless necessity.

[20] Frederick D. Wilhelmsen, *Christianity and Political Philosophy* (Athens, Ga.: University of Georgia Press, 1978), p. 67.

[21] Henri de Lubac, *The Drama of Atheist Humanism* (Cleveland and New York: Meridian Books, 1963), p. 5.

[22] John Keble, ed., *The Works of Mr. Richard Hooker*, 3 vols. (Oxford: Oxford University Press, 1874), Preface ii. 1.

23 *Ibid.*, Preface iii, 10.
24 *Ibid.*, Preface iii, 16.
25 *Ibid.*, Book I. viii, 3.
26 *Ibid.*, Book I. viii, 8.
27 *Ibid.*, Book I. viii, 9.
28 *Ibid.*, Book I. xiv, 5.
29 Quoted in R. C. Zaehner, *Mysticism Sacred and Profane* (Oxford: Oxford University Press, 1967), p. 144.
30 Polanyi, *op. cit.*, p. 311.
31 *Ibid.*, p. 280.
32 *Ibid.*, p. 379.

# What Price "Natural Law"?

"Natural" and "law" form a particular symbol pertaining to one mode of discovering the order of goodness, this mode invented by the classical Greek philosophers. They relied on a number of basic experiences and symbolic concepts: a) the *nous* (mind, reason); something divine in man participating in the mind of divinity; b) the distinction between "being" as the immanent order of "things" and "being" as the divine transcendence; c) the realization that man, possessing language and moral discernment, has an order not merely as a "thing" but also as a participating partner of the transcendence.

In modern times these concepts and underlying experiences have been lost. "Mind" and "rationality" to us mean the opposite of what they meant to the Greek philosophers. We have no longer a concept of "man" resembling theirs; the concept of "soul" has disappeared; all values are completely relativized. We cannot, therefore, bring back "natural law" simply by reading the classical texts. The awareness of the order of goodness must be regained, but we have to pay a price for that. It probably requires the kind of deeply shaking experiences that came to members of Soviet labor camps as described by Solzhenitsyn and his friends. It also would include jettisoning our Enlightenment concept of history. Short of such sacrifices we would do well to use the concept "natural law" reluctantly, if at all.

THERE IS AN ORDER of goodness in the universe, and human knowledge can attain to it. The proposition is made here as an assertion and an affirmation. In the context of the question raised by this paper it comes as a premise which, if we did not have it, would leave us without anything to talk about. The statement avoids not only the terms "ethical," and "moral," but also "law," and "nature,"—all of these being words containing opinions where and how the order of goodness may be discovered, which is the question to be explored in this paper. That question, in our time, is raised for us politically. The frequent and urgent demand that we "return" to natural law, to which sometimes is added "and to classical philosophy," is felt in the context of politics and cultural crisis. The word "return," I take it, is not meant as "return to something that has passed out of reality," but rather, "return to the lost knowledge of an undoubted and continuing reality." At issue, then, is above all knowability, and that concerning the order of goodness, by way of "natural law."

"Natural law" and "the order of goodness in the universe" are not to be taken as synonyms. "Natural law," or, in Aristotle's words, *physei dikaion*, is a symbolic form of human consciousness which came with classical Greek philosophy. One cannot assume that "before philosophy" people knew nothing about the order of goodness in the universe. At least Aristotle assumes that they did when he observed that philosophy is rooted in men's "wondering," the root of philosophy, but conceded that a "lover of myth" was also in a sense a "lover of wisdom," for "the myth is (also) composed of wonders."[1] Thus the knowledge of goodness through the symbol of *physis* (nature) has a specific character, a historical setting, and is attended by certain attitudes.

How can one describe these specifics of "natural law"? First, as Aristotle's remark manifests, philosophy, and with it, the symbol of "nature," are historically related to the myth, a complex relationship which includes both a rejection of the myth as mere "opinion" and an attraction to the myth as evidenced by both Plato and Aristotle, the latter being reported to have said, "the older I grow the more I love the myth." At any rate, Eric Voegelin can say without fear of being refuted that both philosophy and myth began with "the primary experience" of the cosmos as a whole, an experience in which the cosmos with the things in it appear to the eye all at once and hence as a whole, which led Xenophanes to exclaim, "the One is God."[2] The distinctive character of the symbol "nature," which does play an important part in Plato, is above all Aristotle's trademark. Eric Voegelin, in a penetrating analysis,[3] has distinguished the older, both mythical and Ionian emphasis on the movement of generation, and Aristotle's more static concept of form/matter, with the soul as the form of body as matter. As a result the former concern with "coming-to-be" gave way to the latter desire to understand things in the autonomy of their own abiding structures. All the same Aristotle in no way can be said to have produced a "nature" conceived as a closed and self-sufficient system. Not only did he devote much attention to the *aitiai* (the reasons, origins, or causes), but even with regard to the apparently self-sufficient form and matter he pointed beyond them:

> We must consider also in which of two ways the nature of the universe contains the good and the highest good, whether as something separate and by itself, or as the order of the parts. Probably in both ways, as an army does; for its good is found in both its order and its leader, and more in the latter; for he does not depend on the order but it depends on him.[4]

Moreover, Aristotle himself was quite aware of the limitations of the form/matter scheme when he tried to apply it to political entities, with constitution as the form and the population as matter, and, upon finding that it did not work, simply dropped the idea. Eric Voegelin answers his own question of why Aristotle narrowed his concept from philosophical awareness of coming-to-be to the metaphysical form/matter concept, as follows:

> The problems of the new thinking about being could obviously be mastered only step by step. The philosophical conception still preserves the nature of being as a coming-to-be that was already given in the primary experience of the cosmos; while the metaphysical concept accentuates the nature of things as being ordered by form. The two tendencies are in tension with each other.[5]

Asking further how this tension came about, Voegelin writes: "When the experience of being differentiates itself from the primary experience of the cosmos, it elicits the new image of the demiurge."⁶ The new discovery of this divine "forming power" must have been as fascinating as it was disturbing, and it led to the dominance of being as form over its coming-to-be. In the process the world of things is dissociated, as "immanence," from the divine "transcendence." Voegelin traces this dissociation in the famous passage about the *aitiai* in *Metaphysics* alpha, where the term *aitia*, he finds, is used in three different meanings: a) as "the causality of an immanent, temporal process regarding phenomena"; b) as "the four *causae* (*causa materialis, efficiens, formalis,* and *finalis*) by which one comprehends not so much things in general but rather those things that primarily belong to the class of organisms,"⁷ in which context man is conceived as an "immanently formed thing that has its fulfillment in thisworldly happiness"; and c) as the *causa finalis* of human action, "the order of human existence through the *nous*." In this area only, Aristotle rejects the infinite regress in the chain of causes as inadmissible, "since otherwise the "*nous*, the highest good, and the meaning of action would be destroyed." The being "of immanence, which we call world, contains no problem of *archē* . . . but only one of infinite progression." The question of "the origin or beginning does not arise from the experience of being but rather belongs to the prephilosophic primary experience of the cosmos. . . . The differentiation that is new in philosophy is the experience of man as a being who experiences the order of being and his own order as something in accord with it."⁸

In Aristotle, as well as in Plato, then, "nature" is a concept reflecting the experience of things in the autonomy of their own organisms, but it also refers to human action and the order of the good, although this second meaning comes with its own set of symbols. In this latter we have, from Anaxagoras, the emphasis on the *nous* (translated as mind, reason, or intellect but richer in meaning). In Plato, the *nous* is called "the god who is the master of rational men,"⁹ or "the immortal element within us."¹⁰ Elsewhere, "judgment and foresight, wisdom, art and law" are placed "prior to hard and soft, heavy and light,"¹¹ which means that mind and its order outrank nature. Accordingly, the human mind finds order in *metalepsis*, participation in the divine mind by that which is "divine" in the soul. Aristotle distinguishes between the *poētikos nous* (active or creative mind) and the *pathētos nous* (the receptive mind).[12] The full meaning of this distinction is realized when we read in *On the Generation of Animals* that *"nous* alone enters in from the outside as an additional factor and . . . it alone is divine; for bodily activity has nothing whatever to do with the activity of *nous.*"[13] Thus what is "right by nature," of which Vico speaks very precisely as that "inner justice by which the intellect is satisfied,"[14] pertains to a contemplative activity of the soul in which divine grace furnishes the creative element.

The Greek legacy of natural law, transmitted to us above all by Aristotle, has been shaped in a dialectic extending over two centuries and based on strong and paradigmatic experiences of the depth of the soul, the beyond of divinity, a kind of identity of the mind with the object of its knowledge, the simultaneity of confusing ignorance and the "desire" for knowledge of the yet unknown, as well as of the new order of life discovered through reason's participation in the transcendence. "Reason," "nature," "right" were philosophical symbols representing above all a way of life, precisely of the paradigmatic experiences. For our purposes, the key experiences are:

a) The "discovery of the mind" (Bruno Snell) as something between "ignorance" and "wisdom," capable of being "moved by the object of thought" even in the midst of ignorance, and, as "the most divine element in us" attaining to truth in contemplation;

b) The differentiation between the things in this world that move by themselves in an autonomous order, and the divine power that gives them form: in other words, between "transcendence" and "immanence";

c) The realization that man, a thing distinguished by language and the capacity for reasoned choice, has an order not merely as a natural organism but, with regard to actions, through participation in the transcendent reality of being.

It does not follow that the term "natural law," or even the classical texts containing this concept, would automatically convey these experiences. In the post-scholastic discussion of the fifteenth to seventeenth centuries, "natural law" meant something like a secure possession of men, an autonomous order unaffected by the existence or non-existence of God. The idea is usually identified with Grotius but can be found already in the German Gabriel Biel who died in 1495, although his book was published in 1501.[15] Later, during the period of the Enlightenment, the concept of nature was enormously enhanced, as it formed a triad with intelligence and energy, nature being the unifying factor, and God no more than a useful hypothesis. The obvious conclusion postulated that knowledge of ultimates could be fully obtained through the positive sciences which thus were seen, at least by some, as the key to the "knowledge of God." As natural science advanced one would even surmise that one had no longer "any need" for the hypothesis of God. These brief remarks serve only as a reminder that the terms "nature," "natural law," "reason," "order" underwent radical changes, so that one cannot assume that "returning to natural law" carries one back to "the texts of classical philosophy," or even that a "return to the texts of classical philosophy" would necessarily include a sharing of the underlying experiences of the Greek philosophers who explored the "open soul." Now these paradigmatic experiences that occurred in the soul of a few privileged men – Socrates, Plato, Aristotle, Confucius, Lao-tse, Zoroaster – are no mere private subjectivities but have the character of public events. They were neither biographic curiosities nor academic incidents but the beginning of a new order of life communicated through a set of philosophical symbols. It is this set of symbols, born from a way of life, that beckons us to a "return," – if possible. There, I have let slip out my secret fear: "if possible." Having done so, I must say more about it. Why should one fear that a return to truth might not be possible? How could truth be separated from us? Could human existence really be eclipsed by something like alienation? One would have to be bold to attempt generalized answers to such questions. On the other hand, concrete evidence abounds, of the kind of the poet speaking about a "wasteland":

> This is the dead land
> This is cactus land
> Here the stone images
> Are raised, here they receive
> The supplication of a dead man's hand
> Under the twinkle of a fading star.
>
> (T.S. Eliot, *The Hollow Men*)

The sample could be multiplied a thousand-fold. It speaks of terrifying realities. Personally, since I am no poet, I should like to continue in the language of conceptual analysis, as I deal with the situation portrayed by T.S. Eliot.

Plato and Aristotle discovered the "inner justice" of human order in the course of discovering not only the soul, but also its depth and its dimension of participation in the divine beyond. This is what Plato means when he calls the *nous* "the god who is the master of rational men." *Ratio*, then, is the mind of the "open soul," the mind that is "drawn" by the divine so that it "desires" knowledge and "loves wisdom." The discovery is not simple and compact but rather differentiated, complex, and existential along with cognitive. Rationality is also a word of great prominence in the last three hundred years. What we mean by "rationality," however, is not merely distant from Plato's and Aristotle's *nous*, but well-nigh hostile to it. From Descartes, with his starting point of systemic doubt and his insistence on "clear and distinct notions," came the concept of reason as a human instrument to gain power over nature. Nature itself was divested of any trace of value, whether "form," or "essence," or "perfection," and defined as *res extensa*, bodies and motion. Hobbes and Locke reiterated that essences either did not exist or were not knowable. The quest for knowledge was not seen as loving desire but rather as a bid for control, through the "laws of mechanics, which are identical with the laws of nature." (Descartes) The corresponding concept regarding human action was "the order of desires," with the substantive idea coming from Hobbes and Locke, and the name from R.M. Unger.[16] Both concepts envisage "reason" as a faculty in the service of power aims. Neither contemplation nor any experience of participation enter into reason any more; indeed, by the middle of the eighteenth century rationality could be defined as "the human mind, left to itself" (Voltaire), while Kant construed reason as the mind's self-sufficient power of giving itself laws. Only one further step in that direction was left: the merging of reason with the mind's quantifying powers, which Comte proposed not only as the acme of all science but also as the fulfillment of history, as, indeed, the third and final age. Comte's proclamation of that age not as a segment of time but as a totalitarian social order to come proves that this extremely

brief sketch describes no mere academic varieties but mental mutations spawning revolutionary practices and their underlying experiences. This is manifested in literary productions at the end of
the eighteenth and the beginning of the nineteenth century which
convert Prometheus from a great criminal into a great hero. Prometheus' rebellion against the gods, then properly understood as
revolution directed at the God of Christianity, became "the cause"
of human emancipation in its various cultural and political enterprises. "Reason," supposedly, required "doing without God." As an
immediate result we have a variety of nineteenth-century revolutionary movements dressing themselves up in the garments of
science (Marx in economics, Comte in sociology, Freud in
medicine). Further along however, the disguise was dropped.
Nietzsche admitted having invented Dionysius as "a figure of Antichrist," and Sartre acknowledged that "Existentialism is nothing
more than an attempt to draw all the conclusions from a consistently atheistic position."[17] The resulting "absurdity of existence" is
now no longer a conclusion but something like a premise of
thinkers, poets, novelists, and essayists, "the natural climax of the
process of secularization which has increasingly characterized the
thought and activity of the modern world."[18]

Hans Urs von Balthasar has defined our situation in this way:

> Modern man has had the frightful misfortune that God in
> nature has died for him. Where religion once flowered like a
> blooming meadow, there is nothing left now but dry clay.
> Perhaps it is better so; perhaps that religion was like the Pon-
> tine Marshes that had to be drained. Nevertheless, the effect
> remains crushing. The Christian is not allowed to avoid this
> experience. He shares it as a human being. . . .[19]

Our share in this experience is not merely that of a fellow human
being but also that of an accomplice. Most of us subscribe to the vision of man's mastery over nature through reason operating as a
power-tool. The notion of history as a continuous human progress
will not be easily dislodged from our minds. In some way we, too,
applaud the freedom that has been built as modern man's pedestal.
At least subconsciously, most of us harbor in ourselves something
of the positivist, of the revolutionary, of the Promethean. At any

rate, no escape is open to us by way of wishing for the insights of a happier age.

So far we have talked of the perversion of reason. In addition, however, there is also the relativization of values. The very concept of value has been psychologized and subjectivized. It was Rousseau who first said that man would not be free except as he obeyed no one and nothing but himself. Kant, in his new "Copernican Revolution," followed suit with a metaphysics of practical reason to which man is alone his own lawgiver, and lawgiving is his most exalted activity in which he becomes like god, without, however, participating in the divine reality. Now, two hundred years later, the idea has trickled down to the comfortable well-off apartment dweller who goes from one institute to another attempting to "create his own values," every four weeks becoming a "new man" in a "new freedom." The task appears feasible because psychoanalysis has given us the notion that value is nothing but the contrived satisfaction of a subconsciously felt need. Where nothing is perceived but subjective "needs" and their artifacted gratification, the distinction of good from evil evanesces. In its place there remains only one relevant question: "Why not?" Nothing throws a sharper light on our situation than the helplessness of people who *know* that there is the order of goodness but have no ability to defend it when someone, in the innocence of nihilism, asks them, wide-eyed, "Why not?" The helplessness is compounded by the misconception that goodness is logically derived from principles one must have learned. The nihilist admits his total unawareness of these supposed principles, and we discover that we do not have them in our grasp, and stand speechless.

As mentioned before, our problem is not this or that philosopher, but an entire environment of "thought and activity" from which oozes a fog of meaninglessness. Thus the relativization of values is reinforced by the varieties of contemporary mysticism, Western or Eastern, all of which culminate in a state of mind "beyond good and evil." In the words of Charles Manson, the murderer on principle: "If God is One, what is bad?" The "cosmic consciousness" experienced under drugs, the nihilism of a Buddhist enlightenment learned at more than one remove from the culture of the East, the cult of the "high" from rock music – all these converge into something that the fourteenth century mystic Suso called "untrammeled freedom," which he defined as "when a man lives according to all his caprices without distinguishing between God and himself, and without looking before or after. . . ."²⁰ "Everything is permitted" is the maxim which Dostoevsky puts into the mouth of this archetypal atheist character, Ivan Karamazov. That formula, in the 1880s still a frightful shock, has now become a taken-for-granted "life-style" of modern suburbia.

Thirdly, there is found, in our contemporary situation, a vast change in the concept of man. To both Greeks and Christians man is essentially a composite being: form and matter, body and soul. "The soul" may sometimes have undergone a little hypostatization, but the concept represented countless and typical experiences in which natural necessity was clearly distinguishable from a freedom of mind and spirit. Thus St. Paul, in Rm 7:13-25, reports of a lower, concupiscent element in him that he contrasts to a higher one which "loves the law," i.e., the divine. The superordination of the soul to the body, and the soul's higher or rational element to the lower or concupiscent one, became the very concept defining humanness. It was a great milestone for all of humanity when, both in Greek philosophy and in Christian doctrine, the "opening of the soul" came into sight as the gateway of true order and goodness. The term itself stems from Bergson, but the reality is one of which men have been aware for more than two thousand years. Eric Voegelin has lamented, in moving words, the "closing of the soul" that resulted in the millennarian "causes" of the Reformation period and the progressive and revolutionary movements of our time. Any "closing of the soul" is, indeed, reason for deep lament: "Behold, O Lord; for I am in distress; my bowels are troubled; mine heart is turned within me; for I have grievously rebelled; abroad the sword bereaveth, at home there is death."²¹ Our affliction today, however, is not only the "closed soul" of the revolutionary, it is also the man who has no soul at all.²² The very word "soul" has hardly any currency, except to denote emotional intensity in jazz. Anthropologists and psychologists are dispensing with the concept (the Jungians excepted), and philosophers pay no more attention to it. Whatever used to be predicated of the soul has been assigned to one single category, a category of process either mechanical, biological, or psychological. Thus man is no longer seen as a composite being. "In yourself 'all is one' " is an Eastern concept meaning that there is no God above, no objective world without, and no hierarchy of order within. In this undifferentiated something into which man has now been merged there is neither sense nor need to distinguish between intellectual and moral virtues, contemplation and action, or, to use a formula from the Mundaka Upanishad, between "higher and lower knowledge,"[23] or Nāgārjuna's "worldly truth" and "absolute truth."[24] Similarly irrelevant would appear St. Paul's "discernment of spirits," indeed, any discernment whatever, spiritual or moral. For in man as the modern world conceives him, there is neither shape nor structure, no sub- or superordination, no possibility of maturing, nor any basis for a common good.

Let us return to the initial statement of our problem. We need to recover the order of goodness, in the form of principles; we are also aware that the order of goodness was formulated in principled form first and foremost by the classical Greek philosophers and their great Christian counterparts. We had to remind ourselves, though, that the principles of "right by nature" were formulated, accompanied, and sustained by other concepts and insights which stemmed from basic experiences of the mystic-philosophers, above all the experience of reason as the soul's participation in the divine *nous*, the givenness of order reflected in things and their "natures," and the awareness of man as a composite of higher and lower elements. These concepts have been not merely undermined but downright eliminated by modern philosophy, psychology, and anthropology. That means that an attempt to return to the natural law of Thomas Aquinas, for instance, would be tantamount to fetching from afar a text written in a language "not understood by the people." We could recover no more than the words. Our contemporaries would not be mentally and spiritually equipped to read these words with sensitivity or even with interest. As for us, who might seek to "return to natural law" by nothing more than reprinting ancient texts, we would stand convicted of laziness. Still, we must obey the demand of our situation. The order of goodness must be recovered, and in the form of principles.

In the bewilderment to find ourselves at such an impasse, we can detect at least one relevant and promising event. That is the recovery, by a number of Soviet Russia's political victims, of true insights into the order of being and goodness. One of the testimonies of this event is the book *From Under the Rubble*, edited by Aleksandr Solzhenitsyn (New York, 1975). Solzhenitsyn, in the lead article ("As Breathing and Consciousness Returns") describes the cultural condition of Soviet Russia:

> The transition from free speech to enforced silence is no doubt painful. . . . But . . . the return of breathing and consciousness, the transition from silence to free speech – will also prove difficult . . . because of the gulf of utter incomprehension which will suddenly yawn between fellow-countrymen. . . . For decades . . . our thoughts straggled in all possible and impossible directions, lost touch with each other, never learned to know each other. . . . Powerful and daring minds are now beginning to struggle upright, to fight their way out from under heaps of antiquated rubbish.

While we are not in the same sense laboring under "enforced silence," in other respects our situation is similar, in that our thoughts are straggling "in all possible and impossible directions" so that we have "lost touch with each other." How did the about-turn in Russia occur?

The Greek equivalent of "about-turn" is *metanoia,* described in Plato's *Republic* as a God-induced movement from the untruth of the shadows to the truth of the light. It has the nature of a personal experience with consequences for all. In Russia, such personal experiences occurred in the extreme jeopardy of the labor camps. Some prisoners discovered that even on the brink of annihilation, with no prospect of worldly improvement, the decision between "decency and indecency" was not merely possible but was what restored the annihilated humanity. They also found that, through these decisions alone, they were linked to others in commonness of the good. At the same time they experienced the dimension of these decisions as one transcending nature and history.[25] Those who had such experiences also found that the continuity with the past was restored, that they were again enabled to understand the symbols, insights, and principles which at an earlier time of their lives they had destroyed with their own hands. These examples teach that "a return" is possible, but also that no return may be possible without something like an annihilating situation, an insight that underlies also Walker Percy's novel *The Second Coming* (New York, 1980). The great Russian precedent does not compel us to wish for a Gulag situation for ourselves. Still, it bears the message that no recovery of order can be had by a merely intellectual *tour de force*: nothing short of a soul-shaking experience can stir up the ashes of lost truth.

One concluding word about the fact that we are impeded in our desire to "return" not merely existentially and spiritually, but also intellectually. Our material wellbeing is most often mentioned as the main obstacle. In fact, however, our prosperity is beginning to look quite shaky to us. Among other barriers against a "return to natural law," however, is our Constitutional positivism. It tends to usurp the place of natural law, just as our political dogma of freedom as absolute goodness tends to crowd out all other aspects of goodness. In both cases we in fact put forward our national achievement as an answer to the question of what is "right by nature." We might have suspected that much as we reacted intolerantly and with irritation to the severe but friendly criticism of our culture by Solzhenitsyn. (Solzhenitsyn again! He seems to be a figure of fate.) At any rate, a "return to natural law" seems to be possible only at a price the full measure and nature of which we do not yet perceive. If I were pressed to name at least one part of that price, I would be tempted to point to our philosophy of history, which mostly stems from the Enlightenment. Enlightenment progressivism and revolutionary futurism, however, have destroyed history as a symbolic form of consciousness in daily life. Now it might seem that the problem of history is hardly relevant to natural law, since history was not present at the birth of natural law and did not attend its further development through the centuries. Since the beginning of Romanticism, however, history has become an indispensable part of our thinking. Solzhenitsyn concludes the Foreword of *From Under the Rubble* with these words:

> It is from out of those dank and dark depths, from under the rubble, that we are now putting forth our first feeble shoots. If we wait for history to present us with freedom and other precious gifts, we risk waiting in vain. History is us—and there is no alternative but to shoulder the burden of what we so passionately desire and bear it out of the depths.

In other words, a recovery of the order of goodness is itself an historical event, but also a rejection of the false teaching about

history. We, no less than Russians, must jettison the illusion that
history is the single ranking object of "philosophy." This would probably require a science of the origin of history as a concept, in the
course of which all kinds of correctives to our contemporary illusions about history would turn up. By way of example, let us look at
the sixteenth-century French thinker Jean Bodin, who distinguished between four "divisions" of history: a) human history:
uncertain, confused, up and down, always involved in "new errors,"
yet building up memory, and moving between fixed natural causality and God's purpose; b) nature: "steadfast," definite, although
sometimes inconsistent, predictable in such constancies as climate
and race; c) mathematical: by which Bodin meant the metaphysical
aspects of numbers and their pertinent human knowledge; d)
divine: God's purpose alone is most certain and changeless, and
humans are lifted up "by divine grace."[26] If this is somewhat crude,
it nevertheless ranks above the pseudo-theologizing speculations of
Hegel, Comte, or Marx. Bodin comes up with four realistic "divisions" which are borne out by experience: first, nature: regular and
coherent, but still "inconsistent" and thus characterized by certain
"freedoms" in spite of its regularity and coherence. Next, human
affairs, unpredictable, uncertain, and meaningless. What Bodin is
saying is the same as our modern absurdists: that the world of
human history does not make sense of itself. They agree with Wittgenstein's dictum: "In the world everything is as it is, and
everything happens as it does happen: *in* it no value exists – and if
it did, it would have no value. . . . It must lie outside the world."[27]
Bodin's third "division," the "mathematical" one, could and does apply to Western natural science which is certain as well as
cumulative, and thus not only belongs to history but constitutes in
itself a bit of unilinear history, in the midst of many "ups and
downs" of human history. Finally, all purpose, all meaning, all rationality is found with God, the ultimate unity and certainty.

These remarks can do nothing more than merely adumbrate the
various problems of "returning to natural law." In the light of what
has been said, one wonders whether it might not be advisable to use
the term "natural law" reluctantly, if at all. The term may create an
illusion that the task is a purely intellectual one, when it actually
leads necessarily through the depths of regenerative experiences.
All the same, "return to natural law!" communicates an imperative

of the highest rank which no sensitive person would dare to overlook or even postpone. It imposes on us a duty to serve humanity, in the truest sense of that word, humanity which is not defined by bread, power, or superstition, but only by the awe-filled love of truth and goodness.

[1] *Metaphysics*, 982b, p. 19.

[2] Cf. Aristotle, *Metaphysics*, 986b, p. 25.

[3] "What is Right by Nature?" and "What is Nature?" in *Anamnesis* (South Bend: Notre Dame University Press, 1978).

[4] *Metaphysics*, 1075b, pp. 12-17.

[5] *Anamnesis*, loc. cit., p. 80.

[6] *Ibid.*, p. 82.

[7] *Ibid.*, p. 84.

[8] *Ibid.*, p. 85.

[9] *Laws*, 713a.

[10] *Ibid.*, 714a.

[11] *Ibid.*, 892b.

[12] *Of the Soul*, 430a, pp. 10-18.

[13] *Ibid.*, 736b, p. 28.

[14] *The New Science*, #350.

[15] Cf. Wilhelm Dilthey, *Weltanschauung und Analyse des Menschen seit Renaissance und Reformation* (Leipzig and Berlin, 1929), p. 279.

[16] *Knowledge and Politics* (New York, 1975).

[17] Quoted in Eric Mascall, *The Christian Universe* (New York, 1966), p. 43.

[18]. *Ibid.*, p. 34.

[19] *Science, Religion, and Christianity* (Westminster, Md., 1958), p. 100f.

[20] Quoted in Norman Cohn, *The Pursuit of the Millennium*, rev. ed. (New York, 1970), p. 177.

[21] Lm. 1:20.

[22] Cf. Robert Musil, *The Man Without Qualities* (London, 1953).

[23] I, 3-4.

[24] Cf. R.C. Zaehner, *The City Within the Heart* (New York, 1981), p. 105.

[25] Cf. Mihajlo Nihajlov, "Mystical Experiences of the Labor Camps," *Kontinent* 2 (Anchor Books, 1977), pp. 103-31.

[26] *Method for the Easy Comprehension of History* (New York, 1945), chapter I.

[27] *Tractatus Logico-Philosophicus* #6.41.

# Augustine's Political Philosophy?

RESPONSIBLE philosophical critique of philosophy is rare, but the few who achieve it today speak with a new tone of authority. Their argument has new weight because the horizon has widened. On the one hand, many excellent books have given us new insight into the order of the myth, "before philosophy." On the other hand, equally impressive research has been done into the antiphilosophical and antitheistic idea structures known as "ideologies," which are at the root of the deep and widespread disorientation of our time. Between these two horizon-points, philosophy has come into view as a whole, so to speak. We see it as the historical event of the discovery of rational human consciousness, set off against the myth as well as against the annihilating tidal wave of ideologies. At the same time, we now "see" it in terms of its own development, with landmarks that can be assumed as familiar in educated discussion. Landmark thinkers, e.g., Descartes and Hegel, serve the need for an historical overview.

I submit that another such thinker is Augustine of Hippo, ranking foremost in the enterprise of philosophizing in the mode of antiquity but with the insights of Christian faith. Unlike other landmark thinkers, Augustine is known only superficially, and even then only through the glasses of erroneous clichés. Furthermore, the element of Christian doctrine in his work tends to block an understanding of Augustine for many modern non-Christian thinkers, although first-rate scholars have never been deterred by the absence of their personal identification with the object of their study.

Looking at Augustine as a philosopher of politics brings up another difficulty. Augustine is mostly known as the originator of philosophy of history. Some have felt that this is the appearance of Augustine when seen from the standpoint of modern times, so that one may well ask whether, in his own time, Augustine really created a philosophy of history.[1] May one not equally ask, then, "Was Augustine a philosopher of politics?" There are no later political theorists who designate themselves "Augustinians." For that matter, though, there are also no philosophers of history who claim to be Augustinians, and yet few people doubt that history, as "the symbolic form of our consciousness," goes back to Augustine. Augustine, then, really did not teach political theory to others.

Still, let us place him in the broad historical context of philosophy from Athens's fifth century B.C. on. For almost 150 years, the Greeks were astonishingly productive in that field of politics. After the brief and labile self-expression of that school of the Greek Enlightenment, the Sophists, there came the deeply serious and mystical response of Plato's *Republic*, and Aristotle's great attempt to build a political science in the framework of fundamental ethics. But then nothing similar happened for hundreds of years. The two Greek productions, one frivolous and the other, attentive and responsive, were not continued and developed. Cicero's works, *The Republic* and *The Laws*, brought nothing new. From Cicero to Augustine, fully 450 years, most philosophers did not touch politics at all. In the fifth century A.D., however, Augustine did give a great deal of attention to politics, and not as an epigone, but in the context of a most innovative ontology, cosmology, anthropology, and ethics. Even this brief glance would tell us that, in view of earlier Church Fathers who dismissed public order from the perimeter of Christian concerns, Christianity, without Augustine, might not have developed a civilization of its own, or else might have developed an apolitical culture resembling, for instance, Buddhism. The rank of a landmark philosopher, then, cannot be denied Augustine even in the field of politics.

# I

FOR REASONS of comparison let us draw up, in schematic form, the work of Aristotle and Plato in political science.

**Plato:** An anthropology centering on an analysis of the three parts of the soul, and an hermeneutics of the basic experiences of *eros, thanatos,* and *daimon*; a concept of justice derived from the hierarchical order of the three parts of the soul; a verbal model of "the idea" of the state in terms of institutional arrangements that would, if realizable, put an end to "the troubles of the world"; an exploration of the four cardinal virtues; a scheme of public education; a concept of man's experience of, and capacity for, participation in the divine source of order, the *nous*; the concept of political rule by the philosopher; a description of the psychological, cultural, and political dynamics of successively deteriorating stages of perverted order, with tyranny as the nadir.

**Aristotle:** An anthropology based on the concept of four ranks of being, and an analysis of the two parts of the human soul; the concept of happiness as the highest good; a descriptive and analytical list of virtues, with justice as that virtue which comprises all the virtues; the concept of the *spoudaios*, the self-ruling mature man who loves the *nous* within him; a genetic theory of the state; an evaluative classification of forms of the state; a sociology of various types of perverted society; an analysis of political crisis; a concept of "the best state."

One should add that both Plato and Aristotle concerned themselves with the state because they were deeply concerned for the *soteria tou einai,* the preservation of being against external adversities and internal disorder. Plato saw the state required by the disease, "the fever," of the "luxurious," i.e., civilized state. Aristotle considered the state a setting required by nature for the secure attainment of a "happy" life in the midst of family, friends, and fellow citizens, which life could be attained only by the *spoudaios,* the man capable of ruling others because he already ruled as king over himself. Both Plato and Aristotle had the most serious doubts about the realizability of their models of salvific political order: Plato said that "the idea" of the state was not a community that could ever be found on earth; Aristotle did not believe that one could find any city with even one or two *spoudaioi*. Still, both saw human life constantly threatened by decline or destruction. The philosopher's task was to identify the cause of this besetting insecurity of being in order to arrange for some means of preventing this. Categorically, the counteraction was called *soteria*, "deliverance, safety." Augustine's Latin equivalent was *salus*, "health, soundness." Certainly Augustine shared Plato's and Aristotle's concern for deliverance from life-destroying adversities. To what extent did this concern motivate his philosophizing on political order?

## II

THAT SEEMS to be the fundamental question to ask in any comparison between Greek political philosophers and Augustine. For an answer, we shall detour by way of Augustine's ontology and physics. Augustine, trained as a rhetor, had absorbed not only Plato and the Stoa, but also Aristotelian physics and metaphysics, then still considered one science. After his conversion he continued on the same course, having already laid his own philosophical foundation in a number of books written at Cassiciacum: *De beata vita, De ordine, Contra academicos, De pulchro et apto.*

One must remember, though, that he lived no longer in the Athens of 800 years ago but in the period of mature Hellenism. For several hundred years all philosophical endeavor had centered on the problem of God. The Stoics had deified the cosmos itself, Plotinus's God was "The One," to whom to ascend was every soul's desire. Aristotle's "Unmoved Mover" was still playing a role in cosmology. Where the philosophers seemed to have groped for an answer, Augustine supplied his from the first book of the Bible: *Deus creator omnium*, God is the creator of all things. From the Bible he also drew an answer regarding God's essence. God had revealed himself to Moses through the words: "I Am Who I Am."

God is "I Am," the one whose essence is existence. Aristotle had attributed to God the origin of movement, Plotinus the essence of unity; Augustine perceived that God is the Existent who creates existing things out of nothing.

The biblical concept, admittedly received in faith, fitted smoothly into the traditional pattern of philosophical inquiry. "Of all visible things, the cosmos is the greatest; of all invisible, the greatest is God. That the world is, we see; that God is, we believe."[2] It served as an argument against the Stoics who had merged the created cosmos with its creator God. It answered, or rather, filled in, the theological gaps in Aristotle. Augustine found the biblical information, which he accepted on the authority of "witnesses," not less but rather better substantiated than the answer the philosophers had attempted. In no wise could he see it in conflict with *scientia*. On the contrary, the insight that things had been willed into existence by the good God brought to Augustine a new insight into these "things" and their nature. In all this, he never left the scope of the philosophical tradition, the inquiry into the rational intelligibility of given reality.

In another respect Augustine continued in the path of Greek philosophy while enriching it with elements of Christian revelation: knowledge was for him, as it was for Plato and Aristotle, a matter of "seeing" (*theoria*). He greatly widened and elaborated the derived notion of "inner vision," by means of which he overcame the argument of the skeptics about the unreliability of the senses. His original turn consisted in applying vision also to the highest good, in Christian terms, the "vision of God." One fully appreciates this when recalling that the sixteenth-century reformers, both Luther and Calvin, declared the ear to be man's most important organ for understanding. The object to be understood, of course, was the word of God which, according to Luther, should be "shouted not written" (*geschrien, nicht geschrieben werden*). That Augustine saved into the Christian doctrine the concept of *theoria* = "seeing" enabled him also to save the concept of the "nature" of things, which had historical consequences of immense importance. It continued to facilitate, well into modern times, an awareness of the givenness of the order of being, independently of human volition. One of the objections to this concept is that the "inner vision" tends to "see" what ought to be rather than what is. This particular objection, however, certainly does not apply to Augustine, as we shall find soon.

Augustine's ontology, centering on the hymn, "Deus creator omnium," was not merely the completion of Greek ontology by means of God, the Existent, as the creator of all that exists. It also answered the question of the relation between goodness and being more satisfactorily than it had ever been answered before. The ancient Greek tendency was to rely more on the clearly observable presence of purpose in existing things. A contemporary philosopher, Hans Jonas, has pointed to this feature in the following words: "In every purpose being opts for itself and against nothingness . . . i.e., the mere fact that being is not indifferent toward itself establishes its difference from non-being as the value basis of all values, the first YES as such."[3]

Resting an ontology solely on observable purposefulness of existing things, however, causes that ontology to do less than justice to the vulnerability and endemic failure of being, i.e., to "adversity." Augustine's ability to trace goodness to God the creator, however, not only facilitated his account of ontic adversity but also set up a court of highest instance, regarding goodness, above nature.

All these problems confront the modern reader with the difficulty that today we are lacking any ontology, so we have accustomed ourselves to an absolute cleavage between truth, the truth of indifferent facticity, on the one side, and goodness on the other. Still, in these matters Augustine is more approachable for the modern mind than others, precisely because Augustine, through his autobiography and his psychology, has anticipated many of the modern attitudes.

## III

AUGUSTINE'S THEORY of "adversity" has two dimensions. The first is the relative absence of perfection in things created from nothing. To begin with, Augustine changed Aristotle's notion of four grades of being:

> Among those beings which exist, and which are not of God's
> essence, those which have life are ranked above those which

have none; those that have the power of generation, or even of desiring, above those which want this faculty. And, among the sentient, the intelligent are above those that have no intelligence. . . . And, among the intelligent, the immortal, such as the angels, above the mortal.[4]

Next comes his concept of *minus esse*, less being, or being "contracted." This brought into his reach an intelligible accounting of the "adversities" through which created beings find themselves endemically threatened. It is important to remember that Augustine lived at a time when deep experiences of acute disaster and threat of annihilation had generated the monstrosity of the Gnostic religion, a radical way of explaining evil achieved by sacrificing any goodness in existing things, including man. It was clearly a case of throwing out the child with the bath. Many besides Augustine felt moved to call Gnosticism a monstrosity, which did not of itself enable them to come up with an alternative explanation.

Where Origen and Plotinus, who tried a philosophical refutation of Gnosticism, had themselves partly succumbed to it, Augustine succeeded brilliantly, helped above all by the notion of *creatio ex nihilo*, creation out of nothingness. Things created out of nothing lack the unlimited existence of God; they are, characteristically, "mutable." *Mutabilitas*, in this context, included the meaning of turning bad, a tendency to nothingness. Hence their need to "preserve such being as they have received."[5]

Aristotle's *soteria tou einai* is recalled, but with expanded scope and greater emphasis. God's creation is good, albeit subject to degeneration from being neither immutable nor immortal. Evil is a special case of mutability in creatures which have desire as well as intelligence: "For will, being a nature which was made good by the good God, but mutable by the immutable, because it was made out of nothing can both decline from good to evil, which takes place when it freely chooses, and can also escape the evil and do good; which takes place only with divine assistance."[6] This explanation of evil is capable of saving the concept of nature, which the Gnostics threw overboard in their anxiousness to account for extreme experiences of earthly misery. "It is not nature, but vice which is contrary to God. For that which is evil is contrary to the good. . . . Further the nature it vitiates is a good, and therefore to this good it is also contrary. . . ."[7]

One should note the function of the term *vitium*: "Things solely good, therefore, can in some circumstances exist; things solely evil, never, for even those natures which are vitiated by an evil will, in so far as they are vitiated, are evil, but in so far as they are natures they are good."[8] The noun, *vitium*, conveys at the same time the ideas of fault, defect, and imperfection, so that human misery can be accounted for by both *mutabilitas* and *voluntas*, will.

Augustine's "reasonable" accounting of evil in a good creation has particular significance today. For we are living with the painful experience of seeing the radical Gnostic doctrine of a totally evil world, contrasted with the faraway reality of complete goodness, come back with social effectiveness, generating the armed movements of modern totalitarianism. They serve as a warning that philosophy cannot escape the responsibility of explaining the anti-tendencies in the midst of things existing. A naive theory of being, based on "seeing" things as they "ought to be," cannot deliver a satisfactory explanation of "adversity" and thus must fail in times of great historical and cultural catastrophes. Augustine's explanation, we note, does not disarm nothingness but rather evil. Nothingness is a given possibility of things created which, however, can be avoided with the help of the good God, the ultimate Existent. Obviously, Augustine's doctrine was opposed to all traditions of antiquity. If, nevertheless, the modern mind has hardly even taken cognizance of Augustine's sophisticated analysis of adversity in human existence, the reason may possibly be found in a new philosophical naiveté, the illusion of progress.

## IV

BEFORE turning to Augustine's ethics, we ought to throw a brief glance at his anthropology. Having rejected the metaphysical dualism of the Manichees, but also that of Plotinus who placed opposite to God the equally eternal reality of matter, Augustine might have succumbed to the danger of a monism rooted in God as the sole existent. Augustine, however, emphatically renews the body-soul dualism of the Greeks, this time in the context of Christian revelation:

What incredible thing it is, then, if some one soul is assumed by Him in an ineffable and unique manner for the salvation of many? Moreover, our nature testifies that a man is incomplete unless a body be united with a soul. This certainly would be more incredible, were it not of all things the most common; for we should more easily believe in a union between spirit and spirit, or, to use your own terminology, between the incorporeal and the incorporeal, even though the one were human, the other divine, the one changeable and the other unchangeable, than in a union between the corporeal and the incorporeal.[9]

Ontology is the backbone of Augustine's ethics, an ethics which he, by a stroke of genius, arranged in two columns. One column consists of accurate and detailed observations of the fallen human race, or, as Machiavelli would say, of "life as it is." The other column, however, is not "the ideal" as against "the real," but an equally empirical observation of god-centered human lives. Neither column consists of mere factual data: "When, therefore, man lives according to himself – that is, according to man, not according to God – assuredly he lives a lie. . . ."[10]

Augustine describes the ways in which fallen man is a plaything of his lower passions, a being having lost the powers of self-control that were once his. "For what is man's misery but his own disobedience to himself."[11] Nor is his analysis to be misunderstood as a neo-Platonist contempt of the body in favor of the soul. The flesh, having been created by the good God, is not in itself evil. Rather, it is the evil will of the soul that causes the corruption of the creature as a whole. Augustine's analysis is as sophisticated as anything emerging from modern psychology, to which it is superior in that it has no need to invent a new and implausible myth.

The other column corresponds, in its function, to Aristotle's treatise on virtues, without, however, taking over Aristotle's confidence in the power of the virtues to do the "saving" job. For Augustine, the virtues have their place, but it is not at the top, for virtues may be resorted to by a will that, while yearning for goodness, is confident of being able to attain it by his own unaided efforts. The virtues of such a will Augustine calls "a perpetual war with vices – not other men's but our own."[12] The reason is that the will which does not cling to the living God has "no proper authority." It follows that

> the virtues which it seems to itself possess . . . are vices rather than virtues as long as there is no reference to God in the matter. For although some suppose that virtues which have a reference . . . only to themselves are true virtues, the fact is that even then they are inflated with pride.[13]

The concept of will used in this analysis is a synonym for "love." "My love is my center of gravity" is the famous formula which Augustine frequently repeated. "The right will, therefore, is well-directed love, and the wrong will is ill-directed love."[14] Identifying will with love, Augustine is able to provide the needed affective element of ethics, which Aristotle found, not very convincingly, in man's love of the highest good not without also referring to man's love for the *nous*, "itself divine or only the most divine element in us."[15] In any case, Aristotle's loving affect is for an "it."

Augustine decisively improves on that by placing the love for the living God, a God addressed as "thou," at the center of the good life. Through the channel of this love, divine grace, secured in Jesus Christ, will heal the defects of fallen human nature and enable man to retrieve the original goodness that created him. This, then, is the "supreme good," the ultimate happiness or, rather blessedness, for which man is destined, even though to get it he has to pass through the gateway of death, just as mankind has to complete the course of history. "There we shall enjoy the gifts of nature . . . not only of the spirit, healed now by wisdom, but also of the body renewed by resurrection."[16] Of this "ultimate consummation" a certain foretaste is possible even in this miserable life,

> when we have such peace as can be enjoyed by a good life. . . . Virtue, if we are living rightly, makes a right use of the advantages of this peaceful condition. . . . This is true virtue, when it refers all the advantages it makes a good use of, and all that it does in making good use of good and evil things, and itself also, to that end in which we shall enjoy the best and greatest peace possible.[17]

Or, again: "it is a brief but true definition of virtue to say, it is the order of love."[18]

## V

FINALLY, we come to Augustine's political theory. Let us remember that Aristotle, having declared the *polis* the highest kind of human association, the one in which man finds it possible to live in "self-sufficiency," goes on to define the "true" forms of government, but then to study elaborately the "perverted" types characteristic of the world in which he lived. Now by contrast, Augustine had already drawn a full and chillingly "realistic" portrait of "the whole viciousness of human life," as he located the "perversion" not in political forms but in culture, the self-perpetuating pattern of habitual sinfulness.

The difference extends into the sociology of the two thinkers. Aristotle found in the "perverted" cities one unbridgeable social gulf, that between the rich and the poor, a gulf that allowed no common concept of justice to be perceived. Augustine's counterpart of that distinction is found in his "two cities." The term is misleading: I would prefer "two loyalties," or "two citizenries." The word *civitas* cannot mean "city" which certainly in antiquity would have meant a walled city with its own independent ruler. Augustine's two *civitates*, however, are neither living separately nor separately organized. They constitute groups readily observable in society who are distinct in terms of basic orientation and attitudes. Individual people, feeling drawn to each other by the love which they have in common, spontaneously form a group short of overt organization. In that sense, Augustine's two *civitates* resemble Aristotle's rich and poor. "The one consists of those who wish to live after the flesh, the other of those who live after the spirit; and when they severally achieve what they wish, they live in peace, each after their own kind."[19] Later, Augustine amplifies his distinction: "The former, in a word, glorifies in itself, the latter in the Lord. . . . The one lifts up his head in its own glory; the other says to its God, "Thou art my glory, and the lifter up of my head."[20]

The radical difference between Aristotle's and Augustine's observations at this point is that Aristotle's groups make government difficult or impossible, while Augustine's bear on the whole destiny of mankind. A further difference is that Augustine's two *civitates* have something basic in common with each other: the human need for peace in this mortal life. "The families which do not live by faith seek their peace in the earthly advantages of this life," while those who cleave to God "use as pilgrims such advantages of time and earth as do not fascinate and divert them from God."[21] Aristotle's rich and poor cannot coexist politically, unless there be a middle class to mediate. Augustine's two *civitates* share political order, albeit each for its own good: "As long as the two cities are commingled, we [i.e., the City of God] also enjoy the peace of Babylon."[22]

## VI

AT THIS POINT, Augustine succeeds in creating a concept of a people that is compatible with historical contingencies. We are aware, of course, of what Aristotle said, in *Poetics* 1451 b, about the unbridgeable difference between philosophy and history, the former bound to statements of universals, the latter given only to "singulars." "By a universal statement, I mean one as to what such and such a kind of man will probably or necessarily say or do. . . ; by a singular statement, one as to what, say, Alcibiades did or had done to him." True to this separation, Cicero had defined a people as "an assemblage associated by a common acknowledgement of right and by a community of interests."[23]

Augustine shows forth the philosophical nature of this statement: Where there is no true justice there can be no right; so he concludes further that "where there is no true justice there can be no people," and that, according to Cicero, there could have been no Roman people. This difficulty disappears, however, when one defines a people as "an assemblage of reasonable beings bound together by a common agreement as to the objects of their love."[24] Peoples entertain multitudes of love, as fallen man does everywhere. An agreement on one of these loves constitutes a people. This is a concept of common culture as empirically created by common values. Contingent realities are here captured in a universal concept: such is the stuff of which philosophy of history is made. Later on, Ibn Khaldûn would add the notion of *asabiyah*, meaning "party spirit, team spirit, esprit de corps," a psychic element accounting for the genesis and decline of peoples.[25]

## VII

THE KEY CONCEPT of Augustine's political thought is peace. In book XIX, 11-17, he transforms Varro's idea of peace into one fitting the new ontology. The result is a complex of different tiers as well as kinds of peace, all of which are in some way related to each other. Through this complex run two main separating lines: eternal peace, ranking as an absolute above the merely relative earthly peace; and peace according to nature opposed as truth to the perverted unjust peace. Still, Augustine feels that there is room for a general remark: "We may say of peace, as we have said of eternal life, that it is the end of our good."[26] Earlier, Augustine has praised "blessedness," eternal felicity, as the highest destiny, not to be undone, for each particular person;[27] he now erects peace as the highest social good, and these two are merely the sides of the same coin. True peace will be ours only in eternal life.

Of peace on the earth, Augustine speaks in such terms as "some peace," "peace of one kind or another," a "mere solace of our misery," "temporal peace." Still, even in the "misery" of this life, "peace is a good so great" that "there is no word we hear with such pleasure, nothing we desire with such zest, or find more thoroughly gratifying."[28] The language resembles that of Aristotle when talking about "happiness"; the shift of content is significant. All men desire to have peace with their own circle, Augustine observes. He might have added that even animals stake out their territory so as to keep their peace within defined limits. Hence the reference to various groups and circles and "the laws of their own peace." The universal again permits referring to particulars, though not without reference to the absolute. The universal he has circumscribed in memorable words: "The peace of the body consists in the duly proportioned arrangement of its parts. The peace of the irrational soul is the harmonious repose of the appetites, and that of the rational soul the harmony of knowledge and action." One notes both, the Aristotelian concept of the soul, and the pervading concept of "nature" with its corollary, the "proper place" or "duly proportioned arrangement."

Augustine continues: "The peace of body and soul is the well-ordered and harmonious life and health of the living creature. Peace between man and God is the well-ordered obedience of faith to eternal law." What strikes us here is the effortless transition from Aristotelian metaphysics of "nature" to insights of Christian doctrine. But he is not finished:

> Peace between man and man is well-ordered concord. Domestic peace is the well-ordered concord between those of the family and those who obey. Civil peace is a similar concord among the citizens. The peace of the celestial city is the perfectly ordered and harmonious enjoyment of God, and of one another in God. Order is the distribution which allots things equal and unequal, each to its own place.[29]

As distinct from eternal peace, peace in this mortal life, as far as the godly citizenry is concerned, consists of "the use of things temporal with a reference to this result of earthly peace in the earthly community."[30] Earthly peace has the peculiar characteristic that it encompasses the two citizenries of mutually incompatible loyalties, the "earthly city" and the "City of God." "The things necessary for this mortal life are used by both kinds of men and families alike, but each has its own peculiar and widely differing aim in using them."[31]

We note the emergence in Augustine's thought of an independent political function beyond and besides the mutually exclusive loyalties within the culture, the perception of an autonomous task of political rule. This was something at which Marx, much as he tried, never succeeded. Marx should be mentioned next to Augustine in this context, because like Augustine he considered the state a necessity brought about by the corruption of human nature, and therefore a temporary phenomenon.

God "did not intend that His rational creature, who was made in His image, should have dominion over anything but the irrational creation."[32] It is "sin which brings man under the dominion of his fellow." The state is necessary only because of men's vitiated natures, as is clear when just war must be waged because of "the wrong-doing of the opposing party."[33] Like Marx, Augustine delivers a scathing critique of society, its injustices, deceptions, discontents, and unreliabilities. Again, like Marx, he sees this world of sinful quarrels and dissensions not as man's true home.

Those who live in faith, the "City of God," live "like a captive and a stranger in the earthly city." Yet, with hope in the highest promises of God and looking forward to true heavenly glory, they "make no scruples to obey the laws of the earthly city, whereby the things necessary for the maintenance of this mortal life are administered."[34] Thus, as this life is common to both cities, so there is a harmony between them in regard to what belongs to it.[35] Still, the obligation to "obey the laws" of the state does not extend to that matter over which the two citizenries are most deeply divided, to divine worship.

Aristotle's supreme good of earthly happiness has become eternal blessedness beyond death and history. One wonders why Augustine might not be supremely disinterested in this world's political order, like Tertullian was before him. Augustine's ontological emphasis on existence, however, does not permit him to discount any existence, not even the most corrupted one. Therefore he conceives of peace in two tiers: God's eternal peace, and relative peace on this earth, "such as we can enjoy in this life, from health and safety and human fellowship."[36] The relative peace includes:

> all things needful for the preservation and recovery of this peace, such as the objects which are accommodated to our outward senses, light, night, the air, and waters suitable for us, and everything the body requires to sustain, shelter, heal, or beautify it: and all under this most equitable condition, that every man who made a good use of these advantages suited to the peace of this mortal condition, should receive ampler and better blessings, namely, the peace of immortality.[37]

This is the counterpart of Aristotle's *soteria tou einai*, the preservation and protection of being in the security of the *polis*. Augustine, however, amends the concept, though not the activity, by pointing out that the real salvation of being can occur only in full union with God, after death. Remarkable, because Augustine acknowledges the legitimacy of earthly needs and their satisfaction; remarkable also because, in the nature of things, that cannot be the last word on the matter. In the "earthly city," where the relationship between earthly and eternal peace is ignored, that group "desires earthly peace for the sake of enjoying earthly goods, and it makes war in order to attain to this peace."[38] But, he adds, "as this is not a good which can discharge its devotees of all distress, this city is often divided against itself by litigations, wars, quarrels, and such victories as are either life-destroying or short-lived."[39] Or, to use Plato's words, because there are always those who live by evil loves, there "is no end of troubles," and human life cannot be ultimately preserved by any human political order. Still, Augustine is far from despising relative goods: "Miserable, therefore, is the people which is alienated from God. Yet even this people has a peace of its own which is not to be lightly esteemed."[40]

Is Augustine then an advocate of *any* kind of political order, as long as it exists? Would he side with Hobbes, or Machiavelli? He would not. First, having referred the relative to the absolute in an intelligible way, Augustine does allow for value gradations within the scope of the relatively good. Thus he says of the Romans, whose virtues he has sarcastically dismissed as "splendid vices," that "they were good according to a certain standard of an earthly state."[41] More important, though, he castigates the will to empire, which he attributes to certain men's proud wish "that all men belonged to them, that all men and things might serve one head, and might, either through love or fear, yield themselves to peace with him! It is thus that pride in its perversity apes God."[42] Within earthly imperfections, this peace, then, is still something that admits of intelligible distinctions, of grades of goodness, and of recognizable perversity.

## VIII

THAT IS ALL. No further concepts of political theory are in Augustine's bag. In particular: no explicit concept of the state, in terms of either genesis or covenant, nor any doctrine about forms of state. On the contrary, Augustine dismisses the problem: "The heavenly city [is] . . . not scrupuling about diversities in the manners, laws, and institutions whereby earthly peace is secured and maintained."[43] Consequently, Augustine can see no point in a project to define or describe "the best state." Nor do offices and constitutional structure interest him. He never even mentions the rule of law. What he has to teach on war is not new. Revolutions are none of his concern. Thus, it hardly adds up to a systematic political theory. All the same, the way in which he puts politics in the total range of "things visible and invisible" provides important principles to guide discernment. What are his accomplishments?

One must recall the historical situation to get some of the answers. After those Church fathers who declared utter unconcern of Christians for the state, Augustine could declare: "The things which this city desires cannot justly be said to be evil, for it is itself, in its own kind, better than all other human good."[44] Not only is the state not unimportant, but among relative goods of this earth it holds top rank, so that Christians have a duty of loyal political participation. On the other side we find those Church fathers who saw in Rome's absorption of many smaller kingdoms a device of God to facilitate the spreading of the Christian Gospel. Foremost among them was Origen. After him, his disciple Eusebius had linked the *pax romana* to Christ's message of peace, so that he saw Constantine as completing a process that had begun with Christ and was continued by Augustus.[45] Here the Christian eschatology of old had turned into a proclamation of complete harmony between Christ and the Roman Empire. This consoling doctrine had been picked up by one Christian thinker after another.

Augustine, in turn, put a full stop to this thinking. Not only did he fail to praise Rome for its "contributions" to Christianity, he also deflated the expectation of an eventual Christian empire or kingdom. Of the Christian emperors, he treated Constantine with something like a polite bow[46] while heaping fulsome praise on Theodosius who had humbled himself before Ambrose. His historical prediction is by no means sanguine, for he looks for no more than sporadic appearances of this or that Christian ruler, rather than steady Christian progress.[47] Finally, one must not forget Augustine's severe prohibition of any speculation on a future millennium on the basis of Revelation XX:4.[48] "At no time does Augustine leave the reasonable horizon of universals."[49]

Looking forward from Augustine, with the benefit of 20/20 hindsight, we observe that Eusebius, bypassing Augustine, as it were, stamped the influence of his imperial theology on the political thought of the Middle Ages. Augustine, in turn, also in a curious way, bypassed the Middle Ages and left his stamp, the stamp of typical Western autonomy, on Luther's faith as well as Descartes's reason. Beyond that, one might say Augustine's philosophy of history has come fully into its own only in the retrospection of modernity, just as Augustine's *Confession* was more deeply appreciated after the appearance of Western psychoanalysis. If Augustine left no systematic political thought in his time, there is, all the same, a Reinhold Niebuhr to testify to the long-range impulses of the fifth-century thinker. Niebuhr's witness certifies that Augustine, in an exemplary way, discharged the function of philosophy to criticize the illusory fascinations of the world with extant political structures and their pretenses.

## IX

FINALLY, how about Augustine's concern for *soteria tou einai*, the preservation of man's being, its deliverance from "the troubles of the world"? This was our first, and fundamental question. It must be said, in all fairness to Plato and Aristotle, that Augustine did more and probed deeper to ascertain the nature and causes of these troubles. He traced them, partly through his ontology, partly through his ethics. Creatures are less perfect than their creator, and a tendency to nothingness is endemic to their existence. God has given them the power to perpetuate their kind, to heal themselves, even to correct their deficiencies. They are still subject to death and disease and, in the case of humans, to a basic corruption of their will. The human soul "has shown itself capable of being altered for the worse by its own will."[50] Hence the human race, that which is "nothing more social by nature," has become the most "unsocial by its corruption."[51] The *City of God* is filled with example after example of the truth of this statement, some taken from Roman history, others from sociological observation. Man, craving to become more than God, becomes less. That is Augustine's analysis which sees circumstances as symptoms of, rather than as causes for, human insecurity and discontent.

The analysis implies the remedy. Man's will has the power to change his nature for the worse but, once vitiated, it has no longer the power to restore itself. The good will is from God but not the evil will. Man, then, is saved only by regaining a closeness to God, but it is God who has opened that possibility once again. The way to the salvation of man's being goes necessarily through death, and resurrection, to an undisturbed enjoyment of the original goodness of his nature. The true blessedness, which is man's highest destiny, is not realized in history and in the world of history. Those who in hope of this destiny see themselves engaged in a "pilgrimage" can enjoy the peace of the heavenly kingdom in hope and in faith, while making, in a detached way, good use of the goods of this life.

While Augustine's emphasis lies on the otherworldly fulfillment, to which he devotes the last three books of his work, his most telling achievement is to have taken the state from the height of its pedestal. The state, administrator of the earthly peace which even in the most corrupt cases is "not to be lightly esteemed," has still the supreme authority, but that authority has none of the salvific elements that we find in Plato and Aristotle. Political order in this world, then, cannot be an "all-or-nothing" proposition. Salvation is of God, and, in this world, represented by those who have spiritual help to give. The limitation of the state's authority in favor of a spiritual order is obviously implied. Augustine is the intellecutal father of the concept of the limited state, even though Pope Gelasius did provide the effective slogan. To this notion of a somewhat demoted secular power corresponds the other one: the concept of pilgrimage as the mode of historical continuity. Pilgrimage is an ongoing movement composed of many particular movements, yet not identical with any one nor with the sum of all. Pilgrimage is history's direction, its goal the peace of God, its attainment assured in Jesus Christ, its mood hopefully joyous. Pilgrimage is not progress; if anything, it is more akin to Hegel's dialectic, without the "self-movement." It is the human response to "the drawing of God's love and the calling of his voice," the response made in a social way, by a body of humans. Through this grand feature of a historical dynamism responding to God's healing grace, Augustine pulls together the threads of his ontology, ethics, politics, and history, a total movement toward the restoration of man's being.

[1] Ernest L. Rortin, "Augustine's City of God and the Modern Historical Consciousness," *Review of Politics* 41/3 (July 1979).
[2] Augustine, *The City of God* (Dods translation) XI, 4.
[3] Hans Jonas, *Das Prinzip Verantwortung* (Frankfurt, 1979), p. 155.
[4] *City of God* X, 6 (hereafter cited only by book and chapter).

[5] XII, 5.

[6] XV, 21 end.

[7] XII, 3.

[8] *Ibid.*

[9] X, 29.

[10] XIV, 11.

[11] XIV, 15.

[12] XIX, 4.

[13] XIX, 25.

[14] XIV, 7.

[15] Aristotle, *Nicomachean Ethics* X, 7.

[16] *City of God* XIX, 10.

[17] *Ibid.*

[18] XV, 22.

[19] XIV, 1.

[20] XIV, 28.

[21] XIX, 17.

[22] XIX, 26.

[23] XIX, 17.

[24] XIX, 24.

[25] Ibn Khaldûn, *The Muqaddhimah* (Princeton: Princeton University Press, 1967); cf. also my *Between Nothingness and Paradise* (Baton Rouge: Louisiana State University Press, 1971), 180 ff.

[26] *City of God* XIX, 11.

[27] XII, 20.

[28] XIX, 11.

[29] XIX, 13.

[30] XIX, 14.

[31] XIX, 17.

[32] XIX, 15.

[33] XIX, 7.

[34] XIX, 17.

[35] *Ibid.*

[36] XIX, 13.

[37] *Ibid.*

[38] XV, 4.

[39] *Ibid.*

[40] XIX, 26.

[41] V, 9.

[42] XIX, 12.

[43] XIX, 17.

[44] XV, 4.

[45] Cf. Wilhelm Kamlah, *Christentum und Geschichtlichkeit* (Stuttgart, 1951), 175 ff.
[46] *City of God*, V, 25.
[47] V, 21.
[48] XX, 9.
[49] Kamlah, *op. cit.*, 320.
[50] *City of God*, XI, 22.
[51] XII, 27.

# The Eternal Meaning
# of Solzhenitsyn

COMPARISONS between Solzhenitsyn and Dostoevsky have become fashionable, though their meaning has been less than clear. Henri de Lubac, in his *Drama of Atheistic Humanism*, has traced the snowballing movement toward the murder of God and man's self-deification that began with Hegel and accelerated by way of Feuerbach, Stirner, Marx, to Nietzsche, with Comte thrown in for good measure. In the drama's fifth act Dostoevsky, and he alone, arrested this formidable momentum of which he himself had been a part before he ascended *de profundis* to the affirmation of faith. The great power of Dostoevsky's work stems from his characters' participation in a battle of superhuman dimensions. Nobody else could bring home to the reader the forces contending in that fight like Dostoevsky, the sole informant with profound philosophical appreciation of the enemy's strongest case. His work, as Ellis Sandoz has put it in his *Political Apocalypse*, amounts to an "anthropology of disorder," his Stavrogins, Verkhovenskys, Ivan Karamazovs to a gallery of nihilistic archetypes. From this frightful ordeal Dostoevsky himself, however, emerged not a radiant victor but rather a battered, bruised, and bloodied warrior whose exclamation of faith comes in his work to hardly more than a stammer. We must hold him as one who saw the promised land without being allowed to enter in.

Is that the character of Solzhenitsyn's work? True, he also fights his way up from the nadir of Communist ideology in which he was raised and which he must at one time have accepted. Like Dostoevsky, he is fully aware of the motive strengths propelling that movement, as when the prisoner Rubin in *The First Circle* rejects for his person the principle that the end justifies the means, and then continues:

> But it's a different matter when we are talking about society as a whole. For the first time in the history of mankind we have an aim which is so sublime that we can really say that it justifies the means employed to attain it.

His characters all know Communist arguments inside out, and so the refutations issue from the point of view of men who "have been over into the future, and it does not work." Rubin has no answer to Sologdin's demand that he prove how the "negation of the negation" is a law capable of predicting change. Rusanov, in *Cancer Ward*, cannot refute the charge that official discrimination on the ground of "social origin" amounts to racism. Yes, in one sense, Solzhenitsyn does fight a battle similar to Dostoevsky's, but if we ask if it is that which accounts for the singular power of his work, we must answer no, "that is not it, at all." Dostoevsky's ordeal need not be repeated; the Russian writer now has other tasks. Already Pasternak understood this. Beyond historical upheavals and clashing power masses he rediscovered man's perennial experiences of life in nature, of personal suffering and death, of love and sacrifice. About such things, Communism has nothing to say, and thus even the best case that can be made out for it bypasses the human soul, the quivering resonator of transcendent realities.

## Solzhenitsyn's Society

PASTERNAK'S was a valiant effort to which ultimate fruition was denied. A pall of great metaphysical sadness hangs over his work, to which one might apply the title of Walter Sullivan's recent book, *Death by Melancholy*. Solzhenitsyn pushes beyond. Even in the midst of apparently bottomless defeat, his characters manage to sustain hope, faith, love; they remain pilgrims on their way to man's ultimate destiny. To be sure, they inhabit a place like hell. *The First Circle* is a "special prison" for scientists who, while serving long terms, are made to give the state their best inventive and creative powers. That prison with its special privileges may be the best there is, but it is still only the topmost range of the Inferno. The beginning and end of the book circumscribe the whole setting: In the first pages, a Soviet diplomat in an anonymous telephone call warns a friend of impending danger, and a new batch of prisoners arrives at Mavrino, the special prison; in the last pages the diplomat, traced by means of an invention made by the Mavrino prisoners, enters the Lubyanka, and a batch of prisoners are transferred from the "First Circle" to Siberia's labor camps. The law of circulation in Soviet society goes from the ingress of prisoners and an innocent act of decency to the egress of old prisoners bound for lower hell, and the ingress of fresh ones into interrogation. The diplomat is snagged by the noose woven by other prisoners. All human beings, victims and torturers alike, are surrounded by harsh cruelty, systematic degradation, ubiquitous suspicion and hostility, petty meanness of officials, and never-ending inefficiency.

### Iron Ring of Environment

THIS SOCIAL SETTING, surely, is one of "alienation." How would a Western writer have dealt with it? A hundred years ago, he would have drawn a picture of defiance, the lone hero against all of "them"; half a century ago he would have piled proof upon proof that evil is the *ens realissimum* and goodness but a vexation of the spirit; nowadays he would have strewn about fragments of persons and events by way of "I told you so" that everything is absurd. Is it not remarkable that nothing of the kind occurs to Solzhenitsyn? True, all of his characters suffer unspeakably from humiliation, contempt, pain, deprivation, loneliness, malnutrition, cold, separation, unfreedom. Yet in the midst of the most inhuman conditions the dozen or so main characters make choices central to their humanity: whether to consent to an assignment of routine drudgery or be sent to a Siberian slave camp, whether or not to divorce a husband who is behind bars, whether to humor a warder's tyranny or to resist it, whether or not to share with fellow prisoners, whether to do honest work or to mark time, whether or not to cooperate as an informer, whether or not to go along with Communist reasoning. Such choices have constituted man's lot; they do not disappear in a tyrannous social system or even in prison, and oppressive injustice excuses nobody from facing them.

*Cancer Ward*, more of a coherent story, deals with Oleg Kostoglotov, arrested for some casual remarks as a student, imprisoned, later exiled to Siberia "for eternity," then dispatched to the hospital on the brink of death from cancer. He responds strongly to treatment, his vital powers reawaken, he falls in love with one of the nurses, and then, more profoundly, with Vega, his female doctor. Discharged from the hospital and thirstily drinking in all manifestations of life as on the first day of Creation, he learns that his exile may be lifted in which case he would be able to marry Vega. An hour later, though, he also learns that the treatments for cancer have destroyed his reproductive powers and that no family life is any longer possible for him. This man receives an unbroken series of heavy blows to all that he values in the world, his friends, studies, family, his Russia, his freedom, his great love: All prospects are denied, all avenues blocked. Yet nothing can destroy his dignity, his love of life. He remains ever unwilling to pay "any price" for survival, he remains the king of his choices, the servant of a higher good. His existence may have been reduced to something like nothingness, but there abides still "the whole unfathomable universe of one man," the soul that presses toward beyonds after beyonds, undaunted by the fearsome nearbys. The iron ring of the environment here is a double one: first the Soviet regime with its repressions, lies, cruelties and degradations, then, within it, the hospital with its treatments which threaten to cause worse evils than those they are meant to cure. The hospital obviously serves as a paradigm of the whole Communist enterprise and the exorbitant price it exacts for the prospect of removing evils from life, without any real knowledge of how its "remedies" will actually work out.

## Intellectual Patrimony

ENOUGH has been said to indicate the nature of Solzhenitsyn's achievement. In one word: He has succeeded in restoring the concept of man to the fullness of humanity. If you think that this is nothing much, please consider the following: From the philosophers of the seventeenth century on, we have come more and more to a view identifying man with only a fragment of his being, a truncated psychology that arbitrarily eliminates one-half of human motivations. From the end of the eighteenth century on, we have been burdened by a notion which Eric Voegelin has called "the contracted self," man in the role of a world-historical loner, both a self-pitying sufferer from alienation and his own self-worshiping savior from all evil. Early in the twentieth century, we encountered the concept of collective man whose salvation and freedom can be attained only en masse and whose destiny is to function as an integral part of the Plan. From a variety of nineteenth-century ideologies we inherited the idea of the activist man, energy devoid of any contemplation and any norm, a source of deeds that allegedly establish their own meaning. Let us look at all these distortions again, and then reflect on how easy or difficult it is these days to have a notion of man apart from any of these biases.

"What makes you think realism must be brutal?" asks the hero of Saul Bellow's *Herzog*. Thomas Hobbes, that's who, and all who like him have reduced man to a self-centered island of arrogant meanness. Hobbes's philosophy based all social order on his wager that man's fondest desire is to do other men in. He was certainly familiar with the Greek philosophers' insights into human nature, as well as the findings of Augustine and Thomas Aquinas. Augustine, that profound psychologist, pointed out that man lives between the poles of two extreme loves: on the one hand *amor sui*, the love of self and its desire for mundane advantages, possessions, victories and the means of pride; on the other *amor Dei*, the love of God, the longing for good, man's restless tendency to press onward to the Absolute, the completion of self through openness toward divine grace. From this full range of motivations, Hobbes cut away the love of God, so that he had left only egoism, a tendency toward violence, envy and pride, all of which he called not an aspect of man, but, mind you, the whole of man. By the end of the eighteenth century the Marquis de Sade had built a whole world-view on essentially the same premise, and William Beckford, Lord Byron, Shelley, Swinburne came to be fascinated by the attraction of demonic evil. Don't take my word for it, read all about it in *The Romantic Agony*, by Mario Praz. Better still, delve into your own mind and find out whether *you* do not attribute to brutality, violence, ruthlessness, egoism, depravity the character of "real" nitty-gritty reality, of an "unblinking" view of truth compared with which the rest pales into a set of nice but "impractical" ideals hanging high up around the walls of one's seldom-used drawing room. Also bear in mind that most people do not live by their own experiences but receive their images and assumptions from our writers, those writers who for three generations have fed us version after version of sick, oversexed, violent, self-seeking, ruthless characters, always protesting that this surely was all there is of man.

Now for the "contracted self" – what a beautifully evocative term – the man who had detached his self from creation, his fellow creatures, from divine grace and from faith, finding himself alone with his reason and inclined to spin out new worlds within himself. Man's relation with reality comes through the paradigmatic experiences of his soul, the experiences of death, birth, love, contrition, friendship. These guidelines were abandoned as the self contracted into the shell of his own mind. Simultaneous with the contraction took place the idolization of this shrunken self: He became Prometheus, his own creator (Marx), the designer of "universal history" (Schiller), the successor of the murdered God (Nietzsche), his own savior from evil (Freud). The "death of God" is not only a fad of contemporary "theologians," it is already found in Hegel and Marx, Nietzsche and Baudelaire. If you incline to shrug off these few as of no consequence, read J. Hillis Miller's *The Disappearance of God*, to see how five great English writers – De Quincey, Browning, Emily Brontë, Matthew Arnold and Gerard Manley Hopkins – found it impossible, much as they wanted to, to overcome their disconnection from God.

All this was Russia's patrimony, too. The Russian intelligentsia had wholly submitted to Western Prometheanism and millenarianism, with Herzen, Belinsky and Chernyshevsky leading on, and only Dostoevsky able to extricate himself from the spiritual mire. All this, in Russia, is now background. The foreground is occupied by the notion of collective man as promoted and cultivated by Soviet officialdom. Here the other half of human motives, the love of self, is denied and repressed, while service to the Party is substituted for the love of God. The moral basis for collectivism is

Comte's *altruism*, that substitute for charity in a world without God. With the denial of the soul goes the denial of personal destiny, so human fulfillment is possible to the collectivity alone. This concept of man is propagated not only by "Socialist Realism" in art and literature, but also by every disciplinary measure of the Party and the state. Under such pressure, men and women have great difficulty in seeing each other as persons. The encounter between "I and Thou" becomes extremely rare and is normally replaced by an impersonal coordination of working functions in which human beings appear as a planned "it." People who would normally draw vicarious experiences from literature now may excite themselves over the greatness of the Proletarian Revolution or the beauty of the Five-Year Plan, where we would experience the first view of Yosemite Valley or the budding of spring.

### The Other Russia

AS WE REALIZE how much of a sober view of man has been lost, can we imagine the greatness of Solzhenitsyn's achievement? Let there be no doubt: He grew up in the Wasteland. The kindly lights which guide us on our groping ways were all but extinct even in his soul. The machinery of power, the impersonal mechanism of planned society, the dry-as-dust formulary of ideology surrounded him everywhere, all avenues open to him required the renunciation of God, soul and humanity.

> Here is no water but only rock
> Rock and no water and the sandy road
> The road winding above among the mountains . . .
> There is not even solitude in the mountains
> But red sullen faces sneer and snarl . . .

Whence then came to him the power once again to see the fullness of man? None of his characters lacks that fullness. Not just his "good guys" but even his Communists can experience life and respond to it:

> Rubin [the doctrinaire Communist among the prisoners] . . .
> took a deep breath of the air with its tang of snow, and ben-

ding down, he scooped up a large handful of the gleaming
white floss at his feet; he rubbed his neck and face with it and
filled his mouth with it. He felt as though his soul had par-
taken of the freshness of the world.

Experiences are the touch of life on man's soul: friendship in
prison, the wonder of woman, love, the happiness of work. Oleg, on
being released from the hospital,

> looked about. This was a young world, turning green. He
> raised his head. The sky spread out, rosy from the sun rising
> somewhere behind the horizon. He raised his head higher. A
> string of feathery clouds – centuries of the finest workman-
> ship had gone into their making – stretched out across the
> whole sky. . . . This was the morning of Creation! The world
> was being created anew solely for Oleg's return: Go! Live!

The soul, open to being, senses participation, the Creation is
good, and our companions, for better or for worse, are of it too.
One has the feeling that the world was being created anew also for
Solzhenitsyn whose eye kindled with love takes all in with the ra-
diance of affirmation. The Communists are fellow beings too, they
make up part of the society. And, mind you, this is not an abstract,
nondescript society, this is Russia, loved and deplored, loved and
lamented, but loved all the same, the holy ground of home, the
cherished language, the solidness of its simple sons and daughters.
On Solzhenitsyn's pages, life is lived above all by men who are lacking in no relationship, whose minds can assess all situations, whose
decisions flow from their souls' openness toward above. Everything
falls into place. In *August 1914* an ensign and secret Communist
argues against Vorotyntsev:

> "Now you're making us carry this corpse, later you'll order us
> to carry that lieutenant. I can tell from his face that he's a
> Black Hundreds." "Yes, I shall. At a time like this, Ensign,
> party political differences are just so many ripples on the
> water." "Party politics – ripples? . . . What about interna-
> tional politics, then? It's because of that that we're fighting,
> isn't it? In that case – what differences mean anything at all?"
> "The difference between decency and swinishness, Ensign,"
> Vorotyntsev snapped back.

In the same work, a conversation between Varsonofiev and a couple of confused students:

> "But is it right to join the army and go to war?" Kotya blinked. "I must say – yes, it is." Varsonofiev nodded emphatically and approvingly. "Why? How can anyone judge?" Varsonofiev unlocked his fingers and spread them in a gesture that embraced the two young men as his equals. "I can't prove it, but I feel it. When the trumpet sounds, a man must be a man, even if merely for his own self-respect. This, too, is something inscrutable. . . ." "What about justice?" Sanya put in doggedly. "Yes. But again not our invented justice, which we have simply thought up to fit our convenient earthly paradise. There is a justice which existed before us, without us, and for its own sake. And our task is to *divine* what it is!"

In *The First Circle*, Solzhenitsyn remarks on his own vocation:

> Aren't writers supposed to teach, to guide? Isn't that what was always thought? And for a country to have a great writer – don't be shocked, I'll whisper it – is like having another government. That's why no régime has ever loved great writers, only minor ones.

One used to say that Poland had two governments, one of the Communist Party, and the other of Cardinal Wyszynski. Now Russia, too, has an authority ranking next to its Party regime, this one a lone man representing all in Russia that is spiritual, right-minded, common-sensed, home-grown. The phenomenon Solzhenitsyn, however, has an importance far transcending Russia. His appearance must be considered one of the great events of our time, of all time. One concluding word is needed: In his books Solzhenitsyn hardly ever mentions God or speaks of religion. He confines himself faithfully to following movements of the human soul, wherever they may lead him, and his work is above all the restoration of man's full image. But for him the path led logically further. In 1971, Solzhenitsyn received his first communion in Russia's Orthodox Church; and during Lent 1972, he addressed a deeply respectful but also deeply concerned letter to Patriarch Pimen, calling on that spiritual head to turn his pastoral attention to the lost sheep of the people of Russia.

# Why Marion Montgomery
# Has To "Ramble"

IN A REVIEW of a book by Cleanth Brooks, Marion Montgomery points to the ultimate goal: "One starts here not simply to learn how to read Faulkner's great work; the deeper lesson is how to move beyond Yoknapatawpha, to understand the relation between life and art." He praises Brooks for knowing "that literature provides a resonant ground for those serious social pleasures through which we pay homage to the community of man, to our strength and weaknesses individually and in concert. The end of such a social encounter is not simply knowledge but understanding."[1] These words – "serious social pleasures," "social encounter," "not simply knowledge but understanding" – stand for what he himself, Marion Montgomery, is pursuing in his trilogy, *The Prophetic Poet and the Spirit of the Age.*[2] The three volumes contain the fruits of research, criticism and evaluation, and yet must be called a meditation, a sensitive man's experiential journey. Evidence of the journey is found in the fact that, while he visits and revisits the same problems and even authors again and again, he not once repeats himself through more than 1300 pages. The journey has a starting point as well as resting areas. The starting point is marked by place and time. Place: the South of Flannery O'Connor and Montgomery himself. Time: again Flannery O'Connor (d. 1964), but also the "now" of the spirit of the age, meaning the perversions of reason and sensibilities during the last 200 years, and their "flowers of evil." Philosophers, political scientists and sociologists have so far been the ones to define our understanding of the spirit of the age. Marion Montgomery feels no need simply to add another book to this literature. He, a poet, focuses the corruptions of our time through the eyes of the prophetic poet, who is calling us back "to known but forgotten truths about being" and who, according to Solzhenitsyn, may bear the burden of functioning as a "second government," as 4olzhenitsyn himself has done in Russia's present darkness.

The prophetic poet or writer finds it necessary to learn discernment between truth and falsehood when falsehood comes dressed in the mantle of reason, science or conventional literature. Flannery O'Connor's reviews for the (diocesan) *Bulletin*, accordingly, were full of remarks on her studies of Husserl, Heidegger, Nietzsche, Pascal, Maritain, Voegelin and others. Marion Montgomery, following her lead, engaged in similar studies which carried him considerably beyond what he found in the notebooks. As the spirit of the age began to emerge with sharper features and shadows, he traced similar phenomena in literary figures: Edgar Allan Poe, Henry James, James Joyce, William Faulkner, T.S. Eliot, Ezra Pound, Ralph Waldo Emerson, Simone Weil and others. This provides three dimensions for each of his volumes: first, the focal figures (Flannery O'Connor in the first volume, Edgar Allan Poe in the second, Nathaniel Hawthorne in the third), second, a company of other literary figures surrounding the central figure without regard to time, and third, philosophers past and present whose concepts provide orientation points for discernment. The discernment itself, the identification of falsehood in our time, constitutes the fourth dimension. In this respect, Marion Montgomery finds a fairly well-plowed ground, thanks to such works as: Hans Urs von Balthasar, *Prometheus* (1947, dealing with the aberrations of the German soul); Albert Camus, *The Rebel* (1951, doing the same for the French soul); Hans Jonas, *The Gnostic Religion* (1958, an effort to grasp the basic falsehood of existentialism through the study of an ancient religion); Henri de Lubac, *The Drama of Atheist Humanism* (1945, focusing on Christianity and its enemies); Eric Voegelin, *The New Science of Politics* (1952), *Science, Politics & Gnosticism* (1968), and also the four volumes of his *Order and*

*History* (1956, 1957 and 1974), all of which works deal with discernment between contemporary ideologies and the history of truth regarding society. Still, we have had no similar work concentrating on the United States. Marion Montgomery has now filled this gap, as well as the gap of a work tracing false consciousness specifically in the area of poetry and literature.

How does one do this? Montgomery is dealing with an object so much impregnated by subjectivity, so tantalizingly elusive through its symbolic nature, so vulnerable to destruction by insensitive criticism, that a coldly academic approach would be self-defeating. This would remain true if he were simply trying to keep one ball in the air, but he juggles with three or even four at the same time. Were he a pedant and an intellectual bully, he would probably take up each of his tasks separately, one after the other. He could then belabor each until he had arrived at a thesis, and, having beaten rival views out of the way, triumphantly nail his colors to the mast, only to launch immediately into the next fray. Still, many critics might have applauded him for having done so. They would have called his work "readable" and "provocative."

It is the great and incomparable merit of Marion Montgomery's trilogy that he scrupulously avoids the obvious approach. His journey is a succession of social encounters, each occasioned by the reading of a literary work or the perception of a philosopher's insight. It is a continuous conversation of author and reader, as author leads the reader from meeting one literary figure to meeting another, maybe centuries away, the conversation skillfully linking encounter with encounter. The conversation turns on problems of human life, or of poetry and literature, or of philosophic consciousness, and is full of meditations on place, time, language, society, vision, nature, history, being. It is an undulating conversation, like ocean waves, the swell providing not only a sensation of up and down, but also a sense of forward motion. The reader is invited to live with this motion: having been at one place previously, he may find the same impulse later moving him again, yet it moves from a different angle in a new perspective. Thus, various lights play on the same question, fostering new recognitions.

Marion Montgomery has been criticized for "rambling."[3] Such criticism has motivated the title of this essay, a title which also parallels the titles of Montgomery's three volumes. If it is true that the medium is the message, then Montgomery's method, which has been called "rambling," contains the message. One may think of Socrates of the *Republic*, reacting to Thrasymachus' leaping at him "like a wild beast" as he demands that Socrates stop his questioning method and supply "a clear and precise statement." When Thrasymachus finishes with his own "statement," Socrates replies:

> We might answer Thrasymachus' case in a set speech of our own, drawing up a corresponding list of the advantages of justice: he would then have the right to reply, and we should make our final rejoinder; but after that we should have to count up and measure the advantages of each list, and we should need a jury to decide between us. Whereas, if we go on as before, each securing the agreement of the other side, we can combine the functions of advocate and judge.[4]

Socrates, with his own "ignorance" as a starting point, prefers to "ramble" in an attitude of waiting for truth rather than trying to possess it. In the case of Montgomery there may be an additional motive for his rambling. He is engaged in a quest and as on any true quest he finds himself face to face, now with a beautiful maiden, then with a fierce beast, and again with a horrifying demon. The woods through which the quest takes him are called "the spirit of the age," extending far back in history. In the nature of his subject he encounters Edgar Allan Poe not in person but in the shape of this or that of his literary works; or Locke behind this or that concept. Each encounter is a new situation in which he is called upon to say what he has to say and to do what is fitting. Every encounter is new, so that, even having been with Hawthorne before, when he sees him again it is a different experience, and through Montgomery's experiences the reader is carried forward. One may say that the three volumes have the character of a novel with a narrator, the difference being that the characters are not fictitious, and that they have shaped and are still shaping our own minds. The character of the novel strikes one as dramatic, not because a plot poses problems, later resolved, but because of the manifest incompatibility of the idea systems clashing with one another—just as de Lubac was struck by "the drama" of "atheist humanism." Since we have spoken of the novel also as a quest, there must be a land in which the wandering occurs, and it must be part of the subject of the work. Marion Montgomery is very much aware of that country, the abode of mankind, the "in-between," where there is the experience of tension between the higher reality of the divine and the lower reality of created things as well as of demonic narcissism, between nature and grace, between tradition and alienation.

Understanding the spirit of the age became a central problem as people realized that it consists not in fads of habit and emotion but rather in the dominant influence of certain idea systems, and that this influence is the source of major disorders. Moreover, they realized that the disorder could not be grasped by means of the categories and analytical methods available at the beginning of the century, and that the philosophical horizon had to be widened in order to define what was going on. Awareness of this responsibility came late. For the fact that it came at all, we have to thank Hitler as well as Marx: Hitler, because the fanaticism of his regime deeply shocked the West when it found itself face-to-face with criminal irrationality in high places, and that in one of the world's most civilized countries; Marx, because he, and members of the equally irrational movement that had sprung from his idea system, compulsively put all their thoughts on paper, so that one could turn to these texts for evidence. Not until the end of the century's first quarter did philosophically minded scholars address themselves to the task of systematically comprehending the unprecedented perversion of reason. They were a little too late for the statesmen, as shown by Neville Chamberlain's firm conviction that in Hitler he was confronted with nothing more than an excessively irredentist nationalist.

Competent scholarship has proven that a far more demonic derailment of reason has occurred. Once this phenomenon had been described as a "variant of theologizing,"[5] the search expanded from political thinkers like Marx to philosophers, poets and writers. By the middle of the century a large number of books had, indeed, begun to form what Voegelin termed "a new science" surrounding the spirit of the age. A suitable word, "modernity," was at hand; another word, "ideology," itself a coinage by the spirit of the age, proved useful for setting off irrational idea systems from genuine philosophy. One began to wonder how far back things had begun to go wrong. Some traced modernity to the French Revolution, others to Medieval precedents. Solzhenitsyn sees the spirit of the age at work since the Reformation; Richard Weaver felt that William of Ockham was the first culprit. Hans Jonas, sitting at Heidegger's feet and struggling to understand a novel and very strange way of thinking, found the key to Existentialism in the ancient Gnostic religion of the first centuries of our era. Eric Voegelin fingered Gnosticism as "the essence of modernity." All this went much further than Plato's and Aristotle's finding, that irrational politics resulted from private but "unlawful" passions in the disordered souls of particular persons who become tyrants. The new scholarship has shown that the unprecedented disorder of modernity stems not from subrational passions but from semirational spiritual perversion, so that it constitutes a perversion of reason perpetrated by reason itself.

Flannery O'Connor, who was mentioned as Marion Montgomery's starting point, was fully aware of this situation. In her library the three volumes of Voegelin's *Order and History* were heavily marked and annotated. She had studied Heidegger and Sartre. Montgomery writes:

> One does not read very far in her work till one becomes aware of her considerable knowledge of Western intellectual history, and of her interest in that history since the Renaissance for a textural purpose in her fiction wider than the immediate locale. It is an interest she develops under the auspices of Saint Thomas Aquinas most particularly. But then, what a range of reading she does under his auspices: Kierkegaard, Heidegger, Marcel, Sartre, Freud, Jung, Eliade, Teilhard, William James, Eric Voegelin. The names go on and on, bracketed by Pascal and Maritain. (I, p. 18)

She is a prophetic poet precisely inasmuch as her fictional characters are molded by the insight into the West's spiritual and intellectual crises she gained through these studies. Marion Montgomery does not limit himself merely to following her. Even the first volume, which centers on Miss O'Connor and her work, overflows his immediate subject. In the next two volumes he engages in his own tracing of inchoate irrationality, often in places where others have not yet looked. Still, the trilogy is no mere history, and his interest in the spirit of the age is but one aspect of his wider interest in the relations between poetic art and nature, thought and things, memory, imagination and reason, the particular and the universal.

He knows, of course, that art is a territory that must not be sullied by the advocacies of politics or philosophical contention. Still, in our age these advocacies keep intruding on art. Montgomery points out that

> in the literature of alienation, as we see it stretching from Milton to the newest *New Yorker* story, alienation is not simply a theme on which the poet practices variation. It is an idea of an experience in whose depth stirs a devouring problem, growing to the point that it threatens not only individual sanity, but the whole community of mind. . . . One encounters in the poet's word the drama of mind and heart in quest of some Word in the word, or some sustaining will, human or immortal or both. We may observe, almost as a measure of the poet's greatness, his troubled engagement of questions larger than the aesthetic. (I, p. 398)

Thus Nietzsche, Locke, Heidegger and Sartre cannot be shooed away as if they were extraneous intruders in the poet's world, just as they, even though unknown, can no longer be separated from the experiences of the man in the street. Still, as Montgomery deals with the minds that we may be accustomed to see as a problem chiefly to philosophers and political theorists, he places them in the company of poets and their characters, precisely in the context of the aesthetic.

Thus, when Montgomery takes up the subject of Nietzsche, he has with him Haze Motes, a Tennesseean country boy having turned Nietzschean (the protagonist of O'Connor's *Wise Blood*) but also Frederick Copleston, the formidable historian of philosophy, and H.L. Mencken. Why this particular company? Mencken, who furiously and insistently attacked the South, the "Bible Belt," as a benighted region, was a leading Nietzschean on the literary scene. In 1918 he published a translation of Nietzsche's *Antichrist*, "along with an introduction in which he berates the 'Protestant' South." Mencken is strongly attracted by the astonishing "spectacle of (Nietzsche's) mind," while Flannery O'Connor sees "a culmination of certain intellectual currents to spectacular pressure in Nietzsche's mind, making him of particular dramatic interest." (I, p. 386 f.) She possessed a copy of Copleston's lecture on Nietzsche to the Aquinas Society of London, first published in 1944.

> What Copleston has to say in his *St. Thomas and Nietzsche* is . . . strikingly applicable to Haze Motes. . . . In the *Antichrist*, there is a sharp attack upon grace, free will, original sin, in a tone very close to Haze Motes's. . . . One must, says Nietzsche have encountered the menace "at close hand, one must have had experience of it directly and almost succumbed to it to realize that it is not to be taken lightly ( – the alleged free-thinking of our naturalists and physiologists seems to me to be a joke – they have no passion about things; they have not suffered – )". . . . The same, one feels, must be said of Mencken as of Nietzsche's naturalists and physiologists. In doing so, one underlines that aspect of Nietzsche which this quoted passage calls especial attention to: the passion in him. . . . His prophecy is born of his imaginative faculty. . . . Because it is a prophecy of passions in the imaginative faculty, Nietzsche is first and last a dramatically appealing figure. . . . [Miss O'Connor's] tribute is that first protagonist Haze, a wild prophet pursuing the Antichrist – and finding him with a devastating effect. (I, p. 387 ff.)

Nietzsche's Zarathustra says: "Let will to truth mean this to you: that everything be changed into the humanly conceivable, the humanly visible, the humanly sensible." To which Montgomery adds: "That is Haze Motes's message, of course – that one can believe only what one can see and touch." (I, p. 390) This brings up the relation between God and nature. Nietzsche argues: "Once the concept of 'nature' was opposed to the concept of God, the word 'natural' necessarily took on the meaning of 'abominable' – the whole of that fictitious world has its source in hatred of the natural – the real! – and is no more than evidence of a profound uneasiness in the presence of reality. . . . *This explains everything.*" From O'Connor's point of view, far from explaining everything, it may possibly explain Protestantism, but "it leaves aside a conception of Christianity which carefully prevents the separation of nature and God." (I, p. 391) At this point, Copleston enters the conversation, pointing out that, in the direction in which Nietzsche

moved, nature itself must at last be denied: "Nietzsche's ideal man
. . . is man perfected in the natural order. St. Thomas would sympathize with this ideal . . . but he would point out that Nietzsche
sins against his own ideal on the one hand, and that his ideal is not a
high enough ideal. Nietzsche thinks too lowly of man . . . he
falsifies the nature of man." Nietzsche finds himself forced into
nihilism; his triumph is not a joyful one, "the optimism in its favor
being necessarily a forced one." (I, p. 394)

Montgomery's approach to Nietzsche demonstrates the manner
in which he comes to grips with the spirit of the age. He does not attempt a complete portrait of our time in the way of Camus (*The
Rebel*) or de Lubac (*The Drama of Atheist Humanism*), nor does he
aim at a systematic treatment of a thinker such as Nietzsche.
Others have done these things before, and Montgomery relies on
their help – in this case, on Copleston's. On the other hand, his focus
is on poets, writers and their concern, which essentially is with
nature. Of Nietzsche, Montgomery remarks that he attracted
"Shaw, Yeats and Lawrence" (as well as Mencken, of course), and
possibly influenced Teilhard de Chardin, who in turn attracted
Flannery O'Connor. Of all aspects of Nietzsche's thought, he is
most interested in what Nietzsche said of the relation of God to
nature, and of humanity in the light of that relation. Also we note
that he does not move in on Nietzsche by himself, and does not
engage in single combat with him. Nietzsche enters his pages
through Montgomery's encounter with other thinkers or
writers – in this case, Mencken, St. Thomas, Flannery O'Connor.
Moreover, the meeting is not dominated by hostility, even when he
characterizes Nietzsche as "a destroyer." (I, p. 392) He has already
granted to Nietzsche the character of "a prophet" and that of a
"dramatically appealing figure," as well as the merit of having provided "ground to a dramatic spectacle for gnostic thought such as it
had lacked." (I, 391) Characteristically, the chapter following the
one we have quoted is entitled: "Getting To Know Haze Motes:
Nietzsche as a Country Boy."

Now we shall turn to the problem of Heidegger. To this Montgomery devotes considerably more space than to Nietzsche: five
chapters, about eighty-five pages, of volume two of the trilogy. We
shall dwell particularly on chapter XVIII, "Old Bossy Disguised as
the White Stag." Earlier Montgomery quoted Tate, who wondered

"why the proponents of the Big Bang Theory of creation have not condescended to acknowledge Poe as their forerunner," upon which Montgomery comments: "The question seems rather why Poe's critics have not seen him more particularly as the forerunner of Martin Heidegger, our contemporary Existentialist." As he deals with Heidegger along with Poe, later on adding T.S. Eliot, Montgomery would not claim that his analysis, in the history of ideas, adds new insights, as he leans on the work of James Collins, David E. Roberts, Leo Strauss and Eric Voegelin, identifying Heidegger's concepts just sufficiently for his own purpose.

Heidegger is the thinker who in our time has prominently raised again the question of *Sein* (being). "How does it stand with being?" He distinguishes being from being-there, *Dasein*. Mankind, he says, has "fallen out" of being; his being-there is altogether meaningless and empty. Mankind feels "being thrown" into this world in which he experiences a basic anxiety (*Angst*) and homelessness. The remedy for this condition of self-alienation is "a recognition of the presence and power of 'Being-itself,' the foundation of all that is" (II, p. 181), Heidegger's term for this world is "what-is-in-totality." At a first glance, the structure of these concepts reminds the reader strikingly of Christian theology: the corruption of the world on one side, and God's creative power and saving grace on the other. Still, Heidegger's Being-itself is not supposed to be a name for transcendent divinity; again and again he insists that it belongs to the immanent reality of time and place, in other words, to history. In fact, Being-itself is yet to come, in the historical future. Its "presence" is a mere anticipated event. Still, in Voegelin's words: "The position of the gnostic thinker derives its authority from the power of being. He is the herald of being, which he interprets as approaching us from the future."[6] Meanwhile, people become really aware of their existence only in death, so that one could say, "I die, therefore I am."

Heidegger's conception of time is dominated by his exclusive emphasis on "the future as the primary phenomenon of temporality, as that kind of anticipation of self and death whereby human reality exists finitely." (II, p. 175) Montgomery points to striking similarities with Poe's *Eureka* and his colloquies, particularly *The Colloquy of Monos and Una*, as well as *Melonta Tauta*. Monos and Una converse "a hundred years after the death of the principals," the "significant record in the colloquy (being) a transposition of the five senses into a sixth sense, 'the first and obvious step of the in-temporal soul upon the threshold of the temporal Eternity.' " From this vantage point the main difficulty is in finding words, and the chief terror lies "not in the prospect of confronting Nothingness but in Poe's belief in the awesome power of words." (II, p. 176) Montgomery sees the parallel in Heidegger: "It is this impasse with words used discursively which turns Heidegger toward word-coinage." (II, p. 182) The word-coinage in turn serves to disguise problems and impasses:

> A human being becomes *Dasein* (being there), social en-counter becomes *Being-with-one-another*. *Being-itself* becomes the antagonist of *what-is-in-totality*. We find ourselves . . . journeying into Swift's Laputa as Gulliver does or accompanying Bunyanesque (but secularized) personae toward an Omega encounter with *Being-itself*, though we come to that point only as fiction. That is, we stage en-counters between *Dasein* and *Being-itself*, as Poe stages an encounter between *Monos* and *Una*. But we find ourselves nevertheless removed from the experience of a dramatic en-counter by the very word-projection. (II, p. 264)

Through this bracketing of Poe with Heidegger, Montgomery turns the reader's eye from the particular philosopher and the par-ticular poet to an area of concern to all: the human need to reflect on the relation between being and nothingness, history and eterni-ty. He criticizes poet and philosopher for approaching this area through concepts void of content, in which emptiness has a tenden-cy to slip into nothingness. Both men elevate inordinately the mind's power to create its own world. Heidegger's *Being-itself* is explicitly meant as something only "understood by the thought." His "problem (is) complicated by his denial of being to that world he calls that-which-is." "Where St. Thomas recognizes that the I AM THAT I AM lives always at the heart of the desert (that-which-is), that the failure to discover that presence reveals a withdrawal in man's will rather than any withdrawal of the Word, Heidegger argues that Being has withdrawn itself from that world and that it is man's task to recall Being-itself through man's conjuring out of emptiness a word that names Being-itself." (II, p. 200) As Voegelin has pointed out, Heidegger goes beyond the utopian images of Comte, Marx and Nietzsche. "In their place Heidegger puts Being-itself, emptied of all content, to whose approaching power we must submit." Montgomery comments: "If this is the case, then it matters little whether the assumption of man's control is exhibited in utopian attempts upon society as in Condorcet or Comte, or through the utopian attempt to make its own private world as with Poe. Poe and Heidegger are cousins to Condorcet and Bentham and Comte, though they react sharply against the empirical or utilitarian gnostic. . . . For the gnostic political or economic activist and the gnostic poet have the same initial goal – the 'decapitation of being' " (Voegelin's concept). There results the illusion of "absolute freedom of the consciousness," in which illusion "lies the sense also of an absolute alienation." (II, p. 281) If Poe provides a dimensional depth to Heidegger's inability to find the answer to obvious questions (e.g., if the "true-self" is a limited gift, who or what has limited it?), Montgomery can point to other thinkers (Pascal, Kierkegaard and Marcel) who have found satisfactory answers. (II, p. 184)

Voegelin's characterization of Heidegger is devastating: "The construct of the closed process of being; the refusal to acknowledge the experience of *philia, eros, pistis* (faith) and *elpis* (hope). . . ." Montgomery adds: "What one has is a 'resolve' (Heidegger's term) out of the *given*, directed toward that given – that is, directed inward upon the self – but with questions of faith in any given set aside." (II, p. 258) This goes for poet as well as philosopher. Where Heidegger denies any "natural understanding" of things and asserts that the wall of "historical understanding" imprisons each consciousness in its own moment of time, he is where Eliot "found himself in 1909 when he wrote 'Preludes,' an attempt to break out of that closed historical world." Twenty years later, "Eliot looks backward at his own entrapment in eighteenth-century historicism as it has been given a concentration upon individual consciousness by nineteenth-century phenomenalism and twentieth-century existentialism. He concludes that Christ, not the historicist philosopher – the phenomenologist – will redeem time. One sees this radically changed position in 'Ash Wednesday'. . . ." (II, p. 193) In this manner, a study of Heidegger turns into a serious conversation about a universal human problem among Heidegger, Poe, Pascal, Kierkegaard, Marcel, Thomas Aquinas, Flannery O'Connor, T.S. Eliot and the reader, with Montgomery the Socratic moderator. The emerging verdict of "false" upon Heidegger in no wise excludes Heidegger from the conversation. Montgomery, himself gentle, speaks with praise of Heidegger's "gentleness . . . in contrast to the worldly excessive and satanic uses of boredom by some Absurdists" (II, p. 260), and furthermore acknowledges Heidegger's "manner of high seriousness" which, however, prompts him to a suggestion "that he misleads himself as well as the reader." (II, p. 262) What Heidegger says must not simply be dismissed.

> He engages in a game of words whose issue is of profound consequence to the struggling consciousness attempting to deal with his words. Now when we examine the game Heidegger plays out with high seriousness, what we discover is that the words he uses disguise simple country truths so that they appear as original discoveries. . . . The family cow, we may conclude, has been decorated to resemble the White Stag. (II, p. 262)

On the other hand, Eliot, when he has come to a full understanding of the chapters on memory in St. Augustine's *Confessions*, "will be prepared to say that 'What might have been' is 'always present' to the seeking self . . . ; consciousness may participate once more in an event of its own past . . . though it is a participation no longer within the dominion of time and place. . . . Eliot has come to see that 'History is a pattern of timeless moments.' " (II, p. 271)

With Emerson, in the first five chapters of volume III, Montgomery comes closest to the heart of the matter: the spirit of the age, and the spirit of the United States in particular. Once again his encounter with one writer occurs in the company of others, in this case, Hawthorne, Poe, Melville, T.S. Eliot, Charles W. Eliot of Harvard, Husserl, Heidegger, Swedenborg and Winthrop. At the outset he warns himself as well as the reader that "as we come to the self-consciousness of thought and turn from the living world upon particular ideas, or upon particular writers and works, we tend to forget the question appropriate to thought – the question of the abiding cause of our turning mind, the cause which is also the wellspring of the very object elected out of existence by our thought." (III, p. 11) Montgomery's wonderment about the spirit of the age has thus a starting point, and an intent, quite different from that, let us say, of Camus, whose *The Rebel* begins: "The purpose of this essay is once again to face the reality of the present, which is logical crime, and to examine meticulously the arguments by which it is justified."[7]

Camus is moved to write by the phenomenon of political irrationality in thought and practice, as is Hans Urs von Balthasar in his *Prometheus* (1947). Likewise, de Lubac's endeavor is to show "an immense drift; through the action of a large proportion of its foremost thinkers, the peoples of the West are denying their Christian past and turning away from God . . . the negation which underlies positivist humanism, Marxist humanism and Nietzschean humanism is not so much atheism . . . as *anti*theism, or more precisely antichristianism . . . matched by a similarity of results, the chief of which is the annihilation of the human person."[8] Voegelin attempts "to apply to the gnosticism of Hegel, Marx, Nietzsche and Heidegger the insights gained by these predecessors, as well as by my own [Voegelin's] *The New Science of Politics*, and to draw more clearly the lines that separate political gnosticism from a philosophy of politics."

These prophetic writers focus philosophically on the great political catastrophe of our time: they explain how the work of foremost thinkers made possible Mussolini and Hitler, Lenin and Stalin. Montgomery's concern is with the mind and imagination of literary artists, concern for "the common ground to both philosopher and poet, a ground explored by the reason of the one and the imagination of the other, those faculties elevated to a separation in those civil wars in which poet and philosopher seem determined to contend with each other. In the inordinate elevation of those faculties – reason, imagination – the division of these gifts speaks a triumph of the presumptuous will." (III, p. 13) What are the literary manifestations of "the presumptuous will"? In Montgomery's answer both poet and philosopher are addressed: "We assume we may, by the authority of our will, inhabit a never-never land – a detached, suspended ground which is freed of memory and desire alike, freed of the anchor of our particular being in that world we never made." (III, p. 15) He comes close to that concept coined, earlier in this century, by Robert Musil, (*The Man Without Qualities*), who spoke of "the Second Reality," followed by Heimito von Doderer (*The Demons*) who called it "the refusal of apperception." Wallace Stevens echoed these other voices when remarking of modern poetry: "It is the poem of the mind in the act of finding / What will suffice." To which Montgomery adds: "That is, we provide ourselves . . . the energy of pride." (III, p. 19)

Emerson's place, in the history of the spirit of the age, is not that of the key figure of the overall process, but he is certainly a key figure in the cultural self-understanding of America, a place he still holds without being seriously examined. The Chinese wall around him built by his defenders moves Montgomery, for once in his work, to the sharp language of argumentative blows. Emerson elevates the "thinking man" to the status of divinity: "In proportion as a man has anything divine in him, the firmament flows before him and takes his signet and form. . . . The great man makes the great thing." (III, p. 28) "The world is nothing, the man is all." (III, p. 33) "If a man is at heart just, then in so far he is God." (III, p. 36) Emerson deceives his readers by a superficially religious tone in which his arguments are clothed, even though his intent is certainly anti-Christian. He carries the religious intent of previous ages into the age of science in which, as he says, the new religion will not "perpetuate the Hebrew anthropomorphic representation of God"; rather, in its place "the central thought of the new religion will therefore be a humane and worthy ideal of God, thoroughly consistent with nineteenth century revelations concerning man and nature."[9] Montgomery comments, "Emerson transfers Calvinistic election from the province of God to that of nature, relying on the new science as a replacement of Biblical revelation. The new world is the world of man's omnipotent mind, of its triumph over nature. The trumpet of humanistic self-sufficiency sounds a mighty fanfare." Montgomery senses, though, that all is not as brave as it appears. "Emerson affords a quasi-religious satisfaction, an illusion of satisfying the strange hunger in man for a world now lost. . . . The reflective mind, wherever one finds it, reveals fallen across it the haunting shadow of some Eden lost. New Eden, the dream city of man, becomes a necessity, then, without which despair in the heart prevents action." (III, p. 96 f.)

Emerson is no reliable support for one's hand, because he is "a gnostic thinker whose influence we have yet to overcome." (III, p. 98) To him, the self is its own end, "the true romance which the world exists to realize will be the transformation of genius into power" (III, p. 62), until "the world becomes at last a realized will – the double of man." (III, p. 63) His self-confidence takes on the form of self-worship: "I am divine. Through me, God acts; through me, speaks. Would you see God, see me, or see thee, when thou also thinkest as I now think." (III, p. 67) In Emerson's wake, the originally God-centered uniqueness of the New World is becoming a national spirit (which increasingly felt called to a destiny among nations through power)." (III, p. 79)

Hawthorne as well as Emerson require a closer look at their Puritan heritage. Winthrop's "covenant" appears a safe enough biblical concept unless one focuses on the particular way in which the New England Puritans used it: a covenant not so much of God with mankind but rather of mankind with God, extended in New England's history into continuous further bargaining. Under it, Winthrop distinguished between "civil or federal liberty" and "natural liberty." Whoever transgresses that "federal" law from within its bounds is an "enemy of God" who must be expelled. (III, p. 163) The concept curiously enough resembles that of St. Juste's "enemy of the people" (away with him to the guillotine!), as well as Lenin's "enemy of the revolution." For those allowed to stay, Winthrop specifies that "such liberty is only justified to the extent that it is edifying – that is, spiritually utilitarian." John Cotton, in his *Way of Life*, issued an outline of Puritan virtues, the chief of which is Industry (III, p. 221), for which the new "technometria" provides as guide a secular "science." Worse yet was the sense of being cut off from the past. "We find that blighting tendency in our current national spirit to a degree almost epidemic. But it too was in Puritan thought from the beginning. For the attempt to anchor the new church-state in the Bible, after severing roots in the older Church, required an interruption of the continuity of human experience." (III, p. 227)

A similar break was made between mankind and nature. Montgomery speaks of "the restless, wandering Puritan spirit to which nature is most likely to be either an intrusion held suspect as diabolic or a challenge set by God to test stoic resolution. That last tribe of Old Israel, the Puritans . . . engages in bargaining with

God endlessly, sharpening its bargaining powers till it triumphs among men." (III, p. 293) Most interesting is the way in which Montgomery can trace the Puritan heritage to later ways of thinking which spring either from rebellion against Puritanism, or seem far distant from the source. Thus, dealing with Henry James, he dwells on the inordinate importance of form. "Form, we have suggested, came to dominate Puritan thought, through the rigidity of 'technometria,' to which was added the rationalization of form by Locke. With such a heavy, religious emphasis upon the mind's propensity to abstraction, that inclination grew to dominance in the American popular spirit." One of the results was Henry's revolt in which "a new pragmatism is defended: words used to aesthetic form itself as the end." (III, p. 171) Thus he can conclude that "James is one of the sons of Calvin, too." (III, p. 176) While acknowledging that "we are richer for his art," he cautions that it is "an art reflecting the intellectual distemper called gnosticism." (III, p. 195)

The terms "gnostic" and "gnosticism" have popped up in these pages as they have in Montgomery's trilogy. Gnosticism was, of course, an ancient religion widespread in the first four or five centuries of our era. A new interest in this religion was kindled in contemporary philosophers who found that modern ideological systems, particularly Existentialism, fit Gnosticism "as if made to measure. . . . In other words . . . lock turns into key and key into lock: the 'existentialist' reading of Gnosticism, so well vindicated by its hermeneutic success, invites as its natural complement the trial of a 'gnostic' reading of Existentialism."[10] Jonas's study, available in German as early as 1934, stimulated vigorous research on the part of other thinkers who were intensely bent on understanding modernity, e.g., Gilles Quispel, Eric Voegelin. The ancient Gnostics taught "knowledge" of an alien God—alien both to man and to the cosmos—and of the world as the creation of a demonic demiurge ignorant of that divinity. This "knowledge" consisted in an elaborate account of how this wicked creation, and mankind's imprisonment in it, came about: the knowledge seen as constituting salvation, a salvation not of humanity but of the divinity, from the results of its own failures.

How could this system lead to an understanding of our time? "Existentialism," wrote Hans Jonas, "which claims to be the explication of the fundamentals of human existence as such, is the philosophy of a particular, historically fated situation of human existence: and an analogous (though in other respects very different) situation had given rise to an analogous response in the past."[11] Thus, understanding Gnosticism could lead to an understanding of Communism, Nazism and Anarchism, as well as Existentialism, as one came to grasp the underlying spiritual experiences: a radical and comprehensive dissatisfaction with everything that exists, a tendency to blame this on the poor organization of the world as a whole, the assumption that there could be salvation from this evil world, and that this salvation consisted in certain processes of human action.[12]

Most modern scholars turning to gnosticism as a heuristic key of modernity were moved by political and moral concerns. Jonas deplored above all the loss of nature as a philosophical ground for all human norms. "That which has no nature has no norm."[13] Eric Voegelin turned his chief attention to the exclusion of God, of transcendence, from political thought, finding in this exclusion the major source of political irrationality. On his copious findings of human order in dependence on God he constructed his view of history, using the concept of "the flowing presence." His and the works of other scholars gave to the term "gnostic" the quality of a pejorative epithet. The words "ideology" and "ideological" entered into an amalgam with "gnostic" to the point of interchangeability. Montgomery, while accepting this meaning of the term, nevertheless differs from the philosophers looking primarily into the conditions of political and moral order. If he finds Gnosticism heuristically useful, it is chiefly in relation to poetry and literature, as they deal with nature, the reality given to us in time and place. Art aims at understanding, which is the dimension of the eternal encountered in the setting of the particular.

What, then, is Montgomery's final word on the spirit of the age? He sees it as "alienation whose cause is perverted love, the turning inward upon the self." (III, p. 263) In this country, unlike Europe, this alienation does not bear the face of a rejected social system or a political cause. Here, it was prepared by Poe, which explains "why the American intellectual community was not so shocked by that literature of the absurd, out of existential thought, which began to trickle westward from Europe early in this century, swelling to flood tide after midcentury, after which alienation becomes a sentimental ideal rather than a symptom of spiritual disease." (III, p. 357) Spiritual disease is the English version of Schelling's concept, "pneumo-pathology." There are other, specifically American causes: "Not only had the evolution of science in the nineteenth century, the immediate grounds for the new detheologizing priests, already softened the effect; the severest of the Pilgrim fathers had done so, too. For to see God as absentee owner of nature, and man as his tenant charged with improving the property, is already a giant step away from God." (III, p. 357 f.) Montgomery has no need to assail the totalitarianisms which, in any event, have not found friendly acceptance on our shores. There is enough for him to do in the world of the artist of language. Since the Renaissance, he says, we have "separated 'thought from action, judgment from vision, nature from grace, reason from imagination.' " (I, p. 51) These separations, repeatedly emphasized by Flannery O'Connor, can be traced in the Puritans, Locke, Poe, Emerson, Whitman, James, as well as many contemporaries. Through this history runs as a scarlet thread "the conclusion that the visible universe has only mental existence." (III, p. 204) The effect stems not merely from science; it is also noticed in the emotional enthusiasm that one "is saved." "One's sense that one is particularly selected by grace as agent in the world tempts to an excessiveness in which one's pride in the specially granted power leads to a distortion of that world in which the power is exercized. Similarly, the intellectual revelation, which is an experience to which grace as a cause is easily excluded, carries the same temptation. . . . The world appears oversimplified. This, too, is the moment of Manichean temptation with which St. Thomas is concerned when he cites Augustine's attack upon that heresy: 'It was a serious  error in those of whom Augustine speaks to assume it does not matter what men think of the created universe so long as they think rightly concerning God. For error in the matter of the universe means false opinion about God.' " (III, p. 205) Those whose thinking about reality is confined by the sides of their skulls he confronts with St. Thomas: "Truth is the self-manifestation and state of evidence of real things. . . . Truth does not exist for itself alone. Primary and precedent to it are existing things: the real. Knowledge of truth, therefore, aims ultimately not at 'truth' but, strictly speaking, at gaining sight of

reality." (III, p. 295 f.) Alienation means self-separation from reality as the result of which there is found a sense of limitless untram-
melled freedom of each subject, which Dostoevsky called "the terrifying new freedom." John Courtney Murray calls the original act of
freedom "the will to atheism."

This act, like the will to faith, "issues forth from the deepest
regions of the self, where freedom is more than choice, where it is
the self recognizing its own existence in the recognition of God or
rejecting its own existence in the refusal of God – and thus lapsing
into absurdity." (III, p. 441) Montgomery traces this absurdity in
American literature. To the political repercussions he makes only
fleeting reference: "Paralleling the rise of the grotesque in art is
the change in political thinking spawned by the Enlightenment.
There comes to be a pressing necessity to annihilate the existing
social order." (III, p. 375 f.)

We have had a number of books casting the acid of angry rejection over the spirit of our age. They are not in error; it is only that
in many cases they do not get us anywhere. Marion Montgomery
stages his encounters with the Sons of Mani in the company of "the
prophetic writers" and the men of ancient wisdom. It is interesting
to watch him as he frequently resorts to the help of Eric Voegelin,
without attempting to account for Voegelin's entire work. He
gratefully accepts from Voegelin the gift of key concepts, e.g., the
"metaxy" – the in-between nature and transcendence, which is the
real habitat of mankind, as well as the concept of "egophany" and
the manipulating "directors of civilization." He profits from Eliot's
struggle and the resulting fruits of deep insight: he concludes his
work with Eliot's lines,

> to arrive where we started
> And know the place for the first time.


The reader who has patience to proceed slowly, leisurely, as
Montgomery visits and revisits "the questions raised by those
separations," will not fall into a fear of despair but feel himself
gently carried. Ancient evil is with us in contemporary form;
modern reason has turned sour; the center does not seem to hold;
truth appears to vanish . . . and yet there are the voices of reality in

the uneasiness and melancholy of Hawthorne, in the Christian grotesque of Flannery O'Connor, in the breakthrough of Eliot. In this company, even the prophets of perdition witness through their sorrow to that which they have lost. For, in Flannery O'Connor's words, "To know oneself . . . is, paradoxically, a form of exile from the world . . . above all, to know what one lacks. It is to measure oneself against Truth, and not the other way around." (II, p. 527)

[1] *Chronicles of Culture* 8, 5 (May, 1984).

[2] I. *Why Flannery O'Connor Stayed at Home*; II. *Why Poe Drank Liquor*; III. *Why Hawthorne Was Melancholy* (LaSalle, Ill: Sherwood Sugden & Co., 1981, 1982, 1984). Hereafter referred to in the text by volume number and page number.

[3] E.g., in the otherwise enthusiastic response by Maclin Horton, *The Hillsdale Review* 2 (Summer, 1983).

[4] *The Republic*, pp. 336, 348 (Cornford translation).

[5] Eric Voegelin, *The New Science of Politics: An Introduction* (Chicago: University of Chicago Press, 1952), p. 25.

[6] *Science, Politics & Gnosticism* (Chicago: Regnery/Gateway, 1968), pp. 45 f.

[7] *The Rebel* (New York: Vintage Books, 1956), p. 3.

[8] *The Drama of Atheist Humanism* (Meridian Books), p. vii.

[9] *Science, Politics & Gnosticism*, p. v.

[10] Hans Jonas, *The Gnostic Religion*, second edition (Boston: Beacon Press, 1963), p. 321.

[11] *Ibid.*

[12] Cf., Eric Voegelin, *Science, Politics & Gnosticism*, pp. 88 ff.

[13] Jonas, *Gnostic Religion*, p. 334.

# Beyond "Democratic Disorder"

THE TITLE OF this essay suggests that a political form, democracy, might be to blame for our current crisis. I submit that no political form is that important. Forms are secondary in politics, capable of helping or hindering, but they are not at the core of political destiny. If we feel like blaming our present decline on democracy as such, let us remember the Swiss, a living historical example assuring us that democracy is fully compatible with a strong sense of purpose and vigorous action when needed. What we now call "democratic disorder" is precisely an absence of purpose, a faltering sense of reality, a shrinking from vigorous action, a failure of nerve. One should look deeper than mere form to discover the sources of such ailments.

Let me suggest that we are observing an advanced state of dissolution of our cultural patrimony, which is Christian. We are a Christian society, a fact that has little to do with the number of faithful and active Christians in our midst, but rather with the foundation of our culture. Western civilization came into existence through the unifying impulse of Latin Christianity. No other religion has ever wielded a similarly powerful influence in the centuries of our existence. The historical metamorphoses of our culture can be understood only in the relations to the Christian origins, even though not all these mutations have worked in favor of Christianity. Modernity, indeed, has been a great movement disparaging and attacking both the Christian Church and its faith. In the course of this movement much of Western life was profanized, meaning that God and the sacred were driven out to the point of disappearance. To a larger extent, though, modernity brought about processes of secularization which, in the act of perverting, maintained Christian modes of thinking and living.[1] Marxism, whose vision of a socialist future is an "immanentization of the Christian eschaton" could not have been spawned in a non-Christian culture. Indeed, all modern ideologies are perverted, secularized varieties of the Christian message of salvation, and the vision of man's transfiguration. Well they may assert the certainties of science in their analysis and prediction, but they require faith all the same, in their case, faith in history, in the Revolution, in psychoanalysis, in collective economics, in the Party: faith grievously misplaced but faith nevertheless.

No need to dwell on the pseudo-religious quality of modern ideologies, which has been sufficiently belabored and is now accepted as correct analysis. Not all of our modern culture consists of ideologies. The ideologies have come to overshadow everything else because, and insofar as, they are organized, armed, and wield a huge club of terroristic power. Still, much of contemporary life, particularly outside of the metropolis, goes on under the peaceful ordering of Christian consciousness. Even when one visits a country in plain political turmoil and economic disarray, like Italy, one is astonished to find the family largely intact. That kind of discovery is by no means confined to Italy. In many parts the tradition of our culture continues, and not merely as a sectarian backwater. Now between the ideologies and the tradition no peace is possible. A deep hostility stems not merely from the ideologists' disparagement of piety, Christian dogma, and the transcendence. This is not a contemporary version of the religious conflicts of the 16th and 17th centuries. Irreconcilable hostility rather is caused by the ideologists' total subversion of the practical order of politics, rooting in their false image of man, their presumption of certainty about future destiny, their quest for total power, their principled polarization of all humans. Thus, wherever ideologies organize and arm themselves for action, the gulf of latent warfare opens between them and the tradition, and ideologists have not been able to close that gulf when they established themselves in the place of a people's government. In Russia, Spain, Yugoslavia, open war did erupt, and that remains a possibility in almost all other Western countries, in the presence of armed ideologies.

If other countries have managed to escape civil war until now, it is because of the existence of a third element, an urbanized middle class committed to neither the Christian tradition nor the ideologies, and occupying most leading positions in society. One may describe them as a class of profanized people. They have rejected the Christian assumption of man's fallen nature and thus have little or no sense of the reality of evil. Conversely they feel no need for God's salvation and manage to put their whole trust in efforts of human enlightenment, which must be called their ultimate hope. For about two hundred years these people have lived on the left-overs of Christian moral capital. They kept the concept of the human soul, using it without visible embarrassment. They spoke easily of human dignity, without being very clear about what it is that dignifies even the lowest and least intelligent man. The equality of men as creatures made in God's image, as well as all alike being sinners, became in their minds a postulate of equality *tout court*. Human freedom, the outreach of consciousness as it overflowed any intended object and also marveled at its own thinking, as well as the freedom of faith-formed-by-love, assured by the evidence of "God's humility," was turned into a limitless ambition for human power. For a while love was still seen as "the greatest" of the excellences, even though it took the disguise of "altruism." Men continued to call each other brothers even while having little use for a common father. Victorian civilization managed to instill considerable residual moral strength into a largely profanized Christian milieu.

Today the leading elements of our culture have come to the end of their tether. This is what we mean when speaking of "democratic disorder." The Christian capital has been used up in the hearts and minds of those who have discarded its regenerating faith. The Enlightenment's vision of a brave new world is known to have been a Fata Morgana. When once there seemed to be something of great promise, there now is nothing. And thus the deepest convictions, long held over as souvenirs of an erstwhile Christian faith, go limp and drop to the ground, like so many worn-through rags. Our judges, even when imposing punishment, often are unsure of its meaning and justification, and frequently doubt whether what is called evil is not merely an effect of circumstances. Professor Walter Berns reports how, at a meeting of the Advisory Council of the National Institute of Law Enforcement and Criminal Justice, he asked this gathering of eminent men of the law; "Why *not* commit crimes?", a question which no one answered, amidst great em-

barrassment.[2] We are materially living by an economic system of
free enterprise which has generated unprecedented wealth, but our
politicians feel a call to play an adversary role toward that system,
and dedicate themselves to an expanding system of freely handed-
out incomes. Educators, while steadily enlarging their apparatus,
lack a vision of purpose. They are largely hostile to the cultural
tradition it is their business to transmit, and to the standards of excellence that form the quintessence of education. One can multiply
these examples *ad libitum*. In the multiple, they may give an impression of so many unfortunate derailments, each of which may
well be "fixed." The full scope of the crisis comes into view only as
we look at countless and typical middle-aged men and women
engaged in desperate quests for "their identity," "their life-styles,"
and "values they will create," "the new person" they will make out
of themselves as they go from one programmed panacea to
another: "I'm OK, you're OK," Transcendental Meditation, "est,"
"touch therapy," "Hare Rama, Hare Krishna," and a multitude of
other similar ones. For a day or a week they believe they have been
saved from the inner void, only to fall back into it with an ever
greater sense of helplessness. Here is the urban educated middle
class, in the final stage of profanization which attends the crum-
bling of the last vestiges of Christian legacy so that no beliefs are
left any more.

Western humanity thus falls into three distinct elements: 1) The
nihilistic ideologists who, under the sway of History deified, believe
*in* nothing; 2) the urbanized and educated middle class of cultural
leaders who know not in what to believe; and 3) those who believe
in the God of Christianity. The first element is "the specter haunting Europe" (Marx, *Communist Manifesto*), the last element
abides on quiet islands of order, as it were, but the profanized-
second element furnishes the leaders of education, the media, the
bureaucracy, and the government. In other words, the power of
making policies and setting our direction is in the hands of people
who are spiritually, intellectually, and morally adrift. This includes
many leaders of the younger generation, the 30-50 year olds who
were still impressionable in the Sixties and came out with their
world in ruins.

The lack of conviction of this element does not mean that they
are lacking in motives. The motives, however, have shallow roots.

Or, to put it in different words, there are motives but no principles. We see an abundance of feelings which are alleged to be capable of serving as reliable guides. Even these feelings still bear the stamp of their Christian origins. Politicians vaunt their "compassion." One need not doubt their sincerity, but the emotion is no longer controlled by understandings of ultimate reality, of human nature, and even of the causal relations between things in this world. Freedom likewise has become a mere emotional aspiration without shape, or relevance to order. Something similar happened to the concept of virtue in ancient Rome: At first it was not any virtuous deed that won the award of glory but only that deed of excellence which served the *salus publica*, the well-being and endurance of Rome. Later, after the Punic Wars, there developed that "excessive lust of glory" which craved sensational fame in the eyes of the masses, by deeds that were remarkable without in any way serving Rome, and in some cases even directed against Rome. "Glory" was taken to be identical with "being a celebrity." As virtue in ancient Rome separated itself gradually from the public good, so now freedom has cast loose from order, community and the Creation. It has become void of any content of value except itself, so that it is experienced in a process of denying, one after another, obligations, limitations, bonds, values, and distinctions. Other motives there are, for instance: perfection (also an adopted child of erstwhile Christian parentage) but now become a brat throwing tantrums in its desire to get, instantly, flawless human institutions, and yelling for a club to go after the parents who are responsible for the flawed ones. And equality is still around, once a humble assumption about the human condition ("we all are in the same boat," "we all alike are sinners," "Christ died to save us all") but now bloated into a domineering, uncompromising imperative, served emotionally rather than rationally, an *idée fixe* perniciously feeding a more and more universalized discontent.

That discontent, in turn, has none of the dignity of genuine rebellion, in Camus' sense. It manifests itself in a whimpering withholding of affirmation and loyalty, in a bleating "nay" towards everything that can be called existing structure. The unsatisfiable emotional drive for equality, the frustrated demand for perfect human performance, the peacelessness of pursuing unshaped freedom, all induce people to withhold allegiance and respect on the grounds that imperfect institutions of order have no right to exist. "There ought to be something better than our penal system." "Our economy consists of sinful institutions." "Nothing but the absolutely safe car can satisfy us." With such attitudes we criticize not merely this or that action or practice, but the entire set of institutions, and ultimately deny piety and loyalty to the nation whose history has nourished us. As we feel that the state no longer deserves our prayers, national security appears as a guilty use of power, compulsory service for its defense a public abomination, and any vigorous foreign policy a part of "imperialism." Thus, while we still have the technology, the money, the weapons, the manpower, we are lacking the mind that can relate these means to the nation's purpose among other nations. Our absence of will, our "failure of nerve," are symptoms of the void at the heart of human beings, who, having lost their beliefs, have no firm grasp on reality. In an editorial, "Ronald Reagan?", the *Wall Street Journal* drew this sketch of the situation: "Four years ago, the political system . . . reached outside the mainstream, for a fresh new face. . . . This time the system is reaching for an old face . . . because it then can have some confidence in where he stands . . . If Mr. Reagan fails, the failure will not be his alone. This week the political news is dominated by an old face speaking an old message. That is an indictment not of Ronald Reagan, but of an entire generation of American political leadership." (July 14, 1980)

## II

IF THE "democratic disorder," then, is properly assessed as stemming from spiritual roots, as a crisis of profanized man and the power he wields in our society, no merely political remedy can avail. New policies, new programs, fewer programs, new parties, even the return of "old men," all these would be tantamount to mere bandaid treatment of a disease of a spiritual core. Our minds are attuned, not to spiritual problems and evaluations, but to political analysis and political recommendations. Our crisis had been rightly diagnosed in terms of the failures of "profanized man" even before 1950. It has been said, that early, that this malady of a spiritual "dead end" requires the cure of a total collapse, not merely what one calls a historical catastrophe, but the kind of collapse that extends into the particular souls of men. Profanization of life can be transcended only in and through suffering: not any kind of suffering, but the extreme suffering in which even the last possibility of life seems to be lost. The human being who undergoes this kind of suffering may then experience that, as he is falling straight down, apparently into a bottomless abyss, he actually is not dropping into nothingness but rather finds himself being carried.[3] Wilhelm Kamlah, who made this statement, arrived at this insight in the World War II situation. Since then, a philosopher's idea expressed in an academic book has been borne out by the great event of the spiritually regenerative experiences of *zeks* in Soviet Labor camps. In the extremity of personal and collective annihilation, men like Solzhenitsyn discovered the divine reality, without help from dogma or *kerygma*. The community of this experience – or rather, of experiences in forms of a variety of religions – shines forth in the title of a witnessing book: *From Under the Rubble*. A number of different individuals, with varying backgrounds, describe the movement of healing from the disorder of a profanized existence, and the resulting emergence "into history." So far, the Soviet Union seems to be the only place where that movement has occurred on a significantly large scale, even though its testimony has stirred the souls of Czechs, Poles, and Hungarians with great power.

It is a fact which we must duly note that Western publics have had great difficulty with Solzhenitsyn's report, and, even more, with the inferences he has drawn from this event (the "event" not being confined to the one Solzhenitsyn but to a great number of Russian *zeks*). His conclusion, in his *Letter to the Soviet Leaders*, that "Christianity is the sole alternative," is a statement of clinical precision. Western leaders, even those of the profanized type, seemed willing to accept that much, even though they immediately placed Solzhenitsyn in the pidgeonhold of a "romantic reactionary." What they could not forgive him, however, was his criticism of the West, particularly as expressed in his Harvard Commencement Speech. Yet, Solzhenitsyn neither rejects the West as an ally nor turns against it in hostility. His criticism is confined to manifestations of disorder which diminish the West's effectiveness in the common fight. Western leading countries, after all, have not undergone an experience of healing suffering comparable to that of the Gulag *zeks*. Solzhenitsyn is far from recommending that we seek such suffering. The early Church discovered and taught the truth that suffering must not be sought but merely patiently endured when it comes. All the same, the United States has not been defeated, occupied, subjected to starvation and to systematic public falsehood. Its citizens have not lived together in situations where both physical and moral existence trembled on the edge of the abyss. I believe that Solzhenitsyn's critique of the West is correct, that his is a friendly criticism one hundred and eighty degrees different from his criticism of the Soviet regime. What is more, his complaint about our shortcomings does apply to the entire West. Some experience comparable to that of the *zeks* might have been had in Germany, where in fact it did occur, but only in desperately few and isolated cases which did not give rise to a movement, as in Russia. Rather the broader healing effect of these experiences was blocked by the desperate endeavor of most people for personal justification, in the face of the collective odium of Nazi guilt falling on Germany.

All this really constitutes an excursus about a question that must concern all who reflect on the problem "Beyond Democratic Disorder." There is, indeed, such a "beyond," but accessible only by a strait gate and narrow way. The wide gate and broad way of conventional politics allows of no hope except that of temporary palliatives. Actually, this is not a new insight. Ever since Augustine's *City of God* Western man has been aware that government, public policy, and administration cannot offer human salvation. That, however, does not mean that the differences between better and worse government deserve to be slighted or despised. They are important, albeit within the limits of politics in the wider range of human existence. It is not only fitting, then, but necessary that we turn to the practical possibilities available to a government consisting not of profanized men, but of persons living in the Christian tradition, even though their hold on it may be tenuous. What can they do? What criteria of order are available to them?

## III

ONE first thinks of *principles,* chiefly because the profanized man is unable to muster any consistency of principle, as he is largely swayed by emotions. Our judicial system, above all its penal code, is badly in need of some restoration of principles. We need a renewal of the principle of punishment, and a new will to discover principles in the face of abortion, sexual libertinism, and drugs. Our foreign policy requires an acknowledgement of principle with regard to Communism, and the Soviet Union in particular. The particular problem we face here is that of a selective moralism which singles out the Soviet Union, from all other countries, for special condemnation, and thus poses the question of morality in foreign policy in a new way.[4] Principle in foreign policy serves as a criterion to distinguish between impermissible compromises which would destroy moral substance, and permissible negotiations which leave the moral code intact. On the other hand, a universal fusion of moral principle with foreign policy in the Carter style of "support for human rights" must be avoided because of its utopianism, tendency to imperialism, and the likelihood of resulting Quixotic policies.[5] On the other hand the policies of ideological and millenarian parties claim to be principled, and are indeed principled in their own way, but the principles themselves are fallacious and irrational. More about this later.

Secondly, a government of persons rooted in the Christian tradition should be capable of more *realism* than profanized men can attain. An editorial in the *Washington Star* on the death of William J. Baroody characterized him as a "profoundly religious man," but continued: "At the same time, this man of values a good many people find old-fashioned if not downright anachronistic, had an extraordinarily cool and discerning eye for trends. . . . Mr. Baroody maneuvered AEI front and center to a position where it is financed by leading foundations and respected by old opponents as well as by a widening – and bipartisan – circle of new friends." (July 31, 1980) The "realism" of tradition-anchored people may manifest itself in a concern for a preservation of structures: political, economic, and cultural. In that perspective, contemporary politics falls into the dichotomy between doctrinaire activism, basically rebellious, and the politics of structure, governed not merely by "piety" in the ancient Roman sense but also by a clear assessment of "real possibilities." The contrasting concern of doctrinaire activists is rather with "possible realities." As one looks at the politics of structure from the point of view of principle, one may find it frequently unprincipled, because it does what is expedient for the structures rather than what is required by doctrine. All the same the concern for structure is essentially a "long view" toward principle. A masterly analysis of a politician of structure is contained in Eugene Davidson's *The Making of Adolf Hitler* (New York, 1977). General von Seeckt, the commanding officer of the Reichswehr in the first decade of the Weimar Republic, was a man of monarchical principle. He made up his mind, however, to serve with utmost loyalty any viable government that would be produced by the Leftist policies of the postwar years and to disregard his own principles, so that his support might serve to preserve the existence of Germany as a political entity. One might call this a case of principled abandonment of principle.

In today's world, a politics of structure finds itself beset with enemies who have exclusive use of slogans of utopian perfection. A traditionalist government must not remain silent under this kind of attack. It must counter with steady and principled *praise for the structures* it protects, as well as for the principle of piecemeal reform as distinct from wholesale destruction. In doing so, there is some danger of confusion regarding that which is to be defended. At least four different structures need to be distinguished:

a) a system of capitalist production and distribution, with its attendant legal framework of private property rights, a system which also produces the power of corporations and financiers;
b) a system of rapidly advancing technology which entails the increasing dependence of all persons on complex networks of technical operations, and requires much subordination of the personal element to impersonal functions; this system is as characteristic of socialism as it is of capitalism;
c) an individualist culture prone to insist on "my thing," "my values," "my life-style," – all anarchistic notions denying not merely authority but also larger community;
d) a system of democratic diffusion of power, with its attendant need to make a success of complex procedures designed to produce decisions out of a multiplicity of wills and interests.

Each of these structural systems tends toward its own kind of evil. Contemporary politics inclines to seize on these evils, universalizing them into a "total critique," or global condemnation, under the formula that evil is "systemic." The truth is that evil, in this as in every other situation, roots in the human heart, and that each system tends to magnify and manifest human evil in its own way. A government committed to the protection of structures must not on account of that commitment excuse itself from counteracting those by-products of the system that have come to threaten both community and individual lives. The cultivation of power is surely a legitimate function of government, but in practicing it one must not turn one's back on goodness.

Thirdly, in Western countries the cause of *freedom* ranks high, possibly highest, among priorities. To this extent, an ideological element is mixed into all Western politics. For freedom, as we have just seen, can be an instrument of anarchical dissolution of society into millions of atoms. On the other hand, it can also nourish a vision of man as a conqueror of nature, or of his own past, and as an omnipotent builder of a blissful future. The latter is the vision of revolutionary humanism and the source of energy for doctrinaire politics. Freedom, as Burke already observed, can be a heady brew. A government of tradition-rooted people must aim to discern ordered freedom from its demonically destructive perversion. There is no getting around the fact that the human quest for freedom involves always man's relation with his Creator, a relation capable of taking the path of faith formed by love, as well as the path of metaphysical revolution resulting in demonic nothingness. Thus beyond all political solutions there is always the need of man for attaining freedom in his own heart, as he wrestles with the forces of corruption within him and looks for the redemption available to him.

On the other hand, freedom today is no longer seen, as it once was, merely as freedom of "society" from the "state." That kind of freedom is still not forgotten where the regime is totalitarian. "What's happening in Poland can be best described as a renaissance of civil society. All the main social and professional groups are following the workers who won a right to organize independent unions."[6] In the industrialized countries of the West, however, the issue frequently is seen as freedom within society, i.e., within nongovernmental economic and social structures. The slogans in vogue are quite individualistic, but one may surmise that underneath there is a desire for the protection of and respect for, patterns of habits, traditional relationships, i.e., values which each person, effortlessly sharing with others, tends to regard peculiarly his own. From the Enlightenment we derived the contempt for what Burke called "prejudices," the order of habitual judgments constituting man's "second nature." Thomas Aquinas insisted that laws should be "just, possible to nature, according to the customs of the country, adapted to time and place." He added that laws should be changed only with great care, for "when a law is changed, the binding power of law is diminished, as far as custom is concerned." The individualistic rhetoric of the Right might therefore benefit by a period of benevolent neglect, as government focuses its concern on the way in which people habitually live in groups and secondary structures.

Thus freedom to move within the easy yoke of habits must be defended today against two threats: a) "the armed violence of doctrinaire politics which destroys all habits in favor of the Party's total organization," and b) the overbearing disposition of " compassionate" governments to overlay habits with ubiquitous regulations and thus to narrow freedom by a multitude of irritating small reins. As one seeks to stop this tendency one need not defend prevailing habits as morally flawless. Their good consists to a large extent in that they are the people's own. One is reminded that after the fall of Napoleon's brother Joseph, who as king of Spain had set up a very enlightened and modern government, the people welcomed their own king at the border. Ferdinand VII, a monster on the throne if there ever was one, was pulled across the border by the people who had put themselves into the horses' harness, welcoming their own bad man as *"El Deseado,"* the "desired one." We should allow ourselves to be taught by this and other historical examples that freedom is not always identical with letter-perfect procedures of election, legislation, and administration. If a society is felt by its members to "fit like a glove," it means that its people move in it with a sense of freedom, no matter what the conditions may be in our eyes.

Finally, a government that is returned to power as the hope for a radically new course of events should aim above all for *sobriety*. It is true that the two alternatives, liberalism/socialism on the one side, and traditionalist conservatism on the other, are political currents pointing in opposite directions, like rivers at a watershed. In the long run they will result in types of social order utterly incompatible with each other. Precisely for this reason, both sides have somewhat the air of a crusade, with fanfares of a "final battle" being heard in the background. Peregrine Worsthorne showed us, ten years ago, that no Labour Party will ever be able to muster the power required to bring about the changes it projects, given the politics of a modern democratic state. He spoke of the 1968 Wilson government in England, but what he said also applies to an American or German conservative administration. The crusading spirit remains confined to words: it has no ability to translate itself into a spirit of sacrifice and unquestioning loyalty sufficient to brave the heavy storms of systemic change. One can therefore say with some confidence that the return to power of a conservative government will be no earthshaking event, just as little as will be the return of a social-democratic party. In our days, the only earth shaking event that is an ever-present possibility is a Communist takeover.

Conservatives aspiring to power thus should avoid the rhetoric of ultimates. Ronald Reagan made a great mistake in repeatedly using Tom Paine's phrase about the power we have "to make the world anew." A similar mistake is to recall John Winthrop's myth of "the city shining on a hill." The mention of "enduring peace" reflects a millennarian mentality, and the word "aggression" belongs to the same group of concepts, all hatched in the heady days of League of Nations' enthusiasm. These are manifestations of utopian enthusiasm[5]/which entails a refusal of sobriety, and that in an age that needs sobriety as much as its daily bread. All the same, it *is* true that Western civilization stands at a political watershed and must choose whether it wants to go in one or the other of opposite directions. Since it can have no power, thought, to wheel on its heels in a sudden resolve, it must content itself with gradual, piecemeal and hardly noticeable change. Meanwhile, a government must appeal to its citizens in terms of competence, realism, sobriety, and personal character. Rather than whipping up enthusiasm, it must seek to bring calm to agitated souls. In the language of Camus, it must restore a sense of *limits*. Its rhetoric must endeavor to make the limits plausible. The most terrifying limit, of course, is a government's inability to bring about a resolution of the spiritual crisis, which also dictates the modest amount of political power it can mobilize apart from war, and maybe even in the presence of war. And we, the intellectuals among citizens, must learn to control our own yearnings for a "new world," as we learn to live in the one we inhabit, affirming our own history and the "real possibilities" it offers.

[1] On the distinction of profanization and secularization cf. Wilhelm Kamlah, *Christentum und Geschichtlichkeit* (Stuttgart, 1951), p. 19.

[2] *Modern Age,* v. 24, no. 1, Winter 1980, p. 20.

[3] *Der Mensch in der Profanität* (Stuttgart, 1949), n. 18.

[4] Cf. my "Foreign Policy and Morality," *The Intercollegiate Review,* Spring 1980, pp. 77-84. Available upon request as IR Reprint No. 92.

[5] Cf. my "Freedom and Rights: What Is To Be Done," *The Review of Politics,* v. 40, no. 2, April 1978, pp. 183-95.

[6] "Poland's Right to Life," *Wall Street Journal,* Dec. 17, 1980.

# The Glory and Misery of Education

LET US PUT before our inner eye five young men in the process of being educated: A teen-age Australian aborigine, a fifth-century Athenian youth studying with Hippias the Sophist, the same youth after he later had become a disciple of Socrates, a young Russian intellectual in the first half of the 19th century, and his great-great-grandson, in our century. What in each case is happening, and why? The Australian boy is being initiated into manhood by instruction in all that grown men know about the higher forces or powers or beings that either cause or govern birth and death, growth and decay, fertility and barrenness. This knowledge makes him a full-fledged member of his society, the order of which consists in myth, symbol, ritual and lore. The Greeks, in the course of two astonishing centuries, "discovered the mind," opening the possibility of truth that transcended the traditions of society. It immediately gave rise to two approaches: that of "enlightened" Hippias who saw the mind as an instrument for the pursuit of private utilitarian ends of power and wealth, and that of Socrates who "desired knowledge" from a sense of wonder, thinking himself ignorant and philosophizing in order to escape from ignorance, and not for any utilitarian end. (This sentence is practically a copy of Aristotle's words in *Metaphysics* I, 982b, 11-27.) Francis Bacon turned his back on this "free science" by taking from Renaissance "white magic" the objective of power and declaring it the chief end of knowledge; Thomas Hobbes sought so to define his terms that he could manipulate men into a society centered on power; and less than three hundred years later the Russian intellectual pursued this very aim by means of studying Fourier, Hegel, Proudhon, Bakunin, and Marx. The emphasis now was no longer on understanding the world but on changing it, and this teleology of education was not confined to revolutionary ideologies but characterized the approaches to natural science, psychology, and sociology. The product of this kind of education is the modern self, characteristically split into self-pity and self-deification or magnification. The sequel to these three hundred years is another phase of education exemplified at present primarily by the modern totalitarian regimes but lagging yet in the major societies of "democracy and capitalism," an education designed to produce docile instruments useful to the totalitarian rulers alone. It may be that these five types exhaust the possibilities of educational variety, in the same way in which the Christian heresies of the first four centuries of our era have set patterns that recur again and again in later periods.

The picture still includes another feature, which, born out of the concept of "free science" (Aristotle, *ibid.*, 982b, 27), has been embodied in an enduring type of institution, the Western-type universities. Born at the height of medieval Latin Christian culture, they were and are unique in human experience, functioning as centers of learning that were in large degree free from requirements of utility, either private or collective. Such institutions could occur because at the time of their founding there were available large bodies of knowledge not relative to, or dependent on, any given political society, its power and needs: Greek science in the form of philosophy, Roman law, and the *doctrina Christiana*. Moreover, there existed an equally non-relative set of "tools of learning" defined, in the medieval syllabus, as grammar, dialectic, and rhetoric. At the universities, young men learned "the structure of language – a language, and hence of language itself – what it was, how it was put together and how it worked. Secondly, he learned how to use language: how to define his terms and make accurate statements; how to construct an argument and how to detect fallacies in argument (his own argument and other people's). "Dialectic, that is to say, embraced Logic and Disputation." (Dorothy Sayers, *The Lost Tools of Learning*) All tools, and the handling of tools, were useful. The utility of the medieval *trivium* had probably the widest spread of any hitherto known human skill, a skill useful to knowledge which in itself was free from utilitarian limitations.

The new departure linked to the names of Bacon, Descartes, and Hobbes brought forth also its own mental tool, "analysis," the taking apart and putting together again of reality, in one's own mind. It was conceived in close connection with mathematics, which in turn appeared no longer as the paradigm of eternal verities but rather as a powerful instrument useful to dominate nature. Henceforward human reason lost its character of the "discovery of the mind" by the great Greek philosophers and came to be conceived as a practical and useful faculty, an instrument of human power. Bacon and Descartes envisaged the conquest of nature as man's "chief and great end," the practical justification of all endeavors of theory. Socrates, Plato, and Aristotle looked on reality in wonderment, and their wondering included the very reason by which man could participate in divine transcendence. Descartes, in order to launch his new enterprise, first "closed" his mind in systemic and absolute doubt. That in turn entailed a systemic suspicion of "prejudices," i.e., anything not having been produced by the instrument of reason in the form of "clear and simple ideas." From there arose a new notion of "free science," or liberty defined as "stripping away" whatever had grown, or had been known or believed on past authority, replacing it with what one had made oneself. From this beginning in turn came the later growth of positivism, the dictatorship of a single method, as a quantitative approach of the physical sciences was declared the sole permissible key to all kinds of knowledge. Hence this exclusivity of one method governed relevance, the object, truth, and even reality itself. It bred the fact-value dichotomy and the exclusion of value from the realm of knowledge, entailing the replacement of philosophy by the supposedly positive science of sociology.

These developments occurred within the institutions of learning which since the Middle Ages had been dedicated to "free science" in Aristotle's sense, "which alone exists for its own sake." The instrumental view of reason, however, imposed on science an inescapable utilitarian goal, the utility being conceived as either private or social, either as pragmatism or as revolutionary remaking of reality. Greek and Christian philosophy were at the same time rejected as "uncertain sciences," and philosophers planted the claim of *certainty* as their distinctive banner, culminating in

Hegel's *Phenomenology of the Mind.* The quest for certainty entailed the removal of the *doctrina Christiana* and exclusive
reliance on the positive sciences or pseudo-sciences. Education
began to lose its core of unity, as universality was replaced with
multifariousness. The ideal of a liberal education lived on, but in the
curiously meaningless version of a wide collection of as many
specialized disciplines as possible. Where philosophy could not be
replaced by sociology, it gave way to the history of a subject. Thus
there are taught the history of ideas, the history of culture, the
history of literature, the history of art or music. The more smatter-
ings of such information, the broader and better an education was
supposed to be. This wine-tasting approach entailed a necessary
neglect of any widely applicable tools of learning, so that the
dropping of the medieval *trivium* was followed by the decline of the
study of language, of logic, and finally even of reading and writing.
In the midst of highly efficient technology and social organization
one can thus observe a rapidly increasing barbarism. As one contemporary teacher reported: "The students are woefully
undereducated, and before I can discuss philosophical theories I
usually have to explain the meanings of basic English words. The
number of students who have some idea of what the Incarnation is
remains at the normal level of approximately one per class (i.e., one
out of fifty). The number of students who find it incredible that
anyone could ever have believed the utterly ridiculous ideas put
forth by Plato and Aristotle seems higher." Entire chunks of
knowledge drop into oblivion. People of today cannot communicate
anymore with the people even of the previous generation. Allusions
are no longer understood. Language shrinks in scope and power of
differentiation. Still, the modern barbarian is no savage, since he is
not privileged to the savage's education in myths, ritual, skills, and
lore. He is more dangerous than the savage because of his well-nigh
unlimited gullibility which puts him at the disposal of any
charismatic Anti-Christ. Hence the misery of education redounds
to the advantage of the demagogue, the feasibility of terroristic
enterprise, the power of mobs, and the disposition for dictatorship.

   In that kind of situation one might even wish for a return to a
previous age, one without colleges, without high schools, one in
which education at a mother's knee and by a father's example suf-

ficed for an ordered human life, in which the feats of heroes and the
competence of master craftsmen served as measures of excellence,
and decency came with proverbs. No such return is possible or even
desirable. From the level of complex technology, an all-engulfing
bureaucratization, specialization of all jobs, computerization
replacing human labor, there is no falling back on earlier versions
of self-sufficiency. Since the education we have pushed millions into barbarism, and since barbarism no longer possesses any redeeming primitive order for us, we cannot evade the task of re-winning
what it was that made meaningful education possible.

A cat learns, a bird learns, a wolf learns. Is human education,
then, essentially nothing more than what occurs between animals?
An animal is prodded into imitation, but instinct supports the
learning process. Instinct holds together the complex societies of
ants or bees. Are we to infer that human order, too, is basically in-
stinctual? The question should be raised, since it comes close to the
hidden premise of anarchism, and, in our time, libertarianism.
Many sociologists have taken to establish animal models for human
education. Men, too, learn to some extent by imitation. Still,
beyond this there extend the vast reaches of education dominated
by human self-reflective consciousness. Man is aware of himself as
a learner as well as a teacher, and most learning is the subject of
disciplines articulated in language and communicated by concepts
as well as by example. Human consciousness not only orders that
which is to be taught, it also overflows the formulae of discipline
and points beyond it, and beyond the teacher, by virtue of its
capacity for infinity. Thus the work of civilization is an artifact not
merely of things but also of human beings. "Man is made" is the
phrase used by Werner Jaeger. (*Paideia* xxxiii)

This phrase may be confused with the saying of Karl Marx, "man
makes himself," meaning emphatically that man is nobody's
creature but the "creator" of his own life. The difference between
Jaeger and Marx is a watershed of world views. Jaeger's central
concept, *paideia*, is not so much a "making" but a *bringing out* of a
given essence, out of the potentiality into actuality. The Greeks
looked on education as a process of "becoming what you are." The
Latin world *educare* is akin to *ducere*, thus carrying the notion of
"leading out." Marx, by contrast, saw human history as a process of

"coming-to-be," an emancipation from non-being, the emancipation conceived as man's own enterprise, unaided, uninspired, and unguided.

A third view implying "making" is that of Giambattista Vico: "In the night of thick darkness enveloping the earliest antiquities . . . there shines the eternal and never failing light of a truth beyond all question: that the world of civil society has certainly been made by men, and that its principles are therefore to be found within the modifications of our human mind." (*The New Science*, #331) Vico obviously uses "making" not in the sense of "producing," like "making a clock," but rather in the sense of "emerging in the stream of human actions," using the latter term with Aristotle's meaning of "acting" as contrasted to "making." (*Nicomachean Ethics* VI, 4) If history is the "making" of men in that it consists of "the modifications of the human mind," education is properly concerned with this latter subject. That places Vico on the opposite side from Marx who denies that consciousness has a history. (*The German Ideology*, Feuerbach) If education is the bringing out of something that is already given, then Marx cannot see anything like human nature, order, or cosmos as given. The place of education is taken by revolution, the "changing of the world." Nor can Marx see anything like Heraclitus' *koinos*, that which people have in common: "To those who are awake, there is one ordered universe common (to all), whereas in sleep each man turns away (from this world) to one of his own." (Diels-Kranz, fr. 89) Again, if the realm of the common is not yet, but is merely a coming-to-be, there could be no subject of education. Aristotle made it clear that men have in common a "desire to know" which in turn he traces back to the experiences of "seeing" the cosmos as a whole. This "seeing," this sense of wonder without any admixture of utilitarian cupidity, is the core of a freedom predicated of science, as well as of man. Here is the concept of liberal education, the education of free men in the setting of a "free science," subject to nobody and to no passion. Without a "free science" there can be no liberal education, as without the "desire to know," which is a common trait of all men, there can be no *koinos*, no reality experienced as essentially common, something that it would be the task of education to "bring out."

These considerations should have thrown sufficient light on Werner Jaeger's phrase, "man is made," to ban every confusion with Marx's superficially similar utterance. It is precisely the experience of a reality common to all men, an experience had in the process of "discovering the mind," which accounts for such concepts as *paideia* and "free science." Today, Aristotle's language in the first chapter of the *Metaphysics* is either forgotten or has moved beyond the scope of common understanding. We have inherited the institutions of liberal education but cast away its premises and its spirit. Under the circumstances, the institutions will operate but not to the end of freedom, either of science or of man. Their effect will be disorder rather than order, asphalt barbarism rather than culture, dissociation rather than community. Still, as the name of democracy keeps before us an ideal which men will again and again try to realize, the name of liberal education will also maintain some sense of obligation that will refuse to die. Given the history of the last three hundred years of Western civilization, are there still any possibilities of regaining an education that deserves the predicate "free?" Putting it differently one may assert that regardless of college catalogues and curricula, a school of liberal education, as soon as it opens its doors, makes to the student an implicit promise, even though neither students nor teachers may be explicitly conscious of it. Still, the promise is grasped by the student retrospectively, in his maturity, when he tries to sum up what his education has given to him. He may wonder what help his education has been in his endeavor to recognize the possibilities of life, along with the requirements for making good use of them. He will rummage through the sediments of his education, looking for tools to help him discern the character of the time in which he lives. Most often, though, mature alumni will ask what visions their college has opened for them regarding the meaning of the whole. Any thinking person needs purpose and insight. If his mind remains unprepared to cope with such questions, it has simply failed him.

This inquiry we have just conducted demonstrates that humans cannot engage in any project, least of all education, without beliefs that cannot be proved right or wrong. All the same, they can be discussed and criticized, and there is a discernible distinction between beliefs rational and beliefs irrational. Prominent scientists have written histories of science showing that all great advances of sciences have relied on beliefs and would not have occurred without beliefs. Whatever one thinks about positivism and quantitative methods, then, its categorical exclusion of beliefs from critical examination is not only untenable but demonstrably most harmful. Educators who are resolved to protect students from this harm therefore must make room in the curriculum for courses dealing seriously and critically with beliefs. One need not go to the opposite extreme of banning any courses using the empirical approach, and even courses dealing with human problems through quantitative methods. Quantitative research will always have its usefulness. Its error lies in the tyranny with which it makes that method into the sole criterion of relevance. That kind of criterion of relevance can in no way be empirically established: it, too, is a belief that cannot be falsified, thus does not belong to science, and as a belief is irrational in that it claims scientific rank in an area where no positive science applies. Thus the exclusion of beliefs from the liberal arts curriculum is a part of positivism which should be vigorously resisted by deans of arts and letters. As beliefs are once again carefully and systematically examined in education it becomes useful to distinguish between beliefs that are hypotheses and other beliefs beyond proof or refutation. These latter, "transcendent beliefs," are the really important ones. They transcend man's subjectivity, both personal and collective; they also transcend nature and history. They regard the whole of which we acknowledge ourselves to be a part. Assuming that we are part of a whole is an integral part of our thinking. Witness, for example the recurring attempt of the great physicists of our time to sketch a portrait of the universe as a whole; witness also the acknowledged need of astronomers for a concept of that within which the ultimate processes of this universe of galaxies occur. The whole, then, has no context: there is no place beyond on which we could stand, even in imagination, to look on the whole as if it were an object. Our wonderment about the whole therefore can have no end. The whole has inescapably the character of a mystery, and our place in it likewise must remain mysterious. Questions concerning it cannot be answered by way of experiment, nor can they be silenced by any compelling proof. If there were such proof our questioning would be stopped once and for all; we would be enclosed by a confining wall of "fact" imprisoning us beyond endurance.

Against this latter possibility, "You must submit because twice two . . . that's mathematics! Just you try to find an objection," Dostoevsky rebelled in the name of human freedom. His rebellion took an indeterminate, even dangerous form: "I agree that twice-two-is-four is a very fine thing; but, after all, twice-two-are-five is rather nice, too." Let us not forget that Dostoevsky puts these words in the mouth of the "underground man," the man produced as a result of modernity, with its claim to "the tower of Babel," "the Crystal Palace," and "the Man-God." Dostoevsky's own work, however, makes clear that he in no way asserted that any belief would suffice if it only averted the prison of sheer fact. We are creatures endowed with reason. The inescapability of beliefs in our thinking and action does not require the silencing of the intellect. Tertullian's *credo quia absurdum* (I believe because it is unreasonable) was superseded by Augustine's *credo ut intelligam* (I believe that I may understand). Beliefs must not be confused with contempt for experience. Arguments about beliefs testify to the seriousness of the believer, and to the compatibility of beliefs with ratio$al critique, always bearing in mind that there are also those kinds of critique which in themselves root in irrational beliefs. Liberal education, then, must focus its main efforts on thinking about and examining our beliefs, studying them not as if they were alien objects, but rather from within, the beliefs as well as their study being seen as an integral part of the "serious play" of life in which we are involved.

That brings us to a second requirement of re-founding liberal education in our day and age. This one has to do with the historical past, both in the narrow sense of "handing down the tradition," and in the wider sense of history as the symbolic form of our con- sciousness. When "tradition" is mentioned, the modern mind associates the term with past "quaintness," with primitive men- talities, characters, and ideas, with crudity in manner and feeling. This is the kind of prejudice generated by "The Whig Concept of History" (the title of a seminal book by Herbert Butterfield), the view that history resembles an escalator, moving steadily upwards, so that its apex is identical with the present for which all the past has been nothing but an unavoidable preparation. The Whig concept of history is only one variety of the "stopping or freezing" of history (Eric Voegelin, *From Enlightenment to Revolution*, p. 84) which means the fallacious establishment, in history, of a point or age to which absolute validity is attributed. This became the hallmark not only of Marx's view of history, but also of Auguste Comte's, and it is this latter version that dominates our thinking about history and engenders the prejudices characteristic of it. Here we have an example of a critique based on irrational beliefs. Thus deans of arts and letters must be able to find teachers of history who are aware that history has meant not only growth, but also, at times, decline, decay, and perversion, so that "later" does not automatically mean "higher."

Life, in a sense, is indeed a movement toward what is new, but no innovation occurs in empty space. A dimension of our environment is the past, the public memory, the tradition. All newness is a *renewal*. Human beings are members of one another, not merely in the plane of the present (roughly what we mean by the useless cliché of "humanity") but also in the dimension of past and future. Every new religion has deep roots in an older one which are not only modified but also preserved in their newness. Every scientific progress relies on work already done and appropriated. Every moral action is taken in the presence not merely of contemporaries, but also of our fathers and our descendants. He who believes he can cut himself off from tradition is not a free man but rather a naked and isolated "self," drifting in icy solitude, debarred from any signposts of direction or hints of possibilities. The *New Yorker* once published the cartoon of a clock which, instead of numbers, only had twelve spots, each saying "NOW!" Rebellious movements of our age have embraced a critique based on irrational belief, a critique elevating that "NOW!" to a substitute for history. As they thought to destroy the past, they also destroyed the future, ending up in nihilism.

Thinking, as many eminent philosophers have pointed out, is largely memory. No memory is purely subjective and individual. What is more, tradition is a public memory, replete with signs and symbols, a memory that undergirds a common culture and political order. Therefore, the passing on of tradition is not an exercise in nostalgia but a solemn obligation of parents, schools, colleges and universities, churches, governments, and judges. As in the case of beliefs, tradition must be transmitted not blindly but critically, being imperceptibly changed in the process of examination. This must not be perverted in an invidious, rebellious, and hostile undertaking. Rather, the critical task must be performed in the spirit of ancient Roman *pietas*, reverently, "as one approaches the wounds of a father," to use Burke's words. Nor must that "piety" be confused with bigotry. Rather it manifests respect, love, and loyalty for everything that bears a human face, for all human questing for the ground, the end, and the way.

This brings us to a third requirement of liberal education regained, and this one most controversial. It concerns the place of Christianity in liberal studies. In a sense, the transmission of the tradition cannot avoid dealing with Christianity. Beyond that, however, there must be courses available that teach Christianity not merely in the context of literature, art, politics and past culture, but in its own right. In other words, such courses must embrace Christianity in its fullness and study it "from within." Such studies must embrace the body of Scripture, the proclamation of the Gospel, dogma as well as kerygma, the developing of the liturgy and of theology, the errant movements of heresy, and constructive ones of monasticism, the mystics and the doctors of the Church, its institutions of moral discipline and its enterprise of mission.

One can readily hear the objections: "Why just Christianity? Why not religion in general, if at all?" "All right, if Christianity is to figure in the curriculum, equal time must be given to other religions, including atheism." "Since Christianity claims to be the true religion, how can you avoid dogmatic indoctrination?" "No, better risk loss of truth than chance of error" (this latter being William James's description of the skeptic's position). To which one may respond as follows: a) "religion" as such is no subject matter; at most it is a branch of psychology which, however, has had great difficulty in grasping what religion is; b) as for comparative religion, it is a legitimate subject, and an important even though very difficult one. It may well be added to Christian studies, but it will not do as a substitute because Christianity has been the source and center of our culture, the ultimate truth that has shaped our past and is still shaping our present, regardless of what attitude to it particular persons may have. We cannot realistically step out of this truth into "another one," we cannot in truth become Hindus or Buddhists. Western civilization came into existence through the unifying impulse of Latin Christianity, and no other religion has played a similar role among us. The historical metamorphoses of our culture can be understood only in their relation to their Christian origins, even where these metamorphoses have emerged as bitter enemies of Christianity. The Hegelian and Marxian systems are nothing if not perverted schemes of the Christian salvation. Finally, as for the skeptic's option, "better risk loss of truth than chance of error," one can put against it the believer's option, "better risk chance of error than loss of truth," but in any case this is a decision which cannot be made in the context of class assignments, tests, and grades, but only in the solitude of each person's heart.

Another objection might point to the traditionally secular concept of the liberal arts college. This may well be granted, but in spite of this admitted secularism, Christian studies have formed, up to the end of the last century, not only an integral part but the crowning part of liberal education. The objection, then, will in fact come from contemporary hostility to Christianity, a hostility which is effective also against liberal education as a concept. All the same, it is a fact that students entering a liberal arts college today come with a different intent than those seeking a Bible college. In some cases this intent is interpreted by the faculty as a kind of general taboo of even the word "God," which, if mentioned by someone in conversation within the college, may lead to an abrupt change of subject or of the conversation itself.

Thus the introduction of Christian studies into the liberal arts curriculum requires a most careful effort of justification. It must be vigorously defended against the fallacious view that sees transcendent beliefs as a denial of thinking. That defense can hardly be successful until the Cartesian concept of reason itself can be shown false. Fortunately, there is much first-class contemporary philosophy that will support such a demonstration. Even then, however, there remains the limitation that the character of liberal education prohibits the offering of Christian studies with a proselytizing intent. One may ask, however, whether that is a limitation of liberal studies or does not really belong to all studies proceeding by means of lectures, recitations, tests, and grades. Some time ago, the dean of one of the foremost Anglican seminaries addressed a parish meeting at my church. Our director of religious education rather heatedly assailed the dean's talk with the demand that religious education should have as its subject "experience." The dean, with great firmness, replied: "Life, indeed, consists largely of experience, but the subject of education is tradition."

Let us say, then, that Christian studies in the framework of liberal education are part of the handing down of tradition. Our entire culture with all its works of art and artifacts bears so much testimony to the Christian religion that without knowledge of what Christianity is about it can never be understood. Beyond this, however, there is another reason for Christian studies; one may also classify it among the utilitarian reasons. Ours is a culture of life in tension. Between time and eternity, nature and transcendence, the world and heaven, the sacred and the profane there are experiential tensions which cannot and should not be resolved. They are the hallmarks of our civilization. Our time is fortunate in the sense that a number of great scholars have brilliantly understood these tensions and have furnished us with a vocabulary for the philosophical articulation of the attendant problems. One who is not even aware of the problem easily becomes the prey of demagogic leaders who collapse the tension into a fallacious identity of god and man, salvation and politics, religion and revolution. Hence the multitude of movements in our time which enlist mass support by holding out the promise of a heaven on earth, a perfect social harmony, an identity of political power and authority. No positivist can grasp the nature of these movements and their totalitarian regimes, since he has barred his mind from understanding transcendent beliefs in general, and the Christian religion in particular. Likewise the student shaped by a liberal education that knows nothing of Christianity, faith, mysticism, and "words adequate to God" (St. Basil's definition of theology), will remain unable to grasp the nature of our time and its political pitfalls.

As one looks at the curricula of our colleges and universities, and the patterns of thinking of our educational leaders, one realizes that the kind of changes proposed on these pages are not easy to come by. Even the skeptic reader, however, cannot help grudgingly admitting that all three, or even one of them, would go far to restore to liberal education the core of meaning which the cafeteria-type curriculum is lacking. There is also the evidence of small colleges who have boldly set out to devise their own education around a core concept, be it Greek philosophy, or Christian religion, or the great books, – all three, incidentally, parts of the grand tradition which educators have a sacred duty to pass on. There is also the evidence of the recent attempt to restore some modicum of liberal education at Harvard College. These are manifestations of a "great refusal," if one may dare to baptize a concept of unholy intent, a refusal to put up any longer with the muddle that today passes for education in so many institutions. In all probability the misery will have to become more sharply unbearable, the suffering personal and yet wide-spread before people begin to run after a real teacher, seize him by the hem of his overcoat, and beg him to take charge of their children. Let us not say that then it will be too late. It may be too late for some of us. But Augustine, finishing the *City of God* in a town besieged, and eventually conquered, by Vandals, was not completing his work "too late." Nor was his master, Jesus of Nazareth, abandoned by his disciples and rejected by his compatriots, crucified "too late." Our civilization has lived in the knowledge that "the future is open, and it is God's." There is no "too late."

# Acknowledgments

"The Autonomous Man," *The Intercollegiate Review*, Summer 1974.

"Loss of Reality: Gnosticism and Modern Nihilism," *Modern Age*, Fall 1978.

"The Loss and Recovery of History," *Imprimis*, October 1977.

"The Homesickness of the New Left," *National Review*, July 28, 1970.

"Two Socialisms," *Modern Age*, Fall 1962.

"The Communist Mind," ISI Pamphlet (original publication).

"Communism and the Notion of the Good," *The Ethical Dimensions of the Political Life*, ed. Francis Canavan (Durham: Duke University Press, 1983).

"Communist Ideology: The Sixth Age," *Center Journal*, Fall 1985.

"National Self-Defense and Political Existence," *The Intercollegiate Review*, March-April 1966.

"Detente and Ideological Struggle," *The Intercollegiate Review*, Fall 1978.

"Foreign Policy and Morality," *The Intercollegiate Review*, Spring 1980.

"Foreign Policy and America's Sense of Destiny," *Center Journal*, Spring 1983.

"Conservatism and the New Political Theory," *Modern Age*, Spring 1979.

"Eric Voegelin's Philosophy and the Drama of Mankind," *Modern Age*, Winter 1976.

"Greatness in Political Science: Eric Voegelin," *Modern Age*, Spring 1985.

"Ideas Have Also Roots," *Modern Age*, Spring 1982.

"Reason and Faith: The Fallacious Antithesis," *Essays on Christianity and Political Philosophy*, ed. George W. Carey (Bryn Mawr, Pa. and Lanham, Md.: Intercollegiate Studies Institute, Inc. and University Press of America, 1984).

"What Price 'Natural Law'?" *American Journal of Jurisprudence*, 1983.

"Augustine's Political Philosophy," *The Christian Vision of Man and Society*, ed. Lynn Morris (Hillsdale, Mich.: Hillsdale College Press, 1984).

"The Eternal Meaning of Solzhenitsyn," *National Review*, January 19, 1973.

"Why Marion Montgomery Has to Ramble," *Center Journal*, Spring 1985.

"Beyond Democratic Disorder," *The Intercollegiate Review*, Spring-Summer 1981.

"The Glory and Misery of Education," *The Intercollegiate Review*," Fall-Winter 1982.